POSTCOLONIAL PASSA————

POSTCOLONIAL PASSAGES

Contemporary History-writing on India

Edited by
SAURABH DUBE

OXFORD

UNIVERSITY PRESS

OXFORD
UNIVERSITY PRESS

YMCA Library Building, Jai Singh Road, New Delhi 110 001

Oxford University Press is a department of the University of Oxford. It furthers the University's
objective of excellence in research, scholarship, and education by publishing worldwide in

Oxford New York

Auckland Bangkok Buenos Aires Cape Town Chennai
Dar es Salaam Delhi Hong Kong Istanbul Karachi Kolkata
Kuala Lumpur Madrid Melbourne Mexico City Mumbai Nairobi
São Paulo Shanghai Taipei Tokyo Toronto

Oxford is a registered trademark of Oxford University Press
in the UK and in certain other countries

Published in India
By Oxford University Press, New Delhi

ISBN 0 19 566508 2

Typeset in Goudy 10.5 on 12.5
by Laser Print Craft, Delhi 110 051
Printed at Pauls Press, New Delhi 110 020
Published by Manzar Khan, Oxford University Press
YMCA Library Building, Jai Singh Road, new Delhi 110001

for
Bernard Cohn
and
Ranajit Guha

Contents

Preface

Books are born in different ways. This one has unusual beginnings. A few years ago, I compiled a rather large anthology, *Pasados poscoloniales*, which carried in Spanish translation some of the important recent writings on the cultural history and the historical anthropology of South Asia. The critical implications of the works reproduced have always extended rather wider. It was not difficult, then, to set up a conversation between these writings and salient scholarship on Latin America, especially through the means of an analytical introduction. Fortunately, *Pasados poscoloniales* has evinced wide interest, quickly taking on an electronic avatar, gradually appearing in 'virtual libraries' in different parts of the Spanish-speaking world. In such circumstances, the nature of the volume also led to queries concerning my plans for publishing it in English. But with the work fulfilling its purpose in the Spanish language, I demurred, dithered, deferred. Till one of the key contributors to *Pasados poscoloniales*, already familiar with its chapters, after reading the introduction (in English), suggested to OUP the possibility of their publishing a similar volume. The outlines of another project began to take shape. Eighteen months later, should *Postcolonial Passages* be understood as a second-coming (or a ghostly English double) of *Pasados poscoloniales*? Actually, not quite. Only two of the pieces from the Spanish work remain in this one, and the introduction has also been entirely recast. Four of the contributors have had to make way for different colleagues. Yet, most of the contributors have stayed—albeit, chiefly providing other pieces—and the birth of *Postcolonial Passages* appears attended by its predecessor, *Pasados poscoloniales*, an original-in-translation.

It would be silly to expect any broadly conceived anthology to entirely exhaust the field(s) it presents. *Postcolonial Passages* is no exception. Rather than claiming to simply 'represent' contemporary history-writing in India, the work makes particular incisions on the corpus of historical scholarship of the subcontinent. Indeed, the book is organized around three broad but specific, overlapping themes: empire and colony; nation and community; and modernity and its margins. At the same time, even on such questions, the volume is less the utterance of the final word, hardly the proclamation of the last hurrah, and more a plea to further reflection, a pointer toward other literatures, an invitation to rethink the insularity of scholarship on South Asia. Academic ghettoes are unfortunate places. Equally eschewing the snare of approaching the worlds of knowledge and the knowledge of worlds through lazily pre-figured, readily framed, already known 'schools' and 'masters', *Postcolonial Passages* brings into conversation (on subjects of history and theory) a variety of disciplinary dispositions and scholarly persuasions. In this way, the book offers critical perspectives, probing the conditions and possibilities of modernity, questioning the projection of the West as history and destiny, querying the connections and complicities between the colonial state and the Indian nation, and exploring the ambiguities and prospects of the postcolonial as a category.

I have now reached that magic moment when I can thank some of those who have not only made this project possible, but also the work on it a pleasure. For the beginnings of wonder: Leela Dube. For the wonder of beginnings: Ishita Banerjee-Dube. For crucial support: Bernard Cohn, Ranajit Guha, David Lorenzen, and Germán Franco, who began by translating *Pasados poscoloniales*, and has since remained my comrade and co-conspirator. For critical dialogue: Dipesh Chakrabarty, Ann Gold, Sandra Greene, Anupama Rao, Ajay Skaria, Guillermo Zermeño, and the contributors to this book, Shahid Amin, Urvashi Butalia, Kamla Bhasin, Partha Chatterjee, Bernard Cohn, Nicholas Dirks, Ranajit Guha, Sudipta Kaviraj, Ritu Menon, Gyanendra Pandey, Gyan Prakash, and (yes, once more) Dipesh Chakrabarty and Anupama Rao. For research assistance (and friendship): Laura Carballido. For belief (and disbelief): my students at El Colegio de México and Cornell University. For editorial sustenance: the editors at Oxford University Press, New Delhi.

The energies and scholarship of two critical intellects and insurgent souls undergird the contours and concerns of *Postcolonial Passages*. Like its predecessor, this book, too, is dedicated to Bernard Cohn and Ranajit Guha, a personal tribute that is shared I am sure by many, many others.

For permission to reproduce copyright materials I thank the following: Bernard Cohn for excerpts from 'Representing Authority in Victorian India', in Eric Hobsbawm and Terence Ranger (eds), *The Invention of Tradition* (Cambridge: Cambridge University Press, 1983), 165–209; The University of Chicago Press for Ranajit Guha, 'Not at Home in Empire', *Critical Inquiry*, 23, (Spring) 1997, 482–93; Taylor and Francis (http://www.tandf.co.uk) for Anupama Rao, 'Problems of Violence, States of Terror: Torture in Colonial India', *Interventions: Journal of Postcolonial Studies*, 3, 1, 2001, 186–205; Princeton University Press for Partha Chatterjee, 'Communities and the Nation', in *The Nation and its Fragments: Colonial and Postcolonial Histories* (Princeton: Princeton University Press, 1993), 221–39, 260–1; Cambridge University Press for Gyanendra Pandey, 'Disciplining Difference', in *Remembering Partition: Violence, Nationalism and History in India* (Cambridge: Cambridge University Press, 2001), 152–74; Kali for Women for Ritu Menon and Kamla Bhasin, 'Belonging', in *Borders and Boundaries: Women in India's Partition* (New Delhi: Kali for Women, 1998), 228–57; Duke University Press for Saurabh Dube, 'Entangled Endeavours: Ethnographic Histories and Untouchable Pasts', *Comparative Studies of South Asia, Middle East and Africa*, 18, 1998, 82–94; Cambridge University Press for Gyan Prakash, 'Reproducing Inequality: Spirit Cults and Labour Relations in Colonial Eastern India', *Modern Asian Studies*, 20, 1986, 209–30; Princeton University Press for Dipesh Chakrabarty, 'Minority Histories, Subaltern Pasts', in *Provincializing Europe: Postcolonial Thought and Historical Difference* (Princeton: Princeton University Press, 2000), 97–113, 275–7; Penguin, India for Urvashi Butalia, 'Blood', in *The Other Side of Silence: Voices from the Partition of India* (New Delhi: Penguin, 1998), 24–40; Duke University Press for (parts of an earlier version of) Saurabh Dube, 'The Presence of Europe: An Interview with Dipesh Chakrabarty', in S. Dube (ed.) *Enduring Enchantments*, a special number of *SAQ: The South Atlantic Quarterly*, 101, 4, 2002, 859–68.

SAURABH DUBE
Mexico City

Terms that Bind: Colony, Nation, Modernity

Saurabh Dube

T he past two decades have seen remarkable renderings of combative histories and critical ethnographies of South Asia, scholarship manifest as newer theoretical practice and novel empirical study. Today, overlapping developments in cultural histories and historical ethnographies that work with South Asian materials constitute an integral part of transcontinental movements in historiography, anthropology, and cultural studies—significant participants in critical discussions of Eurocentric knowledge, salient interlocutors in key debates on postcolonial perspectives.

Such debate and discussion are animated by wider considerations of colonial knowledge and postcolonial difference, multicultural politics and cultural identities—in the academy and beyond, across different continents.[1] On the one hand, in this milieu, the writings intimating newer accents in South Asian scholarship often appear seized upon as a package deal for discussions of culture and power in Third World contexts and postcolonial arenas, overriding thereby their key differences and critical conjunctions. On the other hand, it is precisely because of its variety that this body of work has reworked old issues and initiated new questions in discussions of colony and nation, modernity and community, and historical margins and postcolonial apprehensions. Taken together, the implications and contentions of the newer cultural histories and historical ethnographies of South Asia underline the importance of bringing them into mutual dialogue, presenting some of the salient writings here in the shape of *Postcolonial Passages*. Toward this purpose, my introductory essay locates this work in its larger theoretical context—of the shifts in disciplines and the politics of knowledge—also implicitly indicating the debates and conjunctions among these writings.[2]

I will begin by pointing to certain wide, key transformations in the disciplines of anthropology and history, particularly over the last twenty-five years. Both a confession and a clarification are in order here. It is not only that these developments have an important bearing on the ensuing arguments. It is also that, oriented toward anthropology while being trained in history over the 1980s, and straddling the two since the 1990s, I feel compelled to come to terms with this past. This is to say that I claim neither novelty nor totality for the account ahead. Rather, the tales speak of my learning of the subjects and my unlearning of the disciplines of anthropology and history. They offer an indicative discussion, pointing toward the conditions of possibility for the reading and writing of cultural histories and historical ethnographies, especially their conjunctions, which are contained in *Postcolonial Passages*.

As the next step, I will describe the changing emphases in the study of colony and empire, leading up to the recent, critical developments in this terrain, providing a basis for considering the contributions to colonial cultures offered by this collection. At the same time, the discussion will also set the stage for exploring, in somewhat lesser detail, the terms of nation and nationalism, modernity and history, that underlie the other essays in the volume. These twin measures are barely surprising. By generating important scholarship, including varieties of postcolonial perspectives, work on colonial histories has shaped this book, especially the interplay between its different parts, also suggesting the title of the work.

Aware of the pitfalls of the postcolonial as a category, in these pages *postcolonial* neither intimates a settled stage of history nor insinuates an exclusive form of knowledge.[3] Rather, *postcolonial* suggests here a broad but critical rubric, including in its fold conjoint yet contending perspectives—unravelling the prior presence of colonial apprehensions within contemporary knowledge; questioning the projection of the West as history and destiny; probing the conditions and possibilities of modernity; and interrogating the limits and stipulations of the modern state and the Indian nation. If clear consensus on emphasis and interpretation is difficult to find in this terrain, the very contention and conjunction, debate and dissension here possibly also help to define the central strengths of the postcolonial corpus. Premised upon this prospect, *Postcolonial Passages* gathers together cultural histories and historical ethnographies that carefully question and critically elaborate colonialism and nationalism, empire and community, state and nation, and modernity and its margins, also thinking through the ambiguities and possibilities of the *postcolonial* as a category.

CULTURES IN TIME

Eschewing the ethnographic exploration of the endlessly exotic, forsaking the bare-habits of 'anthropology-land' and 'history-land', imaginatively evoked by Bernard Cohn, writings of anthropologists have shaped distinct, critical readings of culture and power in recent times.[4] Such moves have followed upon various developments, possibly beginning with anticolonial struggles and processes of decolonization in the Third World from the late 1940s until the late 1960s. Important too were events of the 1960s and the accompanying critique of imperialism and racism—embodied, for example, in the dramatic moment of 1968—across different parts of the world, and emergent critiques of reigning paradigms within the discipline.[5] Aspects of the transformations within ethnography become clear through a focus on dominant definitions and critical questions surrounding two key tropes of anthropology. The first is the concept of 'structure' (and its correlate notion of action), until not so long ago a buzz word in social and cultural anthropology. The second is the category of 'culture', for long inscribed as a homogeneous entity, then increasingly authored as a polyvocal endeavour, and now critically written *against* as a dominant enterprise.

First terms first. In understandings of individual and society or action and structure, functionalism and structuralism, two theoretical traditions prominent within the social sciences unto the 1960s and 1970s respectively, accorded primacy to the object(s) of structure over the subject(s) of history.[6] Now, it is important to clarify that the two traditions understand structure differently.[7] While in functionalism, structure refers to a pattern of social relationships, and function shows how these patterns actually operate as system, structure has a more explanatory role on structuralism, referring to the codes underlying surface appearances. At the same time, the two traditions share the common characteristic of privileging structure over action, an emphasis possibly going back to the influence of Durkheim upon these paradigms. Equally, this emphasis appears intimately related to the clear methodological distinctions made by structuralism and functionalism between synchrony and diachrony, or statics and dynamics. This distinction animates the assumption that it is possible to understand the nature of social systems in abstraction from change. As a result, the central place given to the a-temporal predication of human action upon underlying structure in these theoretical traditions often brackets conceptions of the mutual meshing of structure and agency, determinations and denials played out over time.[8]

Elsewhere, I have provided notes toward an adequate conception of structure and practice, emphasizing precisely the intermeshing of these heuristic categories, descriptive devices.[9] My point here concerns the loss of legitimacy of frameworks in which sociological structures simultaneously displaced and orchestrated historical subjects. Was there not an enormous gap between the tenor of such models and the remarkable energies and the wide-ranging passions that went into the making of counter-colonial movements and processes of decolonization witnessed in the decades since the 1940s? What was the relationship between abstract renderings of overwhelming structures and the critical emphasis on political action of historical subjects that was evident in the imaginings and practices surrounding, for example, the events of the 1960s? It will be naive and simplistic to claim that these wider political initiatives somehow extended their radical impulse to bring about—in an unmediated fashion, a wilful manner—transformations in anthropological thinking about structure and practice. I am suggesting rather that the negotiation and the mediation of the experience of these decades took various forms, which included different engagements with the received visions and inherited models of social action and academic practice.[10]

Turning to the 1970s, the consequence of such engagement could be contradictory indeed.[11] In academic arenas, there was a rise in popularity of Marxist models cast in a mould of sophisticated structuralism—a reaction against the iron laws of communist thought, theory stifled by Stalinism, but also efforts toward a refinement of theoretical practice after the failure of the 'spontaneous' politics of the preceding years. These years saw the enormous success too of 'dependency' and 'world systems' theories that interrogated the capitalist and imperialist continuities of Western domination in non-Western theatres through polarities of core and periphery, development and underdevelopment. These explanatory frameworks, despite their many differences, accorded primacy to underlying structures, often turning human action into a mere vector of the relentless unfolding of the irrevocable logic of world capitalism or rendering historical subjects as the places and functions that they occupied in assiduously articulated modes of production.[12]

Yet, these years also saw separate, contending explorations of the relationship between structure and agency. Drawing upon rather different readings of Marx—and also upon readings of a rather different Marx—and elaborating other theoretical frameworks and philosophical traditions, the new, distinct but overlapping formulations went on to challenge the binaries of academic models and political inquiry. These models of 'structuration' and theories of practice variously analysed and unravelled the mutual entailment of structure and agency, social reproduction and cultural transformation.[13] By the end of the 1970s, the writing was on the wall. Mediating and conjoining the polarities of society and individual, of social structure and historical action, the category of practice had become a critical theoretical trope in anthropology.

These developments were part of a larger revaluation of other key concepts in ethnography. The rethinking of the older anthropological understanding of culture as a shared system of values, actions, and beliefs is a case in point. At issue were not merely different efforts—quite in keeping with an important call issued by Clifford Geertz—to cut the concept of culture down to size to ensure its continued relevance.[14] At stake rather was a fundamental reworking of the category of culture that was in tune with the newer emphases on history and temporality, power and processes within a discipline that was in the throes of rapid change, soon to emerge with distinct orientations.

The emerging critical emphasis on practice within anthropology underscored the significance of temporality and process for the discipline. Both ethnographic analyses and social processes were enacted in time, even if much of anthropological endeavour had constituted its (proximate) object precisely by refusing history to the (distant) native, involving as well a 'denial of coevalness' between the ethnographer self and the anthropological other.[15] In a related but distinct move, world systems theory and structuralist-Marxist analyses, among other orientations, pointed to the importance of historical models in anthropological inquiry.[16] Moreover, charting a radically different course from major pathways of cultural anthropology of the 1970s—which could feature apolitical abstractions regarding essential differences across cultures—these diverse analytical approaches pointed toward the centrality of power in social practice and cultural action.[17] Finally, anticolonial nationalism, decolonization, and nation building in the newly independent nations were powerful examples of histories-in-making, intimating that dominant constructions of the enchanted native were ever an instance of ideologies-in-the-making.[18] The chequered and contested character of these processes in non-Western arenas highlighted complex articulations of discursive schemes, disciplinary regimes, and institutional practices. Such productions of power emerged grounded in the contradictory modernities of the metropole and the colony, revealing themselves as much more and much less than timeless exemplars of archaic authority in native theatres.

In the presence of these pasts and the aftermath of such analyses, it became apparent that influential understandings of culture did not see their discrete object(s) of desire—the values, beliefs, symbols, and rituals of a people—as parts of historical processes. Further, there was growing recognition that in such orientations culture appeared as autonomous and independent from the realities of power, which define social relationships, underplaying thereby the marks of difference and patterns of differentiation within cultures.[19] It followed that cultures (and structures) were increasingly set in motion, infusing them with process and power. It ensued that structures (and cultures) appeared ever more unravelled in time, imbuing them with historical practice and contingent agency.[20] More recently, the logic of these transformations within anthropology emerges extended rather further, including through the broader turn to critical theory and interrogations of Western knowledge, which I will soon discuss.[21] The consequences have been truly wide ranging, particularly in the fashioning of wide varieties of historical ethnographies and ethnographic histories, and their transformations through time.

It is widely recognized today that a recent rapprochement has led to novel renderings of anthropology and fresh formulations of history. It is clear too that we are now far past the stage of early methodological discussions and programmatic evaluations that charted the potential relations between the two disciplines.[22] Much has happened in the critical practice of historical anthropology and ethnographic history over the past twenty years.[23] Fieldwork stands cast in a dialogue with the historical imagination. Archival material and non-official sources appear read through ethnographic filters. In key works of this newer body of writing, the blending of history and anthropology has led to distinct analyses and hybrid narratives. Anthropological agendas have been harnessed to historicize institutional arenas and organizing principles of meaning and practice in the past and the present. Historical sensibilities have been yoked to rich ethnographic explorations of the varieties of knowledge of the colonizer and the colonized and the myriad ways of life of dominant and subaltern groups.[24] Accompanying these developments has been an acute realization that the analytical categories and conceptual arenas of anthropology and history—from tribe and community, to myth and ritual, to culture and tradition—emerge attended by complex genealogies of knowledge and power. Animated by the dialectic between empire and enlightenment, prior anthropological 'fields' appear today as articulated by the dynamic between race and reason. If the strange has been made familiar, the familiar has been rendered strange, the better to unsettle and mix up our notions of strangeness and familiarity, in the present and the past.

PASTS IN PLACE

Among writings on South Asia, the single most formative influence for this book has been the work of the collective Subaltern Studies project, and some of its important contributions appear in these pages. Elsewhere, I have argued that the Subaltern Studies endeavour has animated and articulated different orientations, from histories from below through to postcolonial perspectives.[25] Now, the initial impetus for the elaboration of histories from below in South Asia came from debates concerning the place and function of the movements of subaltern groups within anticolonial nationalist struggles in the Indian subcontinent.[26] The Subaltern Studies enterprise emerged from within this debate.[27] Yet, it also went on to overcome the limitations of the earlier contributions.[28] At work was a double movement: a critique of colonial rule (and its imperial and postimperial historiography) and an interrogation of middle-class nationalism (and its nationalist and left biography).

Subaltern Studies has carried forward these theoretical and political emphases even further in recent years. Out of the analyses of anticolonial movements and counter-colonial initiatives of subordinate groups—and of the relationship of these endeavours with middle-class nationalism—there have emerged wider theoretical critiques of state, nation, and modernity in colonial and contemporary India.[29] On the one hand, these writings have questioned the inherited terms of debate surrounding the state and the nation, bringing to the fore plural imaginings of state(s) and con-federal conceptions of nation(s). On the other, they have interrogated the Eurocentrism and the singularity of the modern project of history.

The emphases within this work have extended from an advocacy for the 'small voice of history' that scrambles authoritative pasts to the highlighting of the multiform articulations of the civil-political sphere within a colonial modernity, which exceed the concerns of relentlessly rational and seamlessly secular historiography.[30] The concerns of this project have ranged from contrapuntal readings of subaltern pasts that recognize their articulation of difference, exceeding the self-same identity of 'agency' and 'history', through to calls for representations of the past that can adequately render the pain of the victims of violence of state and nation.[31] As the essays in this volume show, the efforts here form part of a larger endeavour, extending beyond Subaltern Studies, shaped against the grain of dominant designs of history and modernity, laying bare the several seductions of the state and the nation.

These concerns and emphases are signs of the times. They both index and promote a wider process of questioning that is underway in the academy, involving critiques of teleological schemes and foundational histories, interrogating the complex implications of European expansion and the compounded genealogies of Western knowledge. The basis for such questions and critiques lies in two overlapping tendencies, particularly since the mid-1980s. The first concerns acute analyses of the spatial, categorical, and political constructions of the world in the wake of Western modernity—analyses that articulate a wider challenge to Eurocentric canons within the academy. Second, the turn to critical theory within the humanities that has taken the form of close engagements with Continental philosophy—once the preserve of departments of European literatures in the Anglo-Saxon academy[32]—in the fields of literary criticism and cultural studies and the disciplines of history and anthropology. Together, elaborating a larger sensibility toward combative democratic concerns and politics, these closely connected developments also underlie the recent emergence of wide varieties of postcolonial criticism in the academy in both Western and non-Western contexts, foregrounding colonial questions on the intellectual agenda.

COLONY AND EMPIRE

Colony and empire are not new to anthropology and history. If the presence of colonies made anthropology possible, the privileges of empire shaped the Eurocentric predilections of modern historiography in Western and non-Western contexts. Most early ethnographic endeavour neglected history and elided colonialism. It did so by locating the native in what Bernard Cohn has appositely described as a 'never, never land'—not only of the timeless tradition of structural-functionalism, but also of the 'savage slot' and native niche, the gaze and grasp, of anthropology.[33] This tendency persisted in the discipline through its casting of the object of inquiry as the irremediable other, ever denied, as we have noted, the coevalness of time.[34] Until rather later than generally considered, varieties of metropolitan history writing read the distant pasts of imperial territories as footnotes and appendices to Western history. As for histories shaped in colonized countries and newly independent nations, such accounts often emerged as envisioned in the irrevocable image of a progressive West.[35] In newer guises, these enduring imaginings and resilient conceptions continue to beguile and seduce, leading a charmed life in academe and beyond. Yet, as is well known, there have also been significant changes in history and anthropology in recent decades.

In a wider mood of radical critiques of established disciplines, the late 1960s and the early 1970s saw issues of colony and questions of empire make a crucial appearance on the stage of anthropology. There were two entangled endeavours here. On the one hand, there emerged critical debates on the connections and complicities between anthropological practice and colonial projects.[36] On the other hand, influenced by Marxian political economy, dependency theory, and the world systems framework, there appeared a variety of analyses discussing the workings of colonial economies and of the unfolding of the capitalist dynamic of Western European and North American nations in the making of the modern world.[37] As for history writing, since about four decades ago, in the newly independent nations and within Western academic arenas, historians began to construct detailed accounts of particular economic systems spawned by colonialism and specific social structures shaped under imperialism. Here, together with anthropologists, historians also focused on the responses of the colonized to the workings of imperial institutions and colonial power.[38]

There was much of value in such writing, but the central assumptions of this scholarship also left it limited as regards cultures spawned by colonialism. At the risk of ignoring certain exceptions, colonialism was at once elaborated and debated here as a package deal, a highly articulated structure and an inherently co-ordinated system of economic exploitation, social control, and political domination. It followed that in these analyses the terms of argument, the contending positions, rested upon a particular vision of colony and empire. Argued and challenged was the irrevocable trajectory of colonial power as impelling the actions of the colonialists in definite directions, and the compelling logic of colonial processes governing the practices of colonized populations, which were in turn seen as collaborating with or rebelling against imperial authority.

In this otherwise diverse scholarship, containing opposite viewpoints, the very terms of discussion occluded the elaboration of colony and empire as chequered, contradictory, contingent, and contested processes of culture and history, meaning and power. Broadly speaking, either colonialism appeared as homogeneous and monolithic, or it stood dissolved into a series of disparate episodes and diverse encounters in faraway places. If tensions between various colonial agents appeared acknowledged, they did little more than produce occasional ripples on the surface of imperial power, far removed from the core dynamic of colonial projects, or such differences between imperial actors stood as symptoms of the absence of anything as co-ordinated as colonialism. Not surprisingly, a few exceptions apart, such readings and renderings of colony and empire paid little attention to the rituals and practices, the myths and meanings, the symbols and boundaries of Euro-American people in colonial locations—missionaries, administrators, settler communities—as elaborating the constitutive contradictions of colonial cultures.[39]

Several of the recent revisitations of imperial projects and colonial processes in ethnography and history emerge as constructed against the grain of these dominant, earlier assumptions. Aspects of this revision came to the fore in the 1970s in anthropological writings, often influenced by Marxist theory, which located the social representations of marginal groups within wider fields of economic relationships and cultural power in non-Western arenas. For example, both June Nash and Michael Taussig explored the practices of Bolivian tin miners in terms of their contending appropriations of symbols of *gringo* (white, United States) economic power and their critical representations of metaphors of dominant capitalist relations. These practices and representations featured the devil as the (un)fair Tio wearing a cowboy hat and brandishing a cigarette (Marlboro?), and involved a creative interplay between use value orientations and exchange value ends.[40] Such writings pointed toward the need to examine the life forms of peoples of the colony and subjects of capitalism not as mere reactions to colonial projects and capitalist processes, but instead as contentious engagements within complex fields. Engagements and fields both defined by historically located and culturally layered encounters and entanglements between imperial, Euro-American traditions and colonial, non-Western histories.[41] While these were important emphases, over the past twenty years the logic of such revised understandings of colony and empire stands elaborated further. However, before presenting these newer orientations as a series of interlinked propositions, I turn to another significant development in the field of study of colonial cultures.

The far-reaching revisions in the analyses of colony and empire in recent decades have followed two main pathways. On the one hand, as I have noted, discussions of colonial cultures and explorations of imperial locations have played a key role in the theoretical projects and analytical emphases of historical anthropology and ethnographic history. On the other hand, fields of literary study and cultural criticism have produced wide varieties of engagements with colonial discourse, which now extend to diverse disciplines. If the former orientation, put culture into colonialism and the latter writings put colonialism into culture, it is also the case that these developments have not been oblivious to each other.[42] Indeed, Nicholas Thomas's recent statement about studies of colonialism as almost creating 'a post-disciplinary humanities field, in which histories, cultural studies, cultural politics, narratives and ethnographies all intersect and are all open to being challenged' appears already to be old news.[43] Today, the 'blurred genres' that Clifford Geertz remarked upon somewhat over fifteen years ago stand invoked so often that they carry a sense of deja vu.

Yet, beyond the mix-up between disciplinary boundaries lies the salience of different orientations. Here my own preferences run toward understanding the contradictory fabrication of colonial discourses as part of the historical fashioning of colonial cultures. Besides, an inventory of the different developments in literary and cultural writings on colony and empire is not only a task beyond the scope of this introduction, but such a survey will also serve little purpose. Therefore, I will now highlight a few of the critical emphases in such writing that have a bearing both on the arguments ahead and on the wider themes that run through this book. The burden of this discussion will fall upon Edward Said's seminal and polemical study, *Orientalism*.[44] I claim neither the expertise nor the desire to chart every inch of this jagged and jerky terrain. On the other hand, I am acutely aware that Said's key work does not exhaust the field of literary analyses and cultural studies of imperial representation and colonial discourse. At the same time, *Orientalism* provides a useful point of entry to group and point this discussion.

Much more than any other single study, *Orientalism* critically underscored the mutual entailments of European colonialism and empire and Western knowledge and power. Before the publication of the book in 1978 there existed several studies of European images of non-European peoples. Such work identified various stereotypes:

. . .from the monsters at the edges of maps and women with sagging breasts of medieval and Renaissance accounts, to the noble and ignoble savages of the Enlightenment voyages and the nineteenth century; from the simian cannibals of primitive tribes and effete despots of Asiatic civilizations, to representations prevalent today, such as the fanatical Arabs of terrorist journalism and the passive and beguiling women of tourism's Asia.[45]

Clearly, these variously debased and picturesque, seductive and threatening images enjoyed wide prevalence in colonial cultures, and in their current forms continue unabated in contemporary media. At the same time, much earlier work on such European representations, Nicholas Thomas has suggested, tended to be 'documentary rather than critical or analytical', so that an intriguing array of examples was presented, but their 'discursive affiliations and underlying epistemologies' were frequently glossed over.[46] Moreover, most discussions of *Orientalism* seem to have followed its author's own initial remarks about his overwhelming sense of intellectual loneliness while writing the book. Thus, they have assumed the utter singularity of Said's voice and vision, overlooking that there were at the time other critical interventions that sought to articulate related concerns, connected themes.[47] This said, *Orientalism* drew upon but also exceeded the earlier work on images of non-European realms—and other kindred critical concerns—by making a persuasive case for the systematic textual fabrication of the Orient within the intertwined interstices of European knowledge and Western power.

Edward Said's work and ensuing arguments had irrevocably shifted the ground of analytical debate and political discussion on colonial representations of colonized peoples from uncovering the singular biases of determinate depictions to unravelling the deeper domains of discursive domination. This also highlighted the connection and complicity between earlier imperial imaginings and contemporary academic renderings of the Orient. Of course, a fiercely polemical and deliberately provocative work such as *Orientalism* could not but have its own share of gaps, silences, and theoretical tensions. Beyond trivializing critiques and dismissive readings, critical commentaries marked by an ethical engagement with Edward Said's seminal study have pointed out its tendency to homogenize both the field and the tenor of European representations of non-European worlds.[48] On the one hand, this implicitly overemphasized the efficacy of colonial power, underplaying the contradictory and contingent dynamic of empire driven by complex articulations of class and gender, race and sexuality. On the other hand, it accorded little place to the actions and the challenges of the colonized in the making of colonial projects. The problems emerging from such oversights and emphases have sought to be overcome in diverse ways in both historical and anthropological work—about which more in a moment—and in literary and cultural studies.

Over the past two decades, critical theories of colonial discourse and combative readings of Western representations—together with concerns of turf and tenure, and the marketing success of a hybrid label—have helped forge a new field of postcolonial criticism in metropolitan and provincial academic arenas. Wider challenges to Western canons, key renderings of critical theory, and the impassioned energies of Subaltern Studies have all played an important role here. In this new field, the implications and limitations, strengths and weaknesses of earlier critical work on colonial writing, including *Orientalism*, have been variously negotiated and elaborated, extended and exceeded by studies ranging widely in their theoretical emphases and empirical concerns.

Here I point toward three broad orientations in this newer body of work. In *Orientalism*, Said combined the early Foucauldian emphasis on the mutual determinations of knowledge and power and a Gramscian notion of hegemony, thereby eclectically but deliberately bringing together influential strains of anti-humanist thinking with understandings that emphasized human intention and purposive action behind the work of power.[49] Recent, important work within the emergent field of postcolonial criticism appears closer to anti-humanist perspectives, whether it eclectically conjoins Freud, Foucault, and Fanon, or harnesses deconstructionist readings and strategic sensibilities to fashion against-the-grain readings of subaltern subjects.[50] Moreover, important interventions in this field have variously questioned the ethics of according unchallenged efficacy to colonial projects. Particularly significant here have been explorations of the inherent 'ambivalence' of colonial discourse and the disruptive 'mimicry' of colonized subjects, challenging singular conceptions of colonial cultural writings, even as colony and empire often continue to be rendered as somewhat monolithic endeavours in the domain of literary postcolonial theory.[51] Finally, other critical studies have drawn upon historical materials to trace the interplay between the construction, institutionalization, and sedimentation of racial boundaries, gender identities, sexualized subjectivities, and class divisions in explorations of imperial imaginings, colonial cultures, and postcolonial locations. At this point, the intersections between certain strains of contemporary postcolonial literary studies and several stresses within recent historical ethnographies of colonialism become both significant and palpable.[52]

The new critical histories and ethnographies of colony and empire have thought through postulates of overarching colonial structures and overriding imperial systems by exploring the contradictory location and contending agendas of distinct colonizing peoples and diverse colonized groups in the creation of colonial cultures of rule. This has involved discussions of the representations and practices, the boundaries and contradictions of imperial agents, settler communities, and evangelizing missionaries in colonial locations. In brief, there have been ethnographic examinations of the meanings and truths not only of colonized populations but also of colonizing peoples, even if the programmatic desire toward treating the colonizer and the colonized as part of a single analytical field has sometimes receded into the background here. At any rate, such studies have revealed the persistent fault lines and the critical divisions between different agents of colonialism, diverse agendas of empire.[53] On the one hand, the racial mythologies and the 'homespun' lifestyles of colonizers sought to blur such fault lines. On the other, divisions between different colonialist groups also stood highlighted within everyday representations and quotidian practices in distinct contexts.

It follows that the view of colonialism as a monolithic venture, a seamless and homogeneous project stands tested today. At issue here are not only the variations in the colonial endeavours and imperial exertions of different nations and separate epochs, featuring diverse forms of production and exchange, all important distinctions recognized in earlier scholarship. Rather, recent ethnographies and histories have revealed that the conflicting interests and the contending visions of empire of differentially located interests and actors several times drove a single colonial project. At the same time, distinct colonial projects could draw upon each other's models and metaphors, while imbuing them with varied and contrary salience.[54]

All this has further led to close analyses of the relationship between the metropole and the colony. It has become increasingly clear that there were parallels and connections, conjunctions and contradictions between efforts to discipline and normalize subject groups at home and attempts to civilize and control subject populations in the colonies.[55] A corollary to this has been the growing recognition that the impulses of empire and their reworking in the colonies brought about changes at the heart of Western orders, which followed from the wide-ranging nature of imperial power and the far-reaching interaction of Western traditions and colonial modernities.[56] This has led to varied analyses of the many modes and diverse forms entailed by processes of colonization. There have been remarkable studies of the colonization of space, language, and the body;[57] critical discussions of imperial travel, exhibitory orders, and museum collections;[58] deft analyses of colonial writings, discourses, and representations;[59] and striking work on sexuality, race, and desire in the age of empire.[60] The cultures spawned by colonialism have made a striking appearance on the stage of cultural history and critical ethnography.

In several ways, this emphasis has provided a valuable corrective to the reification of an impersonal world capitalist system and the monumentalization of abstract colonial structures, each with their own subterranean dynamic and irrevocable logic, which characterized several influential writings in these arenas.[61] At the same time, the concerns of culture here do not necessarily discount considerations of political economy and state power. Rather, several significant studies in this new genre suggest the importance of elaborating the fluid interplay between forms of representation, terms of culture, practices of history, processes of political economy, strategies of empire, and imperatives of state formation in the metropole and the colony.[62] Here there is no *a priori* privilege accorded to any one of these heuristic domains on grounds of metatheory. Instead, the mutual determinations of these analytical arenas appear better articulated through histories and ethnographies that eschew rigorously formal frameworks and avoid resolutely abstract blueprints.

Such qualified and nuanced understandings of culture and power emerge bound to the recognition that the work of gender variously inflected the terms and processes of colony and empire. These terms extended from the lifestyles of Euro-American peoples in the colony to the politics of colonial representations, from the tensions of empire to the implications of colonial civility, and from the divisions among the colonialists to varieties of material exchanges, museum collections, and exhibitory orders. These processes ranged from the mutual entailments of the metropole and the margins to the colonization of languages and bodies, and from the contradictory location of colonial agents in places of empire to the complex fabrication of imperial cartographies, defining space(s) of wilderness and time(s) of modernity. At the same time, the critical force of gender shaped and structured these different dynamics and diverse dimensions of colonialism's cultures.[63] Here timeless abstractions regarding racial sexuality and colonial desire stand revealed as skewed sketches and coloured pictures, and influential conjunctions of Freud and Fanon have, for example, been re-examined through rereadings of Foucault's corpus and revisitations of colonial archives.[64] The interplay between race, class, and gender—key categories that lose their critical force when ritually invoked as the holy trinity of liberal/left politics—has acquired new meanings through its elaboration within colonial fields and imperial terrain.

What is at stake in the considerable theoretical and empirical achievements of the newer readings of colony and empire, particularly within anthropology and history? My sketch of the recent, interconnected but varied bearings of the historical anthropology and ethnographic history of colonial cultures should have itself suggested that this body of writing does not constitute a homogeneous whole. Rather, palpable tensions and distinct emphases between and across orientations abound in this arena. These stresses bestride writings that chiefly emphasize the productivity of power by focusing on its discursive and institutional entailments and other orientations that explore rather the practices of social subjects as reiterating and reworking, accessing and exceeding the stipulations of dominant meanings and the provisions of established power. These strains straddle work that engages primarily with discourses of culture and power and other readings that ground such considerations within the broader dynamics of political economy. Such stresses and strains appear mirrored, too, in the domain of literary colonial studies. It is critical to keep such distinctions in mind. Rather than seeking immanent resolutions and offering programmatic solutions, the precise plurality and the consequent contention in this scholarship, it seems to me, can be a source of strength for asking and addressing newer questions in the study of colonial cultures. Far from a bland eclecticism, I point to the possibilities of thinking through analytical tensions which are productive to ponder, and this book takes such a possibility as its premise.

The writings in *Postcolonial Passages* address questions of colony and empire in different yet connected ways. Our considerations open with Ranajit Guha's short and incisive, critical and imaginative essay on the imperial uncanny, articulated by the anxiety of empire. Its arguments put a distinctive spin on recent discussions of 'tensions of empire'. For, instead of exploring the disjunctions and contradictions between diverse imperial agents characteristic of several writings on the theme, Guha unravels how the primary terms of the British Empire entailed distinct registers, which betoken 'rather different, though mutually overdetermined, interpretations for their content'. With characteristic candour and creativity, Guha reads three passages of imperial writing while meditating upon key statements of Kierkegaard and Heidegger on fear and anxiety. Thereby, he poses the question: 'Can we afford to leave anxiety out of the story of empire?'

Guha argues that the requirements of a definitive causality, the discourse of law and order, have led colonialist historiography to assimilate the anxiety of empire, its indefiniteness, to a concern for the security of the state, the imperative of threat and fear. This is to say that nothing less than the limits of colonial worlds are at stake in thinking through imperial anxiety. To track this anxiety is to rend the 'triumphalist and progressivist' narratives of expansion and improvement, where enthusiasm forms the guiding strand of imperialism, as mood, mentality, and modality. It is to reveal the tattered texture of empire, where unfreedom was the routine, for the official and for the native, yet where beyond these limits, of the normal and the familiar, there further lay before the colonialist the uncanny of empire. An uncanny that could frighten by its 'incomprehensible dimensions', an uncanny that could terrify by 'the urgency of its insistence upon freedom', revealing 'if only for the duration of a blink, the possibility of not being at home in empire'.

Between fear and anxiety, rituals of power forged the authority of empire. Bernard Cohn considers the construction and representation of British authority in imperial India, the important intervention exhibiting trademark features of the anthropologist-historian's seminal scholarship, elaborating the fashioning of colonial cultures of rule. At the beginning, Cohn deftly moves between discussions of Mughal customs and analyses of British constructions, outlining thereby the cultural constitution of a ritual idiom of colonial authority in the late eighteenth and early nineteenth centuries, until the great rebellion of 1857. This sets the stage for a discussion of the transformation and consolidation of the 'cultural-symbolic constitution of British India' in the two decades following the events of 1857 and their aftermath, including the assumption of the Government of India by the British monarch in 1858.[65] Cohn's focus is on the Imperial Assemblage of 1877 held to proclaim

Queen Victoria the empress of India. The key imperial figure here was Lord Lytton, the Viceroy to India. As for the cast of Indians, the pride of place was given to native princes who were regarded as 'the natural aristocracy' of the subcontinent, but the assemblage also featured other categories of Indians, including 'native gentlemen', landlords, editors, and journalists.

Through a detailed discussion of this spectacle, Cohn unravels the colonial sociology of knowledge, imperial mappings of space and precedence, and enduring genealogies of British custom and Indian conduct. Indeed, in the best traditions of cultural history and historical ethnography, in Cohn's hands a single event becomes the means of wider theoretical and empirical discussion. Thus, his essay interrogates dominant assumptions regarding the given nature, the settled attributes, of colonial power—revealing its complex fabrications, under-scoring the importance of attending to rituals of rulers and representations of rule, and highlighting the necessity of bringing together metropolitan histories and colonial pasts as parts of an interconnected analytical field. Understood as a metaphor for the organization of power, it is not only that the Imperial Assemblage of 1877 became a model for similar rites of imperial authority. It is also that this event has lived on in implicit meanings and embodied forms at the heart of the politics of Indian nationalism—from the early nationalist meetings in the later nineteenth century, to the rituals of rule of the independent Indian state in the twentieth and twenty-first centuries.

In the next chapter, Nicholas Dirks further elaborates the interplay between colonial power and imperial knowledge, part of his wider excursus into the intimate enmeshments of caste, colonialism, and modernity in India in the nineteenth and twentieth centuries.[66] In the essay, Dirks discusses the terms, implications, and legacies of the imperial sociology of the subcontinent. Here neither power nor knowledge appears as unchanging or undifferentiated. Indeed, Dirks begins by outlining the transformations of empire in the middle of the nineteenth century, transformations that led to anthropology supplanting history as 'the principal colonial modality of knowledge and rule', so that, a few decades later, the colonial state in India took the shape of an ethnographic state, privileging ethnological apprehension as the primary means of imperial understanding. This particular regime was driven by the belief that India could be ruled using anthropological knowledge to understand and control its subjects, and to represent and legitimate its own mission. At the same time, its constructions emerged from within 'murky waters' created by a dynamic between the relentless drive of imperial empiricism and colonial anxiety regarding an incommensurable India, the inscrutable Indian. Accordingly, Dirks traces the shifts and differences in colonial projects to order and classify caste in the second half of the nineteenth century, a period that witnessed the increasing institutionalization, canonization, and formalization of such knowledge, especially all-India census and ethnographic surveys, particularly Risley's extraordinary *The People of India* project.

The imperial anxieties and colonial contradictions registered here find distinct configura-tions in Anupama Rao's discussion of violence and the law, torture and the state in colonial India. Her point of entry into the complex relationship between colonial rule, native police, and the terms of torture and punishment is the case of Gunnoo, a young man of an agricultural caste, accused of drowning his five-year-old niece, after stealing her ornaments. In the late summer of 1855, Gunnoo died in custody, after the police allegedly inserted a stick into his anus to extract a confession, setting into motion wide-ranging deliberations, including a judicial enquiry, bringing to the fore the 'discovery' and containment of torture, and the nature of 'truth' produced before the law and the state. Perceptively and critically, Rao sifts through an administrative, judicial, and medical corpus to unravel the contending implications of Gunnoo's death, evoking the multiple registers that index its legal aftermath, highlighting the critical presence of the colonized body in the exercise of imperial power.

Reading 'the developmental narrative of colonial law against the grain', Rao resituates the category and practice of torture within the terms and stipulations of the colonial judicial-penal complex. The determinations of a colonial modernity instituted sharp hierarchies between 'native' regimes of violence and the liberal rule of law, positing colonial subjects as unaware of the distinction between punishment and retribution. Yet, it was precisely here that colonial law also at once participated in the practice of torture and sought to erase its own complicity in this regime. For, the efforts of colonial governance to contain torture constituted transhistorical projections of pain and suffering, validated scientifically by medical discourses that measured the extent of injury and violation. Yet, the novel demands for proof, motive, and intention to apprehend a crime possibly also produced a police force that regarded torture as legitimate in the constitution of legal truth.

I have noted earlier that in discussions of imperial encounters, assumptions of a stimulus-response model between the colonizer and the colonized have been replaced by rather more nuanced and acute conceptions, highlighting that at stake in colonial histories were critical entanglements in complex fields, the interplay between the metropolitan and the vernacular, between meaning and power. In tune with such emphases, Sudipta Kaviraj puts the spotlight on questions of a vernacular modern in colonial conditions, articulating issues of modernity and empire. Deriving from his wider work on the writing and imagination of Bankimchandra Chattopadhyay, Kaviraj's chapter in *Postcolonial Passages* reflects upon how this extraordinary Bengali literary artist addressed a new world with an old palette.[67] Apparently grounded in somewhat modular notions of modernity and tradition, the chapter actually offers a sensitive and probing understanding of a formative figure and founding moment in the literary pasts of a vernacular modernity. Attracted at once to rationalism and its criticisms, 'tormented by the choice between subjection and modernity', Bankim alternated between 'tragic fiction' and 'comic commentary', darkness and laughter, finding his means of addressing this complexity through the work of irony. Through irony, Bankim retained the contradictions of the social world, shaping not the ideas of a Bengali modernity but shaping the very medium for the making of these ideas, refusing the assurance of appointed discursive spaces on offer in the colonial world, since the choice itself was tragic. The imaginative and prescient terms of Kaviraj's analyses reveal, thereby, the different purposes of laughter, tragedy, and irony, the distinct shapes of modernity, forcing us to rethink a literary imagination in the colonial world, but also the historical world of the nationalist imagination.

NATION AND NATIONALISM

The trouble with nationalism is that it refuses to go away. Once lauded as a remarkable achievement of Western history and the European Enlightenment, duly exported to the colonies, today rather separate yet equally persistent, commonplace, dominant dispositions toward nationalism rule the roost. Here I point to three such tendencies, seemingly disparate articulations of nationalism and nation that are actually bound to each other.

First, for sometime now, in media stories and academic analyses, in Western polities and in other arenas, nationalism has frequently appeared as the current, primitive product of the Third World. Here ethnic conflict, religious violence, and primordial nationalism constitute an unholy trinity, signifying lack of democracy and politics of backwardness. Thus, indigent nationalism becomes a durable and dangerous commodity from distant and dark margins, not unlike Latin American drugs and African Caribbean voodoo, all too capable of upsetting the rational orders and the democratic polities of Western places and civilized spaces.[68] Such spectres are ever close at hand, haunting the aggressive instincts of powerful Western states and their Eurocentric nationalist ideologies.

Second, it follows that with ceaseless strategic interests and carefully cultivated histories assiduously woven into their fabric, the moment there is the slightest rending of this surface, these dominant nation-states and their authoritative nationalism(s) assert themselves, belligerently—as event and image. An admittedly dramatic instance, the aftermath of 11 September 2001, is a case in point. Craig Calhoun puts it candidly:

One need be no friend to terrorism to be sorry that the dominant response to the terrorist attacks has been framed as a matter of war rather than crime, an attack on America rather than an attack on humanity. What could have been an occasion for renewing the drive to establish an international criminal court and multilateral institutions needed for law enforcement quickly became an occasion for America to demonstrate its power and its allies to fall into line with the 'war against terrorism'. Militarism gained and civil society lost not only on September 11 but in the response that followed . . . as the US and other administrations moved to sweep aside protections for the rights of citizens and immigrants alike and strengthen the state in pursuit of 'security'.[69]

Here there are divergences but also conjunctions between distinct expressions of nation and nationalism.

For, finally, in the non-Western world today invocations of nationalism and evocations of national culture are often a ruse for authoritarian governments and populist regimes to endorse indigenist visions, and to engender ideologies founded on a cultural rhetoric of innate difference. On offer are terms of majoritarian politics, relentlessly seeking the support of majority publics, statist citizens, which also imbues these processes with a distinct twist. Such native rehearsals of the nation and indigenous stagings of nationalism simultaneously represent, as though in a mirror, the ideals of historical progress and the idioms of manly adulthood, the signs of a mature state in the image of a Western modernity.

Considered together, two points stand out. On the one hand, even as courageous theorists of a brave new world of global culture spirit away nationalism, the beast rears its ahead and announces its presence, through a rear door—but also from the wings—of this apparently novel transnational stage of history. On the other hand, as Ana Maria Alonso has pointed out, a great deal of 'the misplaced concreteness' that bedevils understandings of nation and nationalism, state formation and ethnicity 'results from the uncritical reproduction of common sense that poses intellectual as well as political problems'. This elides efforts to call the 'naturnalness of nationalism and the primordialness of ethnicity into question', also reproducing 'the precepts of nationalism and colonialism on the concept of culture', articulated through overriding demarcations of traditions and modernity, East and West.[70]

Confronting dominant assumptions and commonplace conceptions, in recent times, critical scholarship has emphasized that nation and nationalism are far from being innate ideas, immaculate imaginings, primordial conceptions, or transcendental categories. Rather, across a range of specific contexts and determinate arenas, nationalisms and nations have elaborated wide varieties of historical practice and detailed diverse forms of cultural action, in the pursuit of often-contending agendas and aspirations.[71] At least three, overlapping strands of scholarship have played an important role in developing newer understandings of nation and nationalism. First, acute ethnographic accounts, sociological discussions, and literary explorations of state, nation, and nationalism have questioned familiar understandings of these categories and entities, in the past and the present.[72] Second, related academic efforts have critically considered the interplay between global and transnational processes, on the one hand, and the imperatives of nation and nationalism, on the other.[73] Finally, the body of work associated with Subaltern Studies, along with related scholarship, has held a mirror to the biography of the nation, especially by unravelling the articulation of subaltern nationalisms, the distinctions of anticolonial renderings of the nation, and the terms, limits, and sway of the nation-state.[74]

It will be clear that recent critical writings on nation and nationalism all appear animated and articulated by anti-essentialist sensibilities. Thus, Robert Foster points to a certain shared scholarly sentiment when he writes, 'Neither the nation-as-community nor, therefore, national culture has any essential properties (the arguments of nationalists notwithstanding). Nations and national cultures are artifacts—continually imagined, invented, contested, and transformed by the agencies of individual persons, the state, and global flows of commodities. As an ideology, nationalism (as well as a set of correlated practices, the nation) is perhaps the most compelling and consequential artifact of modern times. But it is nonetheless an artifact, formulated variously, with various effects, in various social and historical contexts.'[75] Yet, such anti-essentialist emphases warrant staying with, thinking through, longer. Consider, for example, that it is not only the nationalist, alluded to by Foster, who assumes that the nation has essential attributes. After all, much of the structuring of modern practices of history writing has taken place under the sign of the nation, which has distinct consequences for the manner in which the nation becomes a taken-for-granted entity in the imagining of pasts and the organization of the discipline. My point is that the newer emphases on considering nations as cultural products, 'imagined communities', and of treating nationalism as at once a historical and a cultural process have revealed key, critical possibilities, but these orientations can come with their own limitations.

On the one hand, to simply reiterate the constructed nature of nationalism can overlook how this very artefact becomes a structure of feeling, a texture of experience, the stuff of peoples' lives. Obscuring the modalities and moments of the transactions and transformations in question, such intellectual moves also tend to underplay 'the relationship between common sense categories of experience and analytical concepts developed in order to understand the processes that produce such [taken-for-granted] categories'.[76] To take these emphases even further, it is critical to examine how the ideologies and practices, pedagogy and performance, assiduously construing nationalism and nation become a part of the world, acquiring pervasive ontological attributes.[77] At stake here are understandings of the production and dissemination of imagined communities within the interstices of and the interplay between the distinct contexts, the particular processes, defining every nationalism, and the acute presence of the inherent naturalness, the already given character, of each nation.[78]

On the other hand, through the means of anti-essentialism, to endlessly demystify the nation, to repeatedly disenchant nationalism, as projects and processes of power, might be to attend to their fabrications and creations, but these analytical measures can also under-enunciate the distinctions and differences that such elaboration embodies. At the heart of these considerations lie issues of power and differences. As I have discussed elsewhere, several strands of recent critical scholarship converge in their tendency toward considering power as a totalized terrain, and casting difference as unsullied alterity, ahead of power.[79] Possibly, such stances lead to unease, even impatience, with anticolonial nationalism(s), led by a middle-class elite, and subaltern articulations of nation and nationalism. The former endeavours appear assimilated to nationalism-as-usual, projects of power defined by modular attributes.[80] The latter efforts stand usually disregarded in favour of subaltern counter-hegemonic endeavours that directly question and resist the nation.[81] There are weighty elisions at work here.

This becomes clear if we turn to just a few of the lessons learnt from the important work of the last two decades on Indian nationalism. Consider, first, that subaltern endeavours in the wider terrain of anticolonial nationalism articulated their visions of freedom and initiatives of independence through frames of meaning and idioms of struggle that accessed and exceeded the aims and strategies of a generally middle-class nationalist leadership. The supplementary nature of subaltern practices straddled their particular imaginary renderings of the nation and their distinct politics of nationalism. Yet, such imperatives of subaltern difference do not mean that middle-class anticolonial nationalism was ever governed by the logic of historical sameness, featuring relentless reproductions of the modular form of the nation earlier assembled in the West, ceaseless copies of an imagined community out of Europe. Briefly put, middle-class nationalism in the colony did not merely reproduce but rather reworked Enlightenment principles and post-Enlightenment traditions to translate and transform the ideals of the sovereign nation and the free citizen through grids of the subjugated homeland and the colonized subject.

Now, to point toward such disjunction and distinction at the core of anticolonial nationalisms is not to posit that, whether in their subaltern incarnation or their middle-class avatar, such endeavour embodied innocent difference, expressing immaculate alterity. The picture is muddier, murkier, as it should be. If we think of middle-class Indian nationalism, the nation appeared imagined here as a community in the 'inner domain' of culture long before its formal articulation in the domain of institutionalized politics, and nation and nationalism stood elaborated in diverse communitarian ways, each challenging univocal conceptions of these categories.[82] Yet, precisely these considerations foreground questions of the supplanting of different, communitarian imaginings of the nation by a dominant vision of the nation-state holding the 'single, determinate, demographically enumerable form of the nation' as the only viable form of community, defining the terms of the modern Indian state.[83] All this also points toward the burden of the 'majority' and male Indian placed on the 'minority' and woman subject—and upon other subaltern, gendered, subjects, too—in the forging of the figure of the Indian citizen, implicitly envisioned in the image of the male, upper-caste Hindu.

For their part, subaltern expressions of nationalism also did not construe ultimately pure verities. Moulded in crucibles of power, they inflected and instated authoritative meanings of state, dominant mappings of nation. With their very difference first recovered by a writing of history that was enacted under the sign of the nation, such pasts and practices crucially highlight the need for a writing that traces the critical entanglements of state and community, the nation and the subaltern. Nothing less than the shared determinations of the work of power and the labour of difference are at stake here—power restlessly inflected by difference, and difference uneasily shot through by power.[84]

Significantly, the essays ahead do not simply succumb to the ready seductions of anti-essentialist impulses. Rather, in distinct ways they address the experiential and ontological attributes of nation and nationalism, the critical interplay between state and community, and the mutual constitution of the majority, Indian, citizen and the minority, gendered, subject. The section, then, opens with a short essay, the concluding chapter of Partha Chatterjee's seminal study, *The Nation and its Fragments*, a book that makes a persuasive case for the difference defining anticolonial nationalism in Asia and Africa.[85] In this chapter, Chatterjee clearly reveals how his emphases do not merely constitute a Third Worldist defence of such nationalist endeavour. Here he interrogates the modern nation-state, focusing on the Indian nation, through a wide-ranging and sophisticated critique of the 'grand narrative of capital' and a spirited endorsement of the 'independent narrative of community' within regimes of modernity. Chatterjee argues that the narrative of capital seeks to suppress the narrative of community, a suppression that also lies at the heart of modern European social theory. On the one hand, the modern state, embedded within this larger narrative of capital, 'cannot recognize within its jurisdiction any form of community except the single, determinate, demographically enumerable form of the nation'. On the other hand, 'by its very nature, the idea of community marks a limit to the realm of disciplinary power'.

There are problems with this sharp separation between state and community.[86] Yet, it is important to stay with, work through, the dramatic distinction—patiently, modestly. I indicate three reasons here. First, by locating narratives of community within regimes of modernity, rather than reifying these as instances of romanticized tradition or as 'pre-modern remnants that an absent-minded Enlightenment forgot to erase', Chatterjee takes an enormous step forward in our understanding of community and modernity, state and nation. Second, in Chatterjee's analyses, community and state are not so much empirical categories, as they describe entities that carry critical epistemological connotations, moral ontological attributes. Finally, these characteristics provide Chatterjee's readings with theoretical rigour and analytical force to think through the categories of the state and civil society, the individual and the community in traditions of modern political thought. They allow him to point toward possibilities of uncovering the contradiction between the two narratives of capital and community embedded within the idea of the modern nation, including anticolonial nationalism, and to suggest other imaginings of community, nation(s), and modernity.

Next, Shahid Amin critically considers community and state, memory and history, the subaltern and the nation, through a many-layered narrative, juxtaposing colonial and nationalist records and vernacular and 'local' tales, reading the archive against the grain and exploring uncertain byways of historical fieldwork. The chapter consists of excerpts from the final section of *Event, Metaphor, Memory,* a remarkable book on a critical event of subcontinental history. On 4 February 1922, a crowd of peasants burnt a police station in Chauri Chaura, a small market town in Uttar Pradesh, killing twenty-three policemen—all in the name of Mahatma Gandhi's *swaraj* (freedom). This led Gandhi, who had visited the Gorakhpur region a year before, to call off the Non-cooperation–Khilafat movement, initiating the lasting lineaments of a nationalist discourse, which has since ceaselessly, simultaneously recalled and forgotten this affair by naming it after the place where it happened, Chauri Chaura. The affair also set into grinding motion the wheels of the colonial law and order machinery, culminating in a massive judicial trial. Amin renarrates this richly documented, dramatic occurrence as a means of unravelling the 'curiously "Gandhian" politics of the peasants before they entered the record as "rioters" ', searching out 'the relationship between Gandhi and his peasant followers', and seeking 'insights into ways of nationalist historiography'.[87] This is to say that he understands Chauri Chaura as event and metaphor, work of history and memory, production of the past and the present. The portions of the larger study on offer here take up these tasks by drawing upon the labour of 'family histories'—the multiple registers of the account straddling even tempos and uneven tempers, weaving regular tones and irregular textures, traversing familiar routes and jagged pathways— critically representing the many lives of Indian nationalism.

Indeed, there are no ready resolutions offered by the narrative, no comfortable guarantees proffered by this history. On the one hand, the attention to 'detail' and the ethic of 'singularity' at the heart of the account—from its reckoning of Gandhi's presence in the cluster of settlements around Chauri Chaura to its exploration of critical distinctions of peasant nationalist attire and practice—make for two simultaneous moves, analytical and descriptive, as theory and story. Here the self-image of nationalism in its dominant telling(s) does not exhaust every passion and all creativity of peasant understandings, local actions, including the ways in which peasants translated, transferred, and transformed 'alien concepts into idioms which fit their everyday lives'. Yet, it is also the case that 'local and familial memories of the event' appear as 'often at variance with, but seldom independent, of judicial and nationalist accounts'—'inescapably tainted or vitiated or coloured in varying degrees by the hegemonic master narratives.' On the other hand, Amin's fidelity to facts, his contrapuntal conjunction of the archive and the field, lead to novel configurations of theory and narrative, and make newer demands upon critical thought and historical practice. For, in the account, analysis is served by description, eschewing overt intervention, so that facts, unexpected and expected, disrupt interpretive assumptions, even speaking for themselves— 'not in the preemptive tones of positivist certainty, but in the uneasy echoes of limiting doubt.'[88]

In authoritative apprehensions and routine representations, the subjects of nationalism and communalism in India have for long appeared as dualities, innately marked off the one from the other, quite as a contending vision, increasingly ascendant today, has equated the Indian nation with the Hindu subject, assiduously, explicitly, vigorously, especially in recent years. Yet, do mutual premises of majoritarian politics, defining the nation and the citizen, in fact bind these competing conceptions? What critical conjunctions stand revealed by analytically and empirically holding together partition and nation, communalism and nationalism, as parts of a common field, made up of shared discursive practices? Can such endeavour hold a mirror to the reciprocal determinations and joint denials of majoritarian nationalisms, 'secular' and 'religious'? In *Postcolonial Passages*, even as the very organization of each essay in the section on 'nationalism and nation' addresses such questions, the issues receive focused attention in the following two contributions.

Gyanendra Pandey's 'Disciplining Difference', drawn from his recent, important book, *Remembering Partition*, takes as its starting point the moment of rupture and genocide that marked the birth of the two nations of India and Pakistan, exploring efforts to nationalize populations, history, and culture as part of claims to nation-statehood, formations of nation-states.[89] Here Pandey asks the question: In front of the blurred boundaries that characterize all nations and nationalisms, how did nationalists in India and Pakistan set about cleansing the sacred space of their nation? How did they define the core citizen, and contain, 'discipline', difference within the nation-state in a wider context of the mutual constitution of violence and community? In the chapter, Pandey focuses on the shadowy shape yet the critical form of the 'nationalist Muslim' within the politics of the Indian nation, and the strenuous efforts of the governments of India and Pakistan to recover and return abducted women of the 'other' religious/national community, both in the aftermath, the wake, of the Partition. He thereby unravels the repeated violence and consistent vagary that have forged the figure of the citizen—marked by the endless anxiety and patterned arbitrariness of state and nation, seizing community, shaping family. Once more, on offer is a history without warranty.[90]

The contribution by Ritu Menon and Kamla Bhasin, taken from their significant study of women and the partition, *Borders and Boundaries*, turns upon three sets of memories, recorded in recent years, straddling and scrabbling the past and the present.[91] These are accounts of a Hindu woman who rejoined her Muslim husband in Lahore after the partition, living there as a convert; of three Muslim sisters who never thought of leaving their home, Lucknow; and of a Sikh woman who came to India in 1947, only to be torn apart by the violence against her community in 1984. The ordinariness of these narratives is remarkable: set in everyday language, drawing upon discourses of community and state, nationalism and nation, yet they imbue these idioms with a distinct twist, their own salience. Not surprisingly, in the most dramatic moment of the three narratives, when the Sikh woman, Taran, speaks of fighting against violence, of losing her country, in 1984, she does so in registers of quotidian heroism and loss. Her telling establishes that accounts such as hers, and those of the Lucknow sisters and the woman in Lahore, require envisioning not in the looking glass of the spectacular, but through recognition of their very ordinary, even routine, quality as bearing critical distinctions, posing challenges to the imagination of the historian, the writing of history. Indeed, in the hands of Menon and Bhasin the three narratives become the means for asking poignant, prescient questions about the gender of state and nation, citizen and community, exploring women's lives as stitched and split by family, community, and nation, and confronting the terms of a bigoted nationalist practice and the requirements of a proactive secular politics. It follows that in dialogue with the other chapters in the section this one too suggests other imaginings of community, nation(s), and modernity.

Margins of Modernity

Recent years have seen serious questioning of the teleological models of the past. Around 1969, his faith in several of the certainties of historical materialism yet unshaken, the British

Marxist historian Eric Hobsbawm chose to define progress in history in—what he then thought of as—minimal terms, the increasing control of human beings over nature.[92] Perhaps unknown to himself, the tireless historian's caution was not out of place. Fairly soon, the rhetoric of revolution was in retreat, the seductions of structuralism were being replaced by the allure of poststructuralism, and potent but ebbing narratives of human liberation were encountering nascent but unmistakable stirrings against enduring representations of Western-style development.

Did a question mark loom over the notion of progress invoked by Hobsbawm? There was no writing on the wall, but new scripts were emerging. It followed that ten years after, when the famous but fickle rock band, Pink Floyd, orchestrated an assault on a rather different wall, yoking disciplinary strategies of institutional regimes to the rhythmic beat of pop culture, perceptions of the dark side of the Enlightenment were gaining in popularity. By now, a conception of progress such as that of Eric Hobsbawm could appear as a sign of dominant Western knowledge, mark of a hegemonic Eurocentric perspective. Twenty years later, an altogether concrete wall, a testimony to the rabid imaginings of the Cold War, came down. Of course, free-market publicists and navel-gazing theorists celebrated the event as the demise of Marxism and the end of history, hyperbole for the close of Soviet-style communism and the triumph of Western capitalism. The blinkers of such ideologues apart, it continues to be widely overlooked that the technocratic conceptions not only of warriors of scientific socialism but also of crusaders of capital articulate totalitarian tendencies, embedded in meaning-legislative reason and generative of social-engineering projects. Such are the shared entailments of overblown visions of capitalist and communist modernities. At the same time, in intellectual worlds in the wake of the fall of the wall, Hobsbawm's proposal of progress could also itself signify a symptom and a consequence of the cunning, artifice, and folly of reason. The questions continue. Not surprisingly, a little over thirty years after Hobsbawm's suggestion not too many humanist scholars or social scientists will uncritically invoke the proviso of progress as the hallmark of history.

Yet, through all these decades and since long before, patterns of progress and blueprints of development lie intertwined with authoritative projections of the trajectory of history and the ends of modernity. Such schemes posit the essential identity of modular forms of institutions and ideologies, systems and structures, discourses and dynamics, seen as the building blocks of universal history. Such fabrication of the essential identity of modular forms—for example, of nation and development, capitalism and modernity—does not deny their mutability or their lack, particularly in non-Western contexts. Rather, these mutations and this lack form part of a singular logic that provides the underlying key and the organizing principle defining the inherent sameness of history. Indeed, the mutability, the lack, and the sameness of the modular forms of history mutually presuppose each other. People everywhere may act variously, but the logic of their actions either conforms to or deviates from the master design of universal history.

It should be clear that to argue in this vein is not to concur with contemporary cultural critiques that conceive of the modern project of History as the endless enactment of Reason—the use of the capital case is deliberate—and tend toward blunt polemic and facile politics. Put simply, they conflate histories of sameness with the sameness of history, overlooking the plurality constitutive of the writing of history, discussed in focused ways a little later, and also varieties of historical practice that have for long struggled with the 'nature' of the past, even reading it against the grain of development in history.[93] Such plurality and practice give the lie to the totalizing cast of impatient critiques of modern historiography, critiques that seize upon the singularity of central conceptions of history only to render history as an inherently singular project. The plurality puts a question mark alike on conservative, liberal, and radical conceptions and postcolonial, postmodern, and primitivist apprehensions, which establish *a priori* correspondence between the object of History and the subject of Reason by turning both into cabalistic caricatures, reinstating thereby the binaries between myth and history, tradition and modernity, magic and rationality.

The problem has deep roots. For long now, in dominant conceptions, history has been a mark of the modern. At least since the Enlightenment, the *telos* of modernity has been designated and dressed up, staged and rehearsed as history. Not surprisingly, a key characteristic of the modern condition concerns its enduring imagining that modernity as history has already happened elsewhere. This generates within the modern a fear of looking unoriginal—in Western arenas and in non-Western theatres. At the same time, a central stipulation of the *telos* of modernity also dictates that its embodied trajectory as history awaits enactment elsewhere, transforming terrain that still requires the magical touch of inexorable progress and unavoidable development, in large doses or small measures. Those peoples who refuse this trajectory appear as forsaking all claims upon universal history, which is a matter of celebration or sorrow. Here reified representations of the exclusive *telos* of a monumental modernity engender fear of tragedy or visions of triumph; and, governed by this singular logic, laments for ravaged tradition and community do battle with celebrations of modern progress and history.[94]

It is important to carefully question these competing conceptions, which valorize an exclusive modernity, or glorify romanticized tradition, but to do so recognizing that far from being mere ideological aberrations, patiently awaiting their inevitable exorcism through superior knowledge, such schemes have pervasive ontological dimensions.[95] This might be to elaborate a 'third space' or to articulate a 'militant middle ground', but it will be to do so following Walter Benjamin's injunction to drive out all trace of development, progress, from the image of history, interrogating the privileged trajectory of a singular, universal history.[96] This will be to underscore the possibilities of alternative articulations of pasts, which question the conceit of a meaning-legislating reason in order to work through contending interpretive rationalities, elaborating plural understandings. The work of margins has important implications here.

Margins carry geometrical designation and logical entailments. Margins are also contentious terrain and contending categories. Margins are attributes of social space, its ends. Margins are also devices of critical thought, its means. In these pages, margins do not merely refer to dispossessed peoples and subaltern groups. They also point toward domains of human knowledge and arenas of historical endeavour subordinated by scholarly schemes in the social sciences and normalized by distinct disciplines in the humanities. I speak here of strategies and blueprints of knowledge that have variously turned critical difference into mind-numbing sameness and transformed a shared humanity into exotic otherness. In this book, margins are fluid terrain that stand rendered as bounded arenas—designated as peripheral by states of erudition, and entailed as disreputable by reasons of governance—but they are also porous borders that interrogate the central claims of dominant knowledge and enlightened power.

In tune with such emphases, my own essay in the volume carries forward key issues relating to historical margins and subaltern pasts through an examination of ritual and resistance, myth and history, and designs of institutional politics and diffuse imperatives of gender in the pasts of an untouchable and heretical group, the Satnamis. Here, colony and nation, far from privileged as the organizing tropes of modern history, find exploration instead through the perspectives of the pasts of a group on the margins of nation and empire. On the one hand, my account begins before the initiation of colonial rule and takes the story through to after the end of empire, thereby suggesting the importance of linkages between the precolonial, the colonial, and the postcolonial. On the other hand, the pasts of a subaltern endeavour do not appear here assimilated to overarching frameworks of colonialism and nationalism. Rather, I discuss the work of empire and the meanings of nation in terms of their place within the lives of the community, ever refracted through the grids of vernacular understandings. Intersecting with but also exceeding, acceding to but equally challenging the terms of ritual power and caste hierarchy, colonial authority and nationalist imperatives, the subaltern Satnamis carved their own visions and practices surrounding sect and caste, myth and history, gender and order, which also instituted dominant designs within the community.

Next, Gyan Prakash elaborates the relationship between production and reproduction, domination and autonomy, caste hierarchy and spirit cults—actively structured and assiduously articulated by ritual practices and mythic meanings—in colonial eastern India.[97] Prakash explores the case of labour relations between *kamias* (bonded labourers) and *maliks* (landlords) in the southern reaches of the province of Bihar. Reconstructing spirit cult practices in the region in the late nineteenth and early twentieth century, he reveals how this complex of ritual practices simultaneously mapped and reproduced unequal relations between kamias and maliks, articulating caste hierarchy and social bondage. Through a close engagement with the work of Pierre Bourdieu, Prakash argues against rule-centred analyses which subordinate human practice to abstract schemes and grand designs—schemes and designs variously holding that 'transactional norms of the caste system', or 'debt relationships', or the 'supply and demand of labour', once in place, simply drove landlords and labourers into actions that reproduced bondage.

Rather, Prakash emphasizes the densely situated, seemingly contradictory, and entirely practical nature of these processes—aimed at distinct and concrete ends, sought by maliks and kamias—in the reproduction of bondage. Here, rituals were not mere executions of pre-existing rules, and spirit cults did not simply reflect unequal relations between kamias and maliks. 'In fact, ritual practices were dynamic events in which social relations were actively reconstructed. Through propitiation of ancestors and spirits, people sought to deal with "good" and "bad" deaths. In doing so, they made spirit cults an arena for the reproduction of social order.' Gyan Prakash not only interrogates the analytical primacy accorded to totalizing taxonomies of caste, but also underscores the complex articulations of indigenous inequalities with colonial domination. He foregrounds histories that defy generative schemes orchestrated by singular overriding metaphors and grand organizing tropes. Thus, historical margins reveal, once again, the need to rethink central theories of the relationship between colonialism and hegemony, ritual and power.

Dipesh Chakrabarty further expands the terms of minority histories by considering alternative articulations of subaltern pasts, providing a distinct twist to the notion of critical margins.[98] His essay begins with familiar dimensions of minority histories, entwined today with multicultural imperatives, part of 'the struggle for inclusion and representation that are characteristic of representative and liberal democracies'. Over the past few decades, the range of minority histories has vastly expanded and even changed historical discourse. Yet, bound as they are to 'public life' and its requirements—widening the reach of history through the impulse of democracy, despite their differences the writings coming together through their mutual acceptance of shared rational and evidentiary rules—such minority histories have not necessarily brought the discipline and the imagination of history to crisis. It is precisely here that Chakrabarty considers the possibility of alternative understandings of minority histories—as relationships to the past made 'minor' or 'marginal', 'inferior' or 'nonrational' by the 'rational' operations of the historian's methods. Such subordinated relations to the past are what Chakrabarty calls subaltern pasts—pasts that resist historicization, casting doubt on the major narratives of the historical discipline, pointing to the limits of the discourse of history, calling attention to the importance of staying with heterogeneities 'without seeking to reduce them to any overarching principle that speaks for an already given whole'.

How does Chakrabarty go about delineating subaltern pasts? Significantly, he thinks through the different voices of the nineteenth-century rebel peasant leaders, Sidhu and Kanu, and the historian Ranajit Guha—and the gap between them—as describing the agency of the Santal god, Thakur, without assimilating these to a third voice. Moreover, Chakrabarty intimates the presence of the medieval in the modern, and indicates the place of the supernatural in our own worlds. He underscores thereby the critical provisos of subaltern pasts within the historical discipline, a relation of difference that is hardly one of mutual exclusion, since difference itself is 'always the name of a relationship, for it separates just as much as it connects'. On the one hand, as moments signifying the intractability of the archive in the work of professional history, belonging to socially subordinate classes and minority identities, but attributes also of subordinate histories of elite and dominant groups, subaltern pasts are products of the weaving of historical narratives. They are 'stubborn knots that stand out and break up the otherwise evenly woven surface of the fabric'. On the other hand, the relations of subordination and difference implied by subaltern pasts themselves return, 'as an implicit element of the conditions that make it possible for us to historicize', revealing that the writing of history 'assumes plural ways of being in the world'. Taken together, subaltern pasts are supplementary to the historian's pasts; emerging as part of history writing, they enable the discipline to be what it is, yet show what its limits are, including bringing to the fore the imperious instincts of the historicizing impulse, the historical discipline. According to Chakrabarty, subaltern pasts may be considered as intimations received of 'a shared, unhistoricizable, ontological now', making 'any particular moment of the historical present out of joint with itself', the irreducible heterogeneity here pointing toward the struggle, 'or even groping, for nonstatist forms of democracy', which are yet to be understood or envisaged completely.

In the last chapter of this section, an excerpt from her book, *The Other Side of Silence*, Urvashi Butalia acutely grapples with what Gadamer has described as the 'experience of history, which we ourselves have' that is 'covered only to a small degree by that which we would name as historical consciousness'.[99] The experience of history that precedes, exceeds, and resists the objectifications of documentary historiography, while making the latter possible—issues discussed in the previous essay. The chapter is the beginning of the story that Butalia tells in the book, a story that begins, 'as all stories inevitably do', with the self. She writes of blood, of her uncle, Ranamama, and her mother, Subhadra. She writes of her own experiences. She writes of stories heard since childhood, stories recalling loss, then recording resentment, and finally registering indifference. In between, Butalia interweaves other tales, which recount some of the other beginnings scattered through the story.

In the narrative, working through the density of stories, of the past and the present, there is the blurring of neat divisions between the private and the public, family and nation, categories and entities that are straddled and scrambled, retained and resisted, imbued with other senses and cadences, invested with distinct textures and sensibilities. In the account, resting upon stories heard earlier and those heard recently, there is the snapping of shreds of family, a rending of the fabric of nation. Yet, there is no set escape from, no ready exorcism of, nation and family, the terms of their haunting present in endless stories—stories told and untold, heard and unheard, old and new. There is perhaps more to discuss regarding the challenges of Butalia's writing to the discourse of history, its critical recuperation of historical margins, but this might be to turn a deaf ear to a telling that does not 'mean to theorize about grand things'. Yet, Butalia does want to ask questions—'difficult, disturbing questions'—with which I leave you, the reader.

AT THE END

By way of an afterword, responding to my queries expressed in an interview conducted over email, Dipesh Chakrabarty offers critical considerations on the presence of the 'universal' and the place of the 'particular', reflecting on questions of history and modernity arising from his recent book, *Provincializing Europe*, questions that are closely bound to the concerns of *Postcolonial Passages*.[100] Here Chakrabarty approaches 'community' as always/already fragmented, also disavowing, at least for himself, the 'representative function' of history, endorsing instead the more diffuse idea of life-worlds, which overlap and intimate different ways of being in the world. Arguing that intellectuals at once inhabit and deny such different ways of being in the world, including through techniques of 'historicism', and claiming that what makes historicism possible is that which resists historicism, Chakrabarty at once builds upon totalizing and non-totalizing tendencies of thought. Far from railing against universals, he finds European thought as providing a limited though critical 'purchase on the life-practices through which we world the worlds', equally emphasizing the 'need to think the universals as part of immanent critiques of structures of domination that predicate themselves on the same universals'. Alongside, Chakrabarty registers the transhistorical pretensions of such universals since they present 'a particular, and not universal, genealogy of thought', while he recognizes the salience of the translational processes, practical and theoretical, through which such universals, concepts and practices, enter other languages and worlds, being made 'one's own' within different, heterogeneous 'histories of belonging'.

Notes

1. A single example should suffice, concerning the impact of the Subaltern Studies project on writings on Latin America, an impulse important for this volume. Not only has there been the formation of a wide-ranging Latin American Subaltern Studies project in the US, but the work of the South Asian collective has found wide discussion in Latin America itself. For the former tendency, see Jose Rabasa, Javier Sanjines, and Robert Carr (eds), *Subaltern Studies in the Americas*, a special issue of *disposition: American Journal of Cultural Histories and Theories*, 46, 1994, published 1996; Ileana Rodriguez (ed.), *A Latin American Subaltern Studies Reader*, Durham: Duke University Press, 2001; and John Beverley, *Subalternity and Representation: Arguments in Cultural Theory*, Durham: Duke University Press, 1999. On the latter initiatives, see, Silvia Rivera Cusicanqui and Rossana Barragan (eds), *Debates Post Coloniales: Una Introduction a los Estudios de la Subalternidad*, La Paz, Bolivia: Sierpe, 1997; *Historia y Grafia*, special number of the journal on 'Historia y subalternidad', guest edited by John Kraniauskas and Guillermo Zermeño, 12, 1999, 7–176; and Saurabh Dube (ed.), *Pasados poscoloniales: Colección de ensayos sobre la nueva historia y etnografia de la India*, Mexico City: El Colegio de México, 1999. Consider also, Florencia Mallon, 'The Promise and Dilemma of Subaltern Studies: Perspectives from Latin American Histories', *American Historical Review*, 99, 1994, 1491–1515; Saurabh Dube, *Sujetos subalternos: Capítulos de una historia anthropológica*, Mexico City: El Colegio de México, 2001; and Saurabh Dube, *Genealogías del presente: Conversión, colonialismo, cultura*, Mexico City: El Colegio de México, 2004.

2. The nature of this introduction warrants an explanation. My effort is to locate recent critical histories and ethnographies of South Asia concerning colonialism, nationalism, and modernity and its margins in the context of wider—transnational, if you must—discussions of these questions. I hope that the move will act as a foil to the tendency to regard this work as entirely exceptional, cutting-edge unto itself, or a one-off oddity, which also reproduces an insular disposition toward scholarship on India. Accordingly, I have also not rehearsed here, for example, debates on the 'transition to colonialism' in the eighteenth and nineteenth centuries or arguments regarding peasant autonomy and middle-class leadership within Gandhian nationalism, as initiated in the 1970s and important till today, especially since they have already found wide summary and survey, discussion and dissemination. This is neither to suggest that we disregard the work of, say, Christopher Bayly on the political economy of colonialism, of Bipan Chandra on nationalism and communalism, nor to imply that critical apprehensions of colony, nation, and modernity are exclusive to Subaltern Studies and related writings. I trust this will become clear through the terms of this introduction, reflected also in the nature of its references.

3. I discuss these questions—and the literature that they have spawned—in Saurabh Dube, *Stitches on Time: Colonial Textures and Postcolonial Tangles*, Durham: Duke University Press, 2004.

4. Bernard Cohn, 'History and Anthropology: The State of the Play', *Comparative Studies in Society and History*, 22, 1980, 198–221.

5. See, for example, Joan Vincent, *Anthropology and Politics: Visions, Traditions, and Trends*, Tuscon: University of Arizona Press, 1990: 225–9, 308–14. See also, George Stocking, Jr, 'Colonial Situations', in Stocking, Jr (ed.). *Colonial Situations: Essays on the Contextualization of Ethnographic Knowledge*, Madison: University of Wisconsin Press, 1991, 3–4.

6. Even as the theoretical assault on functionalism seemed to have exhausted it as a paradigm within anthropology by the mid-1960s, functionalist tenets could continue to be important in the practice of the discipline in several, including non-Western, contexts—for example, maintaining their hold in universities in India—until very recently. Moreover, with structuralism assuming newer forms in conjunction with Marxism in the 1970s, key structuralist-Marxist writings, such as those of Maurice Bloch, could be based upon functionalist premises. S.N. Einstadt, 'Functional Analysis in Anthropology and Sociology: An Interpretive Essay', *Annual Review of Anthropology*, 19, 1990, 243–51; Sherry B. Ortner, 'Theory in Anthropology since the Sixties', *Comparative Studies in Society and History*, 26, 1984, 127–32, 135–41; Vincent, *Anthropology and Politics*, 335–41; and Maurice Bloch, *From Blessing to Violence: History and Ideology in the Circumcision Ritual of the Merina of Madagascar*, Cambridge: Cambridge University Press, 1986.

7. Here I am aware of the key differences within these traditions: for example, between the ethnography of Malinowski and the ethnology of Radcliffe-Brown, or even the tensions between the radical structuralism of Levi-Strauss and the structural analysis of British anthropologists. At the same time, my effort is to underscore the broad orientations toward structure and action within functionalism and structuralism. Bronislaw Malinowski, *Argonauts of the Western Pacific: An Account of Native Adventures in the Archipelagoes of Melanesian New Guinea*, London: Routledge, 1922; A.R. Radcliffe-Brown, *Structure and Function in Primitive Society*, Glencoe: Free Press, 1952; Ortner, 'Theory in Anthropology': 135–8; Vincent, *Anthropology and Politics*: 155–71; and George Stocking, Jr, *After Tylor: British Social Anthropology 1888–1951*, Madison: University of Wisconsin Press, 1995, 233–441.

8. The problems of a break with 'native experience' and of the repression of temporality are very well brought out by Bourdieu. See Pierre Bourdieu, *Outline of a Theory of Practice*, tr. Richard Nice, Cambridge: Cambridge University Press, 1977, particularly pp. 4–9. See also J.A. Barnes, 'Time Flies Like an Arrow', *Man* (n.s.), 6, 1971, 537–52.

9. Dube, *Sujetos Subalternos*.

10. Three interrelated issues bear mention. First, while it is important to recognize the relative autonomy and the internal logic governing continuities and changes within analytical traditions, it will be a mistake to assume that processes of history and transformations in politics affecting inherited mappings of the world are merely external events, located at a leisurely distance from the work of academic disciplines. Second, the questioning of received models that I have mentioned stood revealed in the way the broader lineaments of functionalism within British anthropology were interrogated from at least the late 1940s. This also meant that questions of structure and agency appeared in newer ways in elaborations of theories of action and analyses of processes, particularly from the late 1950s. Involved here were attempts to grapple with discrete and changing political and institutional contexts of the discipline of anthropology, even if the long shadow cast by functionalism was often difficult to shake off easily, a testimony to the gravity and autonomy of analytical traditions. Consider, for example, Max Gluckman, *Order and Rebellion in Tribal Africa*, London: Cohen and West, 1963; Edmund Leach, *Political Systems of Highland Burma: A Study of Kachin Social Structure*, London: G. Bell and Sons, 1954; Edmund Leach, 'Virgin Birth: The Henry Myers Lecture 1966', *Proceedings of the Royal Anthropological Institute*, 1967, 39–50; F.G. Bailey, *Caste and the Economic Frontier: A Village in Highland Orissa*, Manchester: Manchester University Press, 1957; F.G. Bailey, *Stratagems and Spoils: A Social Anthropology of Politics*, Oxford: Basil Blackwell, 1969; Fredrik Barth, *Political Leadership among Swat Pathans*, London: Athlone Press, 1959; Victor Turner, *Schism and Continuity in an African Society*, Manchester: Manchester University Press, 1957; and Victor Turner, *The Ritual Process: Structure and Anti-Structure*, London: Routledge and Kegan Paul, 1969. Finally, although I have confined myself to functionalism and structuralism, in understandings of the vexed relationship between structure and action, other important traditions of the 1960s could, in distinct ways, also privilege the former over the latter. This holds true for different versions of the 'cultural ecology' approach, especially associated with Marvin Harris, which variously externalized the dynamics of history and the terms of meaning understood as practice and process. Interestingly, the influential work of Clifford Geertz opened up distinct possibilities, both in relation to a changing anthropology for a changing world and in its stress upon the orientation of the actor, but also tended to implicitly predicate the terms of practice upon the designs of culture, which is revealed too in *Negara*, his key work of history. Marvin Harris, 'The Cultural Ecology of India's Sacred Cattle', *Current Anthropology*, 7, 1966, 51–64; Clifford Geertz, *The Interpretation of Cultures*, New York: Basic Books, 1973; Clifford Geertz (ed.), *Old Societies and New States: The Quest for Modernity in Asia and Africa*, New York: Free Press, 1963; and Clifford Geertz, *Negara: The Theatre State in Nineteenth Century Bali*, Princeton: Princeton University Press, 1980. On these questions, see also, Ortner, 'Theory in Anthropology', 132–5; and Vincent, *Anthropology and Politics*, 276–83, 308–87.

11. During the 1970s, several communist parties, worried about the 'voluntarist' tendencies of the past decade, staged a revival of orthodox policies by adhering closely to Stalinist modes of bureaucratic organization. At the same time, these years also witnessed the forging of grass-roots socialist initiatives

that were deeply democratic in their decentralized assumptions and antivanguardist visions. Several such ventures were also critically concerned with issues of gender, forging over time key alliances with different forms of radical politics, from environmentalist and peace initiatives, to factory floor and gay liberation endeavours.

12. Louis Althusser and Etienne Balibar, *Reading Capital*, London: New Left Books, 1970; Samir Amin, *Accumulation on a World Scale: A Critique of the Theory of Development*, New York: Monthly Review Press, 1974; Andre Gunder Frank, *Capitalism and Underdevelopment in Latin America: Historical Studies of Chile and Brazil*, New York: Monthly Review Press, 1967; and Immanuel Wallerstein, *The Modern World System*, New York: Academic Press, 1974. See also, Clifford Geertz, 'Culture and Social Change: The Indonesian Case', *Man*, 19, 1984, 511–32; and Patrick Wolfe, 'History and Imperialism: A Century of Theory, from Marx to Postcolonialism', *American Historical Review*, 102, 1997, 380–420.

13. For example, Bourdieu, *Outline of a Theory of Practice*; Philip Abrams, *Historical Sociology*, Ithaca: Cornell University Press, 1982; Anthony Giddens, *Central Problems in Social Theory*, London: Macmillan, 1979; John Comaroff and Simon Roberts, *Rules and Processes: The Cultural Logic of Dispute in an African Context*, Chicago: University of Chicago Press, 1981; Ortner, 'Theory in Anthropology'; Marshall Sahlins, *Historical Metaphors and Mythical Realities: Structure in the Early History of the Sandwich Island Kingdoms*, Ann Arbor: University of Michigan Press, 1981; and E.P. Thompson, *The Poverty of Theory and Other Essays*, New York: Monthly Review Press, 1978. Of course, these writings did not resolve but recalled the problematic of structure and action in distinct ways, questions that continue to be grappled with today.

14. Clifford Geertz, 'Thick Description: Toward an Interpretive Theory of Culture', in Geertz, *The Interpretation of Cultures*, New York: Basic Books, 1973, 4.

15. Johannes Fabian, *Time and the Other: How Anthropology Makes its Object*, New York: Columbia University Press, 1983; Cohn, 'History and Anthropology: The State of the Play'; Ortner, 'Theory in Anthropology'; and Renato Rosaldo, *Ilongot Headhunting 1873–1974: A Study in Society and History*, Stanford: Stanford University Press, 1980.

16. For example, Maurice Bloch (ed.), *Marxist Analyses in Social Anthropology*, New York: Wiley, 1975; Georges Dupre and Pierre Philipe Rey, 'Reflections on the Pertinence of a Theory of the History of Exchange', in Harold Wolpe (ed.), *The Articulation of Modes of Production*, London: Routledge and Kegan Paul, 1980; Wallerstein, *The Modern World System*; and Claude Meillassoux, *Maidens, Meal, and Money: Capitalism and the Domestic Community*, Cambridge: Cambridge University Press, 1981. See also, Bridget O'Laughlin, 'Marxist Approaches in Anthropology', *Annual Review of Anthropology*, 4, 1975, 341–70; and Peter Kriedte, Hans Medick, and Jurgen Schlumbohn, *Industrialization before Industrialization: Rural Industry in the Genesis of Capitalism*, Cambridge: Cambridge University Press, 1981. For earlier anticipations of such orientations, see, Sydney Mintz, *Worker in the Cane: A Puerto Rican Life History*, New Haven: Yale University Press, 1960; Eric Wolf, *Sons of the Shaking Earth*, Chicago: University of Chicago Press, 1959; and Peter Worsley, *The Trumpet Shall Sound: A Study of 'Cargo' Cults in Melanesia*, London: MacGibbon and Keo, 1957.

17. See here the conjunction between anthropology and history represented in Hans Medick and David Warren Sabean (eds), *Interest and Emotion: Essays on the Study of Family and Kinship*, Cambridge: Cambridge University Press, 1984; and Jack Goody, Joan Thirsk, and E.P. Thompson (eds), *Family and Inheritance: Rural Society in Western Europe, 1200–1800*, Cambridge: Cambridge University Press, 1976. Consider too the emphasis on power and historical analysis in the anthropology of law after 1980, discussed in June Starr and Jane Collier, 'Introduction: Dialogues in Legal Anthropology', in Starr and Collier (eds), *History and Power in the Study of Law: New Directions in Legal Anthropology*, Ithaca: Cornell University Press, 1989, 1–28.

18. David Lan, *Guns and Rain: Guerillas and Spirit Mediums in Zimbabwe*, Berkeley: University of California Press, 1985; Jean Comaroff, *Body of Power, Spirit of Resistance: The Culture and History of a South African People*, Chicago: University of Chicago Press, 1985.

19. Talal Asad, 'Anthropological Conceptions of Religion: Reflections on Geertz', *Man* (n.s.), 18, 1983, 237–

59; Gerald M. Sider, 'The Ties that Bind: Culture and Agriculture, Property and Propriety in the New Foundland Village Fishery', *Social History*, 5, 1980, 1–39. See also, Rosemary Coombe, *The Cultural Life of Intellectual Properties: Authorship, Appropriation, and the Law*, Durham: Duke University Press, 1998, 11–15.

20. Works mapping these changes include Marshall Sahlins, *Islands of History*, Chicago: University of Chicago Press, 1985; Greg Dening, *Islands and Beaches: Discourses on a Silent Land—Marquesas 1774–1880*, Honolulu: University of Hawaii Press, 1980; Bernard Cohn, *An Anthropologist among the Historians and Other Essays*, Delhi: Oxford University Press, 1987; William Roseberry, *Anthropologies and Histories: Essays in Culture, History and Political Economy*, New Brunswick: Rutgers University Press, 1989; Gerald M. Sider, *Culture and Class: A Newfoundland Illustration*, Cambridge: Cambridge University Press, 1986; Rosaldo, *Illongot Headhunting*; Comaroff, *Body of Power, Spirit of Resistance*; Michael Taussig, *The Devil and Commodity Fetishism in South America*, Chapel Hill: University of North Carolina Press, 1980.

21. Thus, strategies of multiple 'evocations' of culture in the experimental ethnography of the 1980s have been increasingly replaced in the 1990s by a more combative analytical stance that seeks to write against culture. James Clifford and George Marcus (eds), *Writing Culture: The Poetics and Politics of Ethnography*, Berkeley: University of California Press, 1986; George Marcus and Dick Cushman, 'Ethnographies as Texts', *Annual Review of Anthropology*, 11, 1982, 25–69; Nicholas Dirks, 'Introduction: Colonialism and Culture', in Dirks (ed.), *Colonialism and Culture*, Ann Arbor: University of Michigan Press, 1992, 1–15; John Pemberton, *On the Subject of Java*, Ithaca: Cornell University Press, 1994; and Sherry B. Ortner (ed.), *The Fate of 'Culture': Geertz and Beyond*, Berkeley: University of California Press, 1999.

22. For such earlier discussions, see E.E. Evans-Pritchard, *Anthropology and History*, Manchester: Manchester University Press, 1961; Bernard Cohn, 'History and Anthropology: The State of the Play'; and Bernard Cohn, 'Anthropology and History in the 1980s: Toward a Rapproachement', in Cohn, *An Anthropologist among the Historians*, 50–70; Natalie Zemon Davis, 'Anthropology and History in the 1980s: The Possibilities of the Past', *Journal of Interdisciplinary History*, 12, 1981, 267–75; and William H. Sewell, Jr, *Work and Revolution in France: The Language of Labour from the Old Regime to 1848*, Cambridge: Cambridge University Press, 1980, particularly pp. 10–13. See also, E.E. Evans-Pritchard, 'Social Anthropology: Past and Present—The Marett Lecture', *Man*, 50, 1950, 118–34; and Hans Medick, 'Missionaries in the Rowboat? Ethnological Ways of Knowing as a Challenge to Social History', *Comparative Studies in Society and History*, 29, 1987, 76–98.

23. This is an enormous terrain with distinct emphases, indicated by the following surveys and anthologies. Shepard Krech III, 'The State of Ethnohistory', *Annual Review of Anthropology*, 20, 1991, 345–75; William Reddy, 'Emotional Liberty: Politics and History in the Anthropology of Emotions', *Cultural Anthropology*, 14, 1999, 256–88; John Kelly and Martha Kaplan, 'History, Structure, and Ritual', *Annual Review of Anthropology*, 19, 1990, 119–50; Peter Pels, 'The Anthropology of Colonialism: Culture, History, and the Emergence of Western Governmentality', *Annual Review of Anthropology*, 26, 1997, 163–83; Frederick Cooper and Ann Stoler (eds), *Tensions of Empire: Colonial Cultures in a Bourgeois World*, Berkeley: University of California Press, 1997; Emiko Ohnuki-Tierney (ed.), *Culture through Time: Anthropological Approaches*, Stanford: Stanford University Press, 1990; Dirks (ed.), *Colonialism and Culture*; and Aletta Biersack (ed.), *Clio in Oceania: Toward a Historical Anthropology*, Washington: Smithsonian Institution Press, 1999.

24. See Nicholas Dirks, 'Foreword', in Bernard Cohn, *Colonialism and its Forms of Knowledge*, Princeton: Princeton University Press, 1996, ix–xiv.

25. Dube, *Stitches on Time*.

26. These issues and such writings appear comprehensively charted in Sumit Sarkar, *Modern India 1885–1947*, Delhi: Macmillan, 1983.

27. Ranajit Guha, 'On Some Aspects of the Historiography of Colonial India', in Guha (ed.), *Subaltern Studies I: Writings on South Asian History and Society*, Delhi: Oxford University Press, 1982, 1–7.

28. See the essays in Ranajit Guha (ed.), *Subaltern Studies I–VI: Writings on South Asian History and Society*, Delhi: Oxford University Press, 1982–9.

29. Partha Chatterjee and Gyanendra Pandey (eds), *Subaltern Studies VII: Writings on South Asian History and Society*, Delhi: Oxford University Press, 1992; David Arnold and David Hardiman (eds), *Subaltern Studies VIII: Essays in Honour of Ranajit Guha*, Delhi: Oxford University Press, 1994; Shahid Amin and Dipesh Chakrabarty (eds), *Subaltern Studies IX: Writings on South Asian History and Society*, Delhi: Oxford University Press, 1996; Gautam Bhadra, Gyan Prakash, and Susie Tharu (eds), *Subaltern Studies X: Writings on South Asian History and Society*, Delhi: Oxford University Press, 1999; and Ranajit Guha (ed.), *A Subaltern Studies Reader, 1986–1995*, Minneapolis: University of Minnesota Press, 1997. In addition, such emphases within Subaltern Studies are also elaborated in the books and other writings produced by the members of the collective, which are referred to at appropriate points in this introduction.

30. Ranajit Guha, 'The Small Voice of History', in Amin and Chakrabarty (eds), *Subaltern Studies IX*, 1–12; and Dipesh Chakrabarty, 'The Difference-deferral of (a) Colonial Modernity: Public Debates on Domesticity in British India', in Arnold and Hardiman (eds), *Subaltern Studies VIII*, 50–88.

31. Ajay Skaria, 'Writing, Orality, and Power in the Dangs, Western India, 1800s–1920s, in Amin and Chakrabarty (eds), *Subaltern Studies IX*, 13–58; Ishita Banerjee Dube, 'Taming Traditions': Legalities and Histories in Eastern India', in Bhadra, Prakash, and Tharu (eds), *Subaltern Studies X*, 98–125; Gyanendra Pandey, 'The Prose of Otherness', in Arnold and Hardiman (eds), *Subaltern Studies VIII*, 188–221; and Shail Mayaram, 'Speech, Silence, and the Making of Partition Violence in Mewat', in Amin and Chakrabarty (eds), *Subaltern Studies IX*, 126–64. See also, Saurabh Dube, 'Myths, Symbols, and Community: Satnampanth of Chhattisgarh', in Chatterjee and Pandey (eds), *Subaltern Studies VII*, 121–56; and Ajay Skaria, *Hybrid Histories: Forests, Frontiers, and Wildness in Western India*, Delhi: Oxford University Press, 1999.

32. Wlad Godzich, for example, has discussed the bases and the consequences of this turn to theory in literary criticism. Wlad Godzich, *The Culture of Literacy*, Cambridge, Mass: Harvard University Press, 1994.

33. Bernard Cohn, 'History and Anthropology: The State of the Play', 199; Michel-Ralph Trouillot, 'Anthropology and the Savage Slot: The Poetics and Politics of the Otherness', in Richard Fox (ed.), *Recapturing Anthropology: Working in the Present*, Santa Fe: School of American Research Press: 17–44.

34. Johannes Fabian, *Time and the Other*. See also John Comaroff and Jean Comaroff, *Ethnography and the Historical Imagination*, particularly pp. 1–9; and Nicholas Thomas, *Out of Time: History and Evolution in Anthropological Discourse*, Second Edition, Ann Arbor: University of Michigan Press, 1996.

35. On this issue, for a compelling theoretical discussion see, Dipesh Chakrabarty, 'Postcoloniality and the Artifice of History: Who Speaks for "Indian" Pasts?', *Representations*, 37, 1992, 1–26. Both Frederick Cooper and Sumit Sarkar in their surveys of the writing of history in Africa and India respectively, while pointing to important exceptions, broadly corroborate my claims. Frederick Cooper, 'Conflict and Connection: Rethinking Colonial African History', *American Historical Review*, 99, 1994, 1519–26; and Sumit Sarkar, *Writing Social History*, Delhi: Oxford University Press, 1997, 30–42. See also, Gyan Prakash, 'Subaltern Studies as Postcolonial Criticism', *American Historical Review*, 99, 1994, 1475–94.

36. Important interventions here were Talal Asad (ed.), *Anthropology and the Colonial Encounter*, London: Ithaca Press, 1973; Kathleen Gough, 'Anthropology: Child of Imperialism', *Monthly Review*, 19, 1968, 12–68; Jairus Banaji, 'The Crisis of British Anthropology', *New Left Review*, 64, 1970, 71–85; and, from the perspective of the 'crisis of anthropology', Dell Hymes (ed.), *Reinventing Anthropology*, New York: Pantheon Books, 1972. In a brief but incisive survey, George Stocking has shown that tendencies going back to the 1940s in the United States and the 1950s in France came together in the five years after 1968, in the specific context of the time, so that 'the relation of anthropology to colonialism/imperialism became for the first time a burning issue for anthropologists'. George Stocking, Jr, 'Colonial Situations': 3–4.

37. For example, Frank, *Capitalism and Underdevelopment in Latin America*; and Wallerstein, *The Modern*

World System. A useful survey here is contained in Ann Stoler, '(P)refacing Capitalism and Confrontation in 1995', in Stoler, *Capitalism and Confrontation in Sumatra's Plantation Belt*, Second Edition, Ann Arbor: University of Michigan Press, 1995, vii–xxxiv. See also, Eric Wolf, *Europe and the People without History*, Berkeley: University of California Press, 1982.

38. For two surveys of the vast literature here see, Sarkar, *Modern India*—that both summarizes and orients the reader toward the different writings on the colonial economy and social processes, including diverse South Asian responses to imperial rule—and Cooper, 'Conflict and Connection: Rethinking African Colonial History'. See also, Sarkar, *Writing Social History*: 24–49; and Gyan Prakash, 'Writing Post-Orientalist Histories of the Third World: Indian Historiography is Good to Think', in Dirks (ed.) *Colonialism and Culture*, 353–88.

39. On these questions see, for example, Ann Stoler, 'Rethinking Colonial Categories: European Communities and Boundaries of Rule', *Comparative Studies of Society and History*, 31, 1989, 134–61. See also, Ann Stoler and Frederick Cooper, 'Between Metropole and Colony: Rethinking a Research Agenda', in Cooper and Stoler (eds), *Tensions of Empire*: 1–56.

40. June Nash, *We Eat the Mines and the Mines Eat Us: Dependency and Exploitation in Bolivian Tin Mines*, New York: Columbia University Press, 1979; Taussig, *The Devil and Commodity Fetishism*.

41. For example, Reynaldo Ileto, *Pasyon and Revolution: Popular Movements in the Philippines, 1840–1910*, Quezon City: Ateneo University Press, 1979; Comaroff, *Body of Power, Spirit of Resistance*; Ann Stoler, *Capitalism and Confrontation in Sumatra's Plantation Belt, 1870–1979*, New Haven: Yale University Press, 1985; Rosaldo, *Ilongot Headhunting*.

42. Nicholas Thomas, *Colonialism's Culture: Anthropology, Travel, and Government*, Princeton: Princeton University Press, 1994.

43. Ibid., 18.

44. Edward Said, *Orientalism*, New York: Pantheon, 1978.

45. Thomas, *Colonialism's Culture*, 22.

46. Ibid., 22–3.

47. Alain Grosrichard, *The Sultan's Court: European Fantasies of the East*, tr. Liz Heron, London: Verso, 1998, first published in French in 1979; Anouar Abdel-Malek, 'Orientalism in Crisis', *Diogenes*, 44, 1963, 103–40; Ashis Nandy, *The Intimate Enemy: Loss and Recovery of the Self under Colonialism*, Delhi: Oxford University Press, 1982; and Fabian, *Time and the Other*.

48. Critical assessments of Said's work from within anthropology include James Clifford, 'On *Orientalism*', in Clifford, *The Predicament of Culture*, Cambridge, Mass: Harvard University Press, 1988; and Thomas, *Colonialism's Culture*, 5–7, 21–7. See also, Carol Breckenridge and Peter van der Veer (eds), *Orientalism and the Postcolonial Predicament: Perspectives on South Asia*, Philadelphia: University of Pennsylvania Press, 1993; and Michael Richardson, 'Enough Said', *Anthropology Today*, 6, 1990, 16–19. For critical readings of Said's text from within cultural and literary studies, Bart Moore-Gilbert, *Postcolonial Theory: Contexts, Practices, Politics*, London: Verso, 1997, 34–73; Robert Young, *White Mythologies: Writing History and the West*, London: Routledge, 1990: 119–40; and Balachandran Rajan, *Under Western Eyes: India from Milton to Macaulay*, Durham: Duke University Press, 1999, 15–20. See also, Meyda Yegenoglu, *Colonial Fantasies: Towards a Feminist Reading of Orientalism*, Cambridge: Cambridge University Press, 1998.

49. See particularly, Clifford, 'On *Orientalism*'; and Wolfe, 'History and Imperialism', 407–10. Related arguments about the tensions between the historicist recovery of the humanist subject and its decentring and dissolution within postmodernist analyses have been made for the Subaltern Studies project. Rosalind O'Hanlon, 'Recovering the Subject: *Subaltern Studies* and Histories of Resistance in Colonial South Asia', *Modern Asian Studies*, 22, 1988, 189–224.

50. Homi Bhabha, *The Location of Culture*, London and New York: Routledge, 1994; Gayatri Chakravorty Spivak, 'Subaltern Studies: Deconstructing Historiography', in Ranajit Guha (ed.), *Subaltern Studies IV: Writings on South Asian History and Society*, Delhi: Oxford University Press, 1985, 330–63; and Gayatri Chakravorty Spivak, 'Can the Subaltern Speak?', in Cary Nelson and Lawrence Grossberg (eds), *Marxism*

and the Interpretation of Culture, Urbana: University of Illinois Press, 1988, 271–313. In a different vein, Gauri Viswanathan, *Masks of Conquest: Literary Studies and British Rule in India*, New York: Columbia University Press, 1989. Useful surveys and critical discussions of this body of writing can be found in Young, *White Mythologies*, 141–75; Moore-Gilbert, *Postcolonial Theory*; Leela Gandhi, *Postcolonial Theory: A Critical Introduction*, New York: Columbia University Press, 1998; and Ania Loomba, *Colonialism-Postcolonialism*, London: Routledge, 1998.

51. In terms of these twin emphases that cut two ways I have in mind the work of Homi Bhabha, particularly 'Of Mimicry and Man: The Ambivalence of Colonial Discourse' and the more critical companion essay, 'Signs Taken for Wonders: Questions of Ambivalence and Authority under a Tree Outside Delhi, May 1817', in Bhabha, *The Location of Culture*, 85–92, 102–22.

52. Anne McClintock, *Imperial Leather: Race, Gender and Sexuality in the Colonial Contest*, New York: Routledge, 1995; Ann Stoler, *Race and the Education of Desire: Foucault's History of Sexuality and the Colonial Order of Things*, Durham: Duke University Press, 1995; Inderpal Grewal, *Home and Harem: Nation, Gender, Empire, and the Cultures of Travel*, Durham: Duke University Press, 1996; Lenore Manderson and Margaret Jolly (eds), *Sites of Desire, Economies of Pleasure: Sexualities in Asia and the Pacific*, Chicago: University of Chicago Press, 1997; Antoinette Burton, *Burdens of History: British Feminists, Indian Women, and Imperial Culture, 1865–1915*, Chapel Hill: University of North Carolina Press, 1994; Stephen Greenblatt (ed.), *New World Encounters*, Berkeley: University of California Press, 1993; and Paul Gilroy, *The Black Atlantic: Modernity and Double Consciousness*, Cambridge, Mass: Harvard University Press, 1993.

53. John Comaroff, 'Images of Empire, Contests of Conscience: Models of Colonial Domination in South Africa', *American Ethnologist*, 16, 1989, 661–85; Stoler, 'Rethinking Colonial Categories'; Stoler and Cooper, 'Between Metropole and Colony'; and Jean Comaroff and John Comaroff, *Of Revelation and Revolution: Christianity, Colonialism, and Consciousness in South Africa*, Volume One, Chicago: University of Chicago Press, 1991. See also, Patrick Wolfe, *Settler Colonialism and the Transformation of Anthropology: The Politics and Poetics of an Ethnographic Event*, London: Cassell, 1999. Analyses of 'settler communities' include Vincent Crapanzano, *Waiting: The Whites of South Africa*, New York: Vintage, 1985; and Dane Kennedy, *Islands of White: Settler Society and Culture in Kenya and Southern Rhodesia, 1890–1939*, Durham: Duke University Press, 1987. See also, Virginia R. Dominguez, *White by Definition: Social Classification in Creole Louisiana*, New Brunswick: Rutgers University Press, 1986; and Dane Kennedy, *The Magic Mountains: Hill Stations and the British Raj*, Berkeley: University of California Press, 1996.

54. Ann Stoler, 'Perceptions of Protest: Defining the Dangerous in Colonial Sumatra', *American Ethnologist*, 12, 4, 1985, 642–58; John Comaroff, 'Images of Empire, Contests of Conscience'; Thomas, *Colonialism's Culture*; and Stoler and Cooper, 'Between Metropole and Colony', 13–14.

55. Anna Davin, 'Imperialism and Motherhood', *History Workshop*, 5, 1978, 9–65; John Comaroff and Jean Comaroff, 'Homemade Hegemony', in Comaroff and Comaroff, *Ethnography and the Historical Imagination*, Boulder: Westview Press, 1992, 265–95; Susan Thorne, ' "The Conversion of Englishmen and the Conversion of the World Inseparable": Missionary Imperialism and the Languages of Class in Early Industrial Britain', in Cooper and Stoler (eds), *Tensions of Empire*, 238–62. See also, Mrinalini Sinha, *Colonial Masculinity: The 'Manly Englishman' and the 'Effeminate Bengali' in the Late Nineteenth Century*, Manchester: Manchester University Press, 1995.

56. Edward Said, *Culture and Imperialism*, London: Knopf, 1994; Walter Mignolo, *The Darker Side of the Renaissance: Literacy, Territoriality, and Colonization*, Ann Arbor: University of Michigan Press, 1995; Stoler, *Race and the Education of Desire*; Uday Mehta, 'Liberal Strategies of Exclusion', in Cooper and Stoler (eds), *Tensions of Empire*, 59–86; Uday Mehta, *Liberalism and Empire: A Study in Nineteenth-Century Liberal Thought*, Chicago: University of Chicago Press, 1999; Lora Widenthal, 'Race, Gender, and Citizenship in the German Colonial Empire', in Cooper and Stoler (eds), *Tensions of Empire*: 263–83. See also, V.Y. Mudimbe, *The Invention of Africa: Gnosis, Philosophy, and the Order of Knowledge*, Bloomington: Indiana University Press, 1988; Jose Rabasa, *The Invention of America*, Norman: University

of Oklahoma Press, 1994; and Walter Mignolo, *Local Histories/Global Designs: Coloniality, Subaltern Knowledges, and Border Thinking*, Princeton: Princeton University Press, 2000.

57. Timothy Mitchell, *Colonizing Egypt*, Berkeley: University of California Press, 1988; John Noyes, *Colonial Space: Spatiality in the Discourse of German South West Africa 1884–1915*, Chur: Harwood Academic Publishers, 1992; Walter Mignolo, 'On the Colonization of Amerindian Languages and Memories: Renaissance Theories of Writing and the Discontinuity of the Classical Tradition', *Comparative Studies in Society and History*, 34, 1992, 301–30; Johannes Fabian, *Language and Colonial Power: The Appropriation of Swahili in the Former Belgian Congo*, Cambridge: Cambridge University Press, 1986; David Arnold, *Colonizing the Body: State Medicine and Epidemic Disease in Nineteenth-Century India*, Berkeley: University of California Press, 1993; Megan Vaughan, *Curing their Ills: Colonial Power and African Illness*, Stanford: Stanford University Press, 1991; Satadru Sen, *Disciplining Punishment: Colonialism and Convict Society in the Andaman Islands*, Delhi: Oxford University Press, 2000; and Nancy Rose Hunt, *A Colonial Lexicon of Birth Ritual, Medicalization, and Mobility in the Congo*, Durham: Duke University Press, 1999.

58. Johannes Fabian, *Out of Our Minds: Reason and Madness in the Exploration of Central Africa*, Berkeley: University of California Press, 2000; Mary Louise Pratt, *Imperial Eyes: Travel Writing and Transculturation*, London: Routledge, 1992; Tony Bennett, *The Birth of the Museum: History, Theory, Politics*, New York: Routledge, 1995; Nicholas Thomas, *Entangled Objects: Exchange, Material Culture, and Colonialism in the Pacific*, Cambridge, Mass: Harvard University Press, 1991; Annie Coombes, *Reinventing Africa: Museums, Material Culture, and Popular Imagination in Late Victorian and Edwardian England*, New Haven: Yale University Press, 1994; Tom Griffiths, *Hunters and Collectors: The Antiquarian Imagination in Australia*, Cambridge: Cambridge University Press, 1996; George Stocking, Jr (ed.), *Objects and Others: Essays on Museums and Material Culture*, Madison: University of Madison Press, 1985. See also George Stocking, Jr, *Victorian Anthropology*, New York: Free Press, 1987; Mauricio Tenorio-Trillo, *Mexico at the World's Fairs: Crafting a Modern Nation*, Berkeley: University of California Press, 1996; and Shelly Errington, *The Death of Authentic Primitive Art and Other Tales of Progress*, Berkeley: University of California Press, 1998.

59. David Scott, *Formations of Ritual: Colonial and Anthropological Discourses on the Sinhala Yaktovil*, Minneapolis: University of Minnesota Press, 1994; Stephen Greeblatt, *Marvelous Possessions: The Wonder of the New World*, Chicago: University of Chicago Press, 1992; Greenblatt (ed.), *New World Encounters*; Anthony Pagden, *The Fall of Natural Man: The American Indian and the Origins of Comparative Ethnology*, Cambridge: Cambridge University Press, 1986; Ranajit Guha, 'The Prose of Counter-insurgency', in Guha (ed.), *Subaltern Studies II: Writings on South Asian History and Society*, Delhi: Oxford University Press, 1983, 1–42; Wolfe, *Settler Colonialism and the Transformation of Anthropology*. See also, Richard Helgerson, *Forms of Nationhood: The Elizabethan Writing of England*, Chicago: Chicago University Press, 1992; Vicente Rafael, *Contracting Colonialism: Translation and Christian Conversion in Tagalog Society under Early Spanish Rule*, Ithaca: Cornell University Press, 1988; Christopher Pinney, *Camera Indica: The Social Life of Indian Photographs*, Chicago: University of Chicago Press, 1997; Deborah Poole, *Vision, Race, and Modernity: A Visual Economy of the Andean Inage World*, Princeton: Princeton University Press, 1997; and Marianna Torgovnik, *Gone Primitive: Savage Intellects, Modern Lives*, Chicago: University of Chicago Press, 1990.

60. For example, Manderson and Jolly (eds), *Sites of Desire, Economies of Pleasure*; Ann Stoler, 'Sexual Affronts and Racial Frontiers: European Identities and the Cultural Politics of Exclusion in Colonial Southeast Asia', *Comparative Studies in Society and History*, 34, 1992, 514–51; and Stoler, *Race and the Education of Desire*.

61. Recall the discussion in the section 'Cultures in Time' above.

62. Significant examples include John Comaroff and Jean Comaroff, *Of Revelation and Revolution: The Dialectics of Modernity on a South African Frontier*, Volume Two, Chicago: University of Chicago Press, 1997; Comaroff and Comaroff, *Ethnography and the Historical Imagination*; and Frederick Cooper, *Decolonization and African Society: The Labour Question in French and British Africa*, Cambridge:

Cambridge University Press, 1996. The interplay between these heuristic domains also becomes clear in the better work in the vast field that has explored questions of environment under terms of empire. For two striking examples of such work on South Asia see, Skaria, *Hybrid Histories*; and K. Sivaramakrishnan, *Making Forests: Statemaking and Environmental Change in Colonial Eastern India*, Delhi: Oxford University Press, 1999. Despite the presence of writings such as these, it seems to me, that discussions of colonial cultures on the Indian subcontinent are yet to critically consider the full import of a work such as Christopher Bayly, *Indian Society and the Making of the British Empire*, Cambridge: Cambridge University Press, 1988, and related scholarship.

63. Ann Stoler, 'Carnal Knowledge and Imperial Power: Gender, Race and Morality in Colonial Asia', in Micaela di Leanordo (ed.), *Gender and the Crossroads of Knowledge: Feminist Anthropology in the Postmodern Era*, Berkeley: University of California Press, 1991, 51–101, which includes a useful and large overview of the work in this arena. See also, Helen Callaway, *Gender, Culture and Empire: European Women in Colonial Nigeria*, London: Macmillan, 1987; Mona Etienne and Eleanor Leacock (eds), *Women and Colonization: Anthropological Perspectives*, New York: Praeger, 1980; Irene Silverblatt, *Moon, Sun, and Witches: Gender Ideologies and Class in Inca and Colonial Peru*, Princeton: Princeton University Press, 1987; and Sinha, *Colonial Masculinity*.

64. McClintock, *Imperial Leather*; and Stoler, *Race and the Education of Desire*.

65. Given constraints of space, these sections of Cohn's essay do not appear in *Postcolonial Passages*. Bernard Cohn, 'Representing Authority in Victorian India', in Eric Hobsbawm and Terence Ranger (eds), *The Invention of Tradition*, Cambridge: Cambridge University Press, 1983, 167–79.

66. Nicholas Dirks, *Castes of Mind: Colonialism and the Making of Modern India*, Princeton: Princeton University Press, 2001.

67. Sudipta Kaviraj, *The Unhappy Consciousness: Bankimchandra Chattopadhyay and the Formation of Nationalist Discourse in India*, Delhi: Oxford University Press, 1995.

68. See, Partha Chatterjee, *The Nation and Its Fragments: Colonial and Postcolonial Histories*, Princeton: Princeton University Press, 1993, particularly pp. 3–5. Of course, the emergence of newer nations, global communities, and diverse conflicts in Eastern Europe, for example, complicates these issues in distinct ways, but arguably the dominant disposition toward the non-Western nation is at once retained and elaborated in such cases.

69. Craig Calhoun, 'The Class Consciousness of Frequent Travellers: Towards a Critique of Actually Existing Cosmopolitanism', in Saurabh Dube (ed.), *Enduring Enchantments*, Durham, a special issue of *South Atlantic Quarterly*, 101 (4), 2002, published by Duke University Press.

70. Ana Maria Alonso, 'The Politics of Space, Time, and Substance: State Formation, Nationalism, and Ethnicity', *Annual Review of Anthropology*, 23, 1994, 379, 400.

71. Craig Calhoun puts it like this: As the 'most potent discourse of collective identity', nationalism appears in both projects of unity and division, but this also means that nationalism is not so much 'an adequate explanation of such processes of integration and disintegration' as it is a 'political rhetoric in which many of them are pursued'. Craig Calhoun, 'Nationalism and Civil Society: Democracy, Diversity, and Civil Society', in Calhoun (ed.), *Social Theory and the Politics of Identity*, Oxford: Blackwell, 1994, 308.

72. For example, Thomas Blom Hansen and Finn Stupatat (eds), *States of Imagination: Ethnographic Explorations of the Postcolonial State*, Durham: Duke University Press, 2001; Ana Maria Alonso, 'The Effects of Truth: Representations of the Past and the Imagining of the Community', *Journal of Historical Sociology*, 1, 1988, 33–57; Fernando Coronil and Julie Skurski, 'Dismembering and Remembering the Nation: The Semantics of Political Violence in Venezuela', *Comparative Studies in Society and History*, 33, 1991, 288–337; E. Valentine Daniel, *Charred Lullabies: Chapters in an Anthropology of Violence*, Princeton: Princeton University Press, 1996; Veena Das, *Critical Events: An Anthropological Perspective on Contemporary India*, Delhi: Oxford University Press, 1995; Michael Herzfeld, *Cultural Intimacy: Social Poetics in the Nation-State*, New York and London: Routledge, 1997; Richard Fox (ed.), *Nationalist Ideologies and the Production of National Cultures*, Washington, D.C.: American Anthropological Association, 1990; Akhil Gupta, *Postcolonial Developments: Agriculture in the Making of Modern India*,

Durham: Duke University Press, 1998; Liisa Malkki, 'National Geographic: The Rooting of Peoples and the Territorialization of National Identity among Scholars and Refugees', *Cultural Anthropology*, 7, 1992, 24–44; Michael Taussig, *The Magic of the State*, New York and London: Routledge, 1996; and Brackette Williams, *Stains on My Name, War in My Veins: Guyana and the Politics of Cultural Struggle*, Durham: Duke University Press, 1991. See also Philip Corrigan and Derek Sayer, *The Great Arch: English State Formation as Cultural Revolution*, Oxford: Basil Blackwell, 1985; Paul Gilroy, *'There Ain't No Black in the Union Jack': The Cultural Politics of Race and Nation*, London: Hutchinson, 1987; Achille Mbembe, 'The Banality of Power and the Aesthetics of Vulgarity in the Postcolony', *Public Culture*, 4, 1992, 1–30; Michael Herzfeld, *The Social Production of Indifference: Exploring the Symbolic Roots of Western Bureaucracy*, New York: Berg, 1992; and Gilbert Joseph and Daniel Nugent (eds), *Everyday Forms of State Formation: Revolution and the Negotiation of Rule in Modern Mexico*, Durham: Duke University Press, 1994.

73.   See, for example, Brian Axel, *The Nation's Tortured Body: Violence, Representation, and the Formation of the Sikh 'Diaspora'*, Durham: Duke University Press, 2001; Arjun Appadurai, *Modernity at Large*, Minneapolis: University of Minnesota Press, 1996; Carol Breckenridge and Arjun Appadurai, 'Editors' Comments', *Public Culture*, 1 (1), 1988, 1–4; Fernando Coronil, *The Magical State: Nature, Money, and Modernity in Venezuela*, Chicago: University of Chicago Press, 1997; Robert Foster, 'Making National Cultures in the Global Ecumene', *Annual Review of Anthropology*, 20, 1991, 235–60; Akhil Gupta, 'The Song of the Nonaligned World: Transnational Identities and the Reinscription of Space in Late Capitalism', *Cultural Anthropology*, 7, 1992, 63–79. See also Ulf Hannerz, 'Notes on the Global Ecumene', *Public Culture*, 1, 1989, 66–75; and David Harvey, *The Condition of Postmodernity: An Enquiry into the Origins of Cultural Change*, Oxford: Basil Blackwell, 1989.

74.   For example, Guha (ed.), *Subaltern Studies I–VI*; Partha Chatterjee, *Nationalist Thought and the Colonial World: A Derivative Discourse?*, London: Zed Press, 1986; Chatterjee, *The Nation and its Fragments*; Shahid Amin, *Event, Metaphor, Memory: Chauri Chaura 1922–1992*, Berkeley: University of California Press, 1995; Gyanendra Pandey, *Remembering Partition: Violence, Nationalism and History in India*, Cambridge; Cambridge University Press, 2001; Gyan Prakash, *Another Reason: Science and the Imagination of Modern India*, Princeton: Princeton University Press, 1999; Urvashi Butalia, *The Other Side of Silence: Voices from the Partition of India*, New Delhi: Viking Penguin, 1998; Ritu Menon and Kamla Bhasin, *Borders and Boundaries: Women in India's Partition*, New Delhi: Kali for Women, 1998. For complementary visions, including counterpoints, from elsewhere, see, for example, Florencia Mallon, *Peasant and Nation: The Making of Postcolonial Mexico and Peru*, Berkeley: University of California Press, 1994; Claudio Lomnitz-Adler, *Exits from the Labyrinth: Culture and Ideology in Mexican National Space*, Berkeley and Los Angeles: University of California Press, 1992; and Prasenjit Duara, *Rescuing History from the Nation: Questioning Narratives of Modern China*, Chicago: University of Chicago Press, 1996.

75.   Foster, 'Making National Cultures in the Global Ecumene', 252.

76.   Alonso, 'Politics of Space, Time, and Substance'.

77.   I discuss such questions in Saurabh Dube, 'Introduction: Enchantments of Modernity', in Dube (ed.), *Enduring Enchantments*.

78.   See, particularly, Pandey, *Remembering Partition*.

79.   Dube, *Stitches on Time*; Dube, 'Enchantments of Modernity'. See also Saurabh Dube, 'Introduction: Colonialism, Modernity, Colonial Modernities', in Saurabh Dube, Ishita Banerjee Dube, and Edgardo Lander (eds), *Critical Conjunctions: Foundations of Colony and Formations of Modernity*, a special issue of *Nepantla: Views from South*, 3 (2), 2002, published by Duke University Press.

80.   A classic example is Benedict Anderson, *Imagined Communities: Reflections on the Origin and Spread of Nationalism*, London: Verso, 1983.

81.   For the sake of brevity, see the terms of discussion in the surveys by Alonso, 'Politics of Space, Time, and Substance'; and Foster, 'Making National Cultures in the Global Ecumene'.

82.   Chatterjee, *Nation and its Fragments*; and Gyanendra Pandey, *The Construction of Communalism in*

Colonial North India, Delhi: Oxford University Press, 1990.

83. Chatterjee, *Nation and its Fragments*: 238; Amin, *Event, Metaphor, Memory*; Pandey, *Remembering Partition*. See also, Gyan Prakash, *Another Reason: Science and the Imagination of Modern India*, Princeton: Princeton University Press, 1999: 201–37.

84. These arguments and emphases are elaborated in Dube, *Stitches on Time*.

85. Chatterjee, *Nation and its Fragments, passim*.

86. For a discussion of some of these problems see, Saurabh Dube, *Untouchable Pasts: Religion, Identity, and Power among a Central Indian Community, 1780–1950*, Albany, NY: State University of New York Press, 1998, especially pp. 207–11.

87. Amin, *Event, Metaphor, Memory*, 1–2 and *passim*.

88. Here I am drawing upon and extending the emphases of Peter Redfield, *Space in the Tropics: From Convicts to Rockets in French Guiana*, Berkeley: University of California Press, 2000, particularly pp. xv–xvi.

89. Pandey, *Remembering Partition*, 1 and *passim*.

90. For a discussion of what I call 'history without warranty', see, Saurabh Dube, 'Conversion to Translation: Colonial Registers of a Vernacular Christianity', in Dube (ed.), *Enduring Enchantments*.

91. Menon and Bhasin, *Borders and Boundaries*.

92. Eric Hobsbawm, 'Karl Marx's Contribution to Historiography', in Robin Blackburn (ed.), *Ideology in Social Science: Readings in Critical Social Theory*, Glasgow: Fontana, 1972, particularly pp. 275–6.

93. While the terms of this introduction should say something about the varieties of historical practice that struggle today against projections of universal history, let me offer here a single example concerning such efforts in the past, turning upon Karl Marx's 'Contribution to the Critique of Hegel's Philosophy of Right'. Recall, this text has been critical for discussions of Marx's understanding of religion. Here, even as Marx underscores the reality of religion, he also speaks of the unseating of religion by philosophy in Germany. Yet, what then is to happen to philosophy? Both a simple negation that turns its back to philosophy and an uncritical affirmation of philosophy as reality—according to Marx, the ways of the 'practical' party and the theoretical 'party', respectively—do not provide the answer. Rather, in his country, philosophy calls for its abolition precisely through its realization in history, a projection that stands premised upon a particular configuration of mid-nineteenth-century Germany, a national economy that is also the embodiment of a specific trajectory of thought and practice, from religion to philosophy to history. My point is that in this understanding, a scheme of universal history, orchestrated by the model of a revolutionary France and defined by the principles of plenitude and lack among nations, is at once affirmed and challenged by Marx's projection of German exceptionalism. What is more, the linear emplotment that this schema implies appears critically accompanied by an emphasis upon the fetish of sovereignty, a dialectic whereby for German 'cotton barons and iron heroes' sovereignty internalized is also sovereignty externalized, defining the frontiers and the space of Germany. This latter move, it seems to me, further underlies the actual complexity of the apparently straightforward nature of Marx's historical narrative. Taken together, I am suggesting that to think through such mix-ups, constitutive contradictions, is essential for critical engagements with universal history: Karl Marx, 'Contribution to the Critique of Hegel's Philosophy of Right', in Karl Marx and Frederick Engels, *On Religion*, Moscow: Progress Publishers, 1976, 41–58. On the diversity and complexity of the 'modern' project of history, see, Donald Kelley, *Faces of History: Historical Inquiry from Herodotus to Herder*, New Haven: Yale University Press, 1998, 188–272.

94. All this further implies questions of the relationship between modernity and colonialism, discussed in dialogue with the salient lines of writing in this terrain in Dube, 'Colonialism, Modernity, Colonial Modernities'.

95. Here are issues not only of 'alternative' modernities but also of modernity's 'enchantments'. These find context-bound elaboration in Dube, 'Enchantments of Modernity', where I also indicate the critical work on these questions.

96. On a 'third', or alternative, space, see Bhabha, *The Location of Culture*; but also Dube, *Untouchable*

Pasts. On a 'militant middle ground', see, Michael Herzfeld, *Cultural Intimacy*: 165–73. See also, Paul Gilroy, *Between Camps: Race, Identity and Nationalism at the End of the Colour Line*, London: Allen Lane, 2000.

97. The essay links up with Prakash's larger study of bonded labour. Gyan Prakash, *Bonded Histories: Genealogies of Labour Servitude in Colonial India*, Cambridge: Cambridge University Press, 1990.

98. The chapter is taken from Dipesh Chakrabarty, *Provincializing Europe: Historical Thought and Postcolonial Difference*, Princeton: Princeton University Press, 2000.

99. See also the discussion in the Afterword to this volume. Gadamer cited in Chakrabarty, *Provincializing Europe*, p. 112. Consider, too, Zygmunt Bauman, *Intimations of Postmodernity*, London: Routledge, 1992, particularly pp. ix–x. Butalia, *Other Side of Silence*.

100. The interview had its beginnings as an exchange in the pages of Dube (ed.), *Enduring Enchantments*; Chakrabarty, *Provincializing Europe*.

ONE

Not at Home in Empire

Ranajit Guha

There is something uncanny about empire. The entity known by that name is, in essence, mere territory. That is, a place constituted by the violence of conquest, the jurisdictions of law and ownership, the institutions of public order and use. And when all the conquistadors, consuls, and clerks are taken out, there is little left to it other than a vacancy waiting for armies and bureaucracies to fit it up once more with structures of power and designate it again as empire. As such, it *requires* no homes, if only because the authority, the imperium, from which it derives its form, function, and purpose, is easily sustained by forts and barracks and offices. Yet as history shows, empire is not reconciled for long to this abstracted condition. Caravans seek the shade of the camps, markets their custom in the garrisons, even religions their flock among war-weary souls. Towns and settlements grow, as empire too is seized by the urge to make a home of its territory.

However, this is not an urge the modern colonial empire can easily satisfy. For it rules by a state which does not arise out of the society of the subject population but is imposed on it by an alien force. This irreducible and historically necessary otherness was what made imperialism so uncanny for its protagonists in South Asia, as witness the experience of a British officer, Francis Yeats-Brown, who could, with good reason, describe the first year of his career in the Indian army as 'a jolly life'; and 'yet among these servants and salaams,' he recalled later on in his memoir, *The Lives of a Bengal Lancer*:

I had sometimes a sense of isolation, of being a caged white monkey in a Zoo whose patrons were this incredibly numerous beige race.

Riding through the densely packed bazaars of Bareilly City, . . . passing village temples, cantering across the magical plains that stretched away to the Himalayas, I shivered at the millions and immensities and secrecies of India. I liked to finish my day at the club, in a world whose limits were known and where people answered my beck. An incandescent lamp coughed its light over shrivelled grass and dusty shrubbery; in its circle of illumination exiled heads were bent over English newspapers, their thoughts far away, but close to mine. Outside, people prayed and plotted and mated and died on a scale unimaginable and uncomfortable. We English were a caste. White overlords or white monkeys—it was all the same. The Brahmins made a circle within which they cooked their food. So did we. We were a caste: pariahs to them, princes in our own estimation.[1]

The defining terms of this Englishman's sense of isolation in this passage are not only ethnic—a 'beige race' contrasted to one that is white. The customary coding by colour is mediated here by a sentiment which could easily have passed as fear were it not for the fact that he identifies no particular object as frightening. What comes through is rather an acknowledgment of being overwhelmed by the scale of things. 'I shivered,' he writes, 'at the millions and immensities and secrecies of India.' Number, dimension, and depth are all apparently a measure of the colonizer's difficulty in coping with the responsibility called empire. He feels diminished: used to the freedom of the Western metropolis, he now regards himself as caged in India; born to an open society, he has his status frozen into a castelike structure. The empire has shrunk into an uncanny trap for him, and he seeks refuge in the club. For that is a surrogate for home. Nearly as small as cage or caste, it is still a circle of illumination where he can recognize fellow exiles by their heads bent over English newspapers and their thoughts, like his, turned to a place far away from this outpost of empire—a place called home, 'a world', as he put it, 'whose limits were known'.

Limit, says Aristotle, is 'the terminus of each thing, i.e. the first thing outside which there is nothing to be found'.[2] It is in the nature of limit, therefore, to define the limited by an operation that excludes as much as it includes, and of all possible worlds of known limits there is none more inclusive, of course, than home. A space of absolute familiarity, it makes the members of a family feel secure by the completeness of their mutual understanding. The club, the Englishman's home away from home under the raj, replicated such familiarity to some extent. For those who gathered there at the end of the day understood each other by the signs of a shared culture and a common language. Each of them could say of the others, '[they] answered my beck'.

Conversely, India, standing as it did beyond the limit, was an empty, hence inaccessible, outside. Empty because it had 'nothing to be found' in it for content, and inaccessible because a void is a non-entity one can hardly get to know and relate to. For a limit, to cite Aristotle again, is also 'the substance of each thing' and as such 'the limit of knowledge; and if of knowledge, of the object also'.[3] Beyond limit, hence beyond knowing, India was thus the unhomely opposite of the world of known limits.

Its unknowability for the young soldier was evidently a function of its immeasurability, as indexed by his reference to its 'immensities' as well as to 'a scale' he found 'unimaginable and uncomfortable'. The comfort of a world of known limits derives precisely from the known measure of things. It does so because measure, despite the apparent rigidity of its image in the numerical tables of school arithmetic, is a fluid and indeed necessary process which, according to Hegel, enables quantity and quality to 'pass into each other'.[4] As such, it stands for the essential dynamism of things and their relationships. It is only by understanding the latter that one comports oneself within a given environment and feels at home in it. Which indeed was why the empire had turned out to be so uncanny for Yeats-Brown. He could not find his bearings in a colonial environment where the 'unimaginable' scale of things was beyond his comprehension. What made him feel so isolated was not therefore fear predicated on any given object but simply an indefinite and pervasive anxiety about being lost in empire.

The isolation of rulers from the ruled was integral to the colonial experience in South Asia. It could hardly be otherwise considering that the raj was a dominance without hegemony—an autocracy that ruled without consent. Isolation was therefore a structural necessity. What made it worse and difficult to forget was the absurdity of Britain's claim to have fitted the roundness of colonial autocracy to the squareness of metropolitan liberalism. A sore that refused to heal, it went on festering by being compulsively touched. Symptom of an unredeemably bad conscience, it developed the habit of insinuating itself into all manner of colonial discourse, ranging from homiletics to politics, from the novel to the lyric to the common joke.

Yet in Yeats-Brown's memoir we have this pervasive concern presented to us in an aspect that remains concealed in the standard histories of the empire. This is not a lacuna which is explained by any shortage of material, for there is no such shortage. The responsibility lies rather with historiography itself—with its tendency to misconstrue the evidence of anxiety simply as fear. In this it allows itself to be uncritically influenced by the discourse of law and order, which had little use for the indefiniteness so characteristic of anxiety and assimilates it readily to fear, if only because the latter offers it the assurance it needs of a definitive causality to justify itself. Historiography, with its statist bias, follows suit and reads fear for anxiety.

Consider for instance the following extract from that truly brilliant work of imperial historiography, John Kaye's *History of the Indian Mutiny*. Written in the manner of grand narratives of war and revolution, it has a storyline which follows close on the heel of events, as in Clarendon's history of the other great rebellion of two centuries before, and stops occasionally, like the latter, to allow metonymy to congeal in reflection. Commenting on the Mutiny at one such stop, he speaks of it as an event that caught the government of the day entirely by surprise.

In all countries, and under all forms of government [he writes], the dangers which threaten the State, starting in the darkness, make headway towards success before they are clearly discerned by the rulers of the land. . . . The peculiarities of our Anglo-Indian Empire converted a probability into a certainty. Differences of race, differences of language, differences of religion, differences of customs, all indeed that could make a great antagonism of sympathies and of interests, severed the rulers and the ruled as with a veil of ignorance and obscurity. We could not see or hear with our own sense what was going on, and there was seldom any one to tell us. When by some accident the truth at last transpired, . . . much time was lost. . . . The great safeguard of sedition was to be found in the slow processes of departmental correspondence. . . . When prompt and effectual action was demanded, Routine called for pens and paper. A letter was written where a blow ought to have been struck.[5]

The differences of race, religion, language, and custom which separated the colonizer and the colonized are perceived in this passage as clearly as they are promptly assimilated to a concern for the security of the state. Of no significance in themselves, they are regarded simply as 'a veil of ignorance and obscurity' preventing the rulers from seeing or hearing 'what was going on' and combating sedition. An instance, par excellence, of the prose of counterinsurgency, this gives the phenomenon of isolation an unmistakably disciplinary slant in colonialist historiography and reduces it into one of fear. For the lack of information that made the regime feel so isolated was supposed to have been all about 'dangers which threaten[ed] the State'. Isolation was identified thus with fear—the fear of sedition and rebellion. As such it belonged to a rather different category from what had driven Yeats-Brown to despair. There was nothing in the latter so specific as a nameable 'cause' of fear and none that could be dealt with by something so positive as police intelligence about 'what was going on'.

This is a distinction of some importance—one which we would suggest, following Kierkegaard, is that between fear and anxiety. The former, he says, refers to 'something definite'.[6] It does so as a state of mind related to a threat—like that to which all states, including the colonial state, are subjected, according to Kaye. A threat is detrimental by its very nature—it harms—and the fear it inspires has its definitiveness rooted as much in the character of the region from which the threat comes as in that of the entity marked out for harming.[7] The fear that haunts the British rulers of India in texts like the one cited above is something definite in this Heideggerian sense. It originates in a clearly specified region—namely, the civil society of the subject population and the equally specific object to which the harm is addressed, that is, the raj. However, directedness alone is not enough to make a threat into an agent of fear. It requires the further condition of drawing close without being actually within striking distance, so that the effect it has is heightened by a degree of uncertainty on the part of the frightened.[8] The alarms and panics of La Grande Peur of 1789 and the Mutiny of 1857 were all fearsome precisely because they were charged with such impendency.

There was little in Yeats-Brown's anguish that could be said to be either directed or impending. We have no idea where it came from, nor indeed what in particular it sought for its focus. Far from being definite, it was a phenomenon characterized by a total indefiniteness—one which the two great thinkers mentioned above have helped us to diagnose as anxiety.

'That in the face of which one is anxious is completely indefinite,' writes Heidegger. This is so in two ways, as he goes on to explain:

Not only does this indefiniteness leave factically undecided which entity within-the-world is threatening us, but it also tells us that entities within the world are not 'relevant' at all . . . . The world has the character of completely lacking in significance. In anxiety one does not encounter this thing or that thing which, as something threatening, must have an involvement.[9]

This is how we read the young officer's state of mind in the passage from his memoir cited above. It spoke of no particular entity as the cause of his isolation. For his sense of isolation carried no threat at all; it had neither the regionality nor the directionality characteristic of the latter. It was not that the world around him had ceased to exist. Only the things that constituted it appeared to signify a nowhere and a nothing—an emptiness beyond limit, a nullity rendered incomprehensible by a scale of things beyond measure. Such nothing and nowhere indicate, according to Heidegger, 'that the world as such is that in the face of which one has anxiety'.[10] To be in such a world is not to be at home in one's environment. 'In anxiety one feels "uncanny".'[11]

Can we afford to leave anxiety out of the story of the empire? For nearly two hundred years the answer of colonialist historiography to this question has been one in favour of exclusion. It is not anxiety but enthusiasm that has been allowed to dominate its narratives. The latter is a mood which is consonant with all the triumphalist and progressivist moments of imperialism—its wars of conquest, annexation, and pacification in the subcontinent; its interventions in our environment and our economy by industrialization, monetization, and communication; its project of social engineering by administrative measures and its mission of civilizing by education. Its politics of expansion and improvement, its ethics of courage, discipline, and sacrifice, its aesthetics of orientalism have all been assimilated to this mood by a whole range of rhetorical, analytical, and narratological devices, so that enthusiasm has come to be regarded as the very mentality of imperialism itself. The result has been to promote an image of the empire as a sort of machine operated by a crew who know only how to decide but not to doubt, who know only action but no circumspection, and, in the event of a breakdown, only fear and no anxiety. However, the picture does not look nearly so neat when we step outside official discourse and meet individual members of that crew agonizing like Yeats-Brown over the immensity of things in a world whose limits are not known to them.

During the dying days of the empire, the complexities of this pred cament came to be widely known in the words of another Englishman, George Orwell, who too had gone out to serve the raj. The importance of his essay 'Shooting an Elephant' for our discussion can hardly be overstated.[12] It speaks from a situation which is not quite so aloof as Yeats-Brown's when he writes of his Indian environment as an 'outside' of panoramic proportions viewed by a rider on horseback or a passenger out of the window of his railway carriage. In either case, the scene, described so well in *The Lives of a Bengal Lancer*, is as broad as it is one that is swiftly passing by, so that the observations, for all their anguish, maintain a distance from what is observed. It is an alienating rather than an inviting distance witness to the fact that things have lost their significance in this world which the observer, in his anxiety, can apprehend only as an unparticularized whole.

By contrast, there is nothing that separates Orwell from his scene. Indeed the idea of separation would seem to be altogether out of place in the drama of that morning's events some seventy-five years ago in an obscure corner of Britain's South Asian empire, a small town of Burma called Moulmein. An elephant in a state of *must* had gone berserk, killed its mahout, destroyed parts of a slum, and was on a rampage threatening more lives and properties.[13] The police officer, called to help, felt beleaguered as he found some thousands of the local population closing in to watch him shoot the beast. Packed with crowds and action, this is not just an outline sketched hurriedly from afar. To the contrary, the details of an involvement in a fast-approaching danger clutter the text. Yet as the crisis ticks away, a terrible sense of isolation gathers in the midst of that tumult, lifts off, and extends beyond the town to all of the empire—to all that goes by that name territorially as well as conceptually. It is precisely this unforeseen and somewhat abrupt development that deflects what might have shaped up as fear from its object and turns it into an anxiety addressed to nothing in particular—no elephant, no yellow face which Orwell so intensely dislikes, not even the dilemma of having to destroy the animal he would rather leave alone.

Indeed Orwell himself refers to his own state of mind at this crisis as no ordinary fear. 'I was not afraid in the ordinary sense,' he writes.[14] How then is one to understand this being not afraid in the ordinary sense? Not, we suggest, as an instance of the moral and political revulsion so conspicuously displayed in the opening paragraphs of that essay. He had gone to the East, says the author, without knowing much about it or what to expect there and was shocked to see how tyrannical British rule was in South Asia, how cruelly it oppressed its subjects, and how strongly the latter resented the raj. All of which he found 'perplexing and upsetting'—to the point of being haunted by 'an intolerable sense of guilt', hating 'the dirty work of empire' he was appointed to do as a subdivisional police officer in the imperial service, and about to make up his mind 'that imperialism was an evil thing and the sooner I chucked up my job and got out of it the better'.[15] Above all he was as bitter about what seemed to him 'an aimless, petty kind of . . . anti-European feeling' among the natives as he was about 'the utter silence . . . imposed on every Englishman in the East' when it came to criticizing the regime.[16] A terrible quandary, which he defines as one of being 'stuck between my hatred of the empire I served and my rage against the evil-spirited little beasts who tried to make my job impossible'.[17]

Years later, when the time came for Orwell to be canonized as a great advocate of liberty, sentiments like these would be bracketed with the ideological stance of his novel *Nineteen Eighty-four* and regarded as evidence of his consistent opposition to all tyrannies—Russian as well as British—and of his unfailing commitment to the ideals of liberalism. However, a close reading will show that the earlier text, published in 1936, does not quite measure up to such claims. For one thing, it has no room in it even for the standard liberal value of racial tolerance. It is peppered with phrases that speak explicitly of his disapproval of the Burmese not only for the colour of their skin but for what he obviously perceived as their cultural and moral inferiority. He describes them as gutless, venal, lying.[18] The youth of the town, with whom he was apparently not so popular, are referred to as 'the sneering yellow faces' that met him everywhere, and a crowd of the local poor who had turned out to see the shooting as a 'sea of yellow faces above the garish clothes'.[19] And this racial loathing is laced with a violence which loses none of its ugliness even in the confessional rhetoric as he writes how 'with one part of my mind I thought of the British Raj as an unbreakable tyranny . . . [while] with another part I thought that the greatest joy in the world would be to drive a bayonet into a Buddhist priest's guts'.[20] Furthermore, what is crucial for our understanding of his predicament is that his urge for freedom is obviously not strong enough to inspire him to grasp it when he has a choice to do so. Indeed, the importance of his essay for me lies in its candid documentation of liberalism's failure to act up to its profession of freedom when the crunch comes.

The misreading of Orwell's anguish as the simple cry of a liberal conscience to no small extent owes to a confusion between its two registers. Unclear about the nature of his own despair, he shifts erratically from one to the other, confusing both himself and the reader in the process. Yet it is precisely such confusion that dignifies this otherwise unremarkable belletristic exercise with the authenticity of a moral dilemma. The two registers have rather different, though mutually overdetermined, interpretations for their content. Both speak of the author-official's understanding of his own world but do so from perspectives which are not quite the same.

One of these, briefly noticed above, concerns the uneasy, doubt-ridden, yet dutiful British bureaucrat overwhelmed by his sense of isolation from the people he rules in empire's name and hates as a racially and culturally inferior species who prevent him from properly doing his job. Yet that job, he knows, stands for 'the dirty work of Empire'—an empire that is oppressive, exploitative, and evil. But the evil victimizes its own instruments as well. The latter must not demur, but carry on with their assignments in silence. They have lost their freedom no less than their subjects. Caught between two hatreds—that of the raj and of the natives—Orwell speaks for his colleagues as well. 'Feelings like these,' he says, 'are the *normal* by-products of imperialism; ask any Anglo-Indian official, if you can catch him off duty.'[21]

In other words, we have an interpretation here of colonial rule in one of its aspects, which may appropriately be called normal. For all that is odious about it, it seems to have been absorbed into the ideology and practice of everyday administration where colonizer and colonized are locked in routine transactions. The moral and political doubts the subdivisional police chief has about such transactions are all integral to and indeed consistent with the normalcy of this world. It is a world where the Anglo-Indian official is quite at home in his secondary society—the society of courts, clubs, and bungalows, of tax collection and pig-sticking and crowd control, of servants and salaams, as Yeats-Brown had characterized it—a secondary society kept scrupulously apart from the wider and larger indigenous one. No cry of conscience, Orwell's observations are simply the record of a common, if grumbling, compliance of the worker ant which carries the grain and the honey of empire industriously, incessantly, and ever so obediently to its queen.

What however lifts Orwell's sentiments above the ordinariness of routine is the other register, where his interpretation of the place he has in that unhappy but duty-bound world of colonial dominance acquires a somewhat different spin. Concerned no longer with the feelings of the generic white official out in the East, it is about a dilemma whose universality derives from its being all his own. The terms of this dilemma are known well enough to require no more than a brief recapitulation. Called upon to deal with the rampaging elephant, he had armed himself with a gun but realized on closer approach that it had calmed down and there would be no point in shooting it. However, a large crowd of onlookers, nearly two thousand strong, had already gathered there. 'And suddenly I realized,' he writes, 'that I should have to shoot the elephant after all. The people expected it of me and I had got to do it; I could feel their two thousand wills pressing me forward, irresistibly.'[22]

The suddenness of this realization, emphasized further by temporal markers like 'glimpse' and 'moment', is what alerts us first to its character as a phenomenon of anxiety.[23] For 'anxiety', says Lacan, 'is always defined as appearing suddenly, as arising'.[24] As such it is a signal of the shortest possible duration, as short as 'a blink of the eye', which, according to Kierkegaard, is how a moment is expressed figuratively in his own language, Danish.[25] This is an ancient usage which coincides with its rendering as *nimesha* (alternatively, *nimisha*) in Sanskrit and goes back to the Vedas within the Indian tradition. What it signals is an abrupt break with continuity, with any pre-existing series whatsoever, just as the blink cuts off the steadiness of a gaze. It is precisely in this least of intervals, which relates to time as succinctly and economically as the point does to Euclidian space, that Orwell situates the suddenness of his realization.

And it was at this moment [he writes], . . . that I first grasped the hollowness, the futility of the white man's dominion in the East. Here was I, the white man with his gun, standing in front of the unarmed native crowd— seemingly the leading actor of the piece; but in reality I was only an absurd puppet pushed to and fro by the will of those yellow faces behind. I perceived in this moment that when the white man turns tyrant it is his own freedom that he destroys. He becomes a sort of hollow, posing dummy, the conventionalized figure of a sahib. For it is the condition of his rule that he shall spend his life in trying to impress the 'natives,' and so in every crisis he has got to do what the 'natives' expect of him. He wears a mask, and his face grows to fit it. I had got to shoot the elephant.[26]

'This moment', the *nimesha*, witness to an interpretation that had so abruptly translated the sahib's contest with the elephant into a contest of will between colonizer and colonized, was the signal of an entirely new realization. As such, it stood for a qualitative leap—a 'negation of continuity', as Kierkegaard put it.[27] There was nothing in it that could be regarded as continuous with the hatred he had distributed so evenly between imperialism and its victims in the first register. It would not be possible to transit directly from that to this other register—the register of anxiety. For what distinguished the latter was the suddenness of a leap that ruptured the *taedium mobile* of an imperial administration where conscientious objection was securely yoked to the routine performance of official chores, however evil or ignominious these might have been.

The moment of realization, we have noticed, is also described by Orwell as a 'glimpse'—that is, as an altogether unexpected disclosure. Curiously enough, that glimpse of what he calls 'the real nature of imperialism' turns out, on close inspection, to be rather different from his initial understanding of empire as a tyranny imposed on the natives.[28] In the register of anxiety, by contrast, the emphasis shifts to the colonizer's own loss of freedom. He has no will of his own any more and is controlled 'by the will of those yellow faces behind'. Trapped in the image of the sahib fabricated by sahibs themselves in order to impress the natives, he is now forced to live up to it by doing what natives expect a sahib to do. They expect him to shoot the elephant. He does not want to shoot it. He must shoot it.

What is clearly at issue in this dilemma is freedom and its possibility, which stares our protagonist, the police official, in the face. The suddenness of this confrontation unsettles him; its urgency is fraught with a terror he finds hard to bear. Seized by anxiety, he has to decide whether to throw off his mask or continue to wear it, to assert his own will or be guided by that of others, to play or not to play sahib before the natives—in sum, to shoot or not to shoot the elephant.

In the event, as we know, he decided to act as a white man must and shot the animal. In doing so, he overcame the anxiety of freedom by coming down firmly on the side of unfreedom—an unfreedom articulated doubly as the native's subjection to colonial rule and the colonialist's to native expectation about what he must do in order not to lose face. This was indeed the unfreedom where he was at home as a functionary of the raj acting out the official roles assigned to him and dutifully, if grudgingly, performing his chores. In such a context, the incident of that morning was nothing other than a signal of the uncanny calling out to him to step out of the groove and walk away to freedom. He had heard that call, but a moment's glimpse of the abyss of possibility was enough to make him recoil from the brink. He chose to stay where he was, clinging firmly to the homeliness of the routine and the familiar. The uncanny of empire had frightened Yeats-Brown by its incomprehensible dimensions, by excesses beyond measure. Some twenty years on, it was to frighten Orwell by the urgency of its insistence on freedom.[29]

The essay 'Shooting an Elephant' is therefore no parable of liberal revolt against colonialism. To the contrary, it demonstrates how a liberal conscience succumbed to colonial imperatives. Yet in the very act of doing so, it was singed by anxiety and brought back, however momentarily, from its absorption in the familiar world of the sahib. From that moment the raj would no longer be the same to it again. For it had caught a glimpse of freedom in the flash of time's passing, and had known, if only for the duration of a blink, the possibility of not being at home in empire.

NOTES

1. Francis Yeats-Brown, *The Lives of a Bengal Lancer,* New York: The Viking Press, 1930: 4–5.
2. Aristotle, *Metaphysics: Books Γ, Δ, and ε,* tr. Christopher Kirwan, Oxford: Clarendon Press, 1971: 54, D17.
3. Aristotle, *Metaphysica,* vol. 8 of *The Works of Aristotle,* tr. W.D. Ross, 2nd ed., Oxford: Clarendon Press, 1928: D17.
4. G.W.F. Hegel, *Logic,* tr. William Wallace, Oxford: Clarendon Press, 1975: 161; see pp. 156–61.
5. John Kaye, *History of the Indian Mutiny of 1857–8,* ed. G.B. Malleson, 6 vols, London: W.H. Allen, 1898, 1:374.
6. Søren Kierkegaard, *The Concept of Anxiety: A Simple Psychologically Orienting Deliberation on the Dogmatic Issue of Hereditary Sin,* tr. and, Reidar Thomte and Albert B. Andersen Princeton, N.J. Princeton University Press, 1980: 42; hereafter abbreviated CA.
7. See Martin Heidegger, *Being and Time,* tr. John Macquarrie and Edward Robinson, London: SCM Press, 1962: 179; hereafter abbreviated BT. I rely generally on section 30 of that work for this and related aspects of my argument here.
8. Ibid.: 179–80.
9. Ibid.: 231.
10. Ibid.
11. Ibid.: 233.
12. See George Orwell, 'Shooting an Elephant', in *'Shooting an Elephant' and Other Essays,* New York: Harcourt, Brace & World, 1950: 3–12; hereafter abbreviated 'SE'.
13. Ibid.: 5.
14. Ibid.: 9.
15. Ibid.: 3, 43.
16. Ibid.:3, 4
17. Ibid.: 4.
18. Ibid.: 3, 5, and 7–8 for assertions and innuendoes to such effect.
19. Ibid.: 3, 7.
20. Ibid.: 4.
21. Ibid. (emphasis added).
22. Ibid.: 8.
23. Ibid.: 4, 8.
24. Jacques Lacan, *Freud's Papers on Technique 1953–1954.* vol. 1 of *The Seminar of Jacques Lacan,* tr. John Forrester, ed. Jacques-Alain Miller, New York: W.W. Norton, 1988: 68.
25. see the editorial note on this point: 'The Danish word *Øiblikket* (the moment) is figurative in the sense that it is derived from *Øiets Blik* (a blink of the eye). Cf. the German word *Augenblick*' (CA.: 87: 245, n. 21).
26. 'SE': 8.
27. CA: 129.
28. 'SE': 4.
29. Yeats-Brown mentioned New Year's Eve of 1905 as the date of his first encounter with the uncanny of empire; see Yeats-Brown, *The Lives of a Bengal Lancer*: 3–13. Orwell joined the imperial service in Burma about twenty years later, in 1926.

TWO

Representing Authority in Victorian India

Bernard S. Cohn

By the middle of the nineteenth century, India's colonial society was marked by a sharp disjunction between a small, alien ruling group, British in culture, and a quarter of a billion Indians whom the British effectively controlled. The military superiority of these aliens had just been successfully demonstrated in the brutal suppression of a widespread military and civil revolt which had spread through much of Upper India in 1857 and 1858. In the two decades that followed this military action, a theory of authority became codified, based on ideas and assumptions about the proper ordering of groups in Indian society, and their relationship to their British rulers. In conceptual terms, the British, who had started their rule as 'outsiders', became 'insiders' by vesting in their monarch the sovereignty of India through the Government of India Act of 2 August 1858. This new relationship between the British monarch, her Indian subjects, and the native princes of India was proclaimed in all principal centres of British rule in India on 8 November 1858. In the proclamation Queen Victoria assured the Indian princes that 'their rights, dignity and honour' as well as their control over their territorial possessions would be respected, and that the queen 'was bound to the natives of Our Indian territories by the same obligations of duty which bind us to all our other subjects'. All her Indian subjects were to be secure in the practice of their religions. They were to enjoy 'the equal and impartial protection of the law', and 'due regard would be paid to the ancient rights, usages and customs of India' in the framing and administration of this law. The princes and her Indian subjects were informed by the queen that all would be done to stimulate 'the peaceful industry of India, to promote works of public utility and improvement', and that they 'should enjoy that social advancement which can only be secured by internal peace and good government'.[1]

The proclamation was based on two main assumptions: first, that there was an indigenous diversity in culture, society, and religion in India, and second, that the foreign rulers had a responsibility for the maintenance of an equitable form of government which would be directed not only to protecting the integrity inherent in this diversity, but also to social and material progress which would benefit the ruled.

The proclamation can be viewed as a cultural statement which encompasses two divergent or even contradictory theories of rule: one which sought to maintain India as a feudal order, and the other looking towards changes which would inevitably lead to the destruction of this feudal order. Each of these theories about British rule incorporated ideas about the sociology of India and the relationship of the rulers to individuals and groups in Indian society. If India were to be ruled in a feudal mode then an Indian aristocracy had to be recognized and/or created, which could play the part of 'loyal feudatories' to their British queen. If India were to be ruled by the British in a 'modernist' mode, then principles which looked to a new kind of civic or public order had to be developed. Those adhering to this view desired a representational mode of government based sociologically on communities and interests, with individuals representing these entities.

British adherents of both the feudal and the representational mode of colonial government shared a number of assumptions about the past and present of India, and the continued necessity and desirability of monarchical rule for India. In both modes, although Indians might become associated with their white rulers as feudatories or as representatives of communities and interests, effective system-wide decisions would be made by the British colonial rulers. The British rulers assumed that Indians had lost their right to self-rule through their own weakness, which led to their subjugation by a succession of 'foreign' rulers, stretching back to the Aryan invasions and, in the more recent past, to the British conquest of the preceding imperial rulers of India, the Mughals. The apparent fact of Indian incompetence for self-rule was accepted by all the British concerned with ruling India. What arguments there were among the British were related to whether this incompetence was inherent and permanent, or whether under proper tutelage Indians could become effective enough to rule themselves. The feudal theory could encompass the representational theory and the possibility of evolution of competence, since the British had lived through a feudal stage in their own history, and in analytical terms the Indian present could be seen as the British past. The British polity, society, and economy had evolved into its modern form from this past; hence, theoretically, the present feudal society of India could also evolve into a modern one in the distant future. In terms of policy the members of the ruling group could argue about the political efficacy of supporting landlords, princes, the peasants, or the rising numbers of urban-based Western-educated Indians in terms of a general agreement on the nature of Indian society and the accomplishment of ultimate goals for India, without questioning the existing institutions of colonial rule. [. . .]

THE FORMALIZATION AND REPRESENTATION OF THE RITUAL IDIOM: THE IMPERIAL ASSEMBLAGE OF 1877

The twenty years after the desacralization of Delhi and the final suppression of the uprising of 1857 were marked by the completion of the symbolic–cultural constitution of British India. I will only briefly list the components of the content of this constitution, and then go on to describe how these components were represented in a ritual event, the Imperial Assemblage of 1877, which was held to proclaim Queen Victoria empress of India.

The central political fact was the end of the Company's rule and the establishment of the monarch of Great Britain as the monarch of India in 1858. This act may be seen as the reciprocal of the final desacralization of the Mughal empire. It ended the ambiguity in the position of the British in India, as now the British monarchy encompassed both Britain and India. A social order, with the British crown seen as the centre of authority and capable of ordering into a single hierarchy all its subjects, Indian and British, was established. The Indian princes now were Queen Victoria's 'loyal Indian Feudatories', who owed deference and allegiance to her through her viceroy. The governor-general and the viceroy, being the same person, was unequivocally the locus of authority in India, and all the British and Indians could be ranked in relation to him, whether it be by office held or membership in various status groups. The British operated in India with an ordinal theory of hierarchy, in which individuals could be ranked by precedence—this precedence being based on fixed and known criteria, established by ascription and succession, or achievement and office. For the allied princes an effort had been made by 1876 to group them by region, with a fixed assignment of rank vis-à-vis other rulers in their region. The size of the princes' states, the amounts of their revenue, the date at which they had become allies of the East India Company, the history of their families, their standing in relation to the Mughal empire, and their acts of loyalty towards the British could all be weighed, and an index established to determine the rank of any ruler. This status was then represented at durbars held by governors or lieutenant-governors of the region, or when the viceroy–governor–general went on a progress. A code of conduct was established for princes and chiefs for their attendance at the durbar. The clothes they wore, the weapons they could carry, the number of retainers and soldiers that could accompany them to the viceroy's camp, where they were met by British officials, in relation to the camp, the number of gun salutes fired in their honour, the time of the entry into the durbar hall or tent, whether the viceroy would rise and come forward to greet them, where on the viceregal rug they would be saluted by the viceroy, where they would be seated, how much *nazar* they could give, whether they would be entitled to a visit from the viceroy, were all markers of rank and could be changed by the viceroy to raise or lower their status. In correspondence with the viceroy, the forms of salutation, the kinds of Indian titles which the British would use, and the phrases used in the conclusion of a letter, all were graded, and were seen as marks of approval or approbation.

Similarly, the Indians who were under direct British rule were ordinarily ranked in their towns, districts, and provinces in the durbar books of various officials. The leading men of a district were ranked on the basis of revenue paid, land held, ancestry of their families, and acts of loyalty or disloyalty to the British government. Indian officials and employees of the imperial or provincial government were ranked by office, length of service, and honours achieved, and the masses, by caste, community, and religion.

Immediately after the suppression of the rebellion and the establishment of the queen of England as the 'fountain of honour' of India, investigations were made into the system of Indian royal titles, with the goal of ordering them in a hierarchy. Not only was the system organized, but holders of titles had to 'prove' by criteria established by the British that their titles were legitimate. Henceforth only the viceroy could grant Indian titles, based on the recommendation of local or provincial officials. The basis of entitlement became specified by acts of loyalty, outstanding and long-term service in the government, special acts of charity such as endowing schools and hospitals, contributions to special funds, and 'good' management of resources leading to the improvement of agricultural production. Indian entitlements were for the length of the life of the holder, although in some of the leading families there was the presumption that with demonstrated good behaviour, the successor to the headship of the family would in due course be rewarded by the renewal in the next generation of a title previously held. Honour and titles by the 1870s were closely tied to the expressed goals of the new governmental order, 'progress with stability'.

In 1861 a new royal Order of Indian knights was established—the Star of India. At first, this Order, which included both Indian and British knights, was restricted to twenty-five members who were the most important Indian princes and senior and distinguished British civil and military officers. In 1866 the Order was expanded by the addition of two lower ranks, and by 1877 there were several hundred holders of knighthoods in the Order, which were personal and granted by the queen. The investiture and holding of chapters of the Order added an important European component to the ritual idiom which the British were establishing in India. The accoutrements of the Order were English and 'feudal': a robe or mantle, a collar, a medallion with the effigy of the queen (the wearing of such a human effigy was anathema to Muslims), and a jewelled pendant. The investiture was in the European style, with the reading of the warrant and a presentation of the insignia, the newly entitled knight kneeling before the monarch or her representative. The contractual aspect of the entitlement was painfully clear to the Indian recipients as the accoutrements given had to be returned at the death of the holder. Unlike presentations received from Indian rulers in the past which were kept as sacred objects in treasure rooms to be viewed and used on special occasions, these had to be returned. The statutes of the Order required the recipients to sign a bond that the valuables would be returned by their heirs. Indians also objected to one of the statutes which specified the conditions under which the knighthood could be rescinded for acts of disloyalty. The knighthoods became rewards for 'good service'.

The relationship between the Crown and India was beginning to be marked by tours of India by members of the royal family, the first of these being by the Duke of Edinburgh in 1869. The Prince of Wales went on a six-month tour of India in 1875–6. The royal tours were not only significant in India in terms of the representation of the bond between the princes and peoples of India and their monarch, but were also extensively reported in the British press. On the return of the Prince of Wales, exhibitions were held in major English cities of the exotic and expensive presents which he had received. Ironically, one of the major gifts which the Prince of Wales gave in return was an English translation of the Vedas by Max Müller.

The period of 1860 to 1877 saw a rapid expansion of what might be thought of as the definition and expropriation of Indian civilization by the imperial rulers. Colonial rule is based on forms of knowledge as much as it is based on institutions of direct control. From the founding by Sir William Jones and other European scholars in 1784 of the Asiatic Society of Bengal, there had been a steady development in the accumulation of knowledge about the history of India, its systems of thoughts, its religious beliefs and practices, and its society and institutions. Much of this accumulation was the result of practical experience in law coùrts, in the assessment and collection of revenue and the attendant English imperative to order and classify information. Through this period more and more Europeans came to define what they thought of as the uniqueness of Indian civilization. This definition included the development of an apparatus for the study of Indian languages and texts, which had the effect of standardizing and making authoritative, not only for Europeans but for Indians themselves, what were thought to be the 'classics' of Indian thought and literature. Through the encouragement of the production by Indians of school books, Indians began to write history in the European mode, often borrowing European ideas about the past of India. In the 1860s an archaeological survey was established, with Europeans deciding what were the great monuments of India, which monuments were fit for preservation or for description as part of the Indian 'heritage'. Census operations and the establishment of an ethnographic survey were to describe 'the peoples and cultures of India', to make them available in monographs, photographs, and through statistical tabulations not only to their own officials but to social scientists so that India could be part of the laboratory of mankind. The British believed that Indian arts and crafts had entered a period of sharp decline in the face of Western technology and machine-made products, hence their arts and crafts had to be collected, preserved, and placed in museums. In addition, art schools were founded in major cities where Indians could be taught how to produce sculptures, paintings, and craft products, Indian in content but appealing and acceptable to Western tastes. Indian architectural builders began to construct European-style buildings, but with 'Oriental' decorative motifs. The imperial government established committees to search for and preserve Sanskrit, Persian, Arabic, and vernacular language manuscripts. Educated Indians increasingly were to learn about their own culture through the mediation of European ideas and scholarship. The British rulers were increasingly defining what was Indian in an official and 'objective' sense. Indians had to look like Indians— before 1860 Indian soldiers as well as their European officers had worn Western-style uniforms; now the dress uniforms of Indians and the English included turbans, sashes, and tunics thought to be Mughal or Indian.

The reified and objectified vision of India, its life, thought, sociology, and history were to be brought together to celebrate the completion of the political constitution of India, through the establishment of Victoria as empress of India.

THE ROYAL TITLES ACT OF 1876

On 8 February 1876, for the first time since the death of her husband in 1861, Queen Victoria opened parliament. Much to the surprise of the Liberal opposition, she announced in her speech that a bill would be introduced in parliament to add to her Royal Style and Titles. In her speech she referred to the 'hearty affection' with which her son, the Prince of Wales, then touring in India, was being received 'by My Indian Subjects'. This assured her that 'they are happy under My rule, and loyal to My throne'.[2] She therefore deemed it an appropriate time to make an addition to her Royal Style and Titles.

In a speech on 17 February 1876, the prime minister, Disraeli, reviewed the discussions of 1858 concerning the declaration of Victoria as empress of India. At that time it had been considered premature to make Victoria empress because of unsettled conditions in India. But, he continued, in the subsequent twenty years there had been growing interest about India in Great Britain. The Prince's visit had stimulated a mutual feeling of sympathy in these two countries, and Disraeli had been assured that an imperial title, the exact nature of which was unspecified, 'will give great satisfaction not merely to the Princes, but to the nations of

India'.[3] It would signify 'the unanimous determination of the people of this country to retain our connection with the Indian Empire'.[4] Disraeli, in this speech, stressed the diversity of India, describing it as 'an ancient country of many nations', varying peoples and races, 'differing in religion, in manners and in laws—some of them highly gifted and civilized, and many of them of rare antiquity'. 'And this vast community is governed', he continued, 'under the authority of the Queen, by many Sovereign Princes, some of whom occupy Thrones which were filled by their ancestors when England was a Roman Province.'[5] The hyperbolic historical fantasy voiced by Disraeli was part of the myth later acted out in the Imperial Assemblage. India was diversity—it had no coherent communality except that given by British rule under the integrating system of the imperial Crown.

Thus at the base of the Conservative defence of the bill was the idea that Indians were a different kind of people from the British. Indians were more susceptible to high-sounding phrases, and would be better ruled by appeal to their Oriental imaginations, as 'they attach enormous value to very slight distinctions'.[6] It was argued that, given the constitutional relations between India and Great Britain, the Indian princes were indeed feudatories, and the ambiguity existing in the relationship of the princes to the British paramountcy would be reduced if the British monarch had a title of 'Emperor'. Although some Indian rulers were called 'Prince' in English, their titles in Indian languages were those of kings, for example, maharaja. With the imperial title, the hierarchic order would be clear cut and unequivocal. It was pointed out that Queen Elizabeth had used an imperial title, and that in practice, from Canning's time in India onwards, imperial titles were used to refer to the queen by princes and independent Asian rulers such as the Amirs of Central Asia. The claim was reiterated that the British were successors to the Mughals, who had an imperial Crown which Indians of all status understood. The British, the Conservatives argued, were the successors of the Mughals; hence is was right and proper that India's monarch, Queen Victoria, should be declared empress.

The Royal Titles Act was passed, and it received the royal assent on 27 April 1876. The need to overcome the acrimonious debate, the adverse newspaper coverage, especially as it found its way into Indian newspapers and was discussed by Western-educated Indians, became part of the rationale for planning the Imperial Assemblage. The three principal designers of the assemblage, Disraeli, Salisbury (secretary of state for India), and Lord Lytton (the newly appointed viceroy), realized that the Imperial Assemblage must be designed to make an impact upon the British at home as well as upon Indians.

THE INTENTIONS OF THE PLANNERS OF THE IMPERIAL ASSEMBLAGE

Lord Lytton, the newly appointed viceroy and governor–general, had returned to England from Portugal, where he had been serving as ambassador, and by January 1876 had begun his effort to overcome his 'absolute ignorance. . . concerning India'. This effort included meetings in February with members of the India Office staff and others in London considered 'experts' on India. The most influential was O.T. Burne, who later accompanied Lytton to India as his private secretary and was regarded by Lytton as the originator of the plan for the assemblage.[7]

Lytton chose Burne to be his private secretary to 'help restore friendly and sound relations between India and Afghanistan and at the same time to proclaim the Indian Imperial title, both of which questions,' Burne wrote, 'I was recognized as having a special knowledge.'[8] As was true of most viceroys, Lytton came to India with little knowledge of India or, perhaps more importantly, about the workings of the government of the colony. Most of the highest officials of the Raj rose through the ranks of the civil service, which meant twenty to thirty years of experience and well-entrenched relationship throughout the bureaucracy, as well as a highly developed capacity for political intrigue. Viceroys complained bitterly about the frustrations in implementing their plans and policies, dictated by political positions in England. It fell to the viceroy's private secretary to articulate the viceroy's office with the bureaucracy. Questions of appointments, promotions, postings, and honours initially went through his hands. Viceroys were dependent on the private secretary's knowledge of personal relationships and factions within the bureaucracy, and their capacity to utilize viceregal power effectively in relation to the civil service. After twenty years of experience in various staff positions, Burne had a wide acquaintance with officials in India, and because of his service in Ireland and London was well-acquainted with leading politicians at home.

The planning of the Imperial Assemblage was started in secrecy soon after the arrival of Lytton and Burne in Calcutta in April 1876. A committee was established which included T.H. Thornton, acting foreign secretary of the Government of India, who was to be responsible for relations with the Indian princes and chiefs, and Major General (later Field Marshal) Lord Roberts, quartermaster general of the Indian army, who was in charge of the military planning of the assemblage. Also on the committee was Colonel George Colley, Lytton's military secretary, and Major Edward Bradford of the political department, head of the recently established secret police.

The president of the committee was Thomas Thornton, who had served mainly in positions in the secretariat, having been secretary to the Punjab government for twelve years before acting briefly as foreign secretary. Major General Roberts, who had made a reputation for himself as a logistics specialist, was in charge of planning the camps in Delhi.[9] Lord Lytton was much impressed with Roberts' abilities. It was because of his performance in planning the assemblage that he was selected for command of the British forces in Afghanistan, the keystone to Roberts' later career in India and England.[10]

The committee drew on the ideas and suggestions of a small and influential group of political officers, men who had served for many years as residents or agents of governor–generals in the principal Indian courts. In the earliest stages of the work Major General Sir Henry Dermot Daly, about whom Lytton wrote 'there is universal consensus of opinion that there is no man in India who knows how to manage Native princes as well as Daly',[11] seems to have been part of the group. Daly argued that holding a durbar with all the major princes represented would be impossible because of the jealousies and susceptibilities of the chiefs.[12] The view held by most of the political experts was that 'Questions of precedence and slumbering claims of various kinds would infallibly arise, and heart burnings and umbrage and even more serious difficulties would ensue'.[13] Lytton tried to dissolve the opposition of the political officers by quietly ignoring them, and by insisting that the meeting in Delhi was not to be a durbar but rather an 'Imperial Assemblage'. Thus, in particular, he hoped that the question of precedence would not arise, and, by carefully controlling the visits with the princes, to avoid discussing various territorial claims.[14]

By the end of July 1876, the committee had finished its preliminary planning. The plan was divulged to the viceroy's council and an outline forwarded to London for the approvals of

Salisbury and Disraeli. At this stage, and into August, strict secrecy was maintained, for Lytton feared that early announcement of the plan would lead to an outcry in the Indian press—European and Indian—about details of the plan, and that there would follow a debate as 'unseemly' as that which had marked the Royal Titles Act.

Lytton expected to accomplish a great deal with the assemblage. He hoped it would conspicuously 'place the Queen's authority upon the ancient throne of the Moguls, with which the imagination and tradition of [our] Indian subjects associate the splendour of supreme power!'[15] Hence the decision was made to hold the assemblage at Delhi, the Mughal capital, rather than in Calcutta. At this time Delhi was a relatively small city recovering from the destruction of the rebellion of 1857. The population of the city was treated as a conquered people. One of the 'concessions' announced on behalf of the queen at the assemblage was the reopening of Zinat ul Musajid, long closed on 'military grounds' for public worship, and the restoration to the Muslims of Delhi of the Fatepuri Mosque in Chandi Chowk, which had been confiscated in 1857.[16]

The selection of Delhi as the site also avoided associating the Crown with a distinctly regional centre such as Calcutta or Bombay. Delhi had the advantage of being in a relatively central location, even though the facilities available for a gathering of large numbers were limited. The location of the assemblage was related to British rather than Mughal Delhi, as the site selected was not the large *maidan* (ground) in front of the Red Fort (which had been cleared and which today is the political ritual centre of India), but one near the ridge, on sparsely settled ground, which had been the scene of the great British victory of the Mutiny. The British camp was located on the ridge and to the east going down to the Jamuna river.

The assemblage was to be an occasion to raise the enthusiasm of 'the native aristocracy of the country, whose sympathy and cordial allegiance is no inconsiderable guarantee for the stability. . . of the Indian Empire'.[17] Lytton was striving to develop strong ties between this 'aristocracy' and the crown. He believed that India would never be held by 'good government' alone, that is, by improving the condition of the *ryot* (agriculturalist), strictly administering justice, and spending huge sums on irrigation works.

The assumed special susceptibility of the Indian to parade and show and the key position of the aristocracy were the defining themes of the assemblage, which was, Lytton wrote, to have an effect also on 'public opinion' in Great Britain, and would act as a support for the Conservative government in England. Lytton hoped that a successful assemblage, well reported in the press and displaying the loyalty of the Indian princes and peoples, would be evidence of the wisdom of the Royal Titles Act.

Lytton wanted the assemblage to bind the British official and unofficial communities in India closer together in support of the government. This expectation was not achieved by the assemblage. The governors of both Madras and Bombay advised against holding the assemblage, and for a time it appeared that the governor of Bombay might not even attend. He argued that there was a famine in Bombay and he was needed there; any cost to the central government or the presidency attendant upon participation would be better spent to alleviate the famine. Both governors complained about the disruption caused by having to leave their governments for two weeks with large numbers of their staff to attend the assemblage.

Many British in India, official and unofficial, and several influential British papers saw the assemblage as part of a policy of elevating the *'blacks'*, and paying too much attention to the Indians, because most concessions and acts of grace were directed towards Indians. Lytton wrote that he faced 'practical difficulties of satisfying the European element, which is disposed to be querlesome and avoiding the difficulty of favouring the conquered more than the conquering race'.[18]

The opposition to the plans in London and India was so strong that Lytton wrote to Queen Victoria:

If the Crown of England should ever have the misfortune to lose the great and magnificent empire of India, it will not be through the disaffection of your Majesty's native subjects, but through party spirit at home, and the disloyalty and insubordination of those members of Your Majesty's Indian Service, whose duty it is to cooperate with the Government. . . in the disciplined and loyal execution of its orders.[19]

COLONIAL SOCIOLOGY AND THE ASSEMBLAGE

In analytical terms the goal of the assemblage was to make manifest and compelling the sociology of India. The invitees were selected in relation to ideas which the British rulers had about the proper social order in India. Although emphasis was placed on the princes as feudal rulers and 'the natural aristocracy', the assemblage was also to include other categories of Indians, 'native gentlemen', 'landlords', 'editors and journalists', and 'representative men' of various kinds. In the 1870s a contradiction in the British theory of Indian sociology had become apparent. Some members of the British ruling group viewed India in historical terms as a feudal society consisting of lords, chiefs, and peasants. Other British saw India as a changing society which was composed of communities. These communities could be large and somewhat amorphous, such as Hindu/Muslim/Sikh/Christian/Animist; they could be vaguely regional, such as Bengali or Gujarati; they could be castes such as Brahmans, Rajputs, Baniyas; or communities could be based on educational and occupational criteria, such as, Westernized Indians. Those English rulers who saw India as made up of communities sought to control them through identifying the 'representative men', leaders who were thought to speak for, and who could shape responses from, their communities.

According to the feudal theory, there was a 'native aristocracy' in India. Lytton, in order to define and regulate this aristocracy, planned the establishment of a privy council and a College of Arms in Calcutta. The privy council was to be purely consultative, summoned by the viceroy 'who would keep the machinery completely under his own control'.[20] Lytton's intention was to arrange the constitution of the privy council 'to enable the Viceroy, whilst making parade of consulting native opinion to swamp the native members, and still secure the prestige of their presence and assent'.[21] The plan for a privy council for India quickly encountered constitutional problems and opposition from the council of India in London. A parliamentary act was necessary to establish such a body, and parliament was not sitting through the summer and autumn of 1876. The result, announced at the assemblage, was the naming of twenty 'Counsellors of the Empress', for the purpose of 'seeking from time to time, in matters of importance, the counsel and advice of Princes and Chiefs of India, and thus associating them with the Paramount Power'.[22]

The College of Arms in Calcutta was to be the Indian equivalent of the British College of Arms in London, which would in effect establish and order a 'peerage' for India. Indian titles had been a vexing question for the British rulers of India since the early nineteenth century. There appeared to the English to be no fixed lineally ordered hierarchy or any common system of titles, such as the British were familiar with in their own society. What were thought to be royal titles, such as raja, maharaja, nawab, or bahadur, seemed to be used randomly by Indians, and were not attached to actual control of territory or office, or a hierarchical system of status distinctions.

Coordinated with the establishment of the College of Arms was a plan to present at the Imperial Assemblage ninety of the leading Indian princes and chiefs with large banners emblazoned with their coats of arms. These banners were shield-shaped in the European mode. The crests were also European, with each heraldic device derived from the history of the particular royal house. The representations of 'history' on the crests included the mythic origins of the families, events connecting the houses to Mughal rule, and, particularly, aspects of the past which tied the Indian princes and chiefs to English rule.

The banners were presented at the Imperial Assemblage to attending Indian princes. These presentations were substituted for the former Mughal practice of exchange of *nazar* (gold coins) and *peshkash* (precious possessions) for *khelats* (robes of honour), which had marked previous British durbar practice. By eliminating what had been rituals of incorporation, the British completed the process of redefinition of the relationship between ruler and ruled begun in the middle of the eighteenth century. What had been a system of authority based upon the incorporation of subordinates to the person of the emperor now was an expression of linear hierarchic order in which the presentation of a silk banner made the Indian princes the legal subjects of Queen Victoria. In the British conception of the relationship, Indian princes became English knights and were to be obedient and offer fealty to the empress.

Lytton was aware that some of the more experienced and hard-headed officials, who had served in India and were now members of the secretary of state for India's council, would see the presentation of the banners and the establishment of the College of Arms as 'trivial and silly'.[23] Lytton thought this response would be a great mistake. 'Politically speaking,' Lytton wrote, 'the Indian peasantry is an inert mass. If it ever moves at all it will move in obedience, not to its British benefactors, but to its native chiefs and princes, however tyrannical they may be.'[24]

The other possible political representatives of 'native opinion' were what Lytton scornfully referred to as the 'Baboos', who had been taught to write 'semi-seditious articles in the Native Press, and who represent nothing but the social anomaly of own position'.[25] He felt that the Indian chiefs and princes were no mere noblesse, but 'a powerful aristocracy', whose complicity could be secured and efficiently utilized by the British in India. In addition to their power over the masses, the Indian aristocracy could be easily directed, if appealed to properly, as 'they are easily affected by sentiment and susceptible to the influence of symbols to which facts inadequately correspond'.[26] The British, Lytton continued, could gain 'their allegiance without giving up any of our power'.[27] To buttress his argument, Lytton referred to the British position in Ireland and especially the recent experience with Ionian Greeks, who, notwithstanding the 'good government' which British rule had given them, enthusiastically surrendered àll these advantages for what he termed 'a bit of bunting with the Greek colours on it'. He added, to underline his argument about the Indian aristocracy, 'the further East you go, the greater becomes the importance of a bit of bunting'.[28]

THE ENACTMENT OF THE COLONIAL SOCIOLOGY OF INDIA:
THE INVITEES TO THE IMPERIAL ASSEMBLAGE

At centre stage, according to the designers of the assemblage, were the sixty-three ruling princes who appeared in Delhi. They were described by Lytton as ruling forty million people and holding territories larger than France, England, and Italy.[29] The ruling chiefs and the three hundred 'titular chiefs and native gentlemen' who attended were seen as the 'flower of Indian Nobility'. Lord Lytton wrote:

Among them were the Prince of Arcot and the Princes of Tanjore from the Madras Presidency; the Maharajah Sir Jai Mangal Singh, and some of the principle Talukdars of Oudh; forty representatives of the most distinguished families of the North-Western province, scions of the ex-Royal family of Delhi; descendants of the Saddozai of Cabul, and the Alora Chiefs of Sindh, Sikh Sardars from Amritsar and Lahore, Rajputs from the Kangra Hills; the semi-independent Chief of Amb, on the Hazara border, envoys from Chitral and Yassin, who attended in the train of the Maharaja of Jammu and Chasmere; Arabs from Peshawar, Pata chiefs from Kohat and Derajat; Biluch Tommduis from Dera Ghazi Khan; leading citizens from Bombay; Gond and Mahratha nobles from the Central Provinces; Rajputs from Ajmere and natives of Burma, Central India, Mysore and Baroda.[30]

This litany of names, titles, and places was for Lytton and the English the embodiment of the assemblage. The exotic names, the 'barbaric' titles, and, above all, the elaborate variation in dress and appearance were constantly noted by English observers of the assemblage. The list of invitees included representatives of many of the dispossessed Indian royal families, such as the eldest son of the 'ex-King of Oudh', the grandson of Tipu Sultan, and members of the 'ex-Royal family of Delhi' (the House of the Mughal emperor). The presence of these descendants of the former great ruling houses of India imparted some of the flavour of a Roman triumph to the assemblage. The British conception of Indian history thereby was realized as a kind of 'living museum', with the descendants of both the enemies and the allies of the English displaying the period of the conquest of India. The 'rulers' and 'ex-rulers' were fossilized embodiments of a past which the British conquerors had created in the late eighteenth and early nineteenth centuries. All of this 'history' was brought together in Delhi, to announce, enhance, and glorify British authority as represented by the person of their monarch.[31]

The conjunction of past and present was proclaimed in the first official announcement of the Imperial Assemblage, when it was stated that among those to be invited would be 'those Princes, chiefest and nobles in whose persons the *ambiguity of the past* is associated with the prosperity of the present'.[32] Indians from all parts of the empire and even some Asians from beyond the boundaries were seen in their diversity as a statement of the need for British imperial rule. The viceroy, standing for the empress, represented the only authority which could hold together the great diversity inherent in the 'colonial sociology'. The unity of empire was literally seen as that provided by the superordinate and heaven-blessed British rulers of India. The diversity was mentioned frequently in the speeches which were a feature of the ten days of assemblage activities. At the state banquet before the assemblage, with a mixed audience of Indians in their 'native costumes' and British in their frock coats and uniforms, Lytton proclaimed that if one wanted to know the meaning of the imperial title, all they had to do was 'to look around' and see an empire 'multitudinous in its traditions, as well as in its inhabitants, almost infinite in the variety of races which populate it, and of the creeds which had shaped their character'.[33]

The colonial sociology of India was by no means fixed and rigidly ranked and ordered. The classificatory system was based on multiple criteria, which varied through time and from region to region of India. At the base of the classification were two kinds of criteria, one which the English rulers believed was 'natural', such as caste, race, and religion, and the other, social criteria which could include achievement, education—both Western and Indian, the financing of works of public utility, acts of loyalty performed on behalf of the English rulers, and family history seen as descent and genealogy. What the English thought of as the 'natural aristocracy' of India were at times contrasted with the category of 'native gentlemen', whose status was based on their actions (social criteria) rather than their descent (natural criteria).

Most of the twenty-two Indians who were invited by the Bengal government as 'native gentlemen' were large landholders, controlling extensive estates, such as Hatwa, Darbangha, and Dumroan in Bihar, or men such as Jai Mangal Singh of Monghyr, who had performed loyal service during the Santhal 'Rebellion' and the Sepoy 'Mutiny'.[34]

The Madras contingent of 'nobles and native gentlemen' was led by descendants of two deposed rulers—the prince of Arcot and the daughter of the last Maharaja of Tanjore. In addition to large landholders of Madras presidency, the Indian members of the Madras legislative council and two Indian lower civil servants were among the official guests. The Bombay contingent of 'nobles and native gentlemen' was the most diverse, and was apparently selected for representative qualities. The city of Bombay sent two Parsis, one of whom, Sir Jamesetji Jajeebhoy, was the only Indian at the time to have a hereditary English knighthood, and had been declared head of the Bombay Parsi community by the English government. In addition, there was a leading merchant, thought to be the 'representative member of the Mahommedan community', a government pleader from the Bombay high court, and another successful lawyer. In terms of the 'communities' of cosmopolitan Bombay, there were two Parsis, two Marathas, a Gujarati, and a Muslim. From the rest of the presidency came several large landholders, a judge of small claims court, a deputy collector, a professor of mathematics from the Deccan College, and the Oriental translator to the Bombay government.[35]

LOGISTICS AND PHYSICAL PLANNING:
THE CAMPS, THE AMPHITHEATRE, AND DECORATIVE MOTIFS

By the end of September 1876 guest lists were drawn up and official invitations were sent out. Planning now shifted to the actual physical arrangements for the assemblage, the location and preparation of the sites of the camps which were to provide living accommodation for the over 84,000 people, who were to converge on Delhi late in December. The camps were spread in a semicircle of five miles, taking the Delhi railway station as the starting point. Preparation of the site required the clearing of one hundred villages, whose lands were rented and whose cultivators were prevented from planting their winter crops. Considerable work was involved in developing a road network, water supplies, establishing several bazaars and proper sanitary facilities. As always with a large gathering of Indians in the nineteenth century, the British were greatly concerned about the possibility of an epidemic breaking out, and extensive medical precautions were taken. Labour had to be recruited, much of which came from the villages which were dislocated by the utilization of their fields for the camps. Actual preparation for the building camp sites began on 15 October, with Major General Roberts in overall charge.

The Indian rulers who were invited were instructed to bring their tents and equipage; railway schedules had to be worked out to transport the thousands of retainers and animals that accompanied the rulers. Strict limits were put on the number of followers who could accompany their masters. The number of retainers allowed to each chief was based on their gun salutes, with those honoured by seventeen and above being allowed five hundred; those with fifteen allowed four hundred; eleven, three hundred; nine, two hundred, and those 'feudatories' without salutes were allowed one hundred.[36] The planners estimated that the Indian rulers and their retinues would total 25,600, but, after the event, it was estimated that there had been 50,741 Indians in their own camps, 9741 Indians in the imperial camps, as clerks, servants, and followers, and another 6438 in the 'miscellaneous camps', such as those of the police, post and telegraph, the imperial bazaar, and the visitors.[37] Excluding the camps of the troops—approximately 14,000 in number—attending the assemblage, there were 8000 tents erected in and around Delhi to house the guests. Overall, at least 84,000 people attended the assemblage, of whom 1169 were Europeans.

The central imperial camp, a mile and a half in length and half-a-mile wide, stretched on the flats abutting the north-eastern side of the Delhi ridge and covered the grounds of the pre-mutiny military cantonment. The viceroy's canvas camp complex faced the main road, so that there would be easy access for the great numbers of visitors, European and Indian, whom he would receive in audience. Wheeler, the official historian of the assemblage, described the viceroy's tents as 'canvas houses' and 'the pavilion'—the enormous durbar tent—as 'a Palace'.[38] In this tent the viceroy held court, sitting on the viceregal chair on a raised platform, at the back of which was hung a painting of a stern-visaged, black-attired Queen Victoria, surveying the proceedings. In front of him stretched the huge viceregal rug, with the coat of arms of the imperial Indian government. Chairs were arranged on the rug in a rough semicircle for members of his staff and the important retainers of the chiefs who were to come to pay homage to the newly proclaimed empress and her viceroy. In ranks around the wall of the viceregal tent stood mare and yak tail whisk bearers, dressed in the livery of the viceregal household, and down the sides of the tent behind the chairs were European and Indian troopers. The whole scene was brilliantly lit by gas lamps.

Camped immediately to the right of the viceroy was the governor of Bombay, and to his left the governor of Madras; there then followed the camps of the lieutenant governors. At the south-east end of the imperial camp, adjoining those of the viceroy and the governor of Madras, were the camps of the commander-in-chief of the Indian army and the commanders of the Madras and Bombay armies. These had their own entrances and were almost as large as the camps of the viceroy. At the back of the camps of the viceroy, the governors, and the lieutenant governors were those of the chief commissioners, the resident of Hyderabad, and the agents to the Governor–General for Central India, Baroda, and Rajputana. Access to these latter was by internal roads, as they did not face outwards on to the plains.

Scattered around the plains for a distance of one to five miles were the camps of the Indians, organized regionally. On the eastern side of the ridge, on the flood plain of the Jamuna river and closest to the imperial camp, were those of the Nizam of Hyderabad, the Gaekwar of Baroda, and the Maharaja of Mysore. These were the 'Special Native Camps'. To the front of the imperial camp were those of the Central Indian chiefs, with the camp of Maharaja Scindia of Gwalior closest to that of the viceroy. Two-and-a-half miles to the south were the camps of the chiefs of Bombay Northwest Province and the Central Province. Strung along the west and the south walls of the city of Delhi were the Punjab chiefs, with pride of place being given to the Maharaja of Kashmir, who, at a distance of two miles, was the closest to the imperial camp. The Rajputana chiefs were camped five miles along Gurgoan road, due south of the imperial camp. Five-and-a-half miles along the Kootub road were the camps of the Oudh Talukdars. The Bengal and the Madras nobles were within a mile of the main camp.

There was a marked contrast between the layouts of the European and the Indian camps. The European camps were well ordered, with straight streets and neat rows of tents on each side. Grass and flowers were laid out to impart the touch of England that the British carried with them all over India. The plants were supplied by the botanical gardens at Saharanpur and Delhi. In the Indian camps, spaces were provided for each ruler, who was then left to arrange his camp in his own fashion. To the European eye, the Indian camps were cluttered and disorganized, with cooking fires seemingly placed at random, and with a jumble of people, animals, and carts impeding easy movement. Nonetheless, most European observers commented on how vibrant and colourful the Indian camps were.[39]

The contrast between the imperial camp and the other camps was not lost on some of the Indians. Sir Dinkar Rao, Sindhia's *dewan* (prime minister), commented to one of Lytton's aides:

If any man would understand why it is that the English are, and must necessarily remain the master of India he need only go up to Flagstaff Tower [highest point overlooking the camps] and look down upon this marvellous camp. Let him notice the method, the order, the cleanliness, the discipline, the perfection of the whole organization and he will recognize at once the epitome of every title to command and govern which one race can possess over others.[40]

There is much hyperbole, and perhaps some self-interest, in Sir Dinkar Rao's statement; however, it effectively points to one of the main things which Lytton and his associates wanted to accomplish through the assemblage, which was to represent the nature of British rule as they conceived it, and this was what the camp represented in their own ruling theory: order and discipline, which was in their ideology part of the whole system of colonial control.

THE AMPHITHEATRE AND PRECEDENCE

From the inception of the planning, the question of the seating arrangements for the Indian rulers was seen as the most crucial single question on which the success of the Imperial Assemblage would rest. As we have seen, the problems of precedence which, in the opinion of experts like Daly, bedevilled a durbar had to be avoided. Its terminological transformation into an assemblage allowed Lytton to do this. He insisted that the assemblage would not resemble a durbar 'in its arrangements or ceremonies, of any of the meetings customarily so called',[41] as the actual ritual to proclaim the new title would not be 'under canvas' but in 'the open plain thereby freeing it from questions of precedence, exchange of presents and other impedimentia of an ordinary durbar'.[42] The planners of the assemblage hit upon a unique solution to the seating arrangements for the Imperial Assemblage. It was decided that the princes would be seated in a semicircular grandstand, by their regional groupings, from north to south. The viceroy would be seated on a dais, on his viceregal chair, and with only members of his immediate staff and family group around him. The dais was to be placed in such a fashion that all the Indians, at least in the first row, would be equidistant from the person of the viceroy. Hence none could claim to have superiority over their fellow chiefs. The grandstand was to be divided by province or agency, with the exception of the Gaekwar of Baroda, the Nizam of Hyderabad, and the Maharaja of Mysore, who would be in a special section in the centre of the seats. Each of the major geographic sections was to have a separate entrance, and as the precedence for each of the geographic units was fairly well worked out, there would not arise, the planners thought, the question of cross-regional precedence. There was to be a separate road providing access to the entrances, and the timings of the entries prescribed. European officials were to sit intermixed amongst the Indians, for example the lieutenant governor of Punjab with the Punjab princes and notables, the agent general for Rajputana and the various residents amongst the chiefs from that region. Lytton wrote:

The Chiefs do not so much object to be seated in groups of their own nationalities and province, as to be mixed up and classified with those of other provinces, as in a Durbar. Each chief would proceed from his camp to the Dais assigned to him in a separate elephant procession, in time to receive the Viceroy.[43]

In addition to the pavilion for the seating of the grandees, two large grandstands were erected obliquely facing it for retainers and other visitors. Large numbers of soldiers from the Indian army and princes' armies stood in semicircular ranks facing the pavilion, as did servants and other Indians. Interspersed with the onlookers were large numbers of elephants and horses with their grooms and *mahouts* (riders).

To emphasize the uniqueness of the event the planners developed an overall design motif which could be termed 'Victorian Feudal'. Lockridge Kipling, Rudyard Kipling's father and director of the Lahore Art School, a minor pre-Raphaelite and, to use his own description, a 'monumental ceramicist', was in overall charge of the designing of the uniforms and decorations for the assemblage.

A large hexagon-shaped dais for the viceroy was built facing the pavilion, each side being 40 feet long, for a total of 220 feet around; its masonry base was 10 feet high. There was a broad flight of stairs leading to the platform on which was placed the viceregal throne. Over the dais was a large canopy. The shafts holding the canopy were festooned with laurel wreaths, imperial crowns, gargoyle-like eagles, banners displaying the Cross of St George and the Union Jack. There was an embroidered frieze hanging from the canopy displaying the Rose, Shamrock, and Thistle with the Lotus of India. Also hanging from the shafts supporting the canopy were shields with the Irish Harp, the Lion Rampant of Scotland, and the Three Lions of England. The 800-foot semicircular pavilion in which the chiefs and high government officials were seated was decorated with fleurs-de-lis and gilded lances, the supporters of the canvas displaying the imperial crown. Along the back posts were mounted large silken banners with the coats of arms of the princes and chiefs. Not all observers of the scene were impressed. Val Prinsep, a painter who had been commissioned to paint a picture of the scene, which was to be a collective present from the princes to their new empress, was aghast by what he thought was a display of bad taste. On seeing the site he wrote:

Oh Horror! What have I to paint? A kind of thing that out does the Crystal Palace in hideosity. . .[it] is all iron, gold, red, blue and white. . . . The Viceroy's dais is a kind of scarlet temple 80 feet high. Never was such a brummagem ornament, or more atrocious taste.[44]

He continued:

They have been heaping ornament on ornament, colour on colour. [The viceregal dais] is like the top of a twelfth cake. They have stuck pieces of needlework into stone panels and tin shields and battle axes all over the place. The size [of the whole collection of structures] gives it a vast appearance like a gigantic circus and the decorations are in keeping. [45]

THE IMPERIAL ASSEMBLAGE

On 23 December, all was in readiness for the arrival of the central figure of the Imperial Assemblage, the viceroy, Lord Lytton. The 84,000 Indians and Europeans had occupied their far-flung camps, the roads had been laid out, and the site was complete. The activities of the assemblage were to last for two weeks; the purpose being to mark Queen Victoria's accession to her imperial title as 'Kaiser-i-Hind'. The title was suggested by G.W. Leitner, professor of Oriental languages and principal of the government college in Lahore. Leitner was Hungarian by birth and began his career as an Orientalist, linguist, and interpreter with the English army during the Crimean War. He was educated at Constantinople, Malta, King's College, London, obtained a PhD from the University of Fribourg, and was a lecturer in Arabic and Turkish, professor of Arabic and Muhammadan Law at King's College, London, before he went to Lahore in 1864.[46] Leitner argued that the term 'Kaiser' was well known to the natives of India, having been used by Muhammadan writers in relation to the Roman Caesar, and, therefore, the ruler of the Byzantine empire should be known as 'Kaiser-i-Rum'. In the present circumstance of the British ruler in India it was appropriate, Leitner thought, as it neatly combined the Roman 'Caesar', German 'kaiser', and Russian 'Czar' imperial titles. In the Indian context it would be unique and would not run the risk of being mispronounced by Indians as would the title empress, nor would it associate British rule with such exhausted titles as 'Shah', 'Padishah', or 'Sultan'. It avoided the overt association of the title with either Hindu or Muslim titles.[47]

Lord Lytton had suggested to Lord Salisbury in late July 1876, on either his or Burne's reading of Leitner's pamphlet, that 'Kaiser-i-Hind', was 'thoroughly familiar to the Oriental mind', and 'widely recognized' in India and Central Asia as 'the symbol of Imperial power'. In addition, the title was the same in Sanskrit and Arabic, 'sonorous' and not 'hackneyed or monopolized by any Crown since the Roman Caesars'. Lytton left it to Salisbury to make the final decision on the question of the queen's Indian title.[48] Salisbury agreed to the use of Kaiser-i-Hind and it was duly announced officially in The Times of 7 October 1876. The title drew criticism as being obscure from the distinguished Orientalist R.C. Caldwell, and Mir Aulad Ali, professor of Arabic and Urdu at Trinity College, Dublin, thought it was 'preposterous' as it formed 'the picture of a European lady, attired partly in the Arab, partly in the Persian garment peculiar to men, and wearing upon her head an Indian turban'.[49]

Lytton's arrival at the Delhi railway station was the official commencement of the assemblage. He descended with his wife and two young daughters and his immediate official party from the railway car, gave a brief speech of welcome to assembled Indian rulers and high government officials, briskly shook hands with some of those assembled, and then moved off to mount a train of waiting elephants.

Lord and Lady Lytton rode in a silver houdah, created for the Prince of Wales's visit the year before, mounted on the back of what was purported to be the largest elephant in India, owned by the Raja of Banaras.

The procession, led by troops of cavalry, moved through the city of Delhi to the Red Fort, circled around the Jama Masjid, and then proceeded towards the north-west to the camps on the ridge. The procession route was lined by Indian army soldiers, Indian and British, interspersed between whom were contingents from the princely state armies, outfitted in their 'medieval' armour and bearing Indian weapons. Lytton commented that these native soldiers presented 'a most striking and peculiar appearance. . . a vivid and varied display of strange arms, strange uniforms, and strange figures'.[50]

The procession took three hours to move through the city to the camps. As the viceroy, his party, and other British officials passed, some of the retainers of the Indian princes fell in behind the official party. However, none of the attending princes or Indian notables rode in the procession. As was to be their role throughout, they were there as recipients of largesse and honour given them by their empress, and to be spectators to the British acting on her behalf as the Indian monarch.

The week between Lord Lytton's arrival and grand entry and the day of the assembly held for the reading of the actual proclamation of Victoria's ascension to the imperial throne on 1 January 1877, was taken up with audiences given by Lytton to leading chiefs, various receptions and dinners for distinguished visitors and participants. In all, Lytton gave 120 audiences in his time in Delhi, including return visits to many of the Princes, and received several delegations offering petitions and loyal addresses for the new empress.[51]

The most important of these meetings were the ones held for the princes in the viceroy's reception tent. A prince would appear at an appointed time accompanied by some of his retinue. On entry, depending on his precise status, he would be greeted by the viceroy, who would then present him with 'his' coat of arms embroidered and fixed on a large silken standard. The armorial bearings of the Indian rulers were designed by Robert Taylor, a Bengal civil servant and amateur heraldist. Taylor had first designed coats of arms for Indian rulers on the occasions of the visits of the Duke of Edinburgh in 1869 and the Prince of Wales in 1876. Lord Lytton now decided that in addition to those which Taylor had already created, another eighty were to be created.

The devices which Taylor created related to his conception of the mythic origins of the various ruling houses, their identification with particular gods or goddesses, events in their history, topographic features of their territories, or they incorporated some ancestral emblem associated with a ruling house or even a group of houses. Most of the arms of the Rajputs bore the sun to symbolize their descent from Rama. The Sikh chiefs of the Punjab all had a boar on their banners. The background colour of the device could also be used to denote regional groups of chiefs, some had particular trees or plants which had sacred significance for a particular house. Even events of the Mutiny were represented if they indicated loyalty to the British. At times Taylor's imagination seemed to run out. Kashmir, a buffer state created by the British in 1854 by the installation of a Maharaja over territories held previously by a number of other rulers, had to be satisfied by three wavy lines representing the three ranges of the Himalayas and three roses to represent the beauty of the vale of Kashmir. The armorial bearings were embroidered on large silk standards, 5 feet by 5 feet, in the Roman style; Indian banners, which were silk streamers, were not thought to be the right shape to bear the arms of the new feudal nobility.[52] In addition to the gift of the banner and the coat of arms, the most important of the Indian rulers were presented with a large gold medallion which was worn from a ribbon around their necks. Lesser chiefs received silver medallions as did hundreds of lower civil servants and soldiers, Indian and British.

Not all went smoothly with the presentation of the banners and medallions; the banners proved to be very awkward and hard to handle because of the weight of the brass poles and the fixtures on them, and it was not clear to the Indians what should be done with them. It was thought they might be used in processions by fixing them to the backs of elephants. One British Army officer, who was presenting the silver medallions to several of his Indian troopers in Urdu, was not up to the task of conveying their significance to his men. He addressed his troops as follows: 'Suwars [pigs—he meant sowar, the Urdu word for trooper], your Empress has sent you a billi [cat—he meant billa, a medallion] for you to wear around your necks'.[53] The presentations which were from the empress were meant to replace the giving of khelats and obviate the presentation of nazar, the gold coins. It is significant that the major present was a representation of the British version of the Indian rulers' pasts as represented in their coats of arms.

At noon on 1 January 1877, all was in readiness for the entry of the viceroy into the amphitheatre. The princes and other notables were all seated in their sections, the spectators' grandstand filled, and thousands of Indian and European troops were drawn up in ranks. The viceroy and his small party, including his wife, rode into the amphitheatre to the 'March from Tannhäuser'. As they got down from the carriage six trumpeters, attired in medieval costume, blew a fanfare. The viceroy then mounted to his throne to the strains of the national anthem. The chief herald, described as the tallest English officer in the Indian army, read the queen's proclamation which announced that henceforth there would be the addition of 'Empress of India' to her Royal Styles and Titles.

A translation of the proclamation of the new title was read in Urdu by T.H. Thornton, the foreign secretary of the government of India. Then a salute of 101 salvos was fired and the assembled troops fired feux de joie. The noise of the cannon and rifle fire stampeded the assembled elephants and horses; a number of bystanders were killed and injured, and a large cloud of dust was raised which hung over the rest of the proceedings.

Lytton made a speech in which, as was common in the speeches of viceroys on major occasions, he stressed the fulfilment of their empress's promise in her proclamation of 1 November 1858 of the achievement of a 'progressive prosperity' combined with the undisturbed enjoyment, on the part of the princes and peoples of India, 'of their hereditary honours', and the protection 'of their lawful interests'.

The historic basis of British authority in India was created by 'providence' which had called upon the Crown 'to replace and improve upon the rule of good and great Sovereigns', but whose successors failed

to secure the internal peace of their dominions. Strife became chronic and anarchy constantly recurrent. The weak were the prey of the strong, and the strong the victims of their own passions.

The rule of the successors of the House of Tamerlane, Lytton continued, 'had ceased to be conductive of the progress of the East'. Now, under British rule, all 'creeds and races' were protected and guided by 'the strong hand of Imperial power' which had led to rapid advance and 'increasing prosperity'.

Lytton then referred to the proper codes of conduct for the constituent components of the empire. He first referred to 'the British Administrators and Faithful Officers of the Crown', who were thanked in the name of the empress for their 'great toil for the good of the Empire', and their 'persevering energy, public virtue, and self devotion, unsurpassed in history'. In particular, 'the district officers' were singled out for their patient intelligence and courage on which the efficient operation of the whole system of administration was dependent. All the members of the civil and military services were gratefully recognized by their queen for their capacity to 'uphold the high character of your race, and to carry out the benign precepts of your religion'. Lytton told them that they were 'conferring on all the other creeds and races in this country the inestimable benefits of good government'. The non-official European community were complimented for the benefits which India had received 'from their enterprise, industry, social energy and civic virtue'.

The princes and chiefs of the empire were thanked by the viceroy on behalf of their empress for their loyalty and their past willingness to assist her government 'if attacked or menaced', and it was to 'unite the British Crown and its feudatories and allies that Her Majesty had been graciously pleased to assume the Imperial title'.

The 'native subjects of the empress of India' were told by their viceroy that 'the permanent interests of this Empire demand the supreme supervision and direction of their administration by English officers' who must 'continue to form the most important practical channel through which the arts, the sciences and the culture of the West. . .may freely flow to the East'. This assertion of English superiority notwithstanding, there was a place for the 'natives of India' to share in the administration 'of the country you inhabit'. However, appointment to the higher public service should not only go to those with 'intellectual qualifications' but must also include those who are 'natural leaders', 'by birth, rank and hereditary influence', that is, the feudal aristocracy, which was being 'created' at the assemblage.

The viceroy concluded his speech by reading a telegraphic message from 'The Queen, your Empress', who assured all assembled of her affection. 'Our rule', she cabled, was based on the great principles of liberty, equity, and justice, 'which would promote their happiness' and add to their 'prosperity and advance their welfare'. [54]

The conclusion of the viceroy's speech was greeted by loud cheering, and when this stopped, the Maharaja Scindia rose and addressed the queen in Urdu and said:

Shah in Shah, Padshah, May God bless you. The Princes of India bless you and pray that your *hukumat* [the power to give absolute orders which must be obeyed, sovereignty] may remain steadfast forever. [55]

Scindia was followed by other rulers expressing their thanks and pledging their loyalty. Scindia's statement, which appears to have been unsolicited, his failure to address the empress with the proper title 'Kaiser-i-Hind' notwithstanding, was taken by Lytton as the sign of the fulfilment of the intention of the assemblage.

The activities of the assemblage continued for another four days. These included rifle match, the inauguration of a Royal Cup Race, won fittingly by one of the princes' horses, several more dinners and receptions, and the presentation of loyal addresses and petitions by various regional and civic bodies. There was also an extensive exhibition organized of Indian arts and crafts. The proceedings were concluded with a march by the imperial troops, followed by contingents from the armies of the princes. Long lists of new honours were announced, some princes had their gun salutes enhanced, and twelve Europeans and eight Indians were awarded the title of 'Counsellor of the Empress'. Thirty-nine new members of the Star were created to mark the occasion, and large numbers of new Indian title-holders were created. Thousands of prisoners were released or had their sentences reduced, and monetary rewards were given to members of the armed forces. On the day of the proclamation ceremonies were held all over India to mark the occasion. In all, over three hundred such meetings were held in presidency capitals, in all civil and military stations down to local tahsil headquarters. In the towns, the plans for the occasion were usually drawn up by local Indian officials and included durbars, the offering of poems and odes in Sanskrit and other languages, parades of school children and their being treated to sweets, feeding of the poor, distribution of clothes to the needy, and usually winding up with a fireworks display in the evening.

CONCLUSION

Historians have paid little attention to the assemblage of 1877; at best it is treated as a kind of folly, a great *tamasha*, or show, but which had little practical consequence. It has been noted in histories of Indian nationalism as the occasion when, for the first time, early nationalist leaders and journalists from all over India were gathered in the same place at the same time, but is passed over as mere window-dressing to mask imperial realities. It is also taken as an example of the callousness on the part of imperial rulers who spent large sums of public money at a time of famine.

At the time that it was planned and immediately afterwards, the assemblage received considerable criticism in the Indian-language press as well as in the English papers. It was seen by many, as were Ellenborough's attempts at imperial glorification, as being somehow or other un-English, and the expression of the wild imaginations of Disraeli and Lytton.

Yet the assemblage kept being referred to subsequently by Indians and Europeans as a kind of marker, a before-and-after event. It became the standard by which public ceremony was measured. It may be said the event itself recurred twice—in 1903 when Lord Curzon organized an imperial durbar in Delhi to proclaim Edward VII emperor of India on the exact location where his mother's imperial title was proclaimed, and when, in 1911, also on the same spot, George V made an appearance to crown himself emperor of India. Curzon, a man of enormous energy, intelligence, and almost megalomaniacal belief in his own power to rule India, spent almost six months planning 'his' durbar, and was always at pains to follow the forms which Lytton had laid down. When he did deviate from these he felt constrained to offer detailed and extensive explanations for his changes and additions. If anything, Curzon wanted the Imperial Durbar to be more 'Indian' than the assemblage, hence the design motif was 'Indo-Saracenic', rather than 'Victorian Feudal'. He also wanted more active participation in the event itself on the part of the princes, who were to offer direct acts of homage. This kind of participation became the centrepiece of the 1911 Imperial Durbar, when many of the leading princes, during the durbar itself, individually kneeled before their emperor, in what was termed 'the homage pavilion', which replaced the dais of the viceroy as the centrepiece of the amphitheatre.

What was the significance or consequence not only of the Imperial Assemblage and the Imperial Durbars, but also the ritual idiom created to express, make manifest and compelling the British construction of their authority over India? Did Lytton and his successors accomplish their goals? On one level they did not, as India, Pakistan, and Bangladesh are independent nations today. The idea of the permanence of imperial rule is a half-forgotten curiosity, even to historians who see the events of the period of 1877 to 1947 as a fight over loaves and fishes, or the culmination of the Indian peoples' anti-imperial struggle.

I think, however, there is another way of looking at the question of success or failure, of the intentions of Lytton and his associates and the codification of the ritual idiom. I have focused almost exclusively on the British construction of authority and its representations. When Indians, particularly in the first years of their national movement, came to develop a public political idiom of their own, through their own organizations, what idiom did they use? I would suggest that in effect they used the same idiom that their British rulers employed. The early meetings of the All India Congress Committees were much like durbars, with processions and the centrality of leading figures and their speeches, which became the vehicle through which they tried to participate in the achievement of the values of 'progressive government' and the obtainment of the happiness and welfare of the Indian peoples. The British idiom was effective in that it set the terms of discourse of the nationalist movement in its beginning phases. In effect, the early nationalists were claiming that they were more loyal to the true goals of the Indian empire than were their English rulers.

The first Non-Cooperation Movement of 1920–1 is taken as marking the final establishment of Gandhi as the crucial figure in the nationalist struggle. It was the first time a new idiom was tried out, in the form of non-cooperation and passive resistance. At base this was the first full-fledged and widespread rejection of British authority in India. The movement began with Gandhi's announcement that Indians should return all honours and emblems granted by the imperial government. In doing this Gandhi attacked not the institutions of government, but the capacity of that government to make meaningful and binding its authority through the creation of honours.

Most of Gandhi's contributions to the nationalist movement were concerned with the creation and representation of new codes of conduct based on a radically different theory of authority. These were represented in a series of markings. No longer were Indians to wear either Western clothes or the 'native' costumes decreed by their imperial rulers, but homespun simple peasant dress. The communal prayer meeting, not the durbar-like atmosphere of the political rallies, was where his message was expounded. The Indian pilgrimage was adapted to politics in the form of Gandhi's marches, and the idea of the *padyatra* (the walking of the politician amongst the people) is still part of the political rituals of India.

Yet, the British idiom did not die easily or quickly, and it may still be alive in various forms. The end of the empire was marked where it might be said to have begun, in 1857, with the desacralization of the Mughals' palace, with English officers drinking wine and eating pork. The moment of transfer of authority from the viceroy to the new prime minister of an independent India was marked at the Red Fort by the lowering of the Union Jack at midnight, 14 August 1947, before a huge crowd of jubilant Indians.

Notes

1. 'Queen Victoria's Proclamation, 1 November 1858', in C.H. Phillips, H.L. Singh, and B.N. Pandey (eds), *The Evolution of India and Pakistan 1858-1947: Select Documents*, Oxford: Oxford University Press, 1962, pp. 10–11.
2. Hansard's *Parliamentary Debates* (3rd ser., ccxxvii, 1876), p. 4.
3. Ibid., p. 409.
4. Ibid., p. 410.
5. Ibid., p. 409.
6. Ibid., p. 1750.
7. Lytton to Salisbury, 12 Aug. 1876, I.O.L.R., E218/518/1, p. 367.
8. Major General Sir Owen Tudor Burne, *Memories* (London, 1907), p. 204, and *passim*, for his career.
9. Field-Marshal Lord Roberts of Kandahar, *Forty-one Years in India* (New York, 1900), ii, pp. 91–2.
10. O.T. Burne, 'The Empress of India', *Asiatic Quarterly Review*, iii (1987), p. 22.
11. Lytton to Salisbury, 11 May 1875, I.O.L.R., E218/518/1, p. 147.
12. Ibid., p. 149.
13. L.A. Knight, in his article, 'The Royal Titles Act and India', *Historical Journal* xi, no. 3(1968), pp. 488–507, details many of the current claims to territories and grievances which were felt might surface at the durbar; T.H. Thornton, *General Sir Richard Meade* (London, 1898), p. 310.
14. Lytton to Salisbury, 11 May 1876, I.O.L.R., E218/518/1, p. 149.
15. Lytton to Queen Victoria, 21 April 1876, I.O.L.R., E218/518/1.
16. I.O.L.R. Political and Secret Letters from India, Jan. and Feb. 1877, no. 24, para. 20.
17. Lytton to Queen Victoria, 4 May 1876, I.O.L.R., E218/518/1.
18. Lytton to Salisbury, 30 Oct. 1876, *ibid.*
19. Lytton to Queen Victoria, 15 Nov. 1876, *ibid.*
20. Lytton to Salisbury, 30 July 1876, *ibid.*, p. 318.
21. Ibid., p. 319.
22. *Gazette of India*, Extraordinary, 1 Jan. 1877, p. 11.
23. Lytton to Salisbury, 11 May 1876, I.O.L.R., E218/518/1, p. 149.
24. Ibid.
25. Ibid.
26. Ibid. p. 150.
27. Ibid.
28. Ibid.
29. I.O.L.R., Political and Secret Letters from India, Feb. 1877, no. 24, para. 5.
30. Ibid.
31. For a listing of the major invitees, see *ibid.*, encs. 1 and 2.
32. *Gazette of India*, Extraordinary, 18 Aug. 1876.
33. I.O.L.R., Political and Secret Letters from India, Feb. 1877, no. 24, enc. 11. 'Speech of Lord Lytton at State Banquet'.
34. I.O.L.R., Political and Secret Letters from India, Jan. and Feb. 1877, no. 24, enc. 2.
35. Ibid.
36. I.O.L.R., Imperial Assemblage Proceedings 8, 15 Sept. 1876, Temple Papers, Euro. MSS. F86/166.
37. Figures are given in I.O.L.R., Political and Secret Letters from India, 6 Aug. 1877, no. 140, enc. 8.
38. J. Talboys Wheeler, *The History of the Imperial Assemblage at Delhi* (London, 1877), p. 47.
39. Wheeler, *op. cit.*, p. 47.
40. Quoted in Lady Betty Balfour, *The History of Lord Lytton's Administration 1876–1880* (London, 1899), p. 121.
41. Lytton, 'Memorandum' I.O.L.R. Imperial Assemblage Proceedings 8, 15 Sept. 1876, Temple Papers, Euro. MSS I 86/166, para. 16.

42. Ibid.
43. Ibid., para. 18; see also Thornton, *op. cit.*, app. to ch. 21, 'Note on the Arrangement of the Imperial Assemblage'.
44. Val C Prinsep.: *Imperial India: An Artist's Journal* (London, 1879), p. 20.
45. Ibid., p. 29.
46. G.W. Leitner, *Kaiser-i-Hind: The Only Appropriate Translation of the Title of the Empress of India* (Lahore, 1876), pp. 11–12.
47. Ibid., p. 9.
48. Lytton to Salisbury, 30 July 1876, I.O.L.R., E218/515, pp. 321–2.
49. *Athenaeum* no. 2559 (11 Nov. 1876), pp. 624–5, no 2564 (25 Nov. 1876), pp. 688–9.
50. Lytton to Queen Victoria, I.O.L.R. Letters Despatched to the Queen. 12 Dec. 1876 to 1 Jan. 1877, L218/515/2.
51. Thornton, *op. cit.*, p. 305.
52. R Taylor, *The Princely Armory Being a Display for the Arms of the Ruling Chiefs of India after their Banners as Prepared for the Imperial Assemblage held at Delhi on the First Day of January, 1877.* I.O.L.R. typescript, and *Pioneer Mail*, 4 Nov. 1904 (clipping bound with Taylor, *Princely Armory* in I.O.L.R.).
53. Burne, *Memories*, pp. 42–3.
54. *Gazette of India*, Extraordinary, 1 Jan. 1877, pp. 3–7.
55. Thornton, *op. cit.*, p. 310.

THREE

The Ethnographic State

Nicholas B. Dirks

ᘒᘎᘒᘎᘒ

By the second half of the nineteenth century, the colonial state in India was about to undergo several major transformations.[1] Land, and the revenue and authority that accrued from the relationship between it and the state, had been fundamental to the formation of the early colonial state, eclipsing the formation of Company rule in that ineluctable combination of formal and private trade that itself masked the formidable state-like functions of the Company. But the fact that the rebellions of 1857 so quickly led to general agrarian revolt, and the steadily increasing economic investment in imperial power (propelled both by strategic and economic ones—as for example in the joint stock funding of railway and telegraph infrastructural expansion) made it clear that things had to change. Land tax was still an important source of revenue through the century, as was much of the trade that had been fundamental to the mercantile origins of empire. However, the extractive colonial state increasingly faced other kinds of challenges requiring a new basis for imperium; accordingly, imperial ambition, and anxiety, moved to new levels and concerns. The steady absorption of new lands through the aggressive policies of Lord Dalhousie, that in the taking of Oudh in 1856 had led directly to the Great Rebellion, were brought abruptly to a halt, and policies of indirect rule were mobilized to accommodate, and ultimately appropriate, the incomplete project of colonial conquest. At the same time, the rebellion made it clear that some communities in India could be counted as loyal, as others became doomed to perpetual suspicion. These latter groups were to be substituted by the 'martial' races, as Macaulay's hyperbolic denunciations of effeminate Bengalis were transmuted into state policy. In the new rhetorical economy of colonial rule, political loyalty replaced landed status. And the form of knowledge and argument that seemed most appropriate to assess matters of loyalty rather than revenue was of course knowledge of peoples and cultures. To put the matter in bold relief, after 1857 anthropology supplanted history as the principal colonial modality of knowledge and rule. In even bolder terms, I would label the late nineteenth- and early-twentieth century colonial state in India as the ethnographic state.

When V.S. Savarkar wrote his grand history of 1857, he glossed the bloody events following the Meerut Mutiny as the first Indian war of Independence. The national awakening that grew out of military refusal was an expression for Savarkar of the fundamental injustice of British rule in India. Savarkar wrote of the need for India to attain historical consciousness of itself as a nation, and of the importance of the rebellion for constituting a foundational moment in the emergence of a national history. Savarkar's narrative emphasized the heroic refusal of Indian heroes, ordinary soldiers as well as brave leaders, to accept British domination. He was especially critical of the commonly accepted view that the revolt had little political significance, that it was carried forward merely by the personal vendettas and interests of a few vestiges of an old regime, that indeed it was primarily about Indian concerns over caste and religion voiced in connection with the originary moment of mutiny, concerns that had clearly inflamed the passions of mutineers and rebels alike. He was referring of course to the question of the cartridge.

The mutiny—and for that matter the rebellion—began in the haze of alarm occasioned by the introduction of a new Enfield rifle, the cartridges for which were packed in a combination of beef and pork fat and were to be loaded by the use of the mouth as well as the hands. Fears of pollution were heightened by the growing reach and influence of Christian missionaries, for it was widely assumed that pollution would be used as a technique to usher new converts into the fold. In the years before the mutiny, missionaries had been given increasingly free reign, including within the military where, for example, Colonel Wheler, Commander of the 34th N.I. at Barrackpore, openly preached the gospel to his soldiers. Missionaries had already made clear their frustration that caste was their single most significant obstacle, and spoke of the need to break potential converts of their caste in order to free their souls for possible conversion. Despite the fact that the fat-laden cartridges were speedily withdrawn and sepoys instructed to pack their own cartridges in grease of their choice, their use became the occasion for the first outbreak of resistance in Meerut on 10 May 1857. Eighty-five sepoys who refused the cartridges were placed in irons and sentenced to ten years' imprisonment. Their fellow soldiers rose up in protest, released them, and travelled to Delhi, where they fashioned the dazed and elderly Mughal emperor, Bahadur Shah, as the leader of the revolt. The fall of Delhi was followed by uprisings at many major military stations in the Northwest Provinces and in Oudh, and rebellion steadily grew, continuing through the summer of 1858 before it was finally brutally suppressed and contained by British forces.

Historians have debated the causes and ramifications of the rebellion ever since, in what has ultimately become a referendum on the beneficence of British colonial rule during its first century, as well as an explanation for major transformations in the nature of that rule thereafter. Sir Sayyid Ahmad Khan wrote an account of the revolt just months after it was over, making a number of points with extreme care.[2] While he offered no real sympathy to the rebels, he maintained that there were legitimate issues of grievance that the British needed to understand, despite the absence of any manifest conspiracy. At the same time, he wrote to counter the charge that Indian Muslims were responsible, clearly shown by the events of the revolt to be disloyal. Significantly, Sir Sayyid blamed the revolt on ignorance and insensitivity rather than on more fundamental causes. He wrote that, 'Government has not succeeded in acquainting itself with the daily habits, the modes of thought and of life, and likes, and dislikes, and prejudices of the people'.[3] As a result, Government was ignorant not only of local modes of thought and of life, but 'of the grievances through which their hearts were becoming estranged'.[4] Sir Sayyid was further concerned about the 'passing of such laws and regulations and forms of procedure as jarred with the established custom and practice of Hindustan'. He seemed particularly alarmed about the role of missionization, suggesting that recent events had made, 'all men whether ignorant, or well-informed, whether high or low, fe[el] a firm conviction that the English Government was bent on interfering with their religion and with their old established customs'.[5] Sir Sayyid noted that missionaries not only began to preach with the sanction of Government, but attacked in 'violent and unmeasured language...the followers and the holy places of other creeds: annoying, and insulting beyond expression the feelings of those who listened to them'.[6] He encouraged greater communication between rulers and ruled, and enjoined the British to pay greater attention to issues of cultural respect. For example, he suggested the institution of state darbars, and the distribution of honours to worthy subjects, as well as far more scrupulous attention to questions of prestige and status among the historically disenfranchised Muslim community.

Sir Sayyid, who went on to found the first Muslim university (the Muhammedan Anglo-Oriental College) in Aligarh in 1875, and bore in his title the success of at least one of his recommendations to the British, downplayed the significance of the Great Rebellion because of his own great concern for reconciliation and reform under British rule. Despite his symptomatic critique of the causes of discontent, he focused in particular on the outbreak of the mutiny around the refusal to bite the greased cartridges, which 'did violence to the superstition of the sepoys'.[7] In this, he reassured those British commentators who preferred to attribute the revolt solely to reaction and superstition; at the same time his conservatism was apparent in early years after the rebellion even to many British, particularly those who had been participants in the events of 1857–8, who were aware of the monumentality of Indian disaffection. Nevertheless, his gentle admonishments did not fall on entirely deaf ears. Sir Bartle Frere wrote that Sir Sayyid's essay clearly showed how 'acts of our Government, well meant and well planned, sometimes do more harm than good, simply owing to our disregard for native opinion and our neglect of the maxim that our measures in India should not only be good in themselves but that they should commend themselves to the approval of the natives. We, as a rule, neither take care enough to know what the natives think of our measures, nor to explain the true grounds and objects of our measures to those affected by them'.[8]

It was in fact widely accepted, even by the colonial historians Malleson and Kaye,[9] that there had been serious reasons for Indian discontent. In the years leading up to revolt, British policy under Dalhousie had favoured annexation wherever possible. As Savarkar pointed out with particular bitterness, adoption even within royal families was frequently disallowed in order to justify annexation through the 'doctrine of lapse', in which princely states without proper heirs would be ripe for colonial plucking. There were manifold political as well as economic reasons that the revolt became such a monumental marker in India's colonial history, a moment when Hindus and Muslims, Marathas and Mughals, legendary heroes and yeoman farmers united with countless other unlikely 'conspirators' to challenge British rule and uphold the legitimate claim of the Delhi Emperor. Nevertheless, the British characterized the revolt for the most part as an expression of Indian fanaticism and superstition, as colonial narratives explained the 'heinous massacre of Cawnpore' and the 'barbaric siege of Lucknow' through stories having to do with chapatis, pig fat, and other signs of alien alterity. And even as Savarkar, Sir Sayyid, and other Indian commentators provided alternative narratives for an event glossed variably as the first War of Independence and a serious warning against colonial complacency, the revolt ended up by justifying new forms of colonial power and policy, leading in the end to greater complacency, and contempt, than had been in evidence before. The revolt was ruthlessly suppressed, while leaders of the revolt such as Nana Sahib were turned into fiends and monsters. The year 1857 became the pretext for the conversion of religious difference into an argument about political indifference, even as it served to warn against religious interference and cultural ignorance. The revolt served to justify the assumption of direct crown rule over Company controlled country, and the inauguration of new forms of indirect rule where full military conquest had left off so abruptly in 1856.

On 2 August 1858, Britain announced that India would henceforth be governed 'by and in the name of Her Majesty, and all rights in relation to any territories which might have been exercised by the said Company ... shall and may be exercised...as rights incidental to the Government of India'. Queen Victoria followed her assumption of authority over India with a proclamation, dated 1 November 1858, in which she sought to allay the concerns of her Indian subjects in matters deemed to have been of relevance to the revolt. She announced 'to the native Princes of India that all treaties and engagements made with them by or under the authority of the Honourable East India Company are by us accepted, and will be scrupulously maintained....' She noted that the doctrine of lapse would no longer be used as a pretext for annexation by stating outright that Britain desired 'no extension of our present territorial possessions; and, while we will permit no aggression upon our dominions or our rights to be attempted with impunity, we shall sanction no encroachment on those of others.' Further, she declared an end to aggressive missionization:

Firmly relying ourselves on the truth of Christianity [this opening phrase was inserted by Victoria herself, into the text prepared by her Prime Minister], and acknowledging with gratitude the solace of religion, we disclaim alike the right and the desire to impose our convictions on any of our subjects. We declare it to be our royal will and pleasure that none be in anywise favoured, none molested or disquieted, by reason of their religious faith or observances, but that all shall alike enjoy the equal and impartial protection of the law; and we do strictly charge and enjoin all those who may be in authority under us that they abstain from all interference with the religious belief or worship of any of our subjects on pain of our highest displeasure.[10]

Thus Victoria put a halt to the evangelical enthusiasm that had mounted since Charles Grant had reversed Company policy earlier in the century, even as she gave voice to the growing sense among many Britons that 'Christianity was ... increasingly a mark of their own difference from, and superiority to, their Indian subjects'.[11] Thomas Metcalf writes: 'Despite the presence of dedicated missionaries throughout India, Christianity had become, as the Secretary of State Lord Stanley put it in 1858, to the consternation of his evangelical countrymen, "the religion of Europe"'.[12] Liberalism did not evaporate overnight. Indeed, many liberals celebrated Britain's new-found commitment to religious toleration in the colonies, and the importance of education remained unquestioned after the rebellion. But for the most part reform foundered against the suddenly hardened shoals of cultural difference.

The most common general explanation for the great revolt was the caste system, a marker of difference even as it seemed to contain the ideologies of pollution and exclusion that had ignited fears around the introduction of the new cartridge. In an essay written in April 1858 in which the renowned Indologist Max Muller took up the question of the true meaning of caste in India, he observed that, 'Among the causes assigned for the Sepoy mutiny, caste has been made the most prominent. By one party it is said that too much, by another that too little, regard was paid to caste'.[13] Muller noted remarks by British officers of the total incompatibility of caste with military discipline. He also reported the remarks of many civilians to the effect that 'the Sepoys were driven mad by the greased cartridges; that they believed they were asked to touch what was unclean in order to lose their caste, and that, rather than lose their caste, they would risk everything'. The revolt occasioned an extraordinary proliferation of writing on the subject of caste, much of it by missionaries who felt that the time had come for an intensified assault on caste by the government. Missionaries had been complaining that caste was the largest single impediment to conversion, that the fear of loss of caste dissuaded potential converts from abandoning Hindu practice more than any other doctrinal consideration. Some missionaries had argued that caste should be broken to make conversion possible, an argument that seemed to many in Government as one of the principal causes of the rebellion, in that it provided evidence behind the assertion that the cartridge had been part of a deliberate strategy. But many missionaries sought to seize the moment, suggesting that Christianity should be imposed on India as a treatment, if not a punishment, for the revolt. The Church Missionary Society's Memorial to the Queen put it like this:

The Government of India has professed to occupy a position of neutrality between the Christian and false religions. Such profession, your Memorialists believe, dishonours the truth of God, discourages the progress of Christianity, and is inimical to the social welfare of the Natives... [the] evils which have been fearfully exhibited amidst the revolting cruelties of the present rebellion...can only be effectually counteracted by recognizing the Christian religion as the basis of law and social order.[14]

Alexander Duff, the chief architect and theorist of missionary education in India, was a critic of caste from the time he first came to India with the Church of Scotland Mission in 1829. Like many other missionaries he was concerned that his pupils were overwhelmingly from lower castes, although his opposition to caste segregation in schools clearly discouraged some upper-caste families from sending their children to him. In his early writings he held that caste was a sacred institution: 'Idolatry and superstition are like the stones and brick of a huge fabric, and caste is the cement which pervades and closely binds the whole'.[15] Duff gave voice to what became missionary orthodoxy by 1850, when the Madras Missionary Conference put forward a minute in which it was held that, 'Caste...is one of the greatest obstacles to the progress of the Gospel in India...whatever it may have been in its origin, it is now adopted as an essential part of the Hindu religion'.[16] The Madras Missionary Conference had in fact argued further that, 'Caste, which is a distinction among the Hindus, founded upon supposed Birth-Purity or Impurity, is in its nature, essentially a religious institution and not a mere civil distinction'.[17] When Duff published two volumes in the wake of the rebellion, one entitled, 'What is Caste: How is a Christian Government to deal with it?',[18] he continued to hold that caste was chiefly religious. However, Duff equally held that caste was also civil, simultaneously a social institution and a religious doctrine. Although Duff, more moderate than many of his missionary colleagues, stopped well short of advocating 'an exterminating crusade', he resolved that a Christian government should 'solemnly resolve to have nothing whatever to do with caste'. In the end, Duff was aware both of the limits confronting Government and the reality that caste could only be exterminated by 'the mighty power of the Spirit of God', though he advocated considerably greater support for missions than Victoria finally would concede.

Despite dominant missionary convictions, there were occasional suggestions that the religious and civil components of caste could be separated, and that caste was in large part a social convention as well as a marker of the Hindu faith. Many thought that Indians would hold onto caste distinction far more assertively than they would to their religion. To quote Lord Stanley again:

The difference between the religion and the caste of the Hindoos was like that between the religious creed of an English gentleman and his code of honour; and that just as an English gentleman would resent any attack on his honour, and yet leave persons perfectly at liberty to attack his religion, so did the Hindoo feel with respect to his caste and religion.... The natives would strongly deprecate any interference with their caste, but were open to instruction and persuasion in religion, provided everything was done openly.[19]

Max Muller developed the notion that caste occupied dual domains with rather more sophistication than Stanley, and directly dispensed with the missionary position. He was concerned that in the aftermath of the revolt and its extraordinary repercussions—including the blaming of all Indians for the extreme actions of a tiny minority—most explanations of the nature and meaning of caste misconstrued both the relationship between religious and social domains, and the extent to which modern manifestations of popular religion deviated from classical Hinduism. On the basis of his examination of the ancient Vedas—the source of greatest authority for all Hindus—he held that none of the objectionable traces of caste could be found in the original constitution of Hindu thought. Indeed, Muller announced that,

The Government would be perfectly justified in declaring that it will no longer consider caste as part of the religious system of the Hindus. Caste, in the modern sense of the word, is no religious institution; it has no authority in the sacred writings of the Brahmans, and by whatever promise the Government may have bound itself to respect the religion of the natives, that promise will not be violated, even though penalties were inflicted for the observation of the rules of caste.[20]

However, Muller was also aware that caste as a social formation was little different than the racial, ethnic, religious, and class differences and prejudices that were accepted as natural in most arenas of European social life. He believed that Brahman priests had grafted religious principle onto social prejudice, thus sanctifying forms of caste exclusion in ways that made questions of intervention sensitive at best. Fulminating against sacerdotal self-interest, Muller nevertheless proposed that caste in many of its aspects be viewed as a social etiquette that circumscribed marriage, dining, and other forms of sociality in ways that could easily be recognized, through appropriate social translation, in Europe. He was convinced that as a religious institution caste would die away in time, though he was convinced that 'as a social institution it will live and improve'. Indeed, he suggested that caste, 'which has hitherto proved an impediment to the conversion of the Hindus, may in future become one of the most powerful engines for the conversion not merely of individuals, but of whole classes of Indian society'.[21] In any event, Muller argued that caste could not be abolished in India, and that any effort to do so would 'be one of the most hazardous operations that was ever performed on a living social body'.[22] He argued that Government should not actively sanction caste in three fundamental respects: first, Government should not countenance the treatment of any of its subjects with indignity on account of caste; second, Government should pay no attention to caste in any contract or employment, whether in civil or military service; and third, caste should be ignored in all public institutions. But he strongly averred that India must be allowed to mature in its own time. Like earlier generations of Orientalists, his defensive understanding of India was made at the cost of simultaneously belittling the status of modern institutions in India and cautioning against the introduction of rapid change.

Thus the dilemma of liberalism in 1858. Muller was one of the few Orientalists still defending Indian civilization, while the old breed of Anglicists and Macaulayan liberals—who had at any rate condemned caste outright—was also giving way to an unholy alliance of parliamentary pragmatists and imperial crusaders. In assuming crown rule, Victoria might have announced a new policy of non-interference, but she did so only because of the widespread perception that imperial and missionary interference had just about led to British defeat in India. If caste could not be broken, this was no reason to allow imperial ambitions to fail too. Indeed, by the late nineteenth century, Christian triumphalism was folded into a new kind of imperial nationalism, in which the rule of the world by Britain was sanctioned both by history and faith. The British government shrunk back from its interest in reform as well, ploughing money and concern instead into new technological projects of control and mastery ranging from railways to agricultural canals. The containment of Christian ambition within Europe and the displacement of missionary evangelicalism onto projects of capitalist technological expansion were of course accompanied by the growing sense of irrevocable racial difference. The universal family of Sir William Jones and the racial unity of Aryans posited by Muller became the basis for race theory that cast Britons and Indians in a relationship of absolute difference.[23] Missionary rhetoric was used to celebrate the accomplishments of empire rather than the message of Christ. Even as the empire took on the ideological trappings of a new crusade, missionaries were consigned to the margins of the imperial theatre. Ironically, liberal sentiment took refuge in the margins of missionary frustration both with Indian society and colonial governmental autonomy. Or at least some liberal sentiment was reborn in the unlikely encounters of a few missionaries with subaltern groups in various parts of the subcontinent. While discourses of empire were still largely shared among imperialists and missionaries alike, the internal differences and debates that at certain moments animated the consolidation of imperial authority at other moments became the fault lines of other kinds of histories.

Victoria's proclamation had unambiguously announced that the British would no longer seek to impose their 'convictions on any of our subjects', and that she would 'strictly charge and enjoin all those who may be in authority under us that they abstain from all interference with the religious belief or worship of any of our subjects on pain of our highest displeasure'. She had further declared that in the 'framing and administration of law, due regard would henceforth be paid to the ancient rights, usages and customs of India'. But while it was clear that the British intended by this never to repeat the provocations—explicit government support for missionization, regular usurpation and annexation of ancestral and princely lands, and the introduction of military requirements entailing choices between discipline and pollution—that were seen to have led to the revolt, it was equally clear that the British had little idea what non-interference would really mean. If colonial rule retreated from its active phase of colonizing properties and souls, it could hardly stop interfering with India during the years after the rebellion when Britain sought to consolidate its control and make permanent the assumptions and institutions of imperialism. The notion that 'religion' and 'custom' could be genuinely exempted from any interference fell apart in the face of two fundamental flaws in colonial reason: the first that the British did not know how to define either religion or custom, the second that the phase of high imperial rule required the state to appropriate the civilizing mission from the church, both to justify itself at home and in the colonies.

The policy of non-interference thus necessitated a new commitment to colonial knowledge about the subjects of its rule. If the rebellion had put paid to debates over history that had been seen earlier as sufficient justification for the state's claim over revenue and land control, it made the anthropologization of colonial knowledge necessary for several reasons. Ethnographic knowledge could help explain why the rebellion took place, how to avoid such disaffection in the future, new ways to claim the loyalty of subjects on the basis of custom and culture, and how to delineate the autonomous and proper domains of religion and custom. With such knowledge the British could not only avoid interference but, in time, become the primary protectors of India's tradition. Even as the history of colonial conquest could now be conveniently erased, the primacy of history in the rhetorical debates of imperial policy could yield increasingly to other logics and imperatives. It is in this sense that I have argued that colonial rule took on an anthropological cast of mind in the late nineteenth century.

The anthropologization of colonial knowledge proceeded slowly, and in the context of myriad other interests and processes in this period. However, it can hardly be accidental that the decade of the 1860s saw a veritable explosion in the production and circulation of Gazetteers and Manuals that now included as a matter of course extensive reports on the manners and customs of the castes, tribes, and religions of the specific regions being studied. Colonial authors continued to write history, even as they sought with increased concern to adumbrate the moral and material progress of its imperial domains through these and other writings. However, for the first time they began systematically to compile ethnographic facts as if they were administrative necessities rather than antiquarian curiosities. Indeed, much of the new ethnography emerged as part of primary administrative business rather than independent, leave alone antiquarian, research. Most official ethnography, later reported in Manuals and then in ethnological catalogues, when it did not come from early missionary accounts, was born in the administrative and policing concerns of late nineteenth-century imperial rule, as the British struggled time after time with the problem of non-interference. Missionaries continued to play an important role off stage, generating sufficient publicity for successive crises to develop around the question of what the colonial state could countenance. Was colonialism on the side of barbarism or civilization, and were there occasions when the colonial power had to take a stand? Did the policy of non-interference hold up under the demands of late nineteenth-century high imperialism, when monumental greed and grandeur had to be clothed in the trappings of a civilizing mission, when the moral charter of Christian prosyletization had to be secularized and nationalized as the ground for and justification of imperium? Could an autonomous and sacrosanct sphere of religious belief be separated off from a wide range of customs and practices that periodically leaked into public view and made imperial disinterest appear shocking, even barbaric? And what happened when Indian tradition itself became the subject of colonial discipline? But it was the colonial state, not the church, that became the primary actor; and it was the state that was the authoritative adjudicator of Indian tradition.

Colonial ethnography appropriated barbarism from the missionaries in the late nineteenth century. Barbarism was now of interest to science, its scandal as much a justificatory basis for empire as it was something that had to be controlled and periodically contained in order to celebrate the civilizing mission of empire. But by the end of the nineteenth century, the civilizing mission was less urgent, and yielded increasingly to the imperatives of a colonial science that would contain barbarism both through the policing of tradition and the recording of tradition that so frequently emerged out of policing activities. The Victorian policy of non-intervention thus became the charter for a colonial anthropology: involving the delineation of religion, custom, and tradition on the one hand, and the firm maintenance of public order in an imperial regime that held the colonized in place through the knowledge and enlightened protection of tradition on the other. Barbarism was a sign of colonial difference, producing an ever widening chasm between the subjects and objects of colonial knowledge. And even the benign aspects of tradition, such as the caste system itself, worked both to explain how Indian society could be orderly in the absence of either political authority or tradition, and why it was that Indian society would never become mobilized around the political aims of national self-determination.

After the great rebellion, historical knowledge thus yielded to anthropological knowledge. Caste recapitulated the legacies of tradition, and history was perceived as absent from Indian sensibilities. The Imperial Census represented the apotheosis of this transformation. It also undertook the final conversion of barbarism into civilized data, the transformation of moral condemnation into the moral basis of both science and state. The Census exemplifies ways in which the documentation project of the colonial state attained unprecedented scope, even as the disturbing character of colonial difference became a problem only at the level of documentation. It is perhaps the greatest irony of colonial rule that the very evidence that could finally be accumulated and contained by the extraordinary apparatus of the decennial Census became the basis for the colonial state's ultimate failure to contain both caste and custom. Indeed, it was in relation to the Census that caste resisted the colonial idea of civil society.

H.H. RISLEY, THE CENSUS, AND THE ETHNOLOGICAL SURVEY OF INDIA

Herbert Hope Risley entered the Indian Civil Service in 1873 with a posting in Bengal,[24] where he soon displayed an active interest in W.W. Hunter's statistical survey. In 1875 he was appointed the Assistant Director of Statistics, whereupon he compiled the volume on the hill districts of Hazaribagh and Lohardaga. Although he soon returned to regular service, he was recruited once again several years later to collect detailed information on the castes, tribes, and sociology of Bengal. It was at this time that Risley became convinced that caste endogamy had worked to preserve physical differences among castes in particularly sharp ways. Risley decided to explore whether he could apply to the leading castes and tribes of Bengal, 'the methods of recording and comparing typical physical characteristics which have yielded valuable results in other parts of the world'.[25] Although he was also committed to collecting material about the customs and manners of each group, he felt that there had been far more cultural borrowing and exchange than there had been racial mixing. Using the methods of the French anthropologists Broca and Topinard, Risley began to record the anthropometric details that became the basis for his four-volume work on the Tribes and Castes of Bengal.[26] Risley's book was in fact an expanded edition of the Report on the 1891 Census for Bengal, of which he was the Supervisor.

As Risley took over the reins of the Census and the ethnological establishment in the wake of his commanding work on Bengal, he found himself relying once again on *varna*, and more generally on Brahmanical measures, and opinions, concerning caste rank. Risley seemed unabashed about the scientific status of *varna*, given his own views on the subject of race. He opened his Bengal book with an account of a stone panel at Sanchi, in which the leader of a procession of monkeys is depicted in an act of reverence and devotion to four stately figures 'of tall stature and regular features'. Whereas most Orientalists had interpreted this scene as a simple act of devotion to the life of the Buddha, Risley found a deeper meaning, 'if it is regarded as the sculptured expression of the race sentiment of the Aryans towards the Dravidians, which runs through the whole course of Indian tradition and survives in scarcely abated strength at the present day'.[27] Risley saw this as another expression of the true moral of the great epic, the Ramayana, in which the army of apes who assisted Rama in the invasion of Ceylon were clearly Dravidians: 'It shows us the higher race on friendly terms with the lower, but keenly conscious of the essential difference of type and not taking part in the ceremony at which they appear as patronising spectators'. Risley went on:

An attempt is made in the following pages to show that the race sentiment, which this curious sculpture represents, so far from being a figment of the intolerant pride of the Brahman, rests upon a foundation of fact which scientific methods confirm, that it has shaped the intricate groupings of the caste system, and has preserved the Aryan type in comparative purity throughout Northern India.

So for Risley the judgement of science confirmed the attitude of the Brahman; so for Risley race history, and perhaps as importantly race sentiment, was the key to understanding caste.

These inquiries became the basis for much of the material that Risley assembled in his *Castes and Tribes of Bengal* as well as for the 1891 Census. In retrospect, Risley's reliance on a Brahmanical sociology of knowledge is astounding. He relied almost entirely on Brahmans and other higher castes. He deferred wherever possible to the *Manu Dharma Sastras* and other *puranic* sources that served in part as later commentaries for Manu. And he organized his entire understanding of caste structure and rank according to Brahmanical indices such as the acceptance of food and water, the use of priests, origin stories concerning duties and obligations towards Brahmans as well as about degradation in relation to those duties and obligations, and ritual proximity to and functions relating to Brahmans. Because of his single-minded obsession with the racial origins of caste, he married his own late nineteenth-century version of scientific empiricism with the powerful combination of early nineteenth-century Orientalist knowledge and the clerical Brahmanical opinion that permeated the middle echelons of colonial administration in the localities. Caste might have been justified as a subject of study because it was seen as organizing many administrative matters from famine relief to criminality, but in the same breath it was constituted once again as a Brahmanical ritual system in which the most esoteric forms of social distinction became the basis for administrative knowledge. And despite the efforts of the 1891 Census to downplay matters of social rank and to privilege functional explanations of caste, nowhere did the question of precedence take on greater force than in relation to the Census of 1901.

In 1901 Risley was also appointed the Director of Ethnography for India, both because of his acknowledged pre-eminence as an ethnographer and because the Ethnographic Survey was designed to be conducted in connection with the Census. In 1899, when the preliminary arrangements for the census of 1901 were under consideration, the British Association for the Advancement of Science had recommended to the Secretary of State that certain ethno-graphic investigations should be undertaken in connection with the census operations. These included an ethnographic survey—'or the systematic description of the history, structure, traditions, and religious and social usages of the various races, tribes and castes in India'—and an anthropometric survey, which would entail the measurements of castes directed to determining the physical types characteristic of particular groups. The Association placed its full faith in H.H. Risley:

The results of the census itself constitute, of course, by their very nature, an ethnographical document of great value; and my Council feel that, without overburdening the officers of the census or incurring any very large expense, that value might be increased to a very remarkable degree, if to the enumeration were added the collection of some easily ascertained ethnographical data. They are encouraged to make this suggestion by the reflection that the Census Commissioner is an accomplished ethnographist, well known by his publication on the Tribes and Castes of Bengal, the valuable results of which would be supplemented by the inquiries now proposed.[28]

Risley's acclaim can be seen in the attention paid to anthropometry in the proposed survey. The Secretary of State noted that,

It has often been observed that anthropometry yields peculiarly good results in India by reason of the caste system which prevails among Hindus, and of the divisions, often closely resembling castes, which are recognised by Muhammadans. Marriage takes place only within a limited circle; the disturbing element of crossing is to a great extent excluded; and the differences of physical type, which measurement is intended to establish, are more marked and more persistent than anywhere else in the world.

And so Risley's racial theory and anthropometric preoccupations were endorsed by the British Government, as they appointed Edgar Thurston to assist him in Madras and empowered Risley to oversee the survey across the rest of British India.

In authorizing funds both for the Director of Ethnography and for the various surveys contemplated over and above the Census operations, the Secretary of State commented on the importance of these investigations.

It has come to be recognized of late years that India is a vast storehouse of social and physical data which only need to be recorded in order to contribute to the solution of the problems which are being approached in Europe with the aid of material much of which is inferior in quality.... It is unnecessary to dwell at length upon the obvious advantages to many branches of the administration in this country of an accurate and well arranged record of the customs and the domestic and social relations of the various castes and tribes. The entire framework of native life in India is made up of groups of this kind, and the status and conduct of individuals are largely determined by the rules of the group to which they belong. For the purposes of legislation, of judicial procedure, of famine relief, of sanitation and dealings with epidemic disease, and of almost every form of executive action, an ethnographic survey of India and a record of the customs of the people is as necessary an incident of good administration as a cadastral survey of the land and a record of the rights of its tenants.

Using language that was a direct quotation from Risley, the Secretary of State wrote, 'The census provides the necessary statistics: it remains to bring out and interpret the facts which lie behind the statistics'.[29] No clearer statement could be made of the colonial uses of anthropology, of how by the late nineteenth century the British in India recognized that the task of colonial rule was essentially ethnographic. Virtually no area of governmental policy or activity could be conducted without benefit of extensive anthropological knowledge. The late colonial state was genuinely an ethnographic state.

Risley did not rigidly separate the ethnographic survey, which in the end was never formally completed, from the census, which stands to this day as a monument to Risley's general influence on colonial anthropology and administration. And while Risley scripted much of the above justification for the conduct of ethnography, his interests were relentlessly 'scientific' rather than attuned to the needs of practical administration. With Risley ethnography escaped the province of statecraft, in the end unleashing a political revolution that the British could neither control nor understand. As we would predict, his commentary on caste in the 1901 Census is dominated by his interest in race.[30]

Risley began his chapter on caste by repeating his anecdote about Sanchi and racial consciousness, moving quickly into an impassioned defence of the importance of anthropometry. Demonstrating the terrific strides made over craniology by developments within anthropometry, Risley noted that he had introduced scientific anthropometry to India seventeen years before in the ethnographic survey of Bengal. He explained the significance of this scientific revolution in part to counter Mr Nesfield's 'uncompromising denial of the truth of the modern doctrine which divides the population of India into Aryan and aboriginal'.[31] He then turned to a criticism of the 1891 Census, for not altogether unrelated reasons. He averred that the functional grouping of the census accorded 'neither with native tradition and practice, nor with any theory of caste that has ever been propounded by students of the subject'.[32] He was particularly exercised at the classificatory patchwork that led to such strange affiliations as the grouping within single categories of 'Brahman priests, Mirasi musicians and Bahurupia buffoons', or of the Dravidian Khandaits of Orissa with Rajputs, Jats, and Marathas.

Risley insisted upon the principle of 'social precedence as recognised by native public opinion'. He was convinced that distinctions predicated on the centrality of Brahmans and involving matters of rank on the basis of ritual distinctions would be far more helpful in understanding the nature of the caste system as a whole. He prepared criteria for understanding caste distinction that could have served as research guidelines for the latter-day students of cultural anthropology:

that Brahmans will take water from certain castes; that Brahmans of high standing will serve particular castes; that certain castes, though not served by the best Brahmans, have nevertheless got Brahmans of their own, whose rank varies according to circumstances; that certain castes are not served by Brahmans at all but have priests of their own; that the status of certain castes has been raised by their taking to infant-marriage or abandoning the remarriage of widows; that the status of some castes has been lowered by their living in a particular locality; that the status of others has been modified by their pursuing some occupation in a special or peculiar way; that some can claim the services of the village barber, the village palanquin-bearer, the village midwife, etc., while others cannot; that some castes may not enter the courtyards of certain temples; that some castes are subject to special taboos, such as that they must not use the village well, or may draw water only with their own vessels, that they must live outside the village or in a separate quarter, that they must leave the road on the approach of a high-caste man or must call out to give warning of their approach. In the case of the Animistic tribes it was mentioned that the prevalence of totemism and the degree of adoption of Hindu usage would serve as ready tests.[33]

That Risley was so invested in the minutiae of caste status, to the point of certifying practices such as infant marriage or the prohibition of widow remarriage at a time of active social reform movements across India, and that Risley's investment was in the context of the administrative enumeration of the population of India, suggests both the extent to which caste had been naturalized as the colonized form of civil society, and the way in which an anthropological imaginary dominated colonial knowledge at this time. Anthropology was no longer merely an administrative tool, but an administrative episteme.

Risley returned to the use of *varna* as the basis for enumeration and classification, as befitted both his resort to Brahmanical opinion and his interest in social rank. He clearly believed that present day castes were the 'modern representatives of one or other of the castes of the theoretical Hindu system'. Accordingly, 'In every scheme of grouping the Brahman heads the list. Then come the castes whom popular opinion accepts as the modern representatives of the Kshatriyas, and these are followed by the mercantile groups supposed to be akin to the Vaisyas'. As always, Risley was on less sure ground when he left 'the higher circles of the twice-born', for it was here that the difficulty of classification by rank was legion. Thus his seventh category, after the three twice-born castes and the castes 'allied' to them, was 'castes of good social position distinctly superior to that of the remaining groups'. The degree to which Aryan blood was retained by a group was marked by the direction in which women were exchanged hypergamously or endogamously, and by exchanges of food, water, and services between caste, and thus the eighth category was made up of castes from whom some of the twice-born would take some kinds of food and water. For these 'Sudras' and other mixed castes, Risley was aware that the criteria for social precedence varied considerably by region. Not only did the Sudra category vary greatly in social status, it made up the dominant groups in most parts of western and southern India, where in any case Brahmans would only take food and water from their own caste or sub-caste. In many parts of north and north-west India, exchanges with Brahmans among other castes were possible and determined ritual status among high castes, but strangely it was in these very areas that the status of Brahmans seemed less secure than where no exchanges were countenanced. *Varna* also seemed of little value for non-Hindu populations, but Risley—once again using his extensive research and correspondence of earlier years—noted that, 'In India, however, caste is in the air; its contagion has spread even to the Muhammedans; and we find its evolution proceeding on characteristically Hindu lines'.[34] Risley also contemplated the extent to which caste might be breaking down as a consequence of new ideas and institutions, and determined that technological change such as the introduction and extension of the railways was having a paradoxical effect. Railways worked to diffuse Brahmanical influence, education to expand the reach of Hindu scriptures. While greater 'laxity' in matters of food and drink might be observed in some cases, Risley noted that he observed 'a more rigid observance of the essential incidents of caste'.[35] And Risley repeated his critiques of other theorists of caste (most especially Nesfield), reiterating his own view that the dominant factor in the formation of caste was the conquest of one race by another. Marriage restrictions developed around the two races, and then were further elaborated around the groups that were born of mixed unions. The principle of the caste system rests on the distinctions of race.[36]

Once started in India the principle was strengthened, perpetuated, and extended to all ranks of society by the fiction that people who speak a different language, dwell in a different district, worship different gods, eat different food, observe different social customs, follow a different profession, or practise the same profession in a slightly different way must be so unmistakeably aliens by blood that intermarriage with them is a thing not to be thought of.[37]

And for Risley, the principle was enshrined in the person of the Brahman and the doctrine of karma.

The ultimate proof for Risley of the wisdom of his system was the great number of petitions and memorials to which it gave rise. Census officers had received similar petitions and representations since the first Census, but the announcement by Risley that the Census would be reorganized on the basis of social precedence made the Census into a political instrument in a way it had never been before. Risley noted several major struggles, including an attempt by Khatris of the Punjab and United Provinces to be classified as Rajputs which was ultimately successful, asserting that these efforts vindicated his belief that 'the sole test of social precedence … was native public opinion'.[38] For the most part, of course, Risley used the opinion of just a small group of 'natives', overwhelmingly the class of official Brahmans and higher castes with whom he had such a regular ethnographic correspondence over the years, to develop the textual and ethnographic parameters for the assignment of social status and the determination of categories. And yet he had no real conception that the list of social prece-dence could become a political document rather than a detached scientific survey. He was unable to respond to the politics his system unleashed.

Risley's ethnological report on the 1901 Census of India was republished, with some additions and revisions, as *The People of India* in 1908.[39] The most significant revision was the addition of a single concluding chapter, entitled, 'Caste and Nationality'. Risley wished to address in this chapter the effects of recent social and economic change on caste, as well as to speculate about whether caste would be 'favourable or adverse to the growth of a conscious-ness of common nationality among the people of India',[40] perhaps in response to the clear indications of a developing nationalist movement that had erupted after the partition of Bengal in 1905. Risley obviously believed in the importance of caste; he wrote that it was the cement that held Indian society together. And he had little but scorn for those 'philan-thropic' Englishmen who, on the basis of their experience of Presidency towns, predict the immediate demise of caste. He wrote that 'anarchy is the peculiar peril of a society that is organized on the basis of caste', noting that ancient Indian monarchy had functioned well precisely because it could control caste antipathies, at the same time that it could take advantage of the exclusion of most castes from politics. But for the same reason, caste hardly contributed to the formation of an idea of common nationality. 'So long as a regime of caste persists, it is difficult to see how the sentiment of unity and solidarity can penetrate and inspire all classes of the community, from the highest to the lowest, in the manner that it has done in Japan where, if true caste ever existed, restrictions on intermarriage have long ago disappeared'.[41] British influence, both through the common study among Indian elites of English history and literature, and through the 'consciousness of being united and drawn together by living under a single government',[42] had begun to suggest the possibility of change. However, for Risley, change would have to occur through traditional means, both because the vast majority of Indians were yet untouched by the idea of nationality, and because the construction of an idea of nationality would best be built on the foundation of traditional institutions, such as the village community and the village council, 'the common property of the Aryan people both in Europe and in India'. Thus Risley's racial theory predicated his hope for India's national future, even as politics served as his retreat, even as he cautioned Indian nationalists against the temptation of sudden change. In the most paternalist of ways, he concluded his chapter by advocating the 'orderly development of the indigenous germs of such institutions', warning at the same time that progress would in any case be slow.[43]

Risley's final ethnographic contribution to colonial knowledge thus reiterated the divisiveness of caste, as well as its fundamental compatibility with politics only in the two registers of ancient Indian monarchy or modern Britain's 'benevolent despotism'.[44] He warned Indian nationalists and European liberals not to give in either to 'impatient idealism' or a belief in the force of modern change in India. And he did so by invoking the full authority of an anthropological view of India which reckoned India as fundamentally non-political and caste as essentially divisive. Indeed, caste was the basic obstacle. As he wrote: 'Were its cohesive power withdrawn or its essential ties relaxed, it is difficult to form an idea of the probable consequences. Such a change would be like a revolution; it would resemble the withdrawal of some elemental force like gravitation or molecular attraction. Order would vanish and chaos would supervene'.[45] He did not mention that this revolution would be pitted against British rule in India, rather suggesting that the kind of revolution envisioned perhaps by Indian nationalists would be in the order of a natural disaster. Change could only be gradual, the introduction of something akin to representative politics only the eventual outcome of the cultivation of village forms of political representation and activity. Risley's own antipathy to change, whether expressed in relationship to his implicit advocacy of Brahmanic customs in the face of pressures for social reform, or in his consternation that the enumeration of caste by rank would unleash a politics that his own social theory could not explain, was of course profoundly mired in his commitment to race science. It is hard to think of another 'impartial' observer of society in the Indian context who had so profound an impact on the very society he observed. It is also hard to imagine another figure who so admired India's ancient constitution precisely because of the ways it enshrined a late nineteenth-century European conception of race.

If Risley's views on caste so clearly mark his imperial conceit, they also reflect a curious conjuncture in the history of empire. Risley, whose advocacy of race science was akin to that of Galton and other late nineteenth-century eugenicists, fashioned a peculiar exchange between the racial anxieties of imperial Britain and the ritual anxieties of Brahmans and other higher castes at the turn of the century. While Risley was so obsessively committed to the measuring of skulls and bodies and the appropriation of the enumerative project of the census by his zeal to prove a racial theory of origins, he found a strange kinship with his interlocutors in the imperial theatre of India. Brahmans used their late imperial access to political privilege to deny the political character of their influence. Meanwhile, the British relied on Brahman knowledge; at the same time they denied Brahmans any real relation to the racial privilege they sought, despite all the claims about Aryan affinity, to preserve for themselves. All this was accomplished with the authority of ancient Brahmanic knowledge, both textual traditions that had been authorized by Orientalist knowledge, and ethnographic assumptions that were confirmed by 'native' informants. And so the British enumerators kept returning, despite all the manifold difficulties, to a reliance on the old *varna* scale for their all-India enumerations, even as they maintained a keen interest in caste as fundamentally about rank and social precedence.

At a time of resounding efforts to engage in social reform against Brahmanic privilege, Risley directed the full apparatus of colonial power to the task of using India to prove the truth of racial difference. In his enterprise, he accepted Brahman claims about the superiority of such customs as the prohibition of widow remarriage or the importance of infant marriage, even as he rejected the claims of manifestly non-Aryan racial groups to twice-born status. One imagines that Risley would have set himself up as an ancient Indian monarch if only he could, adjudicating competing claims over status with calipers in one hand and statistical tables about nasal indices in the other. And in his last work on caste he effectively denied the capacity of Indians for the formation of an idea of nationality, let alone self-rule. At a time when India was beginning to mobilize the momentous struggle of nationalism in such early theatres as the struggles of Savarkar and Tilak in western India and the Swadeshi movement in Bengal, Risley used his racial theory of caste to vindicate his views that nationality would be unable to explode the tenacious grip of caste feeling. Race could simultaneously explain Britain's imperial role in India and India's inability to contest it. And while race justified Risley's imperial project, it also became the unfortunate wedge by which Risley's not inconsiderable influence, on the subsequent careers of imperialism and nationalism both, would be felt in the years to come.

If Risley's racial vision gave the Census an especially significant role in the production of modern caste identities in India, it also provided the ideological basis for an even more dramatic contribution to the modern rise of communalism. As Home Secretary to the Indian Government, a position he assumed after his stint as Director of Ethnography, Risley played a key role in the 1903 proposal that Bengal be partitioned into two provinces, in large part because of the political benefits thought to attend the separation of the politically threatening Hindu minority from the majority Muslim population.[46] A few years later, Risley argued strongly against the view of John Morley, Secretary of State for India, that serious political reforms were necessary in the wake of the agitation over the 1905 partition, in particular the Swadeshi movement of 1905–7. Risley was against territorial representation and parliamentary government for India, and used the demand of the newly formed Muslim League for separate electorates to make his case. In the end, the award of separate electorates for Muslims in the Morley-Minto reforms of 1909 was in large part the result of the energetic role played by Risley, who used his ethnological view of India to make one of the most influential, and deadly, decisions of Britain's colonial era.[47] It was this award of separate electorates in 1909 that set the stage for the demand for Pakistan and the eventual partition of the sub-continent.[48] Risley's anthropology worked not so much to retard nationalism as to render it communal. In so doing, it also left a bloody legacy for South Asia that continues to exact a mounting toll.

Thus the anthropological transformation of colonial state interest played out the larger story of empire. In this story, power became an end in itself and never felt checked by the need for legitimation or accountability. As Hannah Arendt has noted,

it is characteristic of imperialism that national institutions remain separate from the colonial administration although they are allowed to exercise control. The actual motivation for this separation was a curious mixture of arrogance and respect: the new arrogance of the administrators abroad who faced 'backward populations' or 'lower breeds' found its correlative in the respect of old fashioned statesmen at home who felt that no nation had the right to impose its law upon a foreign people. It was in the very nature of things that the arrogance turned out to be a device for rule, while the respect, which remained entirely negative, did not produce a new way for peoples to live together, but managed only to keep the ruthless imperialist rule by decree within bounds.[49]

But Arendt did not understand the extent to which these bounds only worked to serve imperial power, substituting culture for civil society, tradition for politics, and total domi-nation for any expectation of a democratic relationship to the exercise of power. This symbiosis was expressed in the development of colonial anthropology, in which ethnographic accounts of the social became quite literally the history of the colonized. Knowledge about India was largely produced by or in terms of the logic of colonial rule, the imperatives and institutions of the colonial state.

It was unfortunate enough that the colonial state began its career in India as an extractive state, disrupting the circuits of political and economic vitality that have been by now so well demonstrated by generations of historians during the long eighteenth century. But in retrospect one might argue that things became worse, in the short and long runs, when the colonial state converted itself from an extractive state to an ethnographic state in the late nineteenth century. Not only did the ethnographic state continue to rule long after its contradictions unleashed the historical inevitability of partition, it also worked to legitimate not just the nationalism of a figure like Savarkar, but also the extreme nationalist ethnographic imaginaries that have converted parody into tragedy time after time in contemporary South Asia. Arrogance and respect combined in the colonial embrace to leave lasting legacies of communal discord and national struggle.

NOTES

1. This essay is a revised version of a paper first delivered at the International Conference on the State in India, held in Kyoto in December 1999. It is based on and summarizes the argument of a longer work, *Castes of Mind: Colonialism and the Making of Modern India.* Princeton: Princeton University Press, 2001.
2. Sir Sayyid Ahmad Khan's *History of the Bijnor Rebellion*, translated with notes and introduction by Hafeez Mallik and Morris Dembo, published by Asian Studies Center, Michigan State University, East Lansing, Michigan.
3. Ibid., p. 122.
4. Ibid., p. 124.
5. Ibid.
6. Ibid., p. 126.
7. Letter of 1869 to Sir John Kaye, from Sir Sayyid Ahmed, dated 14 December 1869, enclosed in ibid.
8. Notes by Frere and Outram of 28 March 1860 in Canning Papers Miscellaneous, no. 558, quoted in T.R. Metcalf, *Aftermath of Revolt.* Princeton: Princeton University Press, 1964, p. 91.
9. See John W. Kaye, *A History of the Sepoy War in India 1857–1858*, 3v., London, 7th edition, 1875; G.B. Malleson, *History of the Indian Mutiny*, 3v., London: 1896.

10. C.H. Philips, et al. (eds). *The Evolution of India and Pakistan, 1857–1947: Select Documents.* London: Oxford University Press, 1962, pp. 10–11.
11. T. Metcalf, *Ideologies of the Raj.* Cambridge: Cambridge University Press, 1964, p. 48.
12. Ibid.
13. F. Max Muller, 'Caste, 1858', in Muller, *Chips from a German Workshop.* London: Longmans, Green, and Co., 1867.
14. Duncan Forrester, *Caste and Christianity.* London. Pub. 1980, p. 57.
15. Quoted in ibid., p. 33.
16. Minute of the Madras Missionary Conference on the Subject of Caste. Printed for the Conference at the American Mission Press, 1850, p. 1.
17. Ibid., p. 4.
18. Calcutta, 1858.
19. Forrester, pp. 55–6.
20. Muller, pp. 318–19.
21. Ibid., p. 355.
22. Ibid.
23. See Thomas Trautmann, *Aryans and British India.* Berkeley: University of California Press, 1998.
24. H.H. Risley, only son of Rev. John Holford Risley, Rector of Akeley, was born on 4 January 1851. He went to Winchester and Oxford, where he was selected for an appointment in the Indian Civil Service before his graduation in 1872. He stayed in India until 1910, when he was appointed as Permanent Secretary in the India Office, a post he only held for a short time, as he died in September 1911.
25. H.H. Risley, *The Tribes and Castes of Bengal.* Calcutta: Secretariat Press, 1891, preface, p. xix.
26. *Man*, nos 112–13, 1901, p. 137.
27. H.H. Risley, *The Tribes and Castes of Bengal.* Calcutta: Secretariat Press, 1891, p. i.
28. Letter from Michael Foster to the Secretary of State for India, December 1899, in Extract No. 3219–32 from the Proceedings of the Government of India in the Home Department (Public)—under date Simla, 23 May 1901.
29. Resolution of the Government of India, Home Department (Public), no. 3919, 23 May 1901, Simla.
30. *Census of India, 1901,* Vol I, Part I, Report, by H.H. Risley, with the assistance of E.A. Gait, Chapter xi, pp. 489–557.
31. Report on the Census, 1901, p. 493.
32. Report on the Census, 1901, p. 538.
33. Report on the Census, 1901, p. 538.
34. Report, p. 543.
35. Report, p. 544.
36. Risley did not believe that caste was confined to India. 'It occurs in a pronounced form in the southern states of the American Commonwealth, where Negroes intermarry with Negroes, and the various mixed races mulattos, quadroons, and octoroons each have a sharply restricted *jus connubii* of their own and are absolutely cut off from legal unions with the white races (555)'.
37. Report, p. 556.
38. Report, p. 539.
39. H.H. Risley, *The People of India,* Second Edition, London, 1915.
40. Ibid., p. 287.
41. Ibid., p. 293.
42. Ibid., p. 294.
43. Ibid., p. 301.
44. Ibid., p. 281.
45. Ibid., p. 278.
46. See, for example, Sumit Sarkar's thorough discussion of this in his, *The Swadeshi Movement in Bengal, 1903–1908.* New Delhi: People's Publishing House, 1973.

47. See Hermann Kulke and Dietmar Rothermund, *A History of India*. New York: Routledge Press, 1986, pp. 271–2.

48. See Ayesha Jalal, *The Sole Spokesman: Jinnah, the Muslim League and the Demand for Pakistan*. Cambridge: Cambridge University Press, 1985.

49. Hannah Arendt, *The Origins of Totalitarianism*. New York: Harcourt Brace, 1979.

FOUR

Problems of Violence, States of Terror: Torture in Colonial India

Anupama Rao

ৎৡৼ৵৶

In a file labelled the 'Nassick Torture Case' in the Maharashtra State Archives, one can find a petition dated 17 October 1855 to Governor-General M. Elphinstone, signed by 1989 inhabitants of the town of Nasik.[1] The petition seeks the reinstatement of one Mohammed Sheikh, Joint Police Officer, or *foujdar*:

We at present learn from the newspaper that the Government has dismissed him [the *foujdar*] from his situation, and on inquiry found that last year a Coonbee had murdered his niece for her ornaments, and was apprehended by the Police peons, who put a stick up his anus for extorting confession, and that the Government has decided that the Foujdar had ordered to do this to the above Coonbee who died while in custody—but we feel certain that the Foujdar could not have ordered to the above effect because in the deceased prisoner's deposition which was taken down before the Government authorities, no mention is made about the Foujdar's orders, nor did the Police peons who were tried and punished say anything in their depositions concerning the Foujdar's orders for putting a stick up the prisoner's anus or for doing other such evil action.

In the absence of any positive proof of the *foujdar*'s innocence, the petitioners are ironically forced to rely on his alleged victim's dying declaration. Reading this petition today, one is tempted to accuse the petitioners of distorting the significance of the victim's last words: they take an omission as a positive indicator, and thus fabricate a version of events that seems to suppress the truth of torture. But the story at stake here cannot be so easily judged. For, as I will discuss, the truth of torture lies not simply in its opposition to the torturer's version of events but rather in a more complex matrix that situates the *foujdar* and his defenders themselves within a regime of violence. To unravel the relationship between the tortured body and the silence surrounding the practice of torture, it is necessary to read the relationship between torture and colonial law. My study aims to acknowledge the ways in which colonial law not only participated in a regime of torture but also sought to erase its own complicity in this regime.

The complexity of the relationship between colonial rule, native police, and violence emerges in the facts and documents that surround the death of the Coonbee. A young man named Gunnoo aged about nineteen is mentioned in this petition only by his caste label, Coonbee, or *kunbi*, a broad and inclusive category of agriculturalists.[2] The significance of caste and class relations alluded to here is drawn out by the surrounding facts of the case. The chain of events began when Gunnoo was accused of stealing the ornaments of his niece Syee, a young girl of five and then drowning her in a well. One witness' deposition testified that Gunnoo denied knowing the girl's whereabouts. However, when police peons 'gave him a slap on the turban . . . a silver Suklee [chain] fell out—on searching him other ornaments were found'. According to the witness, when asked about the girl again, Gunnoo pleaded that the ornaments must have been planted on him and repeated that he did not know Syee's whereabouts. At this point in the public interrogation, the *foujdar* is alleged to have said, 'he [Gunnoo] is frightened in this crowd take him to one side and *Sumjao* him [make him understand]'.[3] Gunnoo was then taken into the cowshed of a prostitute, Lateeb, by seven policemen, and tortured. Afterwards, he was led to the well outside the town in which the girl's body was found. There, Gunnoo confessed to the crime. He died in custody two days later, on 13 August 1854.

It is in the legal aftermath of Gunnoo's death that the particular relationship of torture to colonial rule was at stake. For although a significant body of literature maintains that cultures of terror were essential to the task of colonial governance, British rule in India also sought to oppose, at least on one level, police violence.[4] Thus Gunnoo's death in custody prompted a judicial inquiry that set colonial administrators against the native police. These efforts on the part of colonial law to distance itself from, and even to condemn, excessive violence participated in a larger attempt to fashion colonial rule as a liberal 'rule of law'.

Gunnoo's death in custody and allegations of police torture, however, put the Bombay government in a difficult position. The simultaneous discovery of and efforts to contain the practice of torture produced a political contradiction. Even as they publicly investigated the charge of torture by the police, colonial administrators were animated by an anxiety about the prevalence of torture (what if it facilitated all policing?), and by a consequent reluctance to draw public attention to its practice. Although meant to exhibit the fair and efficient functioning of colonial institutions, the inquiry therefore sought to characterize Gunnoo's death as an extraordinary event. Only a discursive separation of torture from legitimate forms of punishment would allow colonial administrators to punish the policemen guilty of torture while maintaining a commitment to the beneficent face of the colonial regime.

Gunnoo's death can thus serve as a point of entry into a larger set of debates about the reform of penal practices during the mid-nineteenth century. When the critical historian reads the developmental narrative of colonial law against the grain, it becomes possible to resituate the category of torture within the development of the colonial judicial-penal complex and, consequently, the narrative of colonial modernity. I argue that the containment of torture by colonial authorities worked through a contradictory and highly ambivalent relationship with 'modern' legal and forensic knowledge; that the success of colonial modernity lay, ironically, in positing colonial subjects as unaware of the distinction between punishment and retribution.

In what follows, I focus on this process as it becomes visible in two areas. One, in the indictment of 'native' practices of policing as perpetuating the practice of torture. Colonial administrators distanced themselves from such practices, arguing that they illustrated the persistence of precolonial disciplinary practices. The public exposure of torture, which should have implicated the colonial state and its excesses, was in fact converted into a moral victory over a penal regime now characterized as traditional, and barbaric. Second in the significance of new methods of detection such as forensic medicine in overturning native practices of torture. During the latter half of the nineteenth century, colonial officials in Bombay and London increasingly came to focus on the perceived benefits of the nascent field of medical jurisprudence in detecting not only crime but also the excessive use of force by the police in extracting confessions.[5] Torture's crude violation of the body gave way to more rational and objective forms of discovering the truth of violence. New discourses of detection and physical examination became critical for the elaboration of a colonial judicial-penal complex that objectified the body in terms of its pain and suffering.

COLONIAL GOVERNANCE AND NATIVE POLICE

In the investigation into Gunnoo's death, the structural relationship between colonial governance, police practices, and violence to native bodies is exhibited by the colonial state's attempts to scapegoat the actual perpetrators of police torture—the native police. The Bombay government faced the dilemma of balancing the validity of the evidence gathered at the well regarding Gunnoo's murder of his niece, against the possibility that the confession had been extracted through torture, rendering it invalid or highly compromised at best. On the one hand, the police were seen as belonging to the generic category of state servants and functionaries of the law, while on the other the 'native' police were viewed as a special category of colonial subjects who were *outside* the law.

This tension is revealed in the legal documents that circulated after the sessions court sentenced the six police peons who were accused of committing the torture and murder of Gunnoo to four years' hard labour, four months in solitary confinement, and the first seven and last seven days of the month on a *conjee* (rice water or gruel) diet.[6] The court described the acts of these six men as 'atrocious' and truly outside the bounds of law. These crimes were therefore treated as renegade acts committed without the authority of a superior. For this reason, the *foujdar* himself was not named as a defendant in the case. Indeed, in arguments later made in defence of the *foujdar*, it was maintained that such an act, committed 'in great haste', a 'desperate measure' of 'cruelty' done in a 'clumsy manner', could not have been premeditated and therefore could not have taken place under the orders of a government official.[7] This was buttressed by the eyewitness testimony of Alexander Bell, Assistant Superintendent of Police, who testified that Gunnoo had appeared in perfect health when he had seen him at the well immediately after the alleged torture.

However, further inquiry by the high court called the *foujdar's* innocence into doubt. A resolution from the Governor in Council to the Registrar of the *Sudder Adalat* on 30 August 1855 argued that the native police had been let off too lightly; that 'the punishment is far too light to operate as a warning to the Police subordinates in Nassick and throughout the Presidency'. Furthermore, the letter noted that, while ignoring the *foujdar's* participation in extorting a confession, the sessions court marked its knowledge of the use of torture in this case by noting that 'when the Foujdar ordered the unfortunate prisoner to be taken aside he intended that a confession should be retracted from him by threats and ill-usages'. The judiciary 'knew' the settings of torture, its performance in secret, much as it attempted to ignore the initiation of the event at the behest of the *foujdar*. In the name of the just rule of law, the *Sudder Foujdari Adalat* (Supreme Criminal Court) thus initiated a case against the *foujdar*, arguing that, 'It is not fitting the subject and active agents in this crime should be punished while their superior is held blameless because he took care to keep out of sight himself of the outrage perpetrated'.[8]

The possibility that Gunnoo's murder was not simply the act of renegade police peons but perhaps a deliberately ordered, official act moved this case on to a larger stage. For if Gunnoo's death was now not an aberration but a more general police practice, it would be necessary to conduct an inquiry into this practice on the highest levels. Thus in response to a letter dated 20 July 1855 from Elphinstone, the Governor-General of Bombay Presidency, the *Sudder Foujdari Adalat* replied that it thought the law to be sufficient in handling cases of police abuse as well as extraction in the pursuit of revenue collection.[9] Reforming individual practices gave way to an inquiry into the hierarchies of command within the police, and to attempts to discipline superiors who might have ordered the torture while not having themselves performed it. At this point, the reform of the police as an institution confronted their relationship of the police to the law.

It has been argued that the British imposed a rule of law in colonial India by maintaining that precolonial regimes lacked a properly autonomous domain of law, relying instead on law-like structures and modalities of caste and community based adjudication.[10] An autonomous domain of law was also to be a homogenizing one, buttressed by a large-scale ideological shift in native mentalities. Natives had to be taught to do away with categories of difference such as caste, gender, and religion which assumed that different categories of persons were inherently unequal, entitled to different forms and severity of punishment. In fact, however, the colonial state both relied on and worked through such distinctions.[11]

The imposition of a homogeneous system of criminal law also demanded a cadre of police who would involve themselves in the pursuit of criminals, extract confessions and produce testimony, and work closely with the judiciary in punishing criminal offenders while protecting the populace.[12] Because colonial officers mistrusted the native police and considered their reliance on them a necessary evil, the native police force had to be drastically reformed and modernized if it was to implement the legal reforms contemplated by the British government.

As early as 1832, the Select Committee on East India Affairs (Judicial) had discussed the prevalence of torture and suggested that the police force had to be reformed and modernized in order to curtail the use of corporal violence.[13] In response to a query from the committee—'Are you aware whether the practice of torture by the native officers, for the purpose of extorting confessions or obtaining evidence, has been frequently resorted to?'—Alexander Campbell, ex-Registrar of the *Sudder Diwani* and *Faujdari Adalat* (Supreme Civil and Criminal Court, respectively) in Madras replied:

Under the native governments which preceded us at Madras, the universal object of every police officer was to obtain a confession from the prisoner with a view to his conviction of any offence; and notwithstanding every endeavor of our European tribunals to put an end to this system, frequent instances have come before all our criminal tribunals of its use.[14]

Campbell went on to note that policemen above the rank of the common peon often functioned as witnesses to crimes, which literally allowed the police to take the law into their own hands. In 1857, a member of the House of Commons noted the popular conviction that 'dacoity is bad enough, but that the subsequent police inquiry is worse'.[15] This had much to do with the fact that confessions in the presence of the police were seen as adequate for judicial indictment. Magistrates with a poor command of native languages were often unfamiliar with the customary and/or religious codes that regulated persons and communities. They found themselves relying on confessions taken by the police rather than conducting their own inquiries. This suggests that the police often acted in a *de facto* judicial capacity, taking confessions, deciding guilt, and punishing wrongdoers. This exposed the uncertain position of the police in the implementation of law: were they merely law's functionaries, or were they in fact *producing* the evidence which law courts relied upon in the dispensation of justice?[16]

The continuity between the supposed prevalence of torture in traditional repertories of policing and their use under a colonial regime also suggested the colonial state's pedagogical failure in marking a clear separation between the rule of law and corporal punishment. In 1857 officials were still arguing that 'there was a deficiency in the police and in the administration of justice in India.'[17] Interestingly, police reform and attempts to discontinue the use of excessive corporal violence were situated on a continuum with the abolition of other 'horrible practices' such as hook-swinging, infanticide, and *meriah* (human) sacrifice, all 'cruelties which disgraced society in India'.[18] The problems of judicial administration could therefore be linked to native intransigence rather than to failures of colonial governance. Once again, it was the presence of native policemen, rather than the role of the police in a colonial regime, that came to be problematized. By placing police torture alongside a stream of indistinguishable acts of barbarity and violence of varying motivations, British officials confirmed to themselves that the native police were inured to the use of corporal violence in extracting confessions. The police were understood as a *cultural* institution compromised by the fact of being 'native', and hence fundamentally irrational and prone to excess.

The publication of the two-volume *Report of the Commissioners for the Investigation of the Alleged Cases of Torture in the Madras Presidency* in 1855 (henceforth the *Report*) drew attention to torture as a structural problem of policing, rather than an aberrant and extraordinary instance.[19] The *Report* was initially meant to explore complaints about torture in the extraction of revenue in Madras Presidency. The Government of India extended the scope of the report to include the relationship between torture and policing.[20] This itself is instructive of the dissonant relationship between attempts to extract revenue at all cost (revenue demands rose at least threefold during the first few years of settlement in Madras) and the attempt to impose an equitable judicial system on native subjects.

Though there was no comparable investigation in the Bombay Presidency, the *Report* (which was after all a response to massive complaints about torture by natives) sensitized the bureaucracy to the power of a category, such as torture, that could potentially indict colonial penal practices.[21] Hence the anxiety about containing torture travelled across presidencies. This is reflected, for instance, in the production of three separate judicial files on 'torture' that can be found in the Maharashtra State Archives in Bombay confined to the period 1855 to 1857, coeval with the period when the *Report* was released, and a general discussion of reforming the police force was also underway. The *Report* was as much an attempt to bureaucratize the police force and to press for the reform of criminal law, as it was an attempt to publicize the complaints about torture. In this, perhaps, it reflected the colonial conditions of its production, since discourses of improvement masked the attempts to impose more coercive forms of rule over colonial subjects.[22]

The reliance on the native police coupled with the constant suspicion that they were ignorant or even abusive of legal norms produced the paradoxical need to 'police the police'.[23] In a colonial situation, natives were seen as possibly needing protection from the police, rather than being protected by them. The construction of the native police as fundamentally unreliable (because racially inferior) thus produced a problem of surveillance and control *within* the police force. While legal reform was pursued in tandem with the reconceptualization of personhood and property under colonial rule, the problems with police reform suggested a split between the rhetoric of colonial improvement and its personification in the native police were meant to enact the ideologies of rule by law. The discovery of torture represented this split in spectacular fashion, by displacing the question of colonial culpability for perpetuating the practice on to precolonial or traditional practices of policing.

The problematic discovery of torture for the extraction of confessions is symptomatic of the contradictions of a colonial rule that acknowledged customary practices (due to the political necessity of relying on natives), yet stigmatized them through the rhetorics of modernization and improvement. While torture implicated police excess, it also produced 'false' truths, false because contaminated by their connection with corporal violence. Confessions produced under torture were understood to be worthless since they were produced by the threat of force or even death. In Gunnoo's case this would raise the dilemma of how far the administration could believe the admission of his guilt in drowning Syee. This raised the spectre of colonial power as merely theatrical and self-confirming, despotic rather than reasonable.

Racial assumptions about native inferiority produced a severe and intractable problem: was it impossible to maintain legitimate practices of punishment that did not run the risk of transmogrifying into the exercise of excessive force and violence in a colonial situation? The colonial 'rule of law', in a situation of ruling over the racially inferior and culturally backward often demanded the imposition of forms of physical and symbolic violence. Hence assumptions of native incompetence and barbarity were self-fulfilling prophecies that necessarily depended on colonial authorities' discovery of scandals such as the prevalence of torture practised by native police. The repeated attempts to distinguish between moderate and excessive violence become doubly significant in this context.

Colonial rule was represented as inaugurating a new relationship between subjects and subjectifying practices. Colonial governmentality had much to do with instituting a new practice of power that could be clearly distinguished from its precolonial predecessors.[24] Yet the repeated 'discovery' of torture hinted at the fundamental instability of the rule of law and suggested that excessive force supplemented the consolidation of the legal sphere as an autonomous domain. As with Gunnoo's torture, the eagerness to produce a confession and punish him for the brutal murder of a young girl took the form of his extralegal torture by the police. This contradiction exposed the colonial state's fundamental misrecognition of its own role both in producing and disavowing scandalous practices; in recognizing the extent to which a 'new' relationship between the state and its subjects as well as among subjects had itself reorganized the relationship between law and society, between adjudication and excess. The violence at the very heart of colonial governance raises for us the possibility of understanding law as constantly haunted by its other face: naked force and violence.[25]

THE SECRET LIFE OF TORTURE

Along with attempts to reform the native police, a language of bodily integrity and vulnerability became central to judicial discourses that sought to address torture's disregard for the body. If torture assumed the body as a biological fact or datum to be dismembered in order to produce a confession, the colonial judicial regime seems to have operated with another notion of the body—as one eminently available to certain forms of expert knowledge such as forensic medicine. This resulted in a shift in techniques for the production of truth that integrated scientific discourses of the body with changed conceptions of legal proof and criminal culpability. The affective discourse of pain and suffering animated the discussion of torture as a barbaric and uncivilized practice. I now turn to these issues that appear in the Nasik torture case under the broad rubric of medical testimony.

In Gunnoo's case, the credibility of torture came to rest on the bodily signs that could provide evidence capable of convicting the policemen of wrongdoing. Gunnoo's case was decided on 26 December 1854 by Sessions Judge Mr J.W. Woodstock, in Ahmednugger (Ahmednagar) who acquitted the six accused policemen.[26] But this decision was appealed on the grounds that the medical evidence provided before the court was faulty—that the judge had relied on the questionable claim that Gunnoo had died due to the exacerbation of a prior condition, that is, piles.[27]

Colonial officials and upper-level officers of the judiciary in Bombay suggested that part of the problem with this case was the insufficient medical knowledge available to the medical officer when he had first met Gunnoo in prison, as well as the failure of the post-mortem to reveal torture or the excessive use of force with any certainty. The medical evidence was adduced to be of a 'defective character' according to a letter submitted to the medical board by the Governor in Council on 30 August 1855, after the *Sudder Foujdari Adalat* decision.[28] Debates about medical evidence had become critical to the indictment of the police. But they also indexed a new relationship between the body as the primary source of knowledge about police misdemeanour, and the problematic speech of the tortured victim who refused to reveal his experiences due to the fear of further violence. Ironically, this stood in opposition to the assumptions by the police that violence to the body produced a more trustworthy confession than did verbal interrogation.

Gunnoo's dying declaration before Mr Turquand, Joint Acting Magistrate, and Dr Pelly, the Civil Surgeon, indicted the police for having shoved a stick up his anus in a cowshed.[29] But this indictment occurred when it was too late to be of any use, after Gunnoo had been seen by a native doctor as well as a British doctor, who were aware of the pain he was in, but not its origin. This was in large part because Gunnoo had been unwilling to recount his experience in the cowshed, either from shame and humiliation, or fear of further violence in police custody. On the other hand, the common knowledge of beatings by the police and of threats of torture in extracting confessions emerges at various points in the file on this case, indicating that the practice of torture was an open secret. The knowledge of torture was thus situated between the testimony of witnesses and the hesitation of expert medical testimony in pronouncing that torture was the 'real' cause of Gunnoo's death. While the doctors resisted from pronouncing on torture, performing violence upon Gunnoo's truth, eyewitnesses were both necessary yet insufficient in testifying to the existence of torture as a medically quantifiable fact.

Bala Bhow, the First Hospital Assistant, said that when the deceased had complained of pain in his stomach he had 'asked him if he had been beaten—replied he had not—each day deceased complained of greater pain in his stomach', and that Gunnoo had finally admitted to having been tortured by the six policemen. Bala Bhow noted that 'deceased had in one of his stools passed two ounces of pure blood unmixed with faeces—blood dark and thickened'.

Dr Pelly deposed that:

the deceased was brought to the Hospital on the 12th of August and was when he saw him suffering from great pain in the abdomen which increased by the touch of the hand and from other symptoms of acute enteritis that *Gunnoo complained to him of having been kicked and beaten by the police but mentioned no names*—Had no recollection of Gunnoo's saying anything that day about a stick having been thrust up his anus. But on the Sunday morning being much worse he made a deposition to Mr. Turquand the acting Joint Magistrate in his [unreadable] presence accusing the Police of having done so—Gunnoo died at 2 o'clock the same afternoon [my emphasis].

In the prison where Gunnoo had been kept before being taken to hospital on 12 August, Imam Wallud Gottee, a sweeper, deposed to having washed his *dhotur* (the long cloth used to wrap the lower half of the body) which had stains of dried blood upon it. Ahmed Wallud Dawood remembered 'having cleaned a pan of a prisoner confined in the *Foujdar*'s Cutcherry [courthouse] on a charge of murder. [He said he] saw about a handful of blood in it. There was no excrement'.

Gunnoo's own dying declaration is available to us in its paraphrased version, rather than given verbatim.

[Gunnoo] said that on the day of his apprehension the first six prisoners [the police] had taken him to cowshed belonging to a prostitute by the name of Lateeb—shut the door forced him down with his face to the ground which prevented him from being heard and then thrust the handle of a paper or China umbrella 1 1/2 span up his anus twice or thrice *but that* he could not see who did it—That he found his Anus bloody and that the cloth he had on was also stained with blood—and was washed the following day by a Bhungy [an untouchable who 'traditionally' removes nightsoil]—That on his way from the cowshed to the *Foujdar*'s Cutcherry he was beaten by the Police as well as by the Villagers who had assembled none of whom however could he recognize [my emphasis].

Gunnoo's dying declaration exposes the torture but he is unable to name his aggressors since he could not see them while lying face down in the cowshed.

The testimony of eyewitnesses also indicated that when the policemen had taken Gunnoo aside, they 'knew' or could imagine why Gunnoo was taken away from the crowd, without actually having witnessed the violence. The medical practitioners, for their part, focused only on visible, external symptoms that indicated the internal damage Gunnoo had suffered, further corroborated by the testimony of the prison sweeper who spoke about the presence of blood in Gunnoo's stools. This testimony also tallied with the physical evidence of torture immediately after Gunnoo's apprehension, noted by eyewitnesses: '[After] the lapse of 10 minutes according to one witness and half an hour as deposed to by another, the whole party emerged from the premises, the accused Gunnoo resting his head on a policeman's shoulder and his hands clasped on his stomach, the seat as he said of the pain he was enduring. In that condition he was conveyed to the well; in that condition he made his confession, and he was then removed to the chowkee, still in a state of suffering.'[30]

The deposition of witnesses and Gunnoo's dying declaration that he had not seen the faces of his aggressors affirmed secrecy as the precondition of torture's efficacy, while revealing the quality of the 'truth' it was capable of producing. Torture's status shuttled between its secret performance and the means whereby it became visible and public. The above depositions mark such a movement through the reliance on Gunnoo's various injuries as evidence. Between the truth produced by Gunnoo's body (pain and suffering), the veracity of eyewitness accounts, and medical testimony lies the paradoxical logic of torture as simultaneously secret and public.

The Sessions Court confronted two positions on the torture: that it had occurred, and everyone knew about it, or that Gunnoo had lied. Much of the evidence required measuring the intensity of Gunnoo's wounds, and when they had been inflicted. Witnesses mentioned the pain and suffering on Gunnoo's face. In addition, as the Sessions Court argued, the post-mortem should have revealed death due to unnatural causes. Instead, the medical report showed a contradiction in the medical testimony: the medical officer, Dr Pelly, had deposed that Gunnoo's rectum was found unlacerated during the post-mortem while Bala Bhow had given evidence that the anus was 'not usual but extended'.[31] This meant that the medical evidence was unclear about whether Gunnoo had suffered from a prior condition such as piles, that might have manifest the same symptoms as his torture. This was offered as the reason why the prisoner had been taken to hospital and treated without any suspicion about his wounds, until he testified to his torture.

Pelly said that Gunnoo had first been brought to him between 7 and 8 a.m. on 12 August, when Gunnoo had told him he had been kicked and beaten by the police. Pelly had ordered him to be leached and fomented, and the *faujdar* is said to have recorded his deposition.[32] The next morning Gunnoo was worse, and Pelly, suspecting that his patient might not live long, had gone to get Mr Turquand and the Assistant Superintendent of Police, Alexander Bell, who were in the presence of the prisoner when he gave his dying declaration.

Prior to this, on the morning of 11 August, the native doctor Bala Bhow had gone to the *cutcherry*, having been called out on the night of 10 August to inspect the prisoner. On 11 August Bhow administered a purgative, and the earthen pan containing Gunnoo's bloody stools had been cleaned by the sweeper. Bhow applied leaches to Gunnoo's stomach that night at 7 p.m. when Gunnoo confessed to Bhow that the police had mishandled him. The *foujdar* had been informed of this, and Bhow claimed that the *foujdar* went to see Gunnoo that night. Gunnoo had been taken to hospital, where he met Dr Pelly only on 12 August.[33]

Gunnoo's death on 13 August prompted an inquest. One Gangaram Bhoojaree, a member of the inquest who had seen the body at about 5 p.m. on 13 August, and again at 7 p.m., stated that he had not seen any marks of violence on the body, but that Gunnoo's anus was enlarged and his abdomen swollen. He had also seen '3 pieces of intestines which the doctor said were those of the deceased. These were black and in a decomposed state having marks of coagulated blood on them'. Bhoojaree thought that a stick thrust up the anus might have penetrated Gunnoo's abdomen.

When the puisne judges of the *Sudder Foujdari Adalat* reconsidered the evidence gathered by the Sessions Court, they argued that the lower court had been unclear about whether Gunnoo's injuries were 'new' or manifestations of an older complaint of piles. Though puisne judge M. Larken differed from A. Remington in his views on police culpability, he too argued that the medical evidence had fudged the question of where the injuries were located (rectum, intestine, peritoneum), and how old the injuries might be. W.H. Harrison, Acting Puisne Judge, however, seemed to have accepted that Gunnoo was tortured, commenting that '[T]his case should be laid before Government with the object of drawing their attention to the conduct of the Nassick Native Police of all grades who are concerned with this inquiry'. The medical testimony drew on ineffable qualities such as pain and suffering, and attempted to quantify them through a discussion of wounds and their severity. As with the investigation into police misconduct, however, attempts to get at the truth only revealed the extent to which colonial assumptions about native bodies and mentalities compromised that quest.

Talal Asad argues that the quantification of pain—the ability to measure incommensurable acts of suffering by making physical pain a measurable quantity—effected a significant shift in discourses both of suffering and punishment. Understanding pain as a quantity ('more' or 'less') of undifferentiated physical suffering made it possible to understand the experience of violence as something antithetical to the stature of being fully human.[34] This helps explain the British focus on police torture as a native practice that disregarded the relationship between crime and its commensurable punishment. An instrumental conception of pain and the imposition of excessive suffering seemed to lie at the root of such 'native' practices of barbarism, and so confirmed the absence of 'law' as such in precolonial Maharashtra. Any infliction of unjustified force was viewed by the British as torture, regardless of its place in a 'larger moral economy'.[35]

Asad argues that distinctions between ritual forms of inflicting pain on oneself or others and forms of state-sanctioned violence could be collapsed in this model, since pain was assumed to be a transcultural category, singular in its meaning. In British India, early campaigns to abolish *thuggee*, or dacoity, which was thought to be ritually sanctioned by certain communities, or attempts to prevent hook-swinging, self-flagellation, and other forms of 'cruelty' that practitioners inflicted on themselves during religious events were seen to pose the same problem for colonial governance as did the practice of *sati* or infanticide. This meant that different idioms for legitimating the performance of certain violent or cruel acts were glossed, all in the interest of controlling the victim/patient's pain.[36] The inhumanity of excessive violence, and the attempts to porrtray it as a culturally sanctioned form of punishment, meant that it increasingly stood in opposition to the rational and rehabilitative project of penal incarceration.[37] However, the distinction between 'bad' and 'good' pain, between the kind of pain that was an affront to notions of humanity, on the one hand, and that which was necessarily entailed in the movement out of barbarism or primitivism into modern subjecthood, on the other, was understood in a highly interested and motivated fashion in colonial settings.

As with the development of any modern technique for producing or confirming truth, medical jurisprudence was contradictory in its effects.[38] On the one hand, it was lauded as capable of producing a truth of the body and its interior (wounds, lacerations, injuries) more reliable than verbal testimony in cases involving physical injury; on the other hand, it carried the potential to indict the excesses of policing. The double-edged quality to the development of these technologies must be noted, since they both extended and compromised the colonial state's representations of good governance.[39]

CONCLUSION

The status of torture as a threat to the smooth functioning of the judicial apparatus, its status as an aberration, can be found in the repeated mention of the specific acts that constituted Gunnoo's torture in colonial records. The archive's reiteration of the acts of violence, the doctors' measurement of pain and the extent of violation of the body, and most importantly, the attempts to create a place for torture and its significance within the bounds of judicial knowledge, focused on the perils of policing the country, and indicted the police.

As I have suggested throughout, this had to do with the peculiar 'colonial' conditions in which the discovery of torture could be stigmatized as a precolonial traditional practice, instead of being acknowledged as a practice that had gained new salience through the initiation of colonial rule. The colonial authorities' discovery of, but distancing from, the logic of torture confirmed the superiority of a British rule of law.[40] For the colonial state, questions of judicial improvement revolved around the police as an institution with an ambivalent relation to a larger regime of law.[41] The police were critical to the maintenance of law and order, but they also marked people's entry into a regime of law. Colonial administrators were aware of the extent to which the police often took upon themselves the task of disciplining criminals, extracting confessions, or producing evidence, and so, constantly flouted the distinctions between legitimate and illegitimate action. As the Report noted, the police seemed to inhabit a particularly problematic place, one that often exceeded the demands of modern subjectification which requires the subject to produce himself or herself as the net result of a series of overlapping and competing discourses about the body and its insertion into forms of surveillance.[42] Rather, the space of terror and death produced as the result of the (mis) understanding by the police of the injunction to produce truth at all costs meant the annihilation of the criminalized native body. The conceit of colonial law as administering a 'just measure of pain'[43] was profoundly compromised by such a scenario, since it allowed the colonial state to exercise this right through the conduit of the native police.

Foucault argues that the production of truth through confession is particularly 'modern', since it produces subjects who fulfil their bargain to speak the truth because it is in their interest to do so. The problem with torture, however, was that it produced a truth that was never certain of its status in this network. It produced a truth—in Gunnoo's case a deposition of guilt—that was questionable precisely because it was too closely tied to an experience of the body, pain, that was seen as incapable of producing an uncompromised statement. Gunnoo's torture by his unknown assailants produced a problem of knowledge on two fronts. How was the instance of torture itself to be believed when, as the petition noted, neither Gunnoo nor the police peons had initially said anything about it? Second, given Gunnoo's status as a criminal who had committed the violent crime of stealing a young girl's ornaments and drowning her in a well, what were the conditions under which his torture could be viewed as a(n excessive) form of punishment? How was his suffering at the hands of the police to be calibrated, how was penal punishment to be distinguished from violent crime, or revenge? The aims of torture are divided in their purpose. Torture emerges as: (1) a specific repertoire of corporeal violence used by the police; (2) a method of achieving closure, of solving the mystery of Syee's death; (3) a form of retributive action where a criminal who had murdered a young girl was himself violated as a matter of popular justice; and (4) a form of sodomy or brutality as such that sought humiliation as the confirmation of its power.[44]

It is difficult to decipher whether the scandal of torture lay in its commission, or in the modalities through which it was discovered and acknowledged as a public secret (publicity and awareness regarding torture as a problem through the publication of the Madras *Report*, forms of visual medical evidence that seemed to offer incontrovertible proof of Gunnoo's suspicious death, a repertoire of barbaric and violent native practices that disregarded bodily integrity). Much as the policemen who apprehended Gunnoo seemed to have known that he had committed a crime, the Sessions Judge as well as Bala Bhow indicate that they were not surprised that Gunnoo had been tortured before coming into police custody. The police had already mishandled the criminal before he entered prison and courtroom. In arguing that the torturers were 'native police', the Bombay government sought to erase any trace of the colonial government's complicity with his torture. Instead, as I have argued, attempts to refine and modernize penal practices were accompanied by the recognition of 'new' bodily states such as pain and suffering. Torture became problematic only when forms of establishing truth in the context of penal practices were shifting, when there were attempts to distinguish between a moderated or rational use of punishment, and barbaric precolonial practices.[45]

Ironically, it might have been Gunnoo's death that lent his declaration an air of truth. It was his impending death that prompted the revelation of torture in the cowshed to be read as a 'death in custody'. The truth of torture here lay in the victim's death under questionable circumstances, and under great physical pain. The suffering and pain of the prisoner became converted into an inquiry about police procedure and the aberrant use of excessive force. This in turn closed the logic of colonial governance upon itself, which then devoted an extraordinary amount of time and energy to the question of proper policing, the rationale of incarceration, and the value of a measured and moderated exercise of force as opposed to its illegitimate and improper use in extorting confession. I want to suggest that it was as much a problem of the quality of the truth that was produced as it was an attempt to rationalize and impersonalize police practices that created torture as a problem for the colonial government.

The place of torture in the grammar of colonial governance is one that opens up for us a consideration of the colonial body, since it appears as a particularly overdetermined space for the enactment of colonialism's culture—a site upon which the irregularities and excesses of colonial governance were made visible and problematized. In the larger history that speaks of a steady rationalization of penal practices, torture in the colonies would point to the insertion of a form of power that profoundly disturbed the 'rule of law' and the conceits of progress and improvement.

NOTES

1. Judicial Department, Volume 123, 1855.
2. The term *Maratha* was the name given to the landed gentry who identified as a caste community during the late seventeenth century. O'Hanlon argues that ordinary peasant cultivators, or *kunbis*, claimed

Maratha status during the latter half of the nineteenth century as a means of upward mobility. By 1870 a majority of *kunbis* identified themselves as Marathas. Rosalind O'Hanlon, *Caste, Conflict and Ideology: Mahatma Jotirao Phule and Low Caste Protest in Nineteenth-Century India*, Cambridge: Cambridge University Press, 1985.

3. Deposition of Luximan Sukrajee Chowan.

4. Taussig makes a suggestive argument from this perspective. Michael Taussig, 'Culture of Terror—Space of Death: Roger Casement's Putumayo Report and the Explanation of Torture', in Nicholas Dirks (ed.), *Colonialism and Culture*, Ann Arbor: University of Michigan Press, 1992. Fanon discusses such violence as characteristic of settler societies. Frantz Fanon, *The Wretched of the Earth*, tr. Constance Farrington, New York: Grove Press, 1986. We might make a limited distinction between this and the 'liberal' governance of the British colonial state in India which sought to rule through tradition, while maintaining a rhetorical commitment to criminal law's 'equal' application. Radhika Singha, *A Despotism of Law*, Delhi: Oxford University Press, 1998.

5. The link between the prison-judicial complex and medical technologies was critical to the attempts to codify criminal law in British India. For the history of medical jurisprudence in Britain, see Catherine Crawford, 'Legalizing Medicine: Early Modern Legal Systems and the Growth of Medico-legal Knowledge', in Michael Clark and Catherihe Crawford (eds), *Legal Medicine in History*, Cambridge: Cambridge University Press, 1994; and Brenda White, 'Training Medical Policemen: Forensic Medicine and Public Health in Nineteenth-century Scotland', in Michael Clark and Catherine Crawford (eds), *Legal Medicine in History*, Cambridge: Cambridge University Press, 1994. For India, see Chevers who argued that medical jurisprudence could expose the 'lies' of native truth-telling. N. Chevers, *A Manual of Medical Jurisprudence in India Including the Outline of a History of Crime Against the Person*, Calcutta, 1856.

6. One prisoner was found guilty of aiding and assisting in the crime and was sentenced to two years' hard labour and two months' solitary confinement. Two of the police peons were related to Gunnoo and were described as 'enraged' by Syee's murder.

7. Letter No. 727 of 1855, A.R. Grant, Acting Joint Magistrate to H.L. Anderson, Secretary to Government, Judicial Department, 14 September 1855.

8. Minute recorded by W.H. Harrison, Acting Puisne Judge, *Sudder Foujdari Adalat*. The *foujdar* was dismissed from service by an order dated 6 September 1855, and later petitioned that he had been wrongly accused.

9. H.L. Anderson to Secretary, Government, Judicial Department, Letter No. 219 of 1855. Interestingly, I.G. Lumsden's Minute of 17 September 1855 noted that caste hierarchy was the reason why torture and other barbarous practices were tolerated.

10. See V.T. Gune, *The Judicial System of the Marathas*, Yeravada, Pune: Deccan College, 1953; and Singha, *Despotism of Law*.

11. One might think in terms of the differential temporalities involved in homogenizing criminal law on the one hand, while maintaining entire zones of intimate life as separate and distinct, as, for instance, in the recognition of religiously inflected personal laws that concerned issues pertaining to women, such as, marriage, inheritance, or maintenance. Personal laws too came under the reforming zeal of the colonial state, however, when they could be removed from the sphere of the religious and inserted into a discourse of humanity, as, for instance, in the attempts to categorize *sati* as a barbaric offence to human sensibilities. One of the most important effects of this distinction between a homogeneous domain of modern Anglo-Indian law on the one hand, and personal law and customary practices on the other, was to maintain a core of the traditional or religious at the very heart of the consolidation of colonial law. See Singha 1998 for the prehistory of the 'successful' codification of criminal law by the Indian Penal Code in 1861, inaugurated by the Draft Penal Code of 1837. For a range of arguments about the consequences of the hypostasization of 'personal law', see Uma Chakravarti, *Rewriting History: The Life and Times of Pandita Ramabai*, New Delhi: Kali for Women, 1998; Anupama Rao, 'Understanding Sirasgaon: Notes towards Conceptualising the Role of Law, Caste and Gender in a case of "Atrocity" ', in Rajeswari Sunder Rajan (ed.), *Signposts: Gender Issues in Post-Independence India*, New Delhi: Kali for Women, 1998; Kumkum Sangari, 'Politics of Diversity: Religious Communities and Multiple Patriarchies', *Economic and Political Weekly* 30 (51), 23 December:

3287–3310 and 30 (52), 30 December: 3381–89, 1995. Susie Tharu, 'The Impossible Subject: Caste and the Gendered Body', *Economic and Political Weekly*, 31 (22), 1 June: 1311–15, 1996.

12. Though I do not discuss it here, precolonial regimes rarely resorted to penal incarceration. Sumit Guha notes that fines, beatings, and mutilation figure as important means of punishment. Imprisonment was rarely used by the Marathas in western India before 1818, when the area known as the Deccan came under British rule. Sumit Guha, 'An Indian Penal Regime: Maharashtra in the Eighteenth Century', *Past and Present* 147: 101–26, 1995. See Yang for a discussion of the colonial prison. Anand Yang, 'Disciplining "Natives": Prisons and Prisoners in the Early Nineteenth Century', *South Asia* 10(2): 29–45, 1987.

13. I should note here that the use of the term 'torture' by colonial officials seems to attach itself generically to forms of corporeal discipline, to any method of inflicting excessive pain as a form of punishment.

14. *Select Committee Report* [Judicial], p. 114.

15. *Parliamentary Debates*, 11 June 1857, column 1602.

16. Benjamin suggests that it is precisely this uncertain, liminal character of the police (understood as both form and function) that implicates law in the moment of founding or originary violence. Walter Benjamin, 'Critique of Violence', *Reflections: Essays, Aphorisms, Autobiographical Writings*, tr. Edmund Jephcott, New York: Schocken Books, 1978. In his lectures on governmentality and elsewhere, Foucault suggests that the modern, Western biopolitical state is characterized by an extraordinary reliance on the police function. Michel Foucault 'Governmentality', in Graham Burchell, Colin Gordon, and Peter Miller (eds), *The Foucault Effect: Studies in Governmentality*, Chicago, IL: University of Chicago Press, 1991.

17. Column 1607, House of Commons, 11 June 1857.

18. Ibid., Column 1610. See Nicholas Dirks, 'The Policing of Tradition: Colonialism and Anthropology in Southern India', *Comparative Studies in Society and History* 39(1): 182–212, 1997; Sanjay Nigam, 'Disciplining and Policing the "Criminals by Birth" ', *Indian Economic and Social History Review* 37(1): 131–64, 1990a; Sanjay Nigam, 'The Development of a Disciplinary System, 1871–1900', *Indian Economic and Social History Review* 37(3): 257–88, 1990; Singha; Rajeswari Sunder Rajan, *Real and Imagined Women*, London: Routledge, 1993.

19. See Peers for details regarding the socio-political situation of Madras Presidency that prompted the report, in addition to details about the problematic position of the colonial police force in British India. D.M. Peers, 'Torture, the Police and the Colonial State in Madras Presidency, 1816–1855', *Criminal Justice History* 12:29–56, 1991. Singha argues that the *Report* solidified racial distinctions between British and native; that the 'primary address was to the British public, to reassure them that the natives could not possibly believe that the European functionaries condoned torture', Singha 1998: 305.

20. The *Report* assumes special importance when attempts at reform such as the Select Committee Report, the 1837 Draft Penal Code, and criticisms of local policing practices can be viewed as having reconfigured the relationship of law to truth, so that evidence and confession came to occupy a radically different place in the adjudication of crime. The *Report*'s indictment of judicial functionaries was sidelined, and the focus rested on how to produce credible evidence. As I suggest in my analysis of Gunnoo's torture, it was the *quality of truth* that was significant, and not the indictment of those who administered justice.

21. The Bombay government mooted the idea of a similar report for Bombay, maintaining that Regulations XII and XIII, Chapter 1, Sections 8–10 of 1827 covered cases of bribery, extortion, and other abuse of police authority. However, the Bombay government appointed a special torture commissioner for a short period.

22. Ranajit Guha, 'The Prose of Counter-insurgency', in Ranajit Guha and Gayatri Spivak (eds), *Select Subaltern Studies*, New York: Oxford University Press, 1988.

23. David Arnold, *Police Power and Colonial Rule: Madras 1859–1947*, Delhi: Oxford University Press, 1986.

24. H.K. Fukazawa, *The Medieval Deccan: Peasants, Social Systems and States, Sixteenth to Eighteenth Centuries*, Delhi: Oxford University Press, 1991; Sumit Guha; V.S. Kadam, 'The Institution of Marriage and the Position of Women in Eighteenth Century Maharashtra', *Indian Economic and Social History Review* 25(3): 341–70, 1988.

25. Benjamin; Critique of Violence; Fanon Wretched of the Earth.

26. The *Sudder Foujdari Adalat* deliberated the case on 17 January, 28 March, 4 April, 2 May, and 16 May 1855.

27. The testimony of Gunnoo's aunt became useful in this context. She remembered that Gunnoo had complained of stomach-ache due to piles a month earlier, and noted that he had looked weak.

28. The medical board argued that medical jurisprudence was part of the training of medical officers in the Company's service, and there was no reason to recommend further training.

29. Turquand was commended by the government for his thorough investigation of the case and for alerting the Sessions Court about its importance, while Woodward was characterized as remiss in conducting a thorough investigation.

30. In his minute, however, Puisne Judge Remington suggested that the evidence did not clearly indict the policemen. The eyewitness account also contrasts with Alexander Bell's statement that Gunnoo had looked alright when he saw him at the well.

31. The medical board argued that there was no want of knowledge exhibited by Dr Pelly, who had examined the victim; that he had not been directly asked by the Sessions Judge about the cause of death, but had reported that Gunnoo's rectum was extended, which could either have meant that it was open, or swollen. It was the Sessions Judge who had not asked Pelly which one it was in this instance. Letter of 14 September 1855.

32. This deposition was not included in the Sessions Court proceedings as it was said to be the same as the one recorded the following day.

33. The court noted that contrary to Bhow's claim to having been informed about Gunnoo's condition on the night of 10 August, he had been informed at 4 p.m. that afternoon. He only went in the next morning to see Gunnoo. The court also faulted Bhow for waiting until 12 August to send Gunnoo to hospital.

34. This is very different from the trials of ordeal, divine intervention, and other forms of punishment that Gune mentions as prevalent in Maharashtra from 1300 to 1800. Sumit Guha's work on precolonial Maharashtra suggests that the types of punishment administered for crime more often than not bore little resemblance to the methods prescribed by Sanskrit texts on *dandaniti*, or penal law. He argues that the thoroughly political and decentralized character of punishment—i.e., the sovereign was not the only person who had the capacity to punish—was reflected in the extent to which forms of punishment remained uncodified and therefore open to bargaining and negotiation. 'The individual lived in several penal jurisdictions apart from that of the king and his ministers; he or she might be subject to punishment in various degrees by the caste, the village community, the chief of the merchants, the preceptor [*dharmadikari*] and the head of the family', Sumit Guha 'An Indian Penal Regime' 1995: 110.

35. Talal Asad, 'On Torture, or Cruel, Inhuman, and Degrading Treatment', in Arthur Kleinman, Veena Das, and Margaret Lock (eds), *Social Suffering*, Delhi: Oxford University Press, 1988: 288.

36. Dirks, 'Policing of Tradition'; Lata Mani, *Contentious Traditions: The Debate on Sati in Colonial India*, Berkeley: University of California Press, 1998.

37. This is Foucault's point in *Discipline and Punish: The Birth of the Prison*, New York: Vintage Books, 1995. Rejali argues that torture is essentially modern, that it is a practice integral to the security state. He suggests that this turns Foucault's argument on its head. Darius Rejali, *Torture and Modernity: Self, Society, and State in Modern Iran*, Boulder, CO: Westview Press, 1994. Asad argues that Rejali misunderstands Foucault's argument for a shift in the very conception of power, rather than the sublation of one set of practices (torture) by more rational ones. He rightly suggests that torture's power emanates from the secrecy surrounding its practice, but I would go a little further still, and argue that it is the method of making torture nevertheless visible, its status as open or public secret, from whence it derives its power.

38. The development of medical jurisprudence was influenced by the systems of justice that obtained in Britain and the Continent. In the latter instance, the body occupied a critical place in the highly adversarial and inquisitorial judicial system. This made for the development of an elaborate medical knowledge of wounds and injuries supported by the state in the form of generous remuneration for medico-legal expertise. 'Indeed, Continental writings on forensic medicine can be considered subspecies of the legal literature on proof and procedure'. In England medical jurisprudence began to develop only after 1800. Initial developments in medical jurisprudence can be traced to Scotland, where the first Chair of medical jurisprudence was established at the University of Edinburgh in 1807. A similar Chair was established in

Glasgow only in 1839, though medical jurisprudence had been taught extramurally at the Portland Street Medical School since 1826 Crawford, 'Legalising Medicine', p. 99 and *passim*.

39. Photography, first used in India in 1840, fingerprinting technology used by the police by 1891, and the pseudo-science of anthropometry extended the reach of this scopic regime even further, convinced that the capture of external traits provided a significant indication of deeper structures of vice and depravity. See Pinney on the significance of these visual signs. Christopher Pinney, *Camera Indica: The Social Life of Indian Photographs*, Chicago, IL: University of Chicago Press, 1998.

40. Rejali argues that torture by police and military forces is coeval with the modern exercise of power. Documents regarding torture and other human rights abuses in Algeria, Israel, Latin America, Northern Ireland, and South Africa, to name a few obvious instances, confirm both the secrecy that accompanies the practice of torture, and the extent to which the police and military draw on a shared repertoire of torture instruments and methods. Rejali, *Torture and Modernity*.

41. Foucault (1991) refers to the police as a critical component in the elaboration and control of population, the primary means through which disciplinary power manifests itself in the guise of 'security'. In these instances policing functions as a concept metaphor for thinking about the work of a disciplinary regime modelled on the police form. Foucault, 'Governmentality'.

42. Michel Foucault, *The History of Sexuality*, New York: Vintage Books, 1990.

43. Michael Ignatieff, *A Just Measure of Pain: The Penitentiary in the Industrial Revolution, 1750–1850*, New York: Pantheon Books, 1978.

44. I am grateful to Rajeswari Sunder Rajan for alerting me to this.

45. In Gunnoo's case, the state understood his drowning Syee as a crime against the state.

ADDITIONAL REFERENCES

Agamben, Giorgio, *Homo Sacer: Sovereign Power and Bare Life,* tr. Daniel Heller-Roazen, Stanford, CA: Stanford University Press, 1998.

Amery, Jean, *At the Mind's Limit: Contemplations by a Survivor on Auschwitz and Its Realities*, tr. Sidney Rosenfeld and Stella P. Rosenfeld, New York: Schocken Books, 1986.

Ballhatchet, Kenneth, *Social Policy and Social Change in Western India: 1817–1830*, London: Oxford University Press, 1957.

Burchell, Graham, Colin Gordon, and Peter Miller (eds), *The Foucault Effect: Studies in Governmentality*, Chicago, IL: University of Chicago Press, 1991.

Burney, Ian A., *Bodies of Evidence: Medicine and the Politics of the English Inquest, 1830–1926*, Baltimore, MD: Johns Hopkins University Press, 2000.

Chatterjee, B., 'Cornwallis and the Emergence of Colonial Police', *Bengal Past and Present*, July–December: 1–11, 1983.

Cheah, Pheng, and Elisabeth Grosz, 'The Body of the Law: Notes towards a Theory of Corporeal Justice', in Pheng Cheah, David Fraser, and Judith Gorbich (eds), *Thinking Through the Body of the Law*, New York: New York University Press, 1996.

Cox, Edmund, *Police and Crime in India*, New Delhi: Manu Publications, 1976. Originally published 1910.

Dandaviveka of Vardhamana Upadhyaya, tr. Bhabatosh Bhattacharya, Calcutta: The Asiatic Society, 1973.

Das, Veena, 'Language and Body: Transactions in the Construction of Pain', in Arthur Kleinman, Veena Das, and Margaret Lock (eds), *Social Suffering*, Delhi: Oxford University Press, 1998.

Derrida, Jacques, 'Force of Law', in Drucilla Cornell, Michael Rosenfeld, and David Gray Carlson (eds), *Deconstruction and the Possibility of Justice*, New York: Routledge, 1992.

DuBois, Page, *Torture and Truth*, New York: Routledge, 1991.

Montstuart Elphinstone, *Selections from the Minutes and Other Official Writings of the Honourable Monstuart Elphinstone, Governor of Bombay*, ed. G.W. Forrest, London: Richard Bentley and Son, (1884) 1821.

Fisch, Jorg, *Cheap Lives and Dear Limbs: The British Transformation of the Bengal Criminal Law, 1769–1817*, Wiesbaden: Franz Steiner Verlag, 1983.

Percival Griffith, *To Guard My People: The History of the Indian Police*, London: Benn, 1971.

Guha, Ranajit, 'Torture and Culture', *Frontier* (23 January): 9–15, 1971.

Hanson, Elizabeth, 'Torture and Truth in Renaissance England', *Representations* 34: 53–84, 1991.

Kaplan, Martha, 'Panopticon in Poona: An Essay on Foucault and Colonialism', *Cultural Anthropology* 10(1): 85–98, 1995.

Langbein, John H., *Torture and the Law of Proof*, Chicago, IL: University of Chicago Press, 1977.

Minow, Martha, *Between Vengeance and Forgiveness: Facing History after Genocide and Mass Violence*, Boston, MA: Beacon Press, 1998.

Rosalmid, O'Hanton, 'Issues of Widowhood: Gender and Resistance in Colonial Western India', in Douglas Haynes and Gyan Prakash (eds), *Contesting Power: Resistance and Everyday Social Relations in South Asia*, Berkeley: University of California Press, 1992.

Police Torture and Murder in Bengal. Reports of Two Trials of the Police of the District of Burdwan in August and September 1860, confirmed by the Sudder Nizamut, Calcutta: Savielle and Cranenburgh Printers, 1861.

Rao, V.D., 'A Note on the Police of the City of Poona', *Journal of Indian History* 36: 223–8, 1958.

Report of the Commissioners for the Investigation of Alleged Cases of Torture in the Madras Presidency, Submitted to the Right Honourable Governor-in-Council of Fort Saint-George, Madras: Fort St George Gazette Press, 1855.

Roy, Sripati, *Customs and Customary Law in British India*, Delhi: Mittal Publications, 1986. Originally published 1910.

Steele, Arthur, *The Hindu Castes: Their Law, Religion and Customs*, Delhi: Mittal Publications, 1986.

Wagle, Narendra K., 'A Dispute between the Pancal Devajna Sonars and the Brahmans of Iune regarding Social Rank and Ritual Privileges: A Case Study in the British Administration of Jati Laws in Maharashtra, 1822–1825', in Narendra K. Wagle (ed.), *Images of Maharashtra: A Regional Profile of India*, London: Curzon Press, 1980.

Welsh, Alexander, 'The Evidence of Things not Seen: Justice Stephen and Bishop Butler', *Representations* 22: 60–88, 1988.

FIVE

Tragedy, Irony, and Modernity

Sudipta Kaviraj

இ৳৵৵৩

Irony could not develop before the age of reflection, because it is constructed from something false which by means of reflection disguises itself behind a mask of truth.

Vico

A civilization develops over a long history something like a grammar of vision, an optics on which its aesthetic practice is based. Artists and their audiences see objects in the world, the world itself, its various possibilities through that grammar of seeing. This can perhaps be clarified by an analogy with painting. It is like a palette of primary colours which constitute a structure which restricts and forms possibilities at the same time. Traditions of high culture develop in this manner a palette of feelings, sentiments, ways of describing, feeling, perceiving things of the world.

There is no universally admissible, neutral manner of seeing the social world, the view from nowhere; there cannot be a view that is not of a certain kind. This optics of the literary field is created by aesthetic traditions—usually a complex mixture of explicit and unannounced preferences, ways of shaping things by giving forms, names, destinies which are always at work within the work of authors. It goes without saying that though these are deep structures, with all that this implies, these are not beyond history. Historical requirements affect and transform them, though these demands are neither constant nor linear, happening everyday or in a specific direction. Aesthetics are in the nature of structures of resources which are always available for individual crafting; and through the pressures of such crafting of resources to demands, new items are added to aesthetic structures or their forms are changed. The celebrated Indian term for this grammar is of course the theory of *rasa*: Indian aesthetic uses a palette of the nine primary rasas as its basic generative structure. But the grammar is a historical thing and presupposes a world. The theory of rasas emerged from reflection and perception in a certain kind of world, where objects and possibilities were structured in a specific way. The world that emerged from colonial contact and the sensibility that this generated was fundamentally different. It is this peculiar position in a world that is being historically reconstructed which forced reflexivity upon artists and writers of the period. Bankimchandra was an artist of tradition in a very technical sense. His palette was a traditional one of the primary rasa structure. Often it is easy to describe his tropes, the specific literary operations taking place within his texts, entirely in terms of traditional *alankara* terms—*upama, utpreksa, yamaka, vyajastuti,* even the most conventional of these stylistic features, the *anuprasa.* Yet his art was entirely different from that of his successful contemporaries many of whom had chosen objects, styles, or compositions which, in a world of invading modernity, still sought to retain a whole, unfractured aesthetic tradition. Turning their backs to the historical changing world, they could take refuge in traditional composition. Some, like Vidyasagar, experimented with a new language, though still seeking legitimacy from its obvious kinship with sonorous Sanskrit. But none took the risk, the enormous danger, of turning round and facing the world of modernity with that traditional palette in hand. Vidyasagar's objects of aesthetic depiction and narrative were Sita, Shakuntala, figures who were traditionally depicted by that palette.[1] Thus the characteristic poses, the moods, the emotions suited the palette. Bankim chose figures of a different kind, either living in modernity or thinly living in the past but already experiencing modern forms of suffering, a whole world of emotions, moods, poses, situations that were not formerly the task of this palette to analyse or portray. I think that was why Bankimchandra's art could find no serious imitator or successor,[2] but still has the power of all genuine origins, their ambiguity, their mixture, their duality, their intrinsically transient character. He was neither of this world, nor of the other; yet his art was in a sense adequate to the complexities of both. His aesthetic can be set against that of classical Sanskrit literature and, at the same time, that of the modern. For most other artists in the Bengali language such a double comparison would be wholly inappropriate. Vidyasagar's characters experience traditional emotions of *vatsalya, karuna,* etc., not the indescribable emotions of modernity. Tagore's figures not only experience the new emotions, but have found a new language in which to adequately express themselves. They have been given a new palette. Only in Bankim is the world new, and the palette old. And this transient adequacy gave to his art an indescribable and incomparable dignity. This is why Bankimchandra fashioned the Bengali sense of modernity, because he was the first to teach them to wonder at this phenomenon of history reflexively. He was the first to create something like the rasa of modernity, for which the earlier primary colours of the palette of feelings was inadequate. To contend with the structure of feeling that modernity created in this world slowly growing aesthetically unfamiliar, he had to mix and experiment with rasas. The eventual rasa of modernity, if we can so call it, is fundamentally tragic, and it mixes two primary colours which traditional aesthetics never brought into contact. These are the moods of tragedy and laughter.

In terms of narrative form as well, Bankim relied quite openly and heavily on the resources of traditional Indian aesthetics. His narratives were called novels but were actually structured more like traditional dramas or narratives. His irony of the babu and the world of colonial powerlessness uses constantly and with consummate skill the earlier forms of the vyajastuti. Even his material depictions of nature, or his physical description of women, come straight out of an aesthetic canon which goes back into ancient texts and is at the same time solidly present in the folk optics of nature and femininity, both *prakriti* to classical theory. At the same time, the taste of Bankim's aesthetic is unquestionably modern. In Bankim's efforts to create this new aesthetic the most significant element, because it is also the most contradictory, is his use of irony. Classical Sanskrit and early Bengali literature[3] had long and powerful precedents of poetic compositions of intricate irony. He assumed and extended this line in one sense. Yet, what he did with it, the way he extended and added on to it, the way he made it perform new functions of meaning are astonishingly modern. Irony and self-irony are indeed very close and enormously distant. The literary or stylistic techniques are common, the rasa is radically distinct. Self-irony is both a crowning achievement of irony and an overturning of its conventional form.

Traditional societies often find the identity of others puzzling, to puzzle about the self is an unmistakably modern form of reflection. Settled traditional societies were marked by an assumed sense of self which was rarely a matter of debate and, except in some rare occurrences, never a matter of personal intellectual search or deliberate construction. To construct an identity is an essentially modern activity, and it is part of a history which offers various possibilities of existence for individuals and groups. In a fundamental sense both individuals and groups can, under philosophical conditions of modernity, choose what they would like to be.

The modern absorption with the self has some interesting and contradictory aspects. Thinking about the self is always mildly narcissistic, it gives consideration of the problems of the self great significance but it also implies the necessity of a certain detachment. To look at a face in a mirror is still a project of distancing and detachment, and detachment implies in its train the existence of different possible ways of constructing the self and a life that tries actively to fashion the self's form.

Formerly, intellectuals often described and reflected about why other people were different. European travellers and chroniclers did not merely observe the strange customs of other cultures but also made interesting hypotheses about the reasons for these. Al Biruni, to take an outstanding example from the Indian tradition, speculated about the Brahmanical ways of the Hindus. But typically, neither the Europeans nor the Arabs or the Indians worried about what they were themselves or presented it to themselves as an intellectual problem. Being something was taken for granted, at least it was not considered problematic; it was the being of the other, how people could be different from what people should normally be like, which raised problems.

To turn the self into a problem, either philosophically or sociologically, is a wholly modern idea. And to discover the self is a potentially tragic process. Through the process of reflexiveness, the self is tormented by desire and failure, by its increasing sense of inadequacy, assailed by desires to become something other than what it at this moment is. It can be claimed that Bankim is the first writer in Bengali, and surely one of the first in any Indian language, to turn the self into a problem and investigate its possibilities of construction. He is also one of the very early thinkers to appreciate its historicity, the fact that people can become what they wish to be and not merely stay what they immediately are.

I wish to suggest that it is this reflection on the self as a construct which directs Bankim to his distinctive style of humour. It is a commonplace that Bankim is one of the great writers of humour in the Bengali language. But humour can exist in literary works in many different forms, and to understand what it really does for a particular author it is important to find out in exactly what specific way it exists in his art. In both the literary traditions that Bankim knew, variety is greatly applauded. Modern Western fictional traditions which Bankim knew encouraged the mixing of humour both in the seeing of the world and the telling of the story. Classical Indian literary doctrine was, if anything, even more explicit about the great merits of mixed compositions. The theory of the *Natyasastra*, for instance, encourages mixtures between different primary artistic modes like dance, vocal music, drama. It also encourages the mixture of the rasas with the injunction to respect the difference between the *sthayi* and the *vyabhichari*, without which the work of art loses coherence of signification. Yet those mixtures were meant for pleasing the audience, enhancing the attraction and aesthetic value of the object of art. Bankim's humour arises from a different and, in my view, much deeper source, as the only recourse in his personal and historical predicament. Traditional theory uses fine distinctions between different aspects or forms of *hasya—upahasa, atihasa*.[4] Implicitly, this sort of differentiation of the rasa deploys an implicit norm of moderation, because *atihasita* is a mode of excess, whereas *upahasita* is a subtler way of using the margin of signification that is rendered possible by restraint, by way of understatements. Still, despite this enormously impressive palette of the hasyarasa, traditional forms of wit and humour were insufficient for Bankim, for the rasa or bhava of his historical and biographic experience, of loneliness, incomprehension by his contemporaries, the peculiar melancholy of living in an alienating and intractable history, of an overwhelming feeling of unfulfilment, and the sorrows of discovering the self. It is this predicament—of a self which could not be justified but yet could not be condemned simply because it was too close, inalienable, too dear, simply because it was the self—which makes him look for techniques of transforming the earlier aesthetic of humour into the new, somewhat darker form. Bankim in many ways invents self-irony as the mode which is aesthetically adequate to modernity. Although Bankim made some crucial moves towards the formation of nationalist discourse, its object was still tentative, provisional, fragile in his imagination. He could not draw from it the kind of assurance that later nationalists drew, which meant that they did not require irony to the same extent. They had sorted out the contradictions, or could robustly pretend that these had disappeared. Thus given their disposition to the social and historical world, they did not require irony towards the self; indeed, they suppressed any irruption of doubts as to the seriousness and justifiability of this enterprise.

It is also a commonplace that Bankimchandra was one of the creators of the imaginative world of the modern Bengali. He does not look very successful if we try to count his followers. He led no movement. He founded no church. He did not announce a new political utopia. His contributions to the forming of the Bengali world of modernity are, I have tried to argue, far deeper. Though he did not shape ideas themselves, he shaped the medium with which ideas are made. His own perception of modernity might not have found favour with many, but he gave to the modern Bengali the palette with which it became possible, for the first time, to paint intellectual and imaginative pictures of modernity. His contribution to Bengali literature is well known; what I have been concerned to argue is that he inaugurated a modern, mature form of historical self-reflection, and he shaped a language which had the richness, subtlety, variety, suppleness to engage in such a task, and since then, though transformed several times by others, this language has remained the most fundamental, if also the most invisible, instrument through which the Bengali has tried to cope with the mysteries of living in the peculiar historicity of modern times.

Inevitably, because of their historical context, most thinking Bengalis of his generation reflected on the causes of colonial subjection and the nature of British rule. Only a few, like Bhudev Mukhopadhyay, had the breadth of vision and the philosophical temperament to turn this engagement towards a theoretical reflection on modernity itself. Between the two of them, who were contemporaries, Bankimchandra's reflection had a greater dramatic quality, because of his gradual revision of his earlier enthusiasm for rationalist doctrines—he had a most agitated, tense, self-correcting self to contend with. Bhudev was saved from the necessity of irony about the self by the relative stability and consistency of his views. Since Bankim changed his own views, there is a subtle necessity of tempering the criticism by humour, because on both sides of the ideological divide, in the person who criticized and the person who was the object of this criticism, between the man who attacked and undermined and the man who felt undermined, in a sense, was the same self, in its two temporal versions. His youthful views were not rejected by another person, but by the necessarily ironical mode of a later self. His irony is the direct opposite of Vico's—it could not have arisen before the age of reflection, but inside it is truth which expresses itself by assuming the disguise of falsehood.

Although irony is so evident and remarkable in Bankim's art, its predominant theme is not an engagement with the small embarrassments of the everyday but the movement of history, and his general sense of history is essentially tragic. Evidently, this kind of irony, though a form of humour and depending on the formal aesthetic of laughter, is quite compatible to the tragic sense of history so noticeable in his reflections on modernity. About modernity's dimensions, structures, and trends Bankimchandra's historical thought is admirably clear and unhesitating, but interestingly, it does not pretend that it is at all clear about the future. Bankim's considerable reading of contemporary European social theory—he was very familiar with Comte, Mill, and Spencer, and knew of Hegel and the French philosophers—had not persuaded him to accept any of the great philosophies of history and the assurance these uplifting narratives provided in the face of the fragility of things that modernity had brought about. His acuity of analysis of the present did not tempt him to declare that he saw the future with any degree of clarity—something that later nationalists of much less historical perspicuity announced without hesitation. Bankimchandra was therefore left with a peculiar vision of history. History was of the greatest significance because all things social were malleable, in flux, rendered provisional; it was consequently necessary to achieve a rational understanding of the process of the present as history. Yet it did not yield any clear picture of what would emerge in the future, except images of improbable utopian colour, captured in the complex symbolism of his obsessive dreams. There is particularly one sequence which appears often in varying forms, as a dream of some of his fictive characters, as a dream of his secret self—Kamalakanta. This is the image of a splendid golden icon tossed in the dark waters of time, again a traditional image, but most appropriate to his sense of modernity. History, the way he reflected on it and made it an object of serious reflection, was a wholly modern theme, but he had successfully derived from the great stock of images of the classical past its most appropriate symbolic image.

On the Darkness of History

In Bankim's writing, the question of British colonial administration was broadened, at the best points, into a question of modernity in general. And the question of modernity broadened, at the best points of his performance, into a philosophic reflection on time. It has been argued persuasively that modernity alters the nature of temporality.[5] From a cyclical repetitive ontology of time, European theoretical thought and later popular consciousness emerge by degrees into a conception of future time as an opportunity, as a broad field of creative activity in which natural and social things can be shaped according to collective human desires. The problem was not so much the plasticity of the social world, but rather the difficulty in arriving at some commonly accepted decision/project about what to do in that time.

In a very general way, modernity brings in an identical change in India, from a time that is given to a time that is made, that is, formerly, time is not seen as an opportunity in which well-conceived social or political projects can be carried through. Individual lives have to be lived, in dignity and humility, within terms which are forever set, over which human beings have no control, not to speak of sovereignty. Over a period of about a hundred years, this wholly passive attitude towards time changes into a conception far more active, occasionally superficial, oversimplified, hasty, unintelligently optimistic. But the steps and the exact context of this change were very different from the narrative of modern temporality in the West. The coming of the new time could not appear the same to Indians for two reasons. The optics or ontology of the world through which they saw the coming of modernity, what it unfolded in front of their interpreting minds, was also quite different. While modernity in Europe was primarily an experience of liberation, in India its main element was a narrative of subjection. Bankimchandra's work is interesting precisely because he shows how the earlier optics of time slowly gives way to the possibility of another.

In traditional Indian thought, time was a dark god, sometimes insufficiently distinct from death. Indeed, there is a peculiar indeterminacy, ambiguity in Indian thinking about the precise kind of reverence that is to be accorded to time. Time is evidently irresistible, its ravages inescapable for human lives, but this elicits a response that is more of awe than of regard. Time, kala, is thus given a peculiarly fearful reverence, because of its affinity to death. In traditional Indian consciousness, the metaphors of time are chosen in accord with this predominant sentiment. Time is a river, but a dark river, carrying everything towards an inescapable destruction (laya), finishing annulment, non-being. But this river of time carrying everything along does not surprise people with destruction. It does not do anything sudden, episodic, frightful in the sense of a catastrophe; it is the inevitable definition of life as being towards death. The waters in the river of time are dark, a metaphor appropriate in two ways: the traditional meaning was that time represents intractability, impenetrability, what it does is beyond control and comprehension. In Bankim, history is often related to this river of time. The dream sequence in Kamalakanta reveals what lies as it were in the cultural unconscious of the Bengali intellectual; the two most intense modern experiences of history and colonial subjection appear in this dream through their most appropriate traditional metaphors, of the mother goddess and of the dark waters of time. Kamalakanta sees, under the influence of opium, when truth reveals itself to him in the illusion of dream, that the idol of the motherland, golden and immeasurably precious, is being swept away in the terrifying dark river of time. Some new elements can be discerned in this use of metaphors—displacements to deal with the peculiar features of modernity. Formerly the river of time was merely dark, representing a cognitive impenetrability and a helplessness that all creatures share in. Now there is a clear suggestion of the waters of time getting turgid and muddy, so that the figure of the motherland is subjected to a greater defilement. And its helplessness is not the frailty of all creatures in the face of time, the intimation of mortality; it is the more cruel desertion by destiny, a fate of subjection to the power of others. Death is a great calamity, but it falls to everybody and is therefore a great leveller. Subjection, by contrast, is a bitter fate that falls to some, not to others. It causes a strange kind of bereavement, a strange and partial death; a people can observe the bereavement of its own liberty, mourn, paradoxically for itself.

In another way too Bankim is a figure hesitating at the gates of modernity, of traditional and modern story-telling and fictional aesthetics. Indeed it is possible to argue that there are two fictional aesthetics struggling in his art, of very different kinds, with very different ideas about what depiction in art is about, and who are the figures and actions that deserve the celebration of art. In most traditional cultures, such a figure would be heroic—of a type who is entirely in harmony with the values and ideals of his society and willing to make great sacrifices for them. It is this form of extraordinariness of individuals and their lives which were celebrated in traditional art. No doubt Bankimchandra himself created a number of such figures in his fictional art, though the world in which they live is almost always marked by some complexity. They are not in consonance with a world already given, but a world to be made and whose sanction already lies in the desire of the people around them. Of course, this too involves an idea inextricably connected with modernity, of the plasticity of the relations out of which the social world is made. These heroes create a new national order rather than re-establish one which had been temporarily ruptured, though, without doubt, this is often accompanied by a restorative rhetoric.

But I find something else in Bankimchandra's art which is even more decisively a product of modern consciousness: the perverse attractiveness of Kamalakanta as an extraordinary individual. *Kamalakanta*, I have argued, is quite central to Bankim's art, because it puts the question of colonial powerlessness at the centre of vision, as a nagging, unforgettable fact. But his figure is interesting not only because of his subtle and subliminal politics, but also for a purely artistic reason. If artistic attention is the mark of a hero, then Kamalakanta is certainly one in Bankim's fiction; and it is also true that the whole business of the world in the *daptar* revolves around him. The world unfolds to us through his eyes. And he is not only the master in this world of words, in the fictional world of action, in the court drama too he is the central figure, because he faces the court in a doubly unequal battle. On one side, he is a single, entirely lonely individual against the whole structure of colonial justice. On the other hand, he is not alone, he has the support of a huge historic civilization; all its subtlety, intelligence, evasiveness, refinement are given to him to exploit and embody for this single occasion, because he has made the terrible choice, to be its representative, against all odds. On this level, of course, his adversaries are unevenly matched with him; their culture is shallow, imitative, insecure, inauthentic. He answers their questions with the assurance of an intelligence of a thousand years.

The astonishingly modern quality of Kamalakanta lies in the fact of his being an anti-hero, a hero who is a congeries of totally negative qualities but this heroism being still an act of deliberate choice. In fact, he accomplishes the most amazing series of displacements in the aesthetic of fictional figures. Kamalakanta is not a success in any conceivable sense at all in terms of earlier, more straightforward aesthetics. Indeed, he is unlike the heroes typical of traditional narrative forms—unlike the colourful figures of Bankimchandra's own fictional works, unlike the more problematized heroes of later high Bengali novels including Tagore, unlike again some of the types created by Saratchandra Chattopadhyay drawing upon the slightly inverse heroism of the terrorists, at once mysterious, dangerous, attractive to the middle class. The obliqueness with which Kamalakanta stands is much more radical, unamenable to the standard technique of being redeemed by the love of women, who represent the disinterested, uncorrupted higher intelligence of this society, as happened to the terrorists in the novels. Though shunned by middle-class society, the terrorists' ability to attract the admiration of women showed the possibility of standards by which they could be redeemed to more straightforward norms of fictive glory. Their return to unremarkable domesticity, the site of normalcy and acquiescence in norms, is simply narratively unreported. Kamalakanta is unamenable to this mildly deviant formula of Bengali fiction; his obliqueness, his ability to remain unreconciled, is far more radical than the practical violence of the terrorist figures, than their cult of radicalism of the act. Kamalakanta is wedded entirely to the principle of radicalism of thought, the radicalism of daring to think unlike everyone else. He is the single great hero of uncompromising critical thought that high Bengali literature of the early period produced—desolate, incomparable, inimitable in his peculiarity, ceaselessly lamenting the fate of subalternity, reflecting the darkness of history, but not allowing that to reduce his enjoyment of the comic spectacle of the everyday. He lives in a world of laughter framed in a subtle and unstated sorrowfulness. He is a character in Bengali literature without a forerunner or a successor, and in that sense the most interesting figure in Bankimchandra's art. There is no other way to understand Bankimchandra except to understand the laughter and darkness in the world of Kamalakanta.

Can we make some coherent sense of all that I have said about Bankimchandra Chattopadhyay? What kind of a person was he? What sort of historical discourse did he live within? Historical remembrance is a notoriously mixed fact; being remembered is a process of the accretion of meanings on to texts. Texts are not merely set in history in a broad sense, they also set in motion little histories themselves. What sort of history did Bankim set in motion, or contribute to? It is often seen as an obligatory task of the history of ideas to look with persistence for the 'coherence' of a mind. It is interesting to see why minds like Bankim's, with their opulent gifts, found it hard to decide to be coherent.

All history is contradictory, but not in the same sense or to the same extent. The history of colonial societies is ridden with contradiction in particularly fundamental ways. The puzzlements of colonial intellectuals arose from the unmerciful way history offered them the gift of modernity, in a way in which it was inextricably related to a destiny of subjection. Unlike as in Europe, modernity came to India in the form of a primarily external proposal as a theory and an external agenda as practice. The Enlightenment, for all its later complexities, had begun with a 'happy' history in Europe. Its authors were happy writers, for its protagonists saw the processes of modernity as one which spread liberty across social life. The historical situation of the colonial writer was tragic because of the unjustness of the choices facing him. If he chose modernity, he had to choose subjection as its condition, or so it appeared to him. If he chose autonomy, he had modernity as a necessary price. These two positions developed into two separate discourses, which made exchanges across their boundaries increasingly difficult.

Most intellectuals decided to think in and through one of these discursive forms—the young Bengal with modernity, indigenists with the discourses of tradition, and in the peculiar cultural history of colonial Bengal, it required a certain kind of courage to speak either discourse. But for both there was at least the assurance of an appointed discursive space, with their common arguments, languages, and set audiences. Some, like Bankim, failed or refused to make the choice and saw the structure of this choice itself as tragic. Their intellectual positions were bound to be more lonely than the others'. Hemmed in between two large circles of discourse which sought to deny them any space, what they said was constantly in danger of being assimilated into one of the two dominant forms. They had to struggle constantly against such assimilation. Their inability to turn decisively away from the two sides of their history, their continual interrogation of both, condemned them to a form of 'unhappy consciousness'. Their solution was to remain contradictory in their consciousness, for to be consistent was not to be open to all the human possibilities that history had placed before them.

The gift of history, bestowed by a modern Western education, appeared to them a deeply ambiguous one. They had learnt from it to think of their lives—singly and collectively—in the frame of linear time, and in terms of the rational capacity to construct the present and future. But in their condition, this made a self-conscious existence more difficult. History must have appeared to them a strange mixture of disclosure and concealment captured in Hegel's phrase, the hieroglyph of reason.

There is a peculiar relation of adequacy between the experience of this history and the kind of literary art that Bankim created. Alternating between a tragic fiction and a comic commentary, a view of the world filled with darkness and a view of the everyday filled with laughter, attracted to both rationalism and its critiques, both enlightenment and religion, tormented by the choice between subjection and modernity, he had discovered a way of dealing with all this complexity in irony. Irony allowed the contradictions of the world to be retained without recourse to a reducing consistency. Between its solemnity and travesty, its darkness and laughter, he had fashioned a language that was adequate to express the sense of the world as it appeared to his particular unhappy consciousness.

NOTES

1. Compare, for instance, Vidyasagar's texts, *Sakuntala and Sitar Banabas*.
2. However, a number of people tried to copy his success, like Damodar Mukhopadhyay's sequels to his famous novels in *Mrnmayi* and *Nababnandini*. In a general sense, of course even authors like R.C. Dutt could be called his imitators, but they do not produce a body of artistic work which forms a totality with an internal coherence, and which could be called a distinctive form.
3. Before Bankim several distinguished writers had engaged in satirical compositions on the Bengali social world; Iswarchandra Gupta was the best known among them.
4. After the great canonical text of the *Natyasastra*, most others make fine distinctions between different forms of *smita* and *hasita*. The *Rasatarangini* of Bhanudatta, a text influenced by the *vyapti* ideas of *nyaya*, makes distinctions between *vihasita, upahasita, apahasita, atihasita*, etc. They also make a distinction between *svanistha* or *atmastha* and *paranistha* or *parastha*. Bhanudatta, *Rasatarangini* (ed. Devdutt Kaushik), New Delhi: Munshiram Manoharlal, 1980: 128ff. But this form of *atmastha* humour is quite distinct from Bankim's self-irony.
5. Most persuasively argued by Reinhart Koselleck in *Futures Past*, Cambridge, MA: MIT Press, 1985: 3–20.

SIX

Communities and the Nation

Partha Chatterjee

❧⳾✦⳾❧

Kamalakanta had been called in as a witness in court in a case of petty theft. Both magistrate and counsel were eager to get on to his testimony, but the preliminaries were proving to be difficult, since Kamalakanta, with the extreme analytical skills found only among the mad, had raised a series of unanswerable objections to the oath he was required to take. Finally, those difficulties had somehow been overcome and the identity of the witness was being recorded.

> The lawyer then asked him, 'What jati are you?'
> K: Am I a jati?
> Lawyer: What jati do you belong to?
> K: To the Hindu jati.
> Lawyer: Oh, come now! What varna?
> K: A very very dark varna.
> Lawyer: What the hell is going on here! Why did I have to call a witness like this? I say, do you have *jat?*
> K: Who can take it from me?
> The magistrate saw that the lawyer was getting nowhere. He said, 'You know there are many kinds of jati among the Hindus, such as Brahman, Kayastha, Kaibarta. Which one of these jati do you belong to?'
> K: My lord! All this is the lawyer's fault! He can see I have the sacred thread around my neck. I have said my name is Chakravarti. How am I to know that he will still not be able to deduce that I am a Brahman?
> The magistrate wrote, 'Caste: Brahman'.[1]

Those who know Kamalakanta will recall how, in Bankim's trenchant narration, he shows up, with his madman's logic, the utter madness of all the claims to rationality made on behalf of colonial reason.[2] In this particular piece, Bankim uses Kamalakanta's uncolonizable voice to mock the trappings of colonial justice, including the way in which it required an unambiguous classification of caste to locate and fix the identity of the colonial subject. Kamalakanta here does not dwell very long on the ambiguities that the 'modern' forms of social knowledge face when confronted with a term such as *jati*. But we can already guess that those ambiguities will, in fact, be literally endless.

THE MANIFOLD USES OF JATI

Consider the ways in which the word jati can be used in any modern Indian language. I take as an example the word as used in Bengali. Pick up any standard Bengali dictionary and look through the entries under jati. (It would be useful to remember that these dictionaries themselves have been compiled according to European models so as to conform to the requirements of modern forms of knowledge.) It will first give the Sanskrit etymology of the word: *yan* (to originate, to be born) + *ti*, a noun that literally means 'birth', 'origin'. This will be followed typically by at least a dozen different senses in which the word can be used. Jnanendramohan Das, for instance, lists, among others, the following:

1. *jati* as origin, such as Musalman by birth, Vaisnav by birth, a beggar by birth [*jatite musalman, jatbhikhari*]
2. classes of living species, such as human *jati*, animal *jati*, and bird *jati*.
3. *varna* following from classifications according to *guna* and *karma*, such as Brahman.
4. *vamsa, gotra, kula* [lineage, clan], such as Arya *jati*, Semitic *jati*.
5. human collectivities bound by loyalty to a state or organized around the natural and cultural characteristics of a country or province [Jnanendramohan adds in English 'nation; race'], such as English, French, Bengali, Punjabi, Japanese and Gujarati.[3]

Let us pass over the other, technical, uses of the word in logic, grammar, music, rhetoric, and the like, and concentrate on these—its uses as a category of social classification. Haricharan Bandyopadhyay lists most of the above uses but adds, curiously, to (3)—the sense in which jati is used to denote 'caste' in Indian sociology—a derivation from the Persian *zat*.[4] Jnanendramohan too takes note of this alternative derivation but restricts it to the non-Sanskritic word *jat*, presumed to be a corruption of jati and used in Bengali in all of the first three senses. Finally, in order to clarify our criteria for translation (since, in this particular case, we are discussing the terms of political discourse in India in the English language), let us note that a Sanskrit-Bengali-English trilingual dictionary gives as the English equivalents of jati the following: 'species, caste, birth, family, universals'.[5]

Between (1) and (5) above, the range of meanings available to the word *jati* is immense. It is not surprising that Kamalakanta in court should have found it so easy to play around with the word. Indeed, he could have gone on endlessly, describing himself as belonging to the human jati, the Indian jati, the Bengali jati, the jati of madmen, even (one suspects, with some degree of pride) the jati of opium addicts. One could, obviously and without any contradiction, belong to several jati, not simultaneously but contextually, invoking in each context a collectivity in which membership is not a matter of self-interested individual choice or contractual agreement but an immediate inclusion, originary, as it is by birth. We should not be surprised therefore when political discourse permits the imagining of collective solidarities to slide from one particular form to another, each activated contextually but proclaiming each time a bond of kinship, a natural bond that unites all who share the same origin and who therefore must share the same destiny.

Consider the form of imaginative construction of large political solidarities through the union of several jati. ...Bhudeb Mukhopadhyay is giving us his picture of the nationalist utopia emerging out of a counterfactual past.[6] In the grand council that meets after the new emperor of India has been crowned, the following proposal is made:

Although India is the true motherland only of those who belong to the Hindu jati and although only they have been born from her womb, the Musalmans are not unrelated to her any longer. She has held them at her breast and reared them. Musalmans are therefore her adopted children.

Can there be no bonds of fraternity between two children of the same mother, one a natural child and the other adopted? There certainly can; the laws of every religion admit this. There has now been born a bond of brotherhood between Hindus and Musalmans living in India.   .

Remember that for Bhudeb Indian nationalism is synonymous with Hindu nationalism. But he is also a nationalist of a perfectly modern kind, because in this imaginary council a constitution is promulgated more or less along the lines of the German Reich, with strongly protectionist economic policies which succeed, in this anti-colonial utopia, in keeping the European economic powers at bay. Yet in order to think of a nation that includes both Hindu and Musalman jati, albeit under the leadership of Hindus, Bhudeb has to use the language of kinship.

Nevertheless, this imputation of kinship is clearly contextual. Bhudeb would have been horrified if, for instance, someone had appealed to these imputed affinal ties to make a case, let us say, for marriage between Hindus and Muslims or, for that matter, for eating the same food. Identities and solidarities within the language of jati are contextually defined. The language affords the possibility of imagining new bonds of affinity, but it does this precisely by imposing restrictions on their free flow. There are no substantive affinities that define identity regardless of context.

It is political discourse of the modern kind which insists that these collectivities have a fixed, determinate form, and, if there are several to which an individual can belong, that there be a priority among them, so that it becomes imperative to ask: 'Are you a Muslim first or a Bengali first?' 'Are you a Bengali first or an Indian first?' Since these are questions that recur constantly in contemporary political discourse in India, we must ask what it is that seeks to erase the contextuality of a concept such as jati and give it the fixity that was demanded of Kamalakanta in court.

COMMUNITIES: FUZZY AND ENUMERATED

Sudipta Kaviraj has recently argued that a fundamental change effected in the discursive domain of modern politics in the colonial period was the impoverishment of the earlier 'fuzzy' sense of the community and an insistence upon the identification of community in the 'enumerable' sense.[7] Earlier, communities were fuzzy, in the sense that, first, a community did not claim to represent or exhaust all the layers of selfhood of its members and, second, the community, though definable with precision for all practical purposes of social interaction, did not require its members to ask how many of them there were in the world. The colonial regime, once firmly in place in the second half of the nineteenth century, sought to fashion the conceptual instruments of its control over an alien population precisely by enumerating the diverse communities that, in the colonial imagination, constituted the society over which it had been destined by history to rule. Bernard Cohn, in a well-known piece, has shown how caste and religion became established both conceptually and instrumentally as the 'sociological keys' to the numerical description of Indian society.[8] That this classificatory scheme did not reside exclusively in the colonial imagination is also documented by Cohn, because it shaped in turn the subsequent forms of mobilization seeking representation in the state domain—representation, that is, by caste or religion.

To us, situated on this side of the divide represented by postcolonial politics and poststructuralist theory, the move by a colonial power toward the enumeration of Indian society by ethnic communities seems almost natural. One of the fundamental elements in the colonial conceptualization of India as a 'different' society was the fixed belief that the population was a mélange of communities. The conservative opinion said to have dominated imperial policy in the post-Mutiny decades considered this an irredeemable racial characteristic: it was foolish to think that Western education would somehow improve the moral quality of a colonized people and turn them into individuals fit to inhabit a liberal-democratic society. If the colonial state was to seek legitimacy, it had to do so by picking out and bringing over to its side the 'natural leaders' of the various communities. This theory of representation informed even the constitutional reforms of the late colonial period.

Mature colonial thought adopted this fairly obvious position because, after all, it could not countenance the idea that subject peoples might constitute, in the same way that advanced people did, a singular and true political community such as the nation. At the same time, if 'communities' rather than 'nation' were what characterized this society, those communities had to be singular and substantive entities in themselves, with determinate and impermeable boundaries, so insular in their differences with one another as to be incapable of being merged into larger, more modern political identities.

Nationalists, of course, rejected this presumptuous postulate that India could never become a nation. What is curious is the way in which, despite the establishment of a postcolonial regime, an underlying current of thinking about the sociological bases of Indian politics continues to run along channels excavated by colonial discourse. The most obvious example of this is the notion of majority and minority communities defined in terms of criteria such as religion, language, or tribe and applied over a variety of territorial units ranging from a part of a district to the country itself. The other example is the continued preoccupation with precise calculations of proportionality in demands both for and against 'reservations', not only for the statutorily designated Scheduled Castes and Tribes but also for that contentious category of 'backward castes'. And finally, although caste enumerations have been banished from the schedules of the census in independent India, it is remarkable how tenaciously political discourse clings on to the idea of representation by enumerable communities: virtually every discussion on Indian elections looks for supportive evidence in the complicated political arithmetic of caste and communal alliances, calculations taken seriously into account even in the electoral strategies of parties and candidates. Therefore, even if we dismiss the sociological view that declares India to be a mere collection of discrete communities as a peculiarly colonial construct, we are apparently still left with a brand of postcolonial politics whose discursive forms are by no means free of that construct.

'COMMUNITY' IN POSTCOLONIAL POLITICS

I think, however, that there has been a transformation in the terms of political discourse. It would be too facile to make the criticism that all our forms of modern politics are merely the unfortunate legacy of colonialism. It is true, of course, that the fuzziness which enabled a wide variety of solidarities ranging from subcaste to gender to nation to be encompassed under the single rubric of jati has come under great strain when those solidarities have been forcibly inserted into the grid of the modern regime of power. On the other hand, it is also true that the modern disciplinary regime in India is itself limited and conditioned by the numerous resistances to its hegemonic sway. The result has been an unresolved tension through which the twin constituents of political discourse within the modern domain—one, the categories of the liberal-democratic state produced theoretically in the West, and the other, the categories that made up the Orientalist construction of India—are continuously being re-created in ever more unrecognizable forms.

In the days when the nation was being produced imaginatively without the actual shape of a state, many possibilities of communities that colonial knowledge would have declared as radically distinct came together into large political solidarities. The period of the Khilafat-Noncooperation movement (1919–22) is an obvious instance. Conventional historiography often explains this solidarity as the result of a conscious policy of 'alliance' pursued especially by Gandhi and the Ali brothers. However, as our example from Bhudeb's utopian history showed, the idiom of love and kinship in which the nationalist imagination sought to cast the relation between the Hindu jati and the Muslim jati can hardly be said to belong to a discourse of group interests and alliances, even when, as in Bhudeb's case, the partnership between different jatis was not on the basis of equality.

More interesting are the instances of sanctions imposed by such political collectivities upon those suspected of deviating from community norms. Ranajit Guha has recently discussed the significance of the 'social boycott' that was a widespread phenomenon at the time of the Swadeshi movement in Bengal in 1905–9.[9] The forms of punishment traditionally imposed for violation of caste rules were at this time imposed on those accused of violating the injunctions of the 'nation'—offences such as trading in foreign goods or collaborating with government officials. Even in the rhetoric of the topmost leaders of the movement, the slide from one sense of *jati* to another seemed fairly unproblematical. Hitesranjan Sanyal's researches among participants of the Noncooperation or the Civil Disobedience movements in Midnapore showed how persuasively, almost with the transparency of the self-evident, the concept of the nation, be it jati, or *des*, 'the country', was made tangible in the concreteness of an imagined network of kinship extending outward from the local structures of community.[10]

I do not believe that the imaginative possibilities afforded by the fuzziness of the community have disappeared from the domain of popular political discourse. On the contrary, I suspect that with the greater reach of the institutions and processes of the state into the interiors of social life, the state itself is being made sense of in the terms of that other discourse, far removed from the conceptual terms of liberal political theory. The notions of representation and the legitimation of authority, for instance, have taken on a set of meanings in the popular domain of contemporary Indian politics that would be impossible to describe, let alone justify, in the terms of a theory of interest aggregation or of the rationalization of authority. Our helplessness in understanding processes such as the elections since 1977 or the sudden rise and demise of 'ethnic' movements or the inexplicable fluctuations in the authority of particular political leaders seems largely due to the fact that we lack a theoretical language to talk about this domain of popular political discourse.

That this lack is critical is shown by the responses in the domain of 'high' discourse to this process of increasing interpenetration of the two domains of politics. There have been, it seems to me, two principal responses, both enabled by the play between the 'pure' theory of the modern state and the theory of Oriental exceptionalism. One response involves the reassertion of the universal truth of the pure theory. Thus, claims are being made all over again on behalf of the citizen as a rational individual, transacting public business in accordance with calculations of rational interest and keeping 'culture' tucked away within the confines of private belief. There are similar claims about the need to separate politics and ethnicity, politics and religion.

In one sense, these claims are paradoxical. Thus, when the 'secular' historian asserts that although medieval rulers may often have acted to inflict damage upon the institutions or followers of a rival religion, there was nothing 'religious' about this—it was all 'politics'—the claim also empties the domain of politics of that culturally rooted sense of moral solidarity that the same historian would need to uphold when talking, for instance, of the struggle of the 'nation' against colonial rule. On the other hand, this same 'modernist' discourse would allow the argument to be made that the policy of reservations by caste is divisive because it is prompted only by sectional political interests and is harmful for such general national concerns as merit and efficiency. Our modern discourse, it would seem, has to insist that although 'politics' may at times be good for the nation, at other times it is best abjured.

There is a further irony. The assertion of a zone of pure politics, while rejecting the colonialist dogma that Indian society is unfit to have a modern state, acknowledges at the same time that the cultural realities in the domain of mass politics can only pollute and corrupt the rational processes of the state. Whether it is communalism or casteism, nepotism or power brokerage, thoughtless populism or the absence of a work ethic, the impact of the popular domain is seen as bearing the mark of an impurity.

Take as an example a recent collection of essays on the politics of caste.[11] The list of writers is a fairly representative sample of the strands of thinking among social scientists writing in Bengali today. (Let me add, since I do not wish to suggest a false standpoint of distance, that this list includes my name as well.) The title of the volume is significant, for it announces itself as a book on the politics of *jatpat*, not just caste but 'casteism', and not only casteism but the entire gamut of divisive politics based on religion, language, or ethnicity. *Jatpat* is a curious word. A very recent entrant into the vocabulary of politics, it cannot be found in any standard Bengali dictionary. It has probably made its way into the lexicon of Bengali journalism and social science from Hindi,[12] and in its use within this sophisticated discourse of rationality and progress, it carries a double imprint of corruption. *Jat* itself, according to our lexicographers, is a corruption of *jati* (or else it is derived from the Persian); *jatpat* pushes it even further into the dark recesses of the 'cow belt' or the 'deep south', where they practise a politics so arcane and medieval that progressive Bengalis can only throw up their hands in despair.

The word *jatpat* also enables one to hierarchize the many senses of *jati*. *Jati* can now be given a proper place within the modern discursive formation by reserving its use to the 'good' community, namely, the nation. The other senses will then connote undesirable forms of community, evidence of the cultural backwardness of the people and describable as the politics of *jatpat*.

The other response in the domain of high discourse involves the assertion that all the forms of the modern state in India today represent the unwelcome intrusion of the West and that 'traditional' institutions, if allowed to function freely, are still capable of devising adequate instruments for the harmonious functioning of large collectivities.[13] This is the theory of Oriental exceptionalism turned around, for it argues, first, that the Orient can create its own brand of modernity and, second, that the Orient could not care less if its modernity qualifies as modern or not by the criteria of the West. What the argument overlooks is the depth to which the processes of the modern state have taken root in the contemporary history of India. It is not the origins but the process of domestication of the modern state in India that is at issue; one does not, unfortunately, have the option of sending this state back to its origins.

THE MODERN STATE AND CIVIL SOCIETY

We can see then that to sort out these problems of correspondence between the terms of discourse in the domains of elite and popular politics, we need to confront the central question of the modern state and its mechanisms of normalization that seek to obliterate the fuzziness of communities. I will end by raising this rather large question. . . .

The crux of the matter concerns the presumed emergence in Western Europe of a domain of civil society and its continued autonomous existence, sometimes in opposition to and at other times supportive of the state. What is this civil society? In a recent essay, Charles Taylor has distinguished between three different senses in which civil society can be identified in the European political tradition:[14]

1. In a minimal sense, civil society exists where there are free associations, not under the tutelage of state power.
2. In a stronger sense, civil society only exists where society as a whole can structure itself and coordinate its actions through such associations which are free of state tutelage.
3. As an alternative or supplement to the second sense, we can speak of civil society wherever the ensemble of associations can significantly determine or inflect the course of state policy.

He then spells out five distinct ideas that historically contributed to the production in Europe of a concept of civil society separate from the idea of the state:

A. The medieval idea that society is not identical with its political organization and that political authority is only one organ among others.
B. The Christian idea of the Church as an independent society.
C. The development within feudalism of a legal notion of subjective rights.
D. The growth in medieval Europe of relatively independent, self-governing cities.
E. The secular dualism of the medieval polity in which a monarch ruled with the intermittent and uncertain support of a body of Estates.

Taylor then describes how these ideas were brought together in two quite distinct ways by Locke and Montesquieu, respectively, to produce two different conceptualizations of the state-civil society relation.

In Locke, (A) is interpreted to mean that society is created before government, through a first contract by which individuals in the state of nature give themselves a society. This society then sets up government as a trust. The implication is that if government should violate its trust, society would recover its freedom against government. (B) is given the meaning of a prepolitical community constituted by a natural law received from God. This now becomes the foundation for subjective rights in (C): no positive law can be valid if it contravenes these rights. This particular combination (A), (B), and (C) produces in Locke the notion of a civil society distinguished from political authority, in which much that is valuable and creative in social life, especially in the sphere of social production, is seen as belonging to the domain of civil society, outside the direction or intervention of the political authority. We can immediately notice the centrality of this notion in the ideological self-representation of English capitalism.

Montesquieu, on the other hand, since he does not presume a prepolitical natural community, does not need to appeal to either (A) or (B). For him, society and political authority are coeval. In order to establish his antiabsolutist doctrine, he brings together (C), (D), and (E) in a form that enables him to distinguish between central political authority on the one hand and a set of entrenched rights, defended by citizens who have a republican sense of patriotic virtue, on the other. His view of society then is that of a balance between two elements, neither prior to the other, which remain as it were in perpetual but creative tension, seeking always to achieve that equilibrium in which both retain their identities without destroying each other.

What is significant in this distinction drawn by Taylor between the two streams of thinking leading to the state/civil society opposition, represented by Locke and Montesquieu, respectively, is the element they share in common. Element (C)—the notion of subjective rights—plays the crucial role in establishing both the distinction between as well as the unity of state and civil society in both these antiabsolutist doctrines. I think this commonality is important especially because of the way in which the history of these two streams of political thinking in Europe becomes implicated in another history—the history of capital. I will return to this point later.

In the meantime, let us note another curious feature shared by both streams. Both Locke and Montesquieu defend subjective rights by appealing to a notion of community. In Locke, this is straightforward. Subjective rights have their source in the prepolitical natural community God creates for mankind: (C) is grounded in (B). People in the state of nature are already constituted as 'subjects' by the community of natural law, even before the emergence of society. They can, therefore, proceed, as already constituted 'individuals', to create through mutual contracts first society and then government, and thereby establish the institutions for the defence of their subjective rights. In Montesquieu, although (C) is related in institutional terms to the equilibrating forces contained in (D) and (E), the ultimate defence of subjective rights is *vertu*, the patriotic spirit of citizens who 'feel shame in obeying any order which derogates from their code' and who 'defend the laws to the death against internal and external threat'. One would be justified, it seems to me, to think of *vertu* as that sense of community which is not prior to the establishment of political authority but coeval with it, which nevertheless regards itself as having an identity distinct from that of the political authority. Why else would the defence of subjective rights against royal encroachment be 'patriotic'?

Subjective rights and the grounding of those rights in community—these are the two features that are common to the otherwise different arguments made by Locke and

Montesquieu. The problems that appear in the subsequent history of the state–civil society relation in Europe are, I think, fundamentally shaped by divergences in conceptualizing the relation between rights and community. These divergences are framed within two extreme positions—on the one hand, abolishing community altogether and thinking of rights as grounded solely in the self-determining individual will, and, on the other, attributing to community a single determinate form, delegitimizing all other forms of community. This subsequent history, I will argue, is intricately tied with the history of capital.

CIVIL SOCIETY AND COMMUNITY

The two streams represented by Locke and Montesquieu were brought together in its most celebrated form by Hegel. Yet, as Taylor notes, the two 'sit uneasily together' in Hegel's new concept of civil society. Let me explore the source of this tension in Hegel.

Hegel, as we know, strenuously resisted the line of argument that preferred to think of the state as having been founded by contract. Contracts follow from the accidental, and entirely contingent, agreements among individual wills. They properly belong to the domain of the 'system of needs' but are too fickle to be the basis of Right itself. Hegel also would not admit that the family, that first elementary moment of social life, was founded on contract. To admit this would mean having to recognize that members of a family, whether adults or children, might have rights against each other and even the right to dissociate from or dissolve the family at will. The would make the primary elements of social life subject to the transient and utterly chaotic accidents of contingent agreements. Contracts, for Hegel, belong neither to the domain of the state nor to that of the family; their place is in civil society.

How, then, is the family formed? Hegel, as we know, begins the *Philosophy of Right* by first establishing subjective will in abstract right. But when he moves to the actualizing of subjective will in the concreteness of 'ethical life', he grounds the first moment—the family—in 'love', which is precisely the free surrender of will and personality. The family is ethical mind 'in its natural or immediate phase', where it 'is specifically characterized by love, which is mind's feeling of its own unity. . . . One is in it not as an independent person but as a member'.[15] I quote some of the other things Hegel has to say about this 'natural or immediate phase' of ethical life because I prefer to read these passages as a suppressed narrative of community, flowing through the substratum of liberal capitalist society, which those who celebrate the absolute and natural sovereignty of the individual will refuse to recognize. Hegel says:

Love means in general terms the consciousness of my unity with another, so that I am not in selfish isolation but win my self-consciousness only as the renunciation of my independence and through knowing myself as the unity of myself with another and of the other with me. Love, however, is feeling, i.e. ethical life in the form of something natural . . . . The first moment in love is that I do not wish to be a self-subsistent and independent person and that, if I were, then I would feel defective and incomplete. The second moment is that I find myself in another person, that I count for something in me. Love, therefore, is the most tremendous contradiction; the Understanding cannot resolve it since there is nothing more stubborn than this point of self-consciousness which is negated and which nevertheless I ought to possess as affirmative. Love is at once the propounding and the resolving of this contradiction. As the resolving of it, love is unity of an ethical type.

The right of the family properly consists in the fact that its substantiality should have determinate existence. Thus it is a right against externality and against secessions from the family unity. On the other hand, to repeat, love is a feeling, something subjective, against which unity cannot make itself effective. The demand for unity can be sustained, then, only in relation to such things as are by nature external and not conditioned by feeling.[16]

Hegel, of course, restricts this substantial unity to the nuclear family, in which it finds its determinate existence as a right against externality and secession in, first, the family property, and second, the male head of the family—husband and father. In doing this, Hegel leads himself into a precarious position, for no matter how hard he tries to resist the idea of the family as based on a contractual agreement in which the members retain their individual rights against each other, he cannot prevent the tide of individualism from seeping into the representations of marriage and inheritance even in the positive law of modern Western societies. Reading these passages today, Hegel's arguments on marriage, gender relations, and inheritance seem to us either quaint, if one takes a charitable view, or outrageously conservative.

I wish to argue, however, that there is another narrative in which Hegel's eloquence on the subject of love will not seem so outmoded. This is the narrative not of the bourgeois family but of community. Think of the rhetoric in which, even in this age of the triumph of individualism, all movements that appeal to the 'natural' solidarity of community speak. They claim precisely the right against externality and secession, they seek determinate existence precisely in 'property' and 'representation' through collectively recognized heads, they speak in the language of love and of self-recognition through the free surrender of individual will to others in the community. One might object that this idea of natural affiliation to a community (or an indeterminate set of communities) does violence to the freedom of choice inherent in the subjective will. It is this objection that becomes the basis for the identification in European sociological theory—fed, let us remember, on large doses of Orientalist literature and colonial anthropology—of all precapitalist Gemeinschaften as the domain of ascription, and hence unfreedom, and of modern associations as the field where freedom and choice can blossom. Hegel's arguments on the family remind us, it seems to me, of the irreducible immediacy in which human beings are born in society: not as pure unattached individuals free to choose their social affiliations (whether gender, ethnicity, or class) but as already ascribed members of society. Liberal individualism seeks to erase this level of immediacy where people are not free to choose the social locus of their birth. Indeed, liberalism seeks to forget that the question of choice here is itself fallacious, for human beings cannot exist as 'individuals' before they are born, and when they are born, they are already ascribed as particular members of society. Liberal theory then can only deal with this phenomenon as accidents of 'natural inequality', which social policies of welfare or equal opportunity must mitigate. It can, in other words, deal with it only in bad faith.

If I am allowed the conceit of reading Hegel against the grain, I will choose to read this subsection of 'Ethical Life' as a narrative of community where subjective rights must be negotiated within the 'ascribed' field of the ethical life of the community. I will also recall here that Hegel makes the family the site for the other great process by which 'individual' subjectivities could be negotiated in society, namely, the education of children,[17] which site too he would not be able to defend against the relentless sway of the modern disciplinary regime of power constantly striving to produce the 'normalized' individual. Against the grain of liberal sociology, I prefer to read Hegel as saying that education properly belongs to the field of the ethical life of the community, and not to the compulsory discipline of the school, the prison, the hospital, and the psychiatrist's clinic. I will not describe this field of community ethical life as one devoid of choice, nor will I give it a place at some early stage in the sequence of development of the bourgeois nuclear family. Rather, I will read this as a narrative that continues to unfold to this day *against the grain* of that other narrative of bourgeois individualism.

To return to Hegel and civil society: families, united within themselves against the externality constituted by other families and each represented by its head—the burgher, the bourgeois—comprise the domain of civil society. This is the domain of particular interests, based on particular needs and the mutual satisfaction of the needs of all through contractually mediated exchange of the products of labour. This is also the domain where the property of each family is mutually protected through the administration of justice. Civil society, in other words, is the well-known domain of the market economy and civil law.

Hegel, however, also includes within civil society a residual category, providing for 'contingencies still lurking' in the system of needs and the administration of justice and for the 'care of particular interests as a common interest'. This residual category includes the police and the corporation. Curiously, in demarcating the limits of public surveillance organized by civil society (Hegel is clearly thinking here of the administrative functions of what was known in eighteenth-century Germany and Italy as 'the police' and which had become the subject of an entire discipline called *Polizeiwissenschaft*),[18] Hegel admits that 'no objective line can be drawn'. In other words, at this interface between family and civil society, no objective line separates the private from the public. The separation can be made only contextually, taking into view specific contingencies. 'These details,' Hegel says, 'are determined by custom, the spirit of the rest of the constitution, contemporary conditions, the crisis of the hour, and so forth.'[19] How is one to read this lack of objective separation between the civil and the familial, the public and the private? What is it that produces this zone of contingency and indeterminacy where 'everything is subjective'? Can one read this as one more instance where a suppressed narrative of community is seeping through the interstices of the objectively constructed, contractually regulated structure of civil society?

A final illustration, and I will stop this strenuous reading of Hegel. Still on the subject of civil society and its residual function of taking care of particular interests as a common interest, Hegel writes:

In its character as a universal family, civil society has the right and duty of superintending and influencing education, inasmuch as education bears upon the child's capacity to become a member of society. Society's right here is paramount over the arbitrary and contingent preferences of parents. . . . Parents usually suppose that in the matter of education they have complete freedom and may arrange everything as they like. . . . None the less, society has a right . . . to compel parents to send their children to school, to have them vaccinated, and so forth. The disputes that have arisen in France between the advocates of state supervision and those who demand that education shall be free, i.e. at the option of the parents, are relevant here.[20]

Once again, I wish to suggest that suppressed narrative is raising its irrepressible head. How else can Hegel suddenly slip in the idea of civil society as 'a universal family'? How can civil society represent itself as a family that, according to Hegel himself, is born not out of contract but out of love, the free surrender of individual wills? By reducing family to the single determinate form of the bourgeois nuclear family, Hegel has narrowed and impoverished its scope. The gap has to be filled in by civil society arrogating the role of a universal family. Ironically, by admitting this, Hegel immediately opens himself to appropriation by that powerful strand of thinking which claims that this role of the universal family can be properly played by the only legitimate community in modern society—the nation—a role that must then be enforced by the disciplinary mechanisms of the nation-state. Hegel becomes complicit in this act of appropriation, not innocently but as an inevitable consequence of his own construction of the system of Right: the contingent contractual domain of civil society must, after all, be unified at the higher, universal level of the absolute idea of Right, embodied in the state as *the* political community.

CAPITAL AND COMMUNITY

I am suggesting, therefore, that this suppression in modern European social theory of an independent narrative of community makes possible both the posing of the distinction between state and civil society and the erasure of that distinction. At one extreme, then, we have arguments proclaiming the sovereignty of the individual will, insisting that the state has no business to interfere in the domain of individual freedom of choice and contractual arrangements. At the other extreme are the arguments that would have the *one* political community, given the single, determinate, demographically enumerable form of the nation-state, assume the directing role in all regulatory functions of society, usurping the domain of civil society and family, and blurring the distinctions between the public and the private. It is to this range of arguments that people must refer when they say that the state–civil society relation in Western thought is not one of simple opposition. I will argue that the possibilities of opposition as well as encapsulation arise because the concepts of the individual and the nation-state both become embedded in a new grand narrative—the narrative of capital. This narrative of capital seeks to suppress that other narrative of community and produce in the course of its journey both the normalized individual and the modern regime of disciplinary power.

The historical specificity of European social thought cannot be described simply by Taylor's conditions (A) to (E). It would not be surprising at all if one finds in the premodern histories of other, non-European, countries similar features in state–society relations. It is also difficult to explain why, if European thought is indeed conditioned by these specifics, people from Poland to the Philippines to Nicaragua should appeal to these philosophers from Britain, France, or Germany to think out and justify what they do to their own societies and states. If there is one great moment that turns the provincial thought of Europe to universal philosophy, the parochial history of Europe to universal history, it is the moment of capital—capital that is global in its territorial reach and universal in its conceptual domain. It is the narrative of capital that can turn the violence of mercantilist trade, war, genocide, conquest, and colonialism into a story of universal progress, development, modernization, and freedom.

For this narrative to take shape, the destruction of community is fundamental. Marx saw this clearly when he identified as the necessary condition for capitalist production the separation of the mass of labourers from their means of labour. This so-called primitive accumulation is nothing else but the destruction of precapitalist community, which, in various forms, had regulated the social unity of labourers with their means of production. Thus community, in the narrative of capital, becomes relegated to the latter's prehistory, a natural, prepolitical, primordial stage in social evolution that must be superseded for the journey of freedom and progress to begin. And since the story of capital is universal, community too becomes the universal prehistory of progress, identified with medievalism in Europe and the stagnant, backward, undeveloped present in the rest of the world.

It could not, however, be entirely suppressed. The domain of civil society, ruled by 'liberty, equality, property and Bentham', could not produce an adequate justification for the lack of freedom and equality within the industrial labour process itself and the continued division of society into the opposed classes of capital and labour. What Marx did not see too well was the ability of capitalist society to ideologically reunite capital and labour at the level of the political community of the nation, borrowing from another narrative the rhetoric of love, duty, welfare, and the like. Notwithstanding its universalist scope, capital remained parasitic upon the reconstructed particularism of the nation. (It would be an interesting exercise to identify in Marx's *Capital* the places where this other narrative makes a surreptitious appearance: for instance, money, the universal equivalent, which nevertheless retains the form of a national currency assigned a particular exchange value by the national state; or the value of labour power, homogeneous and normalized, which is nevertheless determined by specific historical and cultural particularities.)

We must remember that the rise of a public sphere in Europe, which is said to be a space outside the supervision of political authority, where 'opinion could present itself as that of society', was also crucial in connecting a reconstructed cultural identity of the people with the legitimate jurisdiction of the state. It was principally in this public space where, through the medium of print-capitalism, the homogenized forms of a national culture were forged— through the standardization of language, aesthetic norms, and consumer tastes. The public sphere, then, was not only a domain that marked the distinction of state and civil society; by creating the cultural standards through which 'public opinion' could claim to speak on behalf of the nation, it also united state and civil society. Civil society now became the space for the diverse life of individuals in the nation; the state became the nation's singular representative embodiment, the only legitimate form of community.

But community is not easily appropriated within the narrative of capital. Community, from the latter's standpoint, belongs to the domain of the natural, the primordial. Only in its sanitized, domesticated form can it become a shared subjective feeling that protects and nurtures (good nationalism). But it always carries with it the threatening possibility of becoming violent, divisive, fearsome, irrational (bad nationalism). It is not so much the state/civil society opposition but rather the capital/community opposition that seems to me to be the great unsurpassed contradiction in Western social philosophy. Both state and civil-social institutions have assigned places within the narrative of capital. Community, which ideally should have been banished from the kingdom of capital, continues to lead a subterranean, potentially subversive, life within it because it refuses to go away.

Recent attempts in social philosophy to produce arguments from a 'communitarian' standpoint against the dominant orthodoxy of liberal or bureaucratic individualism have sought either to rediscover premodern forms of the political community, lost under the rubble left behind by the onward march of modernity, or to find them among suppressed groups or deviant cults surviving on the margins of normalized society. Alasdair MacIntyre, for instance, sets up his argument against the Enlightenment project of modernity, and by implication against the Nietzschean critique of modernity, by vindicating a classical Aristotelian concept of virtue.[21] In doing this, he has to conjure up the vision of the polis, a determinate political community institutionalizing the practices, goals, and tradition of a moral community. Recent theorists of anarchism have looked for support in the ethnographic evidence on stateless tribal communities or in the practices of marginal utopian communities. And Michel Foucault, seeking in the last years of his life to find the ground for resistance to the all-conquering sway of disciplinary power, located it in the possibility of 'an insurrection of subjugated knowledges', a localized but autonomous and non-centralized kind of theoretical production 'whose validity is not dependent on the approval of the established régimes of thought'.[22]

I am pointing out a different possibility. Looking at the relatively untheorized idea of 'the nation' in Western social philosophy, one notices an inelegant braiding of an idea of community with the concept of capital. This is not an archaic idea buried in the recesses of history, nor is it part of a marginal subculture, nor can it be dismissed as a premodern remnant that an absentminded Enlightenment has somehow forgotten to erase. It is very much a part of the here-and-now of modernity, and yet it is an idea that remains impoverished and limited to the singular form of the nation-state because it is denied a legitimate life in the world of the modern knowledges of human society. This denial, in turn, is related to the fact that by its very nature, the idea of the community marks a limit to the realm of disciplinary power. My hypothesis, then, is that an investigation into the idea of the nation, by uncovering a necessary contradiction between capital and community, is likely to lead us to a fundamental critique of modernity from within itself.

But beyond the intellectual history of Europe, our inquiry into the colonial and post-colonial histories of other parts of the world is more likely to enable us to make this critique.[23] The contradictions between the two narratives of capital and community can be seen quite clearly in the histories of anticolonial nationalist movements. The forms of the modern state were imported into these countries through the agency of colonial rule. The institutions of civil society, in the forms in which they had arisen in Europe, also made their appearance in the colonies precisely to create a public domain for the legitimation of colonial rule. This process was, however, fundamentally limited by the fact that the colonial state could confer only subjecthood on the colonized; it could not grant them citizenship. The crucial break in the history of anticolonial nationalism comes when the colonized refuse to accept membership of this civil society of subjects. They construct their national identities within a different narrative, that of the community. They do not have the option of doing this within the domain of bourgeois civil-social institutions. They create, consequently, a very different domain—a cultural domain—marked by the distinctions of the material and the spiritual, the outer and the inner. This inner domain of culture is declared the sovereign territory of the nation, where the colonial state is not allowed entry, even as the outer domain remains surrendered to the colonial power. The rhetoric here (Gandhi is a particularly good example)[24] is of love, kinship, austerity, sacrifice. The rhetoric is in fact antimodernist, antiindividualist, even anticapitalist. The attempt is, if I may stay with Gandhi for a while, to find, against the grand narrative of history itself, the cultural resources to negotiate the terms through which people, living in different, contextually defined, communities, can coexist peacefully, productively, and creatively within large political units.

The irony is, of course, that this other narrative is again violently interrupted once the postcolonial national state attempts to resume its journey along the trajectory of world-historical development. The modern state, embedded as it is within the universal narrative of capital, cannot recognize within its jurisdiction any form of community except the single, determinate, demographically enumerable form of the nation. It must therefore subjugate, if necessary by the use of state violence, all such aspirations of community identity. These other aspirations, in turn, can give to themselves a historically valid justification only by claiming an alternative nationhood with rights to an alternative state.

One can see how a conception of the state–society relation, born within the parochial history of Western Europe but made universal by the global sway of capital, dogs the contemporary history of the world. I do not think that the invocation of the state/civil society opposition in the struggle against socialist-bureaucratic regimes in Eastern Europe or in the former Soviet republics or, for that matter, in China, will produce anything other than strategies seeking to replicate the history of Western Europe. The result has been demonstrated a hundred times. The provincialism of the European experience will be taken as the universal history of progress; by comparison, the history of the rest of the world will appear as the history of lack, of inadequacy—an inferior history. Appeals will be made all over again to philosophies produced in Britain, France, and Germany. The fact that these doctrines were produced in complete ignorance of the histories of other parts of the world will not matter: they will be found useful and enlightening.[25] It would indeed be a supreme irony of history if socialist industrialization gets written into the narrative of capital as the phase when socialist-bureaucratic regimes had to step in to undertake 'primitive accumulation' and clear the way for the journey of capital to be resumed along its 'normal' course.

In the meantime, the struggle between community and capital, irreconcilable within this grand narrative, will continue. The forms of the modern state will be forced into the grid of determinate national identities. This will mean a substantialization of cultural differences, necessarily excluding as 'minorities' those who would not conform to the chosen marks of nationality. The struggle between 'good' and 'bad' nationalism will be played out all over again.

What, then, are the true categories of universal history? State and civil society? Public and private? Social regulation and individual rights?—all made significant within the grand narrative of capital as the history of freedom, modernity, and progress? Or the narrative of community—untheorized, relegated to the primordial zone of the natural, denied any subjectivity that is not domesticated to the requirements of the modern state, and yet persistent in its invocation of the rhetoric of love and kinship against the homogenizing sway of the normalized individual?

It is this unresolved struggle between the narratives of capital and community within the discursive space of the modern state that is reflected in our embarrassment at the many uses of *jati*. Kamalakanta, if he is still around, is now, I suspect, laughing at us.

NOTES

1. Bankimcandra Chattopadhyay 'Kamalakanter Jobanbandi', in *Bankim Racanabali*, edited by Jogeshchandra Bagal, Vol 2, Calcutta: Sahitya Samsad, 1965, pp. 101–8.

2. For an analysis of the Kamalakanta writings, see Sudipta Kaviraj, 'Signs of Madness: The Figure of Kamalakanta in the Work of Bankimchandra Chattopadhyay, *Journal of Arts and Ideas*, 17–18 (June 1989), 9–32.

3. Jnanendramohan Das, *Bangala bhasar abhidhan*, 2nd edition, Calcutta: Sahitya Samsad, 1988, 1:848–49 1937.

4. Haricharan Bandyopadhyay, *Bangiya sabdakos*, New Delhi: Sahitya Akademi, 1966, 1,936.

5. Govindagopal Mukhopadhyay and Gopikamohan Bhattacharya, A *Tri-lingual Dictionary*, Calcutta Sanskrit College Research Series 47, lexicon no. 1, Calcutta: Sanskrit College, 1966.

6. Bhudeb Mukhopadhyay, 'Svapnalabdha Bharatbarser Itihas', in *Bhudeb Racanasambhar*, edited by Pramathanath Basu, Calcutta: Mitra Ghosh, 1969, pp. 341–74.

7. Sudipta Kaviraj, 'The Imaginary Institution of India', in Partha Chatterjee and Gyanendra Pandey (eds), *Subaltern Studies VII*, Delhi: Oxford University Press, 1992: 1–39.

8. Bernard S. Cohn, 'The Census, Social Structure and Objectification in South Asia', in Cohn, *An Anthropologist among the Historians and Other Essays*, Delhi: Oxford University Press, 1987, 224–54.

9. Ranajit Guha, 'Discipline and Mobilize', in Chatterjee and Pandey, *Subaltern Studies VII*: 69–120.

10. Hitesranjan Sanyal, 'Abhayer Katha', *Baromas* 7 (2), Autumn 1984: 97–128.

11. Sujit Sen (ed.), *Jatpater rajniti*, Calcutta: Pustak Bipani, 1989.

12. Hindi dictionaries list the word *jatpant* under the entry for *jat*, the corrupt form of *jati*, and give as its meaning *biradari*, 'the collective "brotherhood" of a subcaste'. There is also a listing for *jatipanti*, once again a non-Sanskritic Hindi word, which could mean *varna*, 'caste' or 'tribe'. Kalika Prasad, Rajballabh Sahay, and Mukundilal Srivastava, *Brhat hindi Kos*, Banaras: Gyanmandal, 1970.

13. While I do not wish to reduce the importance of the immensely suggestive writings of Ashis Nandy, it nevertheless seems to me that they often lend themselves to this kind of interpretation.

14. Charles Taylor, 'Modes of Civil Society', *Public Culture* 3 (1), Fall 1990; 102–19.

15. G.W.F. Hegel, *Philosophy of Right*, tr. T.M. Knox, London: Oxford University Press, 1967, para. 158, p. 110.

16. Ibid., addition 101, pp. 261–2; addition 102, p. 262.

17. Ibid., para. 175, pp. 117–18.

18. Foucault, of course, makes much of these 'police functions' of the early modern state. See, in particular, his Tanner Lectures at Stanford University, reprinted as 'Politics and Reason', in Michel Foucault, *Politics, Philosophy, Culture: Interviews and Other Writings, 1977–1984*, tr. Alan Sheridan et al., New York: Routledge, 1988, 58–85.

19. Hegel, *Philosophy of Right*, para. 234, p. 146.

20. Ibid., para. 239, p. 148, and addition 147, p. 277.

21. Alasdaire MacIntyre, *After Virtue: A Study in Moral Theory*, London: Duckworth, 1981.

22. Michel Foucault, *Power/Knowledge: Selected Interviews and Other Writings, 1972–1977*, ed. Colin Gordon, New York: Pantheon, 1980, 78–92.

23. Foucault was well aware of the fact that contemporary non-Western cultures contained powerful resources for resisting disciplinary power. This was shown quite dramatically, if rather embarrassingly for many of Foucault's admirers, in his enthusiasm for the Iranian revolt against the shah. Those events, he wrote, 'did not represent a withdrawal of the most outmoded groups before a modernization that is too brutal. It was, rather, the rejection by an entire culture, an entire people, of a modernization that is an archaism in itself.' In their will for an 'Islamic government,' he added, the Iranian people were seeking, 'even at the price of their own lives, something that we have forgotten, even as a possibility, since the Renaissance and the great crises of Christianity: a political spirituality. I can already hear the French laughing. But I know they are wrong.' See Didier Eribon, *Michel Foucault*, tr. Betsy Wing, Cambridge: Harvard University Press,

1991: 281–91; Foucault, 'Iran: The Spirit of a World without Spirit', in *Politics, Philosophy, Culture*, pp. 211–24. Foucault's so-called Iran mistake tells us a great deal about both the possibilities as well as the difficulties of an 'antistrategic' theoretical practice: 'be respectful when singularity rises up, and intransigent when power infringes on the universal.'

24. I have discussed this aspect of Gandhi in *Nationalist Thought and the Colonial World: A Derivative Discourse*, London: Zed Books, 1986, pp. 85–130.

25. I am grateful to Dipesh Chakrabarty for pointing out to me the implications of this formulation. Chakrabarty has argued this point in his *Rethinking Working-Class History: Bengal 1890–1940*, Princeton: Princeton University Press, 1989 and in 'Postcoloniality and the Artifice of History: Who "Speaks for Indian Pasts"?', *Representations* 37, Winter 1992, 1–26.

SEVEN

They Also Followed Gandhi

Shahid Amin

ఌఄఌఌ

Almost in storybook fashion, my account of Chauri Chaura has kept coming up against successive hurdles. Contemporary nationalist tracts have no time for a history of the event, only for its lessons. Authorized postcolonial retellings proffer stereotypical descriptions of colonial violence and nationalist resolve. They fail to account for the actors, men such as Nazar Ali, Abdullah, Dwarka Gosain, and Shikari. In the court the accused decline to speak about their 'criminal' past. They address a judge, not History. This economy of rebel speech leads me to the enforced utterances of Approver Shikari. In this Mir Shikari, the approver of the records, the historian finally has access to the actual words of a leading actor. But the presence of the first person singular is, in this case, inadequate guarantee of the speaker's nearness to his own speech.[1]

Disappointed in one archive, it is the business of the historian to turn to another. During my visits to Chauri Chaura I attempted to grasp the event in the moment of its recall. The riot had already been nationalized, and a memorial, the last nail in the coffin as it were, was now being put in place. In February 1989 I had hastened from Delhi to garner the local people's reactions to this official celebration, choreographed by a local politician who had been elevated to a ministership in Rajiv Gandhi's cabinet. In August 1991 another state minister had unveiled a stone tablet purporting to be the 'Golden History of the Martyrs of Chauri Chaura'.

While interrogating several local narratives of the riot, this chapter concentrates on family accounts from Chotki Dumri. The recollections of Naujadi, the wife of a rioter, and of Sita Ahir, the son of a chaukidar, are deployed to construct the world of the peasant nationalists. These *otiyar*s, to use Naujadi's remarkable Bhojpuri creolization of the familiar 'volunteer', were Gandhi's men all right; everything connected with popular nationalism of that time possessed a generic Gandhian quality. But Naujadi's otiyars were Gandhian in curiously unrecognizable ways.

I seek to chart the distance that separates the volunteers of Gandhi's *Collected Works* from the otiyars of Naujadi's recollection. I also try to explore the possibility, with the help of Sita and Naujadi, of generating an independent narrative, a story which does not have crime for its title. My attempt is not quite successful. This is not because the basic facts of the riot are incontrovertible: the same characters can, after all, be made to play several different parts. The difficulty of my effort to generate an entirely alternative narrative of the event, I might even say its failure, illustrates, rather, the hegemonic power of judicial and nationalist discourse. The subalterns make their own memories, but they do not make them just as they please. The gallows and the prison ensure that, decades later, judicial pronouncements live to be heard even in the familial recall of an event. And so it is with Chauri Chaura. Peasant narratives that I collected were inescapably tainted or vitiated or coloured in varying degrees by the hegemonic master narratives.

The experience of historical fieldwork was not without its ironies. On my very first visit to Chotki Dumri I was taken to meet the *gram pradhan*, a sort of elected village headman who represents the village to the outside world. Sharfuddin, my host, was Mir Shikari's son! He chipped in to 'translate' slightly garbled sentences from an older informant's mouth. Ever so often, as befitted his rank and intelligence, Sharfuddin would, while translating the words of our old companion, underline the dominant nationalist spirit 'of those times'. But he proffered no insights into his father, Shikari, nor did I feel the urge to press him.

Sita Ahir, the leading male narrator, turned out, as his story unfolded, to be the son of a village policeman killed in the riot. He was also the nephew of one hanged for the killing and burning at the police station.

From their story-telling it was apparent that the politicization of the case had altered the state's perception of the rioters: now, documents pertaining to an individual's proven crimes bore the impress of their reverse—a heroic nationalist significance.

THE PRESENCE OF GANDHI

In Dumri the end of the event is remembered for its immediate result, not for its national consequences. Repression, punishment, survival—these are the themes with which Naujadi, Sita, and others close their accounts of Chauri Chaura. They do not locate its significance in the grief the riot caused the Mahatma and the brake it put on the fight against the British. None of the relatives of the rioters framed their stories in terms of what 'Chauri Chaura' meant to an ongoing freedom struggle, or to Mahatma Gandhi for that matter. Not that they have no recollection of Gandhi Maharaj. Gandhi's presence in Dumri is in fact so dominant that it has the effect of displacing every other nationalist actor, apart from the local volunteers, from recollections of the event.

Strands of the tie-up with the district headquarters lie scattered throughout the records. The Dumri unit was formally established by Hakeem Arif, a district functionary; Nazar Ali had gone to Gorakhpur with a request for a drill instructor; Lal Mohammad sent up a written complaint about the beating of volunteers in Mundera Bazaar. The Allahabad judges 'strongly suspect[ed]' that the Dumri leaders had in fact acted upon instructions sent out from the district headquarters.[2] Lal Mohammad Sain, who initially arranged Hakeem Arif's visit to Dumri in January, had sent a letter to Gorakhpur after the beating of the volunteers in

Mundera bazaar. In this 'report', the Sain from Chaura made the standard gestures of political deference:

We therefore report this matter to you, Sirs, so that you could come over and ascertain for yourself. And it is because of you, Sirs, that we have not taken any offensive action, for we would act only after seeking the advice of [you] our officers [*afsars*].[3]

Much was made of this letter in the court. The judges suggested that since the confiscated Congress records contained no evidence of a written reply, 'an oral answer was returned [to Chaura] . . . of such a character that those responsible for it could not commit it to writing'.[4] Gorakhpur, in other words, was instrumental in causing the riot at Chauri Chaura.

Important as these events are for historical reconstruction, they seem to have slipped out of local recall. An erasure caused by time, perhaps? Or could it be that those who recounted 'Chauri Chaura' to me were not privy to all that transpired between Dumri and the district? It is significant that in our long conversations, not a single district nationalist's name ever cropped up. It was Gandhi and the volunteers who peopled the Dumri stories. What we have here are mnemonic traces, perhaps, of a desire to construct a world larger than the local, a world of volunteers from which the Gorakhpur superiors are necessarily absent.

There is in fact hardly any place for the District Congress in local accounts of the event. It is Nazar Ali's letter—*tar* (wire) in Sita's words—summoning an urgent meeting at Dumri which is most strongly remembered. No one seems to recall Lal Mohammad's report, which is lodged as an exhibit in the court records.[5] Hakeem Arif, the Gorakhpur nationalist, who, for the judge, 'definitely formed . . . the local . . . Dumri circle . . . of the non-cooperation movement . . . in January 1922',[6] is similarly displaced by the activities of local volunteers. For Naujadi it is an existing band of volunteers, called into being by Gandhi, who confabulate and organize, unaided by people from Gorakhpur (*apne mein log 'kumeti' kail*). The district headquarters is referred to by Naujadi once as the site of the jail, never as the seat of the Non-cooperation movement.

In Dumri the district does not count. The volunteers owed their existence directly to Gandhi's personal appearance at the Chauri Chaura railway station on 8 February 1921,[7] eleven months before Nazar Ali, Shikari, and others turned full-time volunteers.

In Naujadi's recollection that extraordinary visit is heralded by celestial apparitions—a snake-like figure and two commoner objects appeared over the Mundera-Dumri sky. In response to my question about Gandhi's arrival, Naujadi launches into an intriguing tale of the women lentil-splitters of Mundera being roused from their grindstones by strange stirrings in the sky. These heavenly signs were invariably recognized by their form, but their ominousness was open to debate. The old woman is at some pains to dispel the disbelief that her story might arouse among her listeners. Naujadi begins by eliciting an agreement on some basic propositions first:

Oh regarding Gandhiji! You see sir! Now you are sitting on this cot towards the south, right! And *sirkar* we are labourers, right! . . .

You see! It was the month of Magh. Everybody is splitting dal [in special chakkis in Mundera bazaar]. It was a bazaar day, Wednesday, or Saturday perhaps. Har-har-har-har [the chakkis go round and round], everyone is grinding and splitting dal. And then Babu! From *this* very corner—I am not lying, I tell you—from this very side *it* arose, and then went round and round and round, and formed a complete circle. Then it subsided . . . . Like ash, like smoke in the sky it was.

   People said it's a python, a python has descended from the hills. There was great commotion. Merchants and brokers, labourers and dal-grinders, all went to see this *tamasha*, this sight, from rooftops. Next day a broom [*barhani*] appeared in the southern sky, then a ploughing plank [*henga*]. And then a long twig broom [*kharhara*].*

   God save us now! With this kharhara people and their houses will be swept away. No one, nothing will remain, people said.

Unable to understand all of this, I asked Naujadi to elaborate. 'Everyone will die. All will be lost. It is the end of time [*ant kal*],' she stressed, raising her voice to effect communication. Sharfuddin, the village headman, tried to link all this to the future catastrophe—the riot, the repression, the deaths, and imprisonment—which were to destroy the locality a year later. But for Naujadi the omens, though unsettling, were part of a set of strange happenings. She had heard that shrubs would shoot up into big trees, that and other such happenings would augur Gandhi's arrival in February 1921.†

   Sita Ahir, then the twelve-year-old son of a village chaukidar who was at the station with 10,000 others that day, has a more dignified and evocative recollection of Gandhi-Baba: 'Fair, tall and of slight build, he gave a lecture [*bhashan*].' A few words uttered by Gandhi from the door of a rail carriage here fill up to an entire 'speech', and a brief stopover extends into a day's stay. [*Gandhi-Baba ke dekhle rahlin. Gora, patra-ke rahlan, lamba. Bhashan karlan. Bahut bheer! . . . din-bhar ruklan.*]

He had come by train. He stopped over. People from all over had gathered at the station that day. What a crowd! He was surrounded by his servants and attendants [*chakar*]. At the godown-siding west of the station, money and coins [*kaccha paisa, dabbal*] were being thrown from every direction.* He—he was least bothered! Wearing a dhoti as I do, hands folded *like this*, he went round greeting the people. (*Hamre laikhan dhoti karke . . . hath jore, panchan ke hath joren.*)

   Gandhiji was slightly better built than I. [*Hamse taniye karer rahlan Gandhiji.*][8]

It was a stupendous welcome, by any account. The train carrying the Mahatma stopped at each and every station on the sixty-mile rail stretch that traversed the district from east to west. A leader of the Gorakhpur Congress reception party would first explain Gandhi's message to these wayside crowds. 'After the din and the excitement had subsided Mahatmaji would appear at the door of his carriage and give his message.' Gandhi refused donations en route; people were advised to deposit their gifts with the District Congress Committee.

---

   * *Barhani*: broom used by women when sweeping out the house; *henga*: flat plank dragged along the ground after ploughing, while a man stands on it to give it weight; *kharhara*: broom made of twigs, used for sweeping out leaves and stray rubbish.

   † Gandhi's day-long stay in the district on 8 February 1921 was to give rise to fantastic rumours about his 'message', as understood locally. For an analysis, see my 'Gandhi as Mahatma: Gorakhpur District, Eastern UP, 1921–22', in Ranajit Guha (ed.), *Subaltern Studies III: Writings on South Asian History and Society*, Delhi: Oxford University Press, 1989: pp. 1–61.

   * *Kaccha paisa*: the regionally minted copper coin, used locally for small purchases and the payment of bazaar dues in Mundera: 5 kaccha paisa =1 anna. *Dabbal* ('double'?): the two paisa, or the half-anna, coin. 16 annas= 1 rupee.

However, at Chauri Chaura 'a trader managed to hand something over. Then there was no stopping the people', goes the authoritative account of Gandhi's train journey through Gorakhpur. 'A sheet was spread out and currency notes and coins started raining down. It was a sight.'[9]

There is a close correspondence between the authoritative and remembered accounts: donations figure prominently in both. But Sita, significantly, makes Gandhi's train stop at the godown (*malgodam*), well to the west of the railway station proper. (*Malgodamiya par, tisan ke pacchum!*) In a subsequent retelling Sita suggests that Gandhi's carriage was uncoupled at Chauri Chaura for a few hours. Did the bogie carrying the Mahatma get shunted out to the warehouse, awaiting the next train connection, while the populace milled around it at leisure? There is no evidence of this on record, though on occasion Gandhi's 'compartment was detached [and] . . . drawn up in front of a reserved platform', as happened at Madras Central in September 1920.[10] Should we discount Sita's precise location—'at the warehouse, to the west of the station'—as the site where Gandhi appeared before the people of Chauri Chaura only because it is a fact omitted from the published account? The unwritten rules of historical evidence would suggest we do. Unsure of the right answer I would push the question a bit further. Why should Sita confuse the malgodam and the platform, especially when he makes it a point to distinguish between the two?

Sleepy stations like Chauri Chaura were dominated by their godowns.[11] They were built to facilitate links between local production and consumption with the national and world markets. The warehouse precincts could have accommodated the 10,000 who had gathered to greet Gandhi that day. When Sita makes Gandhi's train stop at the warehouse, he enables us to better appreciate the significance of railside bazaars like Chauri Chaura.

The essence of Gandhi's train tours, which he conducted to personally propagate the message of non-cooperation, lay in the stops he invariably made at numerous stations. This afforded 'an expectant and believing people' to 'come from all quarters within walking reach to meet me'—as Gandhi himself put it in October 1920.[12] 'People groaning under misery and insult' flocked to the meetings he addressed at the bigger towns, and so did many more to meet him from 'within walking reach' of railside marts like Chauri Chaura or Gauri Bazaar (to name just two of the seven stops that Gandhi made that day in Gorakhpur district). Sita Ahir, for instance, had to walk just one mile to the malgodam to be in the presence of Gandhi-Baba. Small stations dominated by warehouses allowed the nationalist public a far better view of the Mahatma than was accorded by monster meetings like the one Gandhi addressed at Gorakhpur on the afternoon of 8 February 1921.[13]

Gandhi was apparently pleased with the crowd and the money collected at Chauri Chaura, as he was with the reception at the next station, Kusmhi,[14] eight miles up the track in the middle of a jungle that, thirty years earlier, had skirted Chotki Dumri itself. But railway stations were also the sites where the *darshan*-seeking public appeared as mobs to the Mahatma.* These 'insistent and assertive crowds' were bent on viewing and touching Gandhi even when he was asleep, and ended up in a 'tug of war' with his companions. They pulled up

---

* *Darshan*: paying homage to a holy object or a saintly person by presenting oneself in the vicinity of the personage.

the shutters of his carriage, lit up torches to quell the darkness, and demanded that Gandhi show himself. Sometimes they even engaged in a slanging match with the Mahatma—as happened on the journey back from Gorakhpur. It was these mobs that Gandhi wanted disciplined by trained volunteers.

When large crowds demanded darshan in the middle of the night, after the Gorakhpur train took a turn at Bhatni junction for Banaras, Gandhi lost his temper: 'I got up and peeped through the window . . . . It was quite cold but, in my temper, I didn't feel it. I pleaded with the people in a raised voice. Their shouting of slogans grew louder.' To Gandhi's angry question—'How could you expect darshan at night?'—the crowd responded with even louder cries: 'Victory to the Mahatma!' 'What was I to do?,' Gandhi wrote twelve days later. 'Should I jump from the window? Should I cry? Should I beat any of them? Should I stay back at the station?' Gandhi hit his forehead twice in anger, but with no apparent effect on the unruly people who had gathered at Salempur station. Gandhi hit himself for the third time. It was then that 'the people got frightened. They asked me to forgive them, became quiet and requested me to go to sleep'. Gandhi's secretary, who 'could not contain . . . [his] anger . . . had the cheek to tell a lie in the very presence of Gandhiji'.

Many of these devotees do not even know how their 'Mahatma Gandhi' looks. A few of them thrust themselves into our compartment, and began to bawl out, 'Who is Mahatma Gandhiji? Who is Mahatma Gandhiji?' I got desperate and said 'I'. They were satisfied, bowed down to me and left the compartment.[15]

Gandhi had formulated elaborate rules for the shepherding of such unruly demonstrators. Large crowds were not to be allowed inside railway stations, and people were to be let in just before 'the notified time of arrival' of Gandhi's train. 'Demonstrators' were to keep 'motionless and silent', and move only under a 'prearranged signal from an authorized volunteer'. Shouts of 'Victory to Gandhi' (and to the Nation) were not to be raised till after the arrival of the train.[16] The reception recounted by Sita Ahir and the midnight madness at Salempur suggest that people at railway stations were quite literally seeing their Mahatma in their own ways, unmindful of the disciplinary cordon that Gandhi had advocated at such sites! To see the unruly platform people only through the bleary eyes of Gandhi is to miss out the Mahatma that got fabricated at and on the way to smaller stations.

'When Mahatma Gandhi was going back on the night of 8 February from Gorakhpur . . . there was a huge gathering at Salempur station to have his darshan', reported a local correspondent in the nationalist weekly *Swadesh*. There was a Barai lad in that gathering. 'It is said that he had asked the wife of a high-caste Brahmin for a [cloth] wrapper to come to the station. She reprimanded him and refused to give him the blanket. The poor soul came shivering to the station, had darshan of the Mahatma and went back.' But the suffering of that young boy—'it was quite cold' that night, though Gandhi in his anger at the darshan-demanding crowd 'didn't feel it'—had become a part of a story. Next morning the village was agog with the rumour that shit was raining all over the house of that mean, anti-Gandhian woman who had denied the boy a blanket. This demeaning punishment was not the end of the story: 'In the end, only when she kept a fast and did ritual praying to the Mahatma did peace finally return to her.'[17]

In Gandhi's own account of the encounter with the Salempur mob, the hero is a local gentleman-nationalist who 'at every station . . . would plead with the people, restrain their eagerness for darshan and persuade them to remain quiet'.[18] In the south-eastern corner of the district, it is this young low-caste lad who goes out into the cold to the nearby station where Gandhi would stop, and, by his personal suffering, humbles a foul-mouthed sceptic—it is the son of the Barai who is the hero for having sought the Mahatma out.

The things that occurred at the station—that is, Gandhi lost his temper, he beat his forehead thrice in anger and thus frightened people into leaving him alone—seem to have been immaterial to the way the Mahatma's presence was felt in the nearby villages. Gandhi's story of his encounter with the Gorakhpuri mobs is enshrined in his *Collected Works*: It forms a part of the discourse of discipline. The stories of the *individuals* who sought Gandhi leaked out that night into an eddy of rumours about the Great One, adding to an imaginative crafting of the figure of Mahatma Gandhi.

'Gandhiji was only slightly better-built than I' [*Hamse taniye karer rahlan Gandhiji*] recalled the eighty-year-old Sita, establishing a physical connection between the people of Dumri and the author of non-cooperation. Naujadi for her part makes another link between Gandhi and his otiyars. Her account commences: 'To begin with, all were otiyars in Chauri Chaura; when Gandhi Maharaj's raj came, there were otiyars.' [*Chauri Chaura mein pahile sab otiyar rahlan; Gandhi-Mahatma ke jab raj ail—otiyar rahlan.*]

The phrase about the Mahatma is significant, for it makes the otiyars contemporaneous with Gandhi-raj. This is a novel perspective on the rule of Gandhi. Gandhi's raj is then not an impending event which had to be divined by a reading of its signs, nor is it an object attainable by militant means.[19] For Rameshar-volunteer's wife the time of the otiyars *was* the time of Gandhi-raj. The proximity created by Gandhi at the Chauri Chaura station on 8 February 1921, 'wearing a dhoti as I do' (Sita), paradoxically left no room for the District Congress Committee.

The presence of Gandhi in Gorakhpur seems to have left no separate space for Shaukat Ali and Mohammad Ali, the two charismatic leaders of the Khilafat movement, aligned to his non-cooperation campaign in India. We know from records of individuals, 'reading out Gandhiji's books and displaying Shaukat Ali's picture along with Gandhi's at Bhopa', the makeshift leather trading bazaar where a large contingent of Muslim peasants and traders and Chamar tanners congregated every Saturday. Mohammad Ali had also made that train journey to Gorakhpur along with Gandhi on 8 February 1921 and addressed the massive meeting at the district headquarters. In the countryside, however, the enthusiasm generated for the Khilafat cause and its high profile leaders was not separate from the popular regard for Mahatma Gandhi. At the Dumri meeting on the morning of the riot, a man 'wearing green glasses', whom Shikari could not identify but 'who from his words appeared to be a Musalman' came forward and 'began to read from a slip of paper', singing a song exhorting the gathering to embrace imprisonment, like Mohammad and Shaukat Ali, for two years' each. The man slipped away after the song, but the crowd which had been bound together by oath by Nazar Ali started its march to the thana to the cry of 'Victory to Mahatma Gandhi'. The pan-Islamic cause of Khilafat and the Indian fascination with the Mahatma were compounded in Dumri that day.[20]

Just as Gandhi was associated in Gorakhpur with a variety of miraculous occurrences—'We have not seen the miracles of the Mahatma; we have only heard of them', testified Sukhari, an accused of Amahiya village, in court[21]—so did his name lend itself as a label for all sorts of public meetings, pamphlets, and of course for that polysemic word 'Swaraj'. Lal Mohammad of Chaura sold two sets of 'announcements in Urdu', most probably exhortations to oppose the British published by the Khilafat Committee of Gorakhpur, 'which he said were Gandhiji's paper'. Shikari, who bought one such appeal in November 1921, priced at a low 2 and 4 pice each, was told 'to take the paper and return it when *Gandhiji asked for it*'.[22] The receipt for the more substantial donations to the Khilafat fund, which bore a superficial resemblance to a one-rupee bank note, though much larger in size, was referred to as a 'Gandhi note' by the peasants of Gorakhpur. Villagers, pro-government sources alleged, interpreted its non-acceptance (as legal tender?) as an act of opposition to the Mahatma.[23] Whether peasants genuinely failed to recognize the difference (as officials in some Awadh districts implied),[24] or whether this was just a conscious manipulation of an ambiguous printed paper to force non-believers into acceptance, we do not know for certain. What is clear, however, is that we have in the 'Gandhi note' an index of the popular tendency to look upon the Mahatma as an alternative source of authority.

However, as local-level volunteer activity entered a more militant phase in late 1921, the coming of Swaraj was perceived—contrary to everything the Congress stood for at that time—in terms of the direct supplanting of the authority of the police.[25] Thus Sarju Kahar, the personal servant of the thanedar of Chaura, testified that 'two or four days before the affair [he] had heard that Gandhi Mahatma's Swaraj had been established, that the Chaura thana would be abolished, and that the volunteers would set up their own thana'.[26]

As the High Court judges observed, the local peasantry 'perceived of it [Swaraj] as a millennium in which taxation would be limited to the collection of small cash contributions or dues in kind from fields and threshing floors, and [in] which the cultivators would hold their lands at little more than nominal rents'.[27] While recruiting volunteers to the newly formed Dumri mandal in January 1922, Nazar Ali and Shikari appear to have held out such promises. 'Shikari and Nazar Ali told me to become a volunteer', testified Sampat Chamar, a labourer from Chaura. 'Shikari told me I would get 2 or 3 bighas of land [at low rent] if I got myself enrolled . . . . So I became a volunteer.'[28] Thakur Ahir, the second approver, was promised a substantial reduction in his rent and also a volunteer's salary just below the current daily wage rate:

Nazar Ali and Shikari and a small boy [Nackched Kahar, the schoolboy who filled the forms] made me a volunteer . . . . I became a volunteer because I was told that the Maharaj's [Gandhi] Swaraj would come and I should [only] have to pay 4 annas a bigha, and would get Rs 8 pay a month.[29]

Surveying the background to the Chauri Chaura riot, the judges of the High Court found it 'remarkable . . . how this name of "Swaraj" was linked, in the minds of the peasantry of Gorakhpur, with the name of Mr Gandhi. Everywhere in the evidence and in the statements made . . . by various accused persons', they found that 'it was "Gandhiji's Swaraj", or the "Mahatmaji's Swaraj" for which they [i.e., the peasants] were looking.'[30] We have it on local testimony that peasant volunteers proceeding to a sabha at Dumri on the morning of 4 February 1922 (hours before the clash with the police was to occur at the Chaura thana, a couple of miles away), claimed that they were 'going to hold a Gandhi Mahatma Sabha' which would bring about 'Gandhi Swaraj'.[31]

What is significant is that the phrase 'Gandhiji's swaraj has come' was used as an exhortation for each and every reversal that the Dumri volunteers brought about that day. When the daroga tried to save the day by apologizing to the crowd and letting it move towards Mundera bazaar, 'then the gathering clapped their hands', jeered that the daroga was 'shit scared', and said 'Gandhiji's swaraj had come to pass'. Once the police had sought to recover lost ground by firing and the crowd had begun brickbatting and clubbing the policemen, leaders like Lal Mohammad and Meghu Tiwari were reported to have shouted: 'Kill the sister-fucker-policemen, Swaraj has come. Burn the thana.' 'Until the thana has been burnt and the police have been killed, there will not be Gandhiji's swaraj,' another man rushing in to join the riot was reported shouting.[32]

According to Harbans Kurmi of Mangapatti, Narayan, Baleshar and Chamru of his village said on their return from the riot that 'they had burnt and thrown away and Swaraj had come'.[33] Or, as Phenku Chamar told the sessions judge in August 1922:

Bipat Kahar, Sarup Bhar and Mahadeo Bhuj were coming along calling out 'Gandhi Maharaj, Gandhi Maharaj' from the north, the direction of Chaura, to [the] south, the direction of Barhampur. I asked why they were calling out 'Gandhi Maharaj' and they said the thana of Chaura had been burnt and razed to the ground [by them] and the Maharaj's swaraj had come.[34]

Of course, all this evidence was produced in the court so as to prove a connection between public proclamations made by individual accused and the crimes for which they were jointly on trial. But this is not reason enough to disregard these paradoxical and cruel cries in the name of Gandhi. First, several analyses of contemporary volunteer activity in other parts of north India suggest that peasant-nationalists were invoking the Mahatma to rough up opponents, punish waverers, and attack bazaars and police stations.[35] Second, the foregoing discussion of the presence of Gandhi suggests that the issue of violence apart, the Mahatma of the peasants was not as he really was but as they had thought him up. This is the case in the villages around Chauri Chaura even today.

Ramji, an untouchable and therefore living in the segregated Chamar quarters on the outskirts of the village, remembers Gandhi's arrival and his message with a profanity that ends up implicating the Mahatma with the riotous actions of the Dumri volunteers!

This son of Puranmasi Chamar (convicted for eight years), Ramji, came to know 'Gandhi Maharaj' only after seeing them. He did not know about him earlier. And Gandhi Maharaj,

did he leave a single village untouched? Oh no! And what did he tell everybody? Just this much: 'Fucking-hell! take back your raj; turn out these mother-fuckers; kick out the Englishman!' In every village this is what people talked, thought and agreed on. You know, this business about the thana—the burning etc.,—all this leads back to him, to Gandhi Maharaj! [Are hamman unke, Gandhi Maharaj ke ta bad mein jiyanal gailin: magar pahilwan hamman nahin jani, magar Gandhi Maharaj ekko gawn choren! Khali ehe kahen, ekar bahin-chodo ee raj apan le la, aa eke sale ke khed da . . . angrej ke kheda! Ehe te hokhe gawn-gawn sarmatiya, uho gaur karen. Hai thanwa-onwa akhir unhi ke jari se jaral.]

At least in this account, everything, including the violence, seems to derive from Gandhi!

It may be argued that it is because of the riot that Ramji Chamar remembers Mahatma Gandhi in such an obscenely violent way. However, there is other evidence to suggest that the Dumri volunteers, in their attempts to do 'Gandhi Mahatma's work',[36] were equipping themselves in a markedly different fashion. Months before the clash with the police, the ways of Nazar Ali and his associates were already at variance with, and often in actual opposition to, the dictates of the Mahatma and the requirements of the District Congress Committee of Gorakhpur.

We therefore turn to the image of the volunteer in Dumri village to chart the career of Nazar Ali, Shikari, and others before the picketing of fish, meat, and liquor shops began; before Bhagwan Ahir, returned soldier-turned-volunteer, was beaten by the police inspector; before Nazar Ali sent letters to other volunteers inviting them to a meeting at Dumri on the morning of 4 February to 'stop at the Mundera bazaar after paying our respects to the daroga'.

OTIYARS

An otiyar (volunteer) was one who begged for his food and who wore gerua (safflower-coloured) clothes.

That is how Naujadi began her account on 18 August 1988. 'It was raining appropriately in patches, for the lunar asterism [nakshatra] was Maggha, and all of us—a small inquisitive set—were sitting in the tiled verandah [osara] of Shikari's old house. Sharfuddin, Shikari's son and the elected village chief, had asked Sita and Naujadi, the two surviving witnesses to Chauri Chaura, to come over to his house. Besides Sharfuddin and myself, there was Shikari's four-year-old grandson, Shikari's daughter, Jaibul, Sita Ahir, Naujadi, and a couple of young men from the village.' The interview with Sita had concluded for the day; it was Naujadi's turn to speak. She said:

'In the beginning there were otiyars in Chauri Chaura. When Gandhi Mahatma's raj came there were otiyars. They asked for alms.' Shikari Babu, 'this gentleman's father', Naujadi points to Sharfuddin, 'was there; Nazar Ali was there, Salamat-father-in-law [bhasur] was there; Nageshar, my devar [husband's younger brother] was there; Rameshar was there'. Naujadi, taken in by this roll call uncharacteristically identifies her husband by his first name and not by the euphemism hamar parani (lit. 'my life'). 'And Awdhi was there. I am telling you the story of that time.' With this temporal emphasis, Naujadi comes round to identifying the otiyars by their attributes. First they got organized, they got together and discussed things (lit. 'did some "committeeing"') among themselves (apne mein log Kumeti kail). And like beggars asking for alms (bhik), they asked for a pinch of grain chutki. 'They had flags, pink, no gerua long shirts (kurta), caps, flags.' She now turns to the otiyar's uniform.

Chauri Chaura mein pahile sab otiyar rahlan. Gandhi-Mahatma ke jab raj ail—otiyar rahlan. Bhik mangat rahlan. Babu-ke dada rahlan.[37] Ohmen Shikari-babu rahlan, Najar Ali rahlan, Salamat-bhasur rahlan . . . Sahadat rahlan, Nagesar, hamre devar rahlan, Ramesar rahlan, Awadhi rahlan . . . Sun tani! Oh-samay ke bat ba!

Okre bad mein inhan-se Sarkar jab apne-mein log 'kumeti' kail, aa chutki mangat rahal, te ohi-mein khat-o rahlan aa dharat-o rahal . . . Mane khat-o apne-mein rahlan, aur dhara-jat rahal jo besi ho.

Khariyani nahin let rahlan.[38] Jaise bhikmanga chutki mangele na? Mange-lan bhik!!—Ohi-tarah log bhik mangat rahlan.

Jhanda rahal, gulabi-kurta rahal—gerua-rang; dhoti rahal, topi rahal, aa jhanda rahal.

In Naujadi's mind chutki, bhik, and gerua clothes together distinguished the otiyars of Chauri Chaura.

CHUTKI, OR THE GIFT OF GRAIN

'They would come abegging and ask for a pinch of grain,' says Naujadi, wife of Rameshar Pasi of Chotki Dumri. Demanding chutki was regarded as evidence of a volunteering past in the court as well. However, chutki was here so closely associated with *chanda* (subscription) as to have become synonymous with it. 'We were all told to collect subscriptions [*chanda* and *chutki*]' is how Shikari's implicit distinction between these two was blurred in the official record of the trial.[39] In the judicial probe, chutki was one fact among many by which the accused were identified as volunteers: donning a Gandhi cap, patrolling the village at night, 'behaving as a policeman' at a fair or a gathering, signing the pledge form—all these formed the set of incriminating evidence.[40]

With Naujadi it was chutki that mattered most. It was what distinguished a real otiyar from a nominal one—her brother-in-law from her husband, for example:

Otiyar khali uhe, chotka [Nageshar-devar] rahal. [As for Rameshar, her husband?]: Are likhaule rahlan, mane mangat nahin rahlan. Uu [Nagesar] mangat rahal—gerua . . . sab pahir le-lena, lugga-kapra. [Ramesar] khali likhaule-bhar rahlan.

Translated, this is roughly what she says: 'It was only he—Nageshar—the younger one, who was the otiyar. As for Rameshar, well he had himself enrolled but never asked for chutki. Nageshar, he would ask for it, he had gerua clothes, the works.'

It was chutki-begging and not enrolment that made a volunteer. And the volunteers asked for chutki, *like beggars*, Naujadi stresses, her voice rising in exasperation at my inability immediately to grasp the meaning of the term. 'Send out a pinch of flour, mother! [*Bhejyo mai, chutki*]' was in fact a mendicant's cry in north India.[41] The housewife, before cooking the day's food, would set aside some lentils, rice, or flour as her share for volunteers. It was not so much the reason as the reasonableness of the demand—'they did not come for it everyday, did they? [*roj nahin-na kahen? . . . dusre-tisre din diyat rahal*]—that Naujadi remembers. Out of the chutki so collected, every third day or so the volunteers would cook their own food; the surplus chutki they would stock up.

This short paraphrase of Naujadi's long statement on chutki provides a housewife's view of the Chauri Chaura volunteers.[42] Nationalism in the guise of the alms-seeking volunteer appeared literally outside Naujadi's door: '*Aa hamar duare-pe aa-ke khara hoilan bhikmanga! Hamre jo-kuch jutal: chaur-dal jutal, pisan jutal, diyai.*' Whatever could be managed, she says—rice, lentils, flour—I gave. Since the peasant household parted with a portion of its food, it fell to the housewife to make arrangements for the upkeep of these full-time peripatetic volunteers.[43] They were not given the leftovers, as was 'the stated rule' with *sanyasis*;[44] otiyars claimed a fraction of the food at the point at which it was to be cooked by the housewife [*grihasthin*].*

Chutki lay in the domain of the domestic. This pinch of grain was what the peasant family volunteered from its own consumption. And unlike *khalihani*, or harvest dues, collected periodically at the threshing floor, chutki-giving tied recipients and donors in a continual, quotidian relationship. In local parlance chutki was not a *huk* (a right) but *bhik* (alms); its recipient was a beggar-like person, not a superordinate claimant.

---

* *Grihasthini* in its proper Sanskritic rendition.

Chutki-giving for non-ascetic or political purposes was not novel in the region: the militant kine protection leagues that had emerged in the 1890s to safeguard the Hindu community's holy cows from being slaughtered by butchers and at Muslim religious ceremonies had laid down elaborate chutki-gathering rules.* 'Each household was directed to set apart at each meal one chutki (equal in weight or value to one paisa) of foodstuff for each member of the family.' And in keeping with the cow-centred discipline of the sabhas, 'the eating of food without setting apart the chutki' was tantamount to eating beef! *Sabhasads* (agents) were deputed to garner these contributions. They were to convert chutki-grain into hard cash and remit the money to regional treasurers.[45]

An analogous network of converting chutki to cash and its onward transmission to headquarters was proposed by the Gorakhpur Congress Committee in 1921. In a front-page notice, *Swadesh*, the nationalist weekly, exhorted 'each and every village . . . claiming faith in Mahatma Gandhi' to 'take out *chutki* . . . and *khalihani*'.[46] Raghupati Sahai, who became the famous poet Firaq Gorakhpuri in later years, was initially in charge of these collections. Maulvi Subhanullah, the District Congress President, replaced him in May 1921. In a public notice Firaq enjoined 'one or two persons in every village to take responsibility for the collection of *muthia* and *khalihani*'. Responsible individuals were to sell the chutki-grain 'in the village or a nearby bazaar' and forward the cash by money order to the District Congress Committee in Gorakhpur. The preferred mode was for collectors to come over to the headquarters and deposit the cash personally.[47] Chutki registers were in existence in villages like Burha Dih near Pipraich, and in Padrauna tahsil.[48] Small wonder then that the 1921–22 budget of the District Congress had estimated an income of Rs 5 lakhs from chutki-muthia collections. A realization rate of ½ *chatanks* chutki daily per house of 10 persons, with a 33 per cent 'discount for unrealized houses', when sold at an average rate of 12 seers to the rupee, yielded an annual value of Rs 509,352 for the entire district.[49] The rate of conversion was arrived at keeping in mind the different foodstuffs—*pisan, chaur, dal* in Naujadi's composite phrase—that were offered as chutki. As the secretary, Gorakhpur Town Congress Committee, told the court, 'various corns [*sic*] were collected in the handfuls [*muthia*], so it was considered that they will sell for 12 standard seers to the rupee.'[50]

For the Congress Committee chutki was a subscription; it was another name for chanda. It had to be collected, forwarded, and accounted for. Lists of authorized chutki and chanda collectors were often published in nationalist newspapers;[51] district accounts ledgers have such entries as 'direct muthia from a Salempur village, Rs 7–12'.[52] Chutki or muthia collections were certainly not meant for the upkeep of local volunteers—there was no provision for this in the budget for 1921–2.[53] When Hakeem Arif came to Dumri on 13 January, 'he told Lal Mohammad and Nazar Ali and (Shikari) to make over to Bhagwati Bania the subscriptions . . . (*chanda and chutki*) collected by us.'[54] This order, Shikari testified in court, was not obeyed. 'Collections . . . made by Lal Mohammad and Nazar Ali' were 'apparently embezzled', said the judge, basing himself on the approver's testimony.[55]

---

* Such chutki or *muthia* (*mutthi*: fist) collections could, for instance, support full-time Sanskrit students at an informal *pathshala*. For an example from north Bihar, see Rahul Sankrityayan, *Meri Jeevan Yatra*, i, Kalkutta, 1951: 21.

THE FEAST OF 4 FEBRUARY 1922

All this is a far cry from Naujadi's idea of chutki. Chutki for Naujadi was what sustained full-time volunteers. It was not a contribution meant for ultimate deposit in the District Congress treasury.[56] Naujadi's otiyars in fact straddled the distance that separated chutki, a public levy, from chanda, a nationalist subscription. The surplus chutki was laid aside (*dharat rahal*) in the village for a suitable public use.[57] According to Naujadi, the big Dumri gathering of 4 February feasted on the chutki collected by the volunteers of Chauri Chaura. Shikari in his statement did not mention the storage and the feast. He alluded, however, to the *gur*, or raw sugar, that had been collected for the meeting.[58] Naujadi maintained that it was a regular feast (and not 'modest provisions', as the judge noted) that took place on the day of the clash with the police:

I mean sweets were there, vegetables were there, rice and dal, this-and-that was there. All this was cooked, they ate, they drank, and only then did they move. [*Aré mitha ail rahal, mane mitha, tarkari ail rahal, dal-chaur ail rahal, dusar-tisar ail rahal . . . banal, khailan-piyalan, tab uthlan.*]

It is difficult to miss the hyperbole in this statement. But it is precisely such excess of description that enables Naujadi to underscore the public and festive nature of that gathering. Here, issues were debated, food consumed, oaths administered, and the march to the thana commenced amidst fanfare:

Are you listening! In the month of Magh there was a gathering here. [*Suni! te Magh-ke mahinna mein inhan bator bhail.*] It is the same month now! There was a gathering; everybody came. All the chutki that had been kept—all that chutki—was sent to the *kali-mai-ke-than*.* It was at the place that the feast took place [*Ohi-ja banal bhandara*]. They ate and drank; thick, real thick garlands were prepared; and then the drums [*dholaks*] started their song.

It was from such a meeting that the otiyars marched, singing and shouting, on to the thana.[59] Note the effervescent nature of the Dumri sabha; and note specially the feast that Naujadi repeatedly emphasizes. Brought up on a diet of Indian anthropology, I wanted to know whether the grain was cooked or offered uncooked, *sattu*-like.[60] At this Naujadi lost her patience:

Now, whether they cooked it or consumed it uncooked [*kaccha*], this I did not see with my own eyes. I didn't see who ate and who didn't, did I? It was in his house—in Mir Shikari's house . . . and in Salamat's house [Shikari's daughter's in-laws'] that all the stuff was kept . . . .
  Everybody, young and old [*larka, parani, manahi*], everybody carted the stuff away. Whether people cooked it and ate it, or they didn't eat it—the stuff left [Shikari's] house.

'I am telling you, all the grain was sent for the feast [*Ajji! sajji jinisiya gail khae-piye ke; Bhandara mein chal gail!*].' The construction of this passage is significant: it is not as if the grain was kept in a storehouse (*bhandar*); in fact, on the morning of 4 February it was sent out to the

---

* The village threshing floor (*khalihan*) was also known as Kali-mai-ka-than, after the small Kali temple, laying adjacent to it.

*bhandara.** Now, bhandara means both a 'storehouse' and a 'feast' (of jogis, sanyasis, etc.). 'Baba-ka bhandara bhar-pur rahe' was a benediction of plenitude that alms-seeking mendicants showered on householders. The beggar's second cry, 'Mhare bhandare mein sajha kar-ke mai, mhare bhandare mein' was an invitation to the alms-giving housewife to share in the mendicant's feast/storehouse in the next world.[61] In Naujadi's recall chutki and bhandara unite the individual volunteer to other volunteers and to the 'paulic' (public) at large. The bhik given to the otiyars remained in the village, but it made a substantial contribution to the success of a major political meeting.

Do the terms bhik, chutki, and bhandara suggest that Naujadi's otiyars should be thought of as sadhus and sanyasis, renouncers, and religious mendicants? I do not think so, for several reasons. First, during her long exposition on chutki, Naujadi nowhere employed these familiar terms. She repeatedly used the descriptive *bhikmanga* (beggar), not baba, which is the generic term for a religious mendicant. 'Baba duare mange dal-o-pisan ho!' is how a Bhojpuri poet was to describe the usual chutki-seeking ascetics of eastern UP.[62] Naujadi, however, refrained from characterizing Nazar Ali, Shikari, or Nageshar, her brother-in-law, as babas in nationalist garb. Even when someone glossed over her comment on gerua clothes with the stock phrase, '*vairagya mein aa gaye*' (they appeared as ascetics), she did not nod her head in assent. For Naujadi the chutki-seekers of 1922 were political activists from the village: all householders whom she knew, and whose physical strength and organizational skill she admired. They begged bhikmanga-like for chutki,[63] but that did not make them sanyasis or ascetics.

Volunteer—a new idea—comes into the village. This term is neither translated into the standard Hindi, swayam sevak, nor absorbed into the more common baba or sanyasi. The word is peasantized. It would not help to translate this peasantization, namely otiyar, any further. The cultural significance of this term would in fact be denied if we failed to accept that peasants play with, transfer, and transform alien concepts into idioms which fit with their daily lives. We do not gain anything by translating one native term into another. So, it would help to stay with Naujadi's otiyars for a little bit longer.

THE COLOUR GERUA AND PROPER NATIONALIST ATTIRE

The chutki-seekers of Naujadi wore *gulabi* (pink) or gerua clothes. In our second meeting in February 1989, Naujadi elaborated on the coloured clothes of the volunteers:

When Gandhi-Baba came—what did he give [us]? He took out [karhlan] otiyars. Otiyars he took out. He first sent word that people should become otiyars. Red, black—no, not black—red—geru . . . everything geru. Then the cap was got dyed, this, whatsitsname, dhoti, was got dyed. And this big flag and lathi . . . And the flag was used for gathering chutki.

Now, the dyeing of dhotis was not the norm in eastern UP and Bihar. *Markin*, that is, machine-made cloth with the distinguishing mark of a Lancashire or Bombay mill, was the cloth most used for dhotis, and it was usually white.[64] Shikari's uncle recalled seeing 'a large number of men' going towards the thana, 'some with yellow and *some with ordinary cloth*'.[65] Where white was the norm,

---

* A sister word, *bhandari*, is still used in Mundera for Sant Baksh Singh's provisioning of the police raiding parties after the riot.

the dyeing of cloth had a special significance attached to it. Dhotis are still dyed primarily for marriages and other ceremonies, and they are dyed by the *rangrez*, the professional dyer commonly pronounced 'angrez'! Buchanan-Hamilton, that trusted companion of medieval and modern historians, comes in handy here. 'The dyers in most parts of the district', he wrote in his notice on Bhagalpur:

are chiefly employed to dye the clothes of those who attend marriage parties . . . and during the three months that the ceremonies last, the dyers make very high wages; but at other times they have little employment.
[Those in the town of Munger] dye chiefly with safflower, with which they give two colours, kusami [*kusumbi*: cloth dyed with safflower, *s.v.* Fallon], a bright pomegranate red, and Golabi a fine red like rose; and each colour is of two different shades . . . . The safflower, *Carthamus tinctorious* or kusum is most in demand.[66]

Gulabi, lal, and geru were used interchangeably by Naujadi; in the court records gerua bastar, red, or simply 'coloured clothes', described the *pahirawa* (dress) of the Chauri Chaura volunteers.[67] In fact the various volunteer corps, as they sprang up in the early 1920s, revealed a marked preference for coloured uniforms.[68] An intelligence report noted that 'the yellow [gerua] shirt' was specially popular among the volunteers in UP. In north Bihar, nationalist battalions were dressed in *khaddar* of 'yellow *ramraj* colour'. Rahul Sankrityayan, who raised one such unit of '*rangin vardi-dhari swayam-sevaks*', also tried his hand at dyeing by looking up the nationalist-chemist P. C. Ray's book on colour.[69] The Bihar Sewak Dal, formed in late 1921 to foment rebellion (*baghawat*), had a wide range of coloured uniforms: white for Hajipur, red for Muzaffarpur, and green dhotis for those enlisting in Sitamarhi district.[70] The UP Provincial Volunteer Board, for its part, reserved these swaraj colours for shoulder straps; it recommended kusumbi and *zafrani* (safflower and saffron) as the preferred colour for khaddar uniforms.[71] All this was in total disregard of Gandhi's express instructions on proper nationalist attire.

For Gandhi, the satyagrahi had to wear white khaddar; coloured clothes were out at least until swaraj was attained. The Mahatma was willing to compromise on certain things: one's bedding, for instance, could still be of 'foreign or mill-made cloth', as there were 'difficulties in the way of immediate self-purification to this extent'.[72] No such difficulty was countenanced for khaddar as apparel. Those who could not afford to buy khaddar worth Rs 5–10 for their clothes 'could certainly borrow this amount . . . and become volunteer(s)'.[73] It was not 'at all difficult', wrote Gandhi in late 1921, to 'use khadi for one's clothes.' A 'very poor man' could 'limit himself to a loincloth, but this should be of khadi'.[74]

The importance of khadi consisted in three qualities: sparseness, coarseness, and whiteness. Handloom silk and woollen clothes were to be abjured, except 'when . . . required by climatic or other urgent considerations . . . . The fashion certainly should be . . . to wear coarse khaddar'.[75] The clothes of the Gandhian volunteer had to be coarse khaddar and white. 'India will lose nothing by wearing only white clothes for some time to come. Let them fill in colours after they have, clad in white, achieved their goal', Gandhi quoted approvingly from an unlikely source. He added: 'We wear white khaddar because we have no time to get it dyed. Moreover, many of us do not like colours, as they are of foreign make.'[76]

In early 1922, at the height of the volunteer movement (96,000 had signed up in UP alone), Gandhi's instructions on proper khaddar-wear were being ignored. 'Hardly 50 could be found dressed in hand-spun khaddar from top to toe' in Allahabad and Banaras. Others 'wore khaddar for outer covering, all the rest being foreign cloth'.[77] In Calcutta, Gandhi ruefully catalogued 'hundreds who have gone to jail know nothing about the pledge, are not dressed in khaddar, are not dressed even in Indian mill-made cloth but have gone to jail wearing foreign cloth, and . . . they have had no training in non-violence.'[78]

WHAT THE OTIYARS WORE

The picture in Chauri Chaura was no different. For Naujadi it was Gandhi all right who had created volunteers, but she was clearer that the otiyars wore gerua than that it was khaddar.[79] In enquiries and testimonies khaddar and gerua often appear as exclusive categories. A report on the occurrence published in *Pioneer* spoke of a 3000-strong 'procession . . . headed by *four or five volunteers in khaddar uniform*'.[80] The unofficial Congress enquiry talked in turn about 'five or six hundred volunteers' all 'clad in gerua-coloured clothes . . . accompanied by a large crowd'.[81] In the first version it was texture, in the second colour, which marked a Chauri Chaura volunteer.

At innumerable places in the court records we get the equation gerua clothes = volunteers.[82] Bhagwan Ahir, himself a leading actor, stated: 'some [were] dressed in white and *some dressed as volunteers*'.[83] Nazar Ali was identified 'as a volunteer as he was in front of the crowd and *was wearing gerua cloth*'.[84] It was not as if no one wore khaddar. Dwarka Pandey of Barhampur mandal was in his khaddar dhoti-kurta when he was put up for identification in the district jail. The magistrate had to make special arrangements—two persons were asked to don khaddar clothes and stand beside Dwarka—to make the identification proceedings seem fair to the accused.[85] But even Dwarka, reminiscing fifty years later, talked about 'a 400-strong contingent of gerua-clad volunteers supervising the conduct of the 5000-strong crowd'.[86]

The distinction between colour and texture breaks down in several recollections in the courtroom. Meghu Tiwari, the chief villain involved in dishonouring the darogain, was denounced as a volunteer who 'used to wear gerua-khaddar . . . before . . . [and] on Chaura riot day'.[87] Identifying eight men from his village, Mahatam of Kusmhi testified: 'They were all dressed in gerua khaddar. They told me they were going to Dumri sabha. *Volunteers wear gerua cloth.*'[88] We are back once again to gerua as the distinguishing marker.

Sarju Kahar, a domestic servant at the thana, was certain that 'the volunteers had on gerua cloth and were crying Mahatmaji's jai. The four men I identified had on gerua cloth'.[89] One of these, Bhagwan Ahir, the subaltern pensioner from the Mesopotamia campaign, was not wearing gerua. On 4 February, Bhagwan was sporting, as usual, his 'khaki sarkari coat', appropriate attire for the drill master of Chaura volunteers. Bhagwan, it seems, never took his jacket off, even while in hiding. Constable Jai Ram arrested him on 10 March in the northern jungle by the river Gandak 'because of his [khaki] uniform'.[90] Such was the metonymic connection gerua/otiyar that Sarju Kahar persisted in identifying Bhagwan-volunteer by his non-existent gerua clothes.

The association of otiyars with a particular colour was so strong that in the courtroom reconstruction of the riot, those proved to be wearing white clothes were presumed to be spectators and not volunteers! The counsels for the accused spent considerable time getting the approvers to admit to this distinction between geru and white. 'I meant by "spectators" the people who were wearing white, not coloured clothes,' Shikari stated at the beginning of his cross-examination. The Defence pushed him further:

I considered the persons wearing coloured clothes to be volunteers. And I thought the persons who were not wearing coloured clothes were not volunteers. Among those 4000 [outside the thana] were volunteers, non-volunteers and spectators.[91]

Thakur, the second approver, also stated under cross-examination: 'the volunteers had on ochre-coloured clothing [gerua bastar].'[92] These were not abstract characterizations. What the approvers made of a man's attire was a matter of life and death for the person in the dock. Shikari had named Shahadat as 'taking part in the riot', but was unclear about his volunteer status. Under cross-examination Shikari replied that Shahadat of Dumri was 'not a volunteer *because* he wore white clothes'. The judge seemed to agree. Among other reasons, Shahadat's clothes were the reason why Holmes of Gorakhpur 'did not think it . . . safe to convict him'.[93] Clothes like Shahadat's testified to the presence of non-volunteers and spectators in the crowd. White, coarse khaddar was not a markedly nationalist sign in Chauri Chaura.

What significance do we ascribe to gerua then? How much 'reflexivity' was there in the wearing of these garments? Were the volunteers conscious that their clothes were different from those prescribed by the Mahatma?

The emphasis on gerua need not imply that the Gandhian creed was thereby divested of all meaning. Naujadi's heroes were clearly imbued with the idea of Gandhi. 'Otiyar' they conceived of as a novel category, a state requiring marked changes in living and attire: witness Nazar Ali, who had sold off his tailoring business ever since he became a volunteer-activist in early 1922.[94] Dyeing their clothes yellow—rather than wearing white and proper khaddar—and doing Gandhi's bidding were not incompatible practices for the Dumri nationalists.

So, for Naujadi and many others, chutki and gerua defined the volunteers.[95] True, these terms have histories of their own.[96] But the old woman has no urge to hurl her otiyars back into the enveloping fold of a context-free meaningful past. Naujadi remembers them in relation to a specific present: 'the time of Gandhi-raj and of the turmoil [utpat] we [hamman] all created' on 4 February 1922. Naujadi's usage of hamman, the first person plural, embraces the otiyars and their families in a collective act of great national significance for which they still await adequate recompense.

WITNESS TO A HISTORY

Sita: Chauri Chaura is really the first 'case' in connection with *Swaraj*.
Naujadi: No doubt about it, it is Chauri Chaura for sure—and Dumri is the place from where everything started . . . . Everybody has got their raj, our raj never came. It's us [hamman] who created the turmoil [utpat], and look what we got—nothing!

The old widow is of course complaining about Rameshar's political pension which, instead of coming to her, is intercepted by local politicos who parade relatives of the rioters in Lucknow and Delhi for their own ends. Naujadi no longer has her paper with 172 written on it. Rajbansi Sainthwar, a politician from Bansgaon tahsil, has taken it away. Her poverty; the bully

Rajbansi; the pension that never comes; the arrival of Gandhi; the sabha at Dumri—all are jumbled together into her poignant statement. Naujadi breaks down and the visiting historian hears himself mumble foolishly: 'What else do I ask you?'

Listen! In the month of Magh chutki-gathering started, and this event also happened in the month of Magh. This kand took place after a year. After one year this, whatsitsname—the sabha—took place. Are you listening! 172 persons there are on my paper, and Rajbansi has taken it away. [Breaks down.] My son had died [and I had to go to Delhi with Rajbansi]. I said to Rajbansi, 'Oh neta', I said, 'I can't make it.' He replied, 'I'll beat your arse blue if you carry on like this.' Eh Babu! hearing this my daughter started crying. Rajbansi also took away a hundred rupees from me. Babua-log, give me something to keep me going.

Naujadi's story is not just about the event of 1922, it is equally about the iniquitous recognition of freedom fighters. Our long conversations somehow missed out on what it felt to be the wife or the son of a convicted rioter. Rather, the memory of privation, when the householder was locked up for eight to fifteen years, or indeed hanged, was enveloped by the quest for the political pension that was now due to the family. Recollections of the riot in Dumri are invariably interspersed with graphic accounts of a recent trip to New Delhi—to 'Rajiv's [Rajiv Gandhi's] house', to Jantar Mantar, or to the Rashtrapati Bhavan. The successful insertion of that infamous event into the life of the nation has both freed and framed familial memories.

Towards Conclusion

'Now Sir! Fathom it after your own heart! How much more can one narrate [*Babu! Apne dil se samajh leen! Ab kahwan le biyan kihal ja*].' So concludes Naujadi.

And so the time has come to stitch this narrative to a close and make an end of our story. In this chapter I have tried to do several things—some may feel too many. I have tried to raise certain questions about the ways of nationalist historiography. 'Chauri Chaura' is a tale of how the celebrated condemnation of a riot by Gandhi paradoxically entitles it to national importance. This outrage, this episode, this kand, has until now been stereotypically forced into the narrative of the freedom struggle. This denotes the quiet confidence, indeed the supreme and not quite warranted confidence, that a dominant ideology has hitherto exuded over a colonial past. At a general level, the story of the riot suggests *how* a particular event is excised from a series in terms of its denouement and consequence, even though it belongs to a set of events similar in almost all respects. A close study of such an occurrence then discloses the tensions which such acts of excision hide within the body of an apparently homogeneous set of events: hours before the clash with the police, the Dumri volunteers were as Gandhian as most other peasant-volunteers in India in the winter of 1921–2. Hours after it, they were criminals.

It is the nationalist requirement to perceive Chauri Chaura differently that precludes a fuller understanding of all these tensions between the leaders and the led, authorized statements and popular understanding, organization and movement. Such tensions characterize all mass movements, nationalism included. The contrary tendency, the antithesis of nationalist historiography as exemplified in colonialist writings, is to see the riot in a common blur of rustic excesses fuelled by local political machinations. This again leaves us none the wiser, for it affords no space from where to write the history of such exceptional and revealing events.

Chauri Chaura is a metaphor both for nationalists and colonialists because it typifies violent police–peasant confrontations under the British Raj. Preparatory to the launch of his second all-India campaign of civil disobedience, Gandhi had in early 1930 'wished to discover a formula whereby sufficient provision can be made for avoiding suspension by reason of Chauri Chaura'. A singular event eight years in the past had by now come to inform an entire nationalist strategy. And in August 1942, when police and railway stations were targeted by student- and peasant-nationalists to force the British to 'Quit India', the governor of UP took recourse to the imagery of a past riot when characterizing the turmoil in the provinces of Uttar Pradesh and Bihar.

. . . there has been a second Chauri Chaura at a police station in Ghazipur, the police station burnt and the staff murdered.

It is not in its violence alone that 'Chauri Chaura' suggests other places, other events, other times. While paying particular heed to the riot outside the thana, I have also looked closely at the internal face of popular nationalism: the demiurgic presence of Gandhi, local elaborations on his teachings, the self-empowerment of volunteers. Chauri Chaura, this work implies, indicates peasant nationalism more generally. . . .

Although the difficulties with the actors' speech in the court and in the nationalist record push the possibility of narrating the event, historical fieldwork—that is, interviews, conversations, and the eliciting of contemporary recollections of a very old event—can feebly attempt to unify extant and emerging accounts. Testimony to the incompleteness of the existing record, familial memories are, however, themselves witness to *another* history, namely the recent nationalization of the event.

The enormous conceptual and narratological complications here are obvious by being on display. So, clearly, I am not suggesting that what we now have on record is the definitive voice and consciousness of the actors as it played itself out in early 1922. I simply note that the problems of capturing 1922 through interviews in 1990 are considerable, as are the pitfalls of a pragmatic reliance on contemporary evidence. Certainly, I have consciously shunned any attempt to use oral history as a seasoning to enliven documentary evidence. My effort has been to arrive at an enmeshed, intertwined, and imbricated web of narratives from every available source. Without venturing into historical fieldwork I would have continued reconstructing the event through court records of 1922 without circumventing the problems that this procedure would have entailed. This, it seemed to me, would yield a somewhat barren archival book, a detailed textual analysis of the judicial archive which gratuitously failed to unearth exciting, alternative accounts which will soon be dead to the historian.

Given the negative charge attached to the event within Indian nationalism, competing contemporary narratives of the riot are largely absent. I have therefore tried to trace the event by teasing out local remembrances of things past. In my encounters with Naujadi Pasin, Sita Ahir, and others, processes and encounters external to 'Chauri Chaura', but not to its retellings, play their part. While according primacy to local speech, I have refrained from simple ethno-reportage. I have sought instead to reproduce specific, personalized, and often eccentric accounts and have ranged, arranged, rearranged these against the authorized texts of historiography: court records, contemporary tracts, ethnological notices, even the dictionary. This is my own historiographical way of shaping events and their recall and their context into a far from final or authoritative text, yet nonetheless one which strives towards a complexity hitherto absent. The historian who seeks to garner memories of an event officially labelled 'crime', cannot escape marching outwards from the archives, for a refusal to recognize the prior presence of law, 'the state's emissary',[97] is unlikely to lead to a better dialogue at the present site of past action.

Writing history in this fashion leads one to constantly ask whether the really complex questions about the production of historical narratives have been answered, or indeed adequately posed. How does the passage of time affect the telling of stories? What structures existed prior to the event? What happens to a storyline in a village now freed from the constraints of law and national condemnation? What approaches to narrative were learned by informants in past listenings and in the telling of stories within other cultural constructions? In the hands of a master practitioner like Natalie Davis, such questions serve as starting points for a deft retelling of how peasants in sixteenth-century France fabricated the narratives of their crimes so as to invoke royal pardon. The telling of these stories lay in their effect, in creating a structure of feeling within readers by which the king's emissaries would be moved, literally, from a world of blood and gore to the domain of mercy.[98]

Important though such questions about narrative are, they were not the questions that animated my conversations in Chauri Chaura. I was more interested in the way local people begin and close their retellings, and in the episodes with which such accounts are made to knit together into a story. In specialist phraseology, it was narrative detail rather than narrative performance that I was after. I was not primarily interested in the articulation of pre-existing codes within situated story-tellings. Must non-literates always exemplify a code when they speak—this is what I ask now that my account of such stories draws to a close. Is their way of speaking with elites not greatly affected by who they speak to, and indeed, by the subject and object of such a 'conversation'? Would not my writing have been different had I refused to approach the archive in the first place? Certainly, but the meaning of 'Chauri Chaura' lies in its ephemeral and metaphoric positioning within the colonial and the national archive in the first instance, and so it seems there was, in a sense, no escape from approaching the task in the way it was approached.

It is worth emphasizing that this book resists the temptation to structure Naujadi or Sita Ahir's recall along identifiably *Indian* or *peasant* patterns. I hope, rather, that this account throws some light on the ways in which many peasants in India relate stories from their public pasts. I have refrained from translating the terms used by these peasants back into pan-Indian cultural constructs, for semantically this would have resulted in a denial of agency to the actors of 1922, and to the present-day recollection of such actions. Ethnographic details which may have appeared as entanglements in the story were placed to prevent any simple or easy understanding of an overarching cultural context. Such unmediated descriptions allow, I feel, an appreciation of the ways in which an existing cultural repertoire is elaborated.

And so the peasantization of volunteers into the novel Bhojpuri term otiyar, and its association—both in Naujadi's and courtroom recalls of witnesses—with chutki and gerua appear as important markers of the ambiguous relationship between Mahatma Gandhi and his peasant followers. The Mahatma of his rustic protagonists was not as he really was, but as they had thought him up. Similarly, otiyars were not what the nationalist elite had willed them to be. The Dumri activists were tough wrestler-like characters who fed on alms, divested themselves of their normal clothing, moved about, and asserted their strength in markedly different attire—and all this in the name of Gandhi. Despite their similarities to Hindu sanyasis, which may even appear compelling, they were perceived then and are remembered now as otiyars, nothing more, nothing less.

Just as I have refused to call Naujadi's otiyars ascetics, so have I refrained from propping local accounts onto stories other than that of 'Chauri Chaura'. The significance of what Naujadi said lies in its validity as *an account* of 'Chauri Chaura', and not in its use as a typology of peasant recollection of upheavals and violent events. The Hindi word for interview, *sakshatkar*, has the sense of physical impression, and I have conceived of my presence in Dumri as a series of conversations, with all the attendant evils and possibilities of such an encounter.

Local and familial memories of the event, we see, are often at variance with, but seldom independent of, judicial and nationalist accounts. Subaltern recollections of historic events— historic because they are on record as infractions of the law which did not go unnoticed or unpunished—are also remembrances of the role of the police and the judge. Novel and emphatic recollections of nationalist activity in the villages similarly yield significant clues about the ways of peasant activists. Therefore the fieldwork in this book is not intended to supersede the colonial and the nationalist archive. Rather, it is placed in a complex relationship of variation to the official record.

Now that nearly all the rioters are dead, the voice of the peasant-actor emerges, both in the court records and in local recall, as an echo of other more powerful and persuasive voices. Exaggeration, conflation, repetition, redundancy, partial and idiosyncratic detail—all are present in this book. As I said, they are here not so much for colour but to delineate the ambiguities and tensions of an officious record.

Incongruence with known facts has not been construed as a lapse of memory, but rather as a necessary element in the stitching together of the story of Chauri Chaura.

EPILOGUE

As the last of the *puraniyas* (the old folk) die, familial recall will lose its intensity and facticity. But ironically, the investment made in 'Chauri Chaura' by local politicians will keep the stories alive. The stories of Gandhi's men, the beating of the volunteers, the firing on the crowd, the attack on the thana, the arrival of the avenging force, the circumstances that saved the locality, the punishment . . . and now the betrayal of these families by New Delhi and the Nation. Shikari's betrayal pales into insignificance against this.

Of course the nation has its own ways of memorializing the event. Now that the riot has been incorporated within the Great Freedom Struggle,[99] a space has been created for a monument so tall that lights flicker over it at night, warning away planes making their way to the airport in Gorakhpur. A marble column *enumerates* the nineteen hanged; it stands as an artifice of postcolonial history. An engraved stone tablet, situated across the railway track from the site of the burnt-down police station, similarly memorializes the event without mentioning a single person from Dumri or Chauri Chaura! Mahatma Gandhi, the progenitor of the non-cooperation movement; Moti Lal Nehru, the impresario of satyagraha in the region(!); Indira Gandhi, the moving spirit behind the memorial—these are the three individuals who mark the beginning, the middle, and the end of this 'Golden History of the Martyrs of Chauri Chaura'! The names of the Chauri Chaura accused are literally missing, even to this day, from every nationalist narrative.

Adjacent to the railway station stands the old Chauri Chaura memorial, inaugurated in February 1924 by the Lieutenant-Governor of that time. This monument, unveiled eighty years ago to honour the dead policemen, has also been nationalized. The legend the colonial masters engraved on it was gouged out by Baba Raghav Das, the prominent Gandhian of east UP, on 15 August 1947.[100] This noble worthy was followed by the postcolonial government, which did more than just smoothen the rough cutting edges of nationalist chisels. It chose to inscribe 'Jai Hind' on the police memorial, the slogan with which prime ministers of India end their independence day perorations from the Red Fort in Delhi. Both policemen and rioters, it now appears, laid down their lives for the Nation.

While embracing the colonial Indian policemen, this nationalist memorial manages nevertheless to underline one particular difference—that between Hindu and Muslim citizens of independent India. A close look at the names of the policemen killed, each given a niche where their relatives burn commemorative lamps, reveals that the Muslim names are written in Urdu and the Hindu names in Hindi! Further, while the names in Urdu are engraved, the lettering in Hindi is simply painted over. Clearly, the colonial government, which associated Hindi with subversive nationalism and found Urdu less threatening, had originally engraved all the names in Urdu, that being the vernacular most often used in administration. An influential postcolonial figure must have then ordered the plastering over of the Urdu writing for the Hindu names! But the Hindu names were not re-engraved in Devanagari. Re-engraving was passed over, perhaps because of budgetary constraints, for a shoddier painted inscription in Hindi.

This monument to the policemen killed at Chauri Chaura is testimony to the ways of the majoritarian nationalist discourse in India even today. All the policemen killed by nationalist peasants now belong to 'India's past'. But the 'essential' difference—Hindu and Muslim—surfaces surreptitiously through this notorious process of nationalist erasure and reinscription.

A few years ago the otiyars received yet another gift from the nation. A super-fast train named Shaheed Express in honour of the Chauri Chaura 'martyrs', was started between Delhi and Gorakhpur. Inaugurated on 2 October, Gandhi's birthday, it terminates ironically at the district headquarters, at a railway station which falls some fifteen miles short of Chauri Chaura.

And now, finally, even that irony has lost some of its poignancy. The train has in fact been extended. It now touches Chauri Chaura, but does not stop at that station. Another existing train, which once connected Gorakhpur and the smaller towns en route to the provincial High Court city of Allahabad, has been rechristened the Chauri Chaura Express. The memorialization of Chauri Chaura is far from over: it is now a routine, everyday affair.

NOTES

1. I am here borrowing Veena Das's characterization of Shikari's testimony. See her 'Subaltern as Perspective', in Ranajit Guha (ed.), *Subaltern Studies VI: Writings on South Asian History and Society*, Delhi: Oxford University Press, 1984: 315–16. See also Renato Rosaldo, 'From the Door of his Tent: The Field-worker and the Inquisitor', in J. Clifford and G.E. Marcus (eds), *Writing Cultures: The Poetics and Politics of Ethnography*, Berkeley: University of California Press, 1986.

2. Judgment, High Court, pp. 16–17. Greater details of references and abbreviations used in the notes to this chapter are contained in Shahid Amir, *Enent, Metaphor, Memory: Chauri Chaura 1922–1992*, Berkeley: University of California Press, 1996.

3. Extract from the District Khilafat Committee's [confiscated] Papers: '*Amad-ke kagzat ka Ragister*', Exh. no. 95, CCR. I have modified the translation from the one given in the High Court judgment, p. 16.

4. Judgment, High Court, p. 16.

5. Exh. 95, CCR.

6. Judgment, Sessions Judge, p. 9.

7. For Gandhi's reception at Chauri Chaura, see Shahid Amin, 'Gandhi as Mahatma: Gorakhpur District, Eastern UP, 1921–22', in Ranajit Guha (ed.), *Subaltern Studies III: Writings on South Asian History and Society*, Delhi: Oxford University Press, 1984: pp. 19–20.

8. Interview with Sita Ahir, Chotki Dumri.

9. The quotations in this paragraph and the estimate of the crowd at Chauri Chaura are from 'Mahatmaji ki Aguani', Report by Pandit Shyamdhar Mishra, in *Swadesh*, 13 February 1921, p. 3.

10. 'Some Illustrations', 22 September 1920, CWMG, xviii, p. 273.

11. See Amin, *Event, Metaphor, Memory* pp. 21–40.

12. 'Necessity of Discipline', 20 October 1920, CWMG, xviii, p. 361. The next quotation in this paragraph is also from the same source.

13. For an account of Gandhi's Gorakhpur meeting, see Shahid Amin, 'Gandhi as Mahatma', pp. 21ff.

14. *Swadesh*, 13 February 1921, p. 3.

15. 'What to Do When One Loses One's Temper', 20 February 1922, CWMG, xviii, pp. 373–5; Mahadev Desai, *Day-to-day with Gandhi* (Secretary's Diary), iii, Varanasi, 1965: 264.

16. 'Democracy "versus" Mobocracy', 8 September 1920, CWMG, xviii, pp. 242–4. For an analysis of Gandhi's attempt at 'mob control', see Ranajit Guha, 'Discipline and Mobilize', in Chatterjee and Pandey (eds), *Subaltern Studies VII*, Delhi: Oxford University Press, 1992.

17. This rumour was reported by Sri Murlidhar Gupt from Majhauli in *Swadesh*, 16 March 1921, p. 5. I discuss this and several other rumours about the 'powers' of Mahatma Gandhi in 'Gandhi as Mahatma', pp. 1–61.

18. CWMG, xviii, p. 374.

19. For a brief discussion of these two themes, see Shahid Amin, 'Gandhi as Mahatma', pp. 52–3.

20. The statement about the singing of songs at the Dumri sabha is taken from Shikari's testimony, CCR, II, p. 9. While describing a non-cooperation meeting at the tahsil town of Hata on 31 January 1921, Shikari had earlier recalled: 'A Panditji standing on a [stool] . . . recit[ed] Mohammad Ali's mother says "son die for the Khilafat" ', CCR, I, p. 165; see also above p. 88. For similar singings by itinerant minstrels (and the text of the second song), see Qazi Mohammad Adil Abbasi, *Tahrikh-Khilafat*, New Delhi: Tarraqi Urdu Board, 1978: 190. I am emboldened by family ethnography and fieldwork into hazarding the guess that many more Muslim urban dwellers than peasants had committed these two songs to heart.

21. CCR, I, p. 919.

22. Testimony of Shikari, CCR, II, p. 1 (Emphasis added).

23. *Gyan Shatki*, February 1921, p. 404.

24. See for instance the official handbill, 'Khabardar', issued by the Deputy Commissioner of Rae Bareli, encl. in Jawaharlal Nehru Papers, pt II, File 129, NMML.

25. See 'Some Instances of the Highhanded Methods of Non-Cooperation Volunteers', encl. to Bihar Government letter dated, 5 December 1921, Home Pol. File 327/I/1922, NAI.

26. *Tajwiz Awwal*, p. 358, CCR.

27. Judgment, High Court, p. 9.

28. CCR, I, p. 712.

29. CCR, II, p. 21.

30. Judgment, High Court, p. 9. The evidence about Lal Mohammad in the next sentence comes from the testimony of Shikari before the Sessions Judge, p. 1.

31. Evidence of Mindhai, cultivator of Mahadeva, and Birda, cultivator of Bale, CCR, II, pp. 512–13.

32. CCR, II, pp. 250, 337, 348, 349.

33. CCR, II, p. 525.

34. CCR, p. 516.

35. See Majid Hayat Siddiqi, *Agrarian Unrest in North India: The United Provinces, 1928–1922*, Delhi: Vikas, 1981; Kapil Kumar, *Peasants in Revolt: Tenants, Landlords, Congress and the Raj in Oudh, 1886–1922*, Delhi: Manohar, 1984; Stephen Henningham, *Peasant Movements in Colonial India, North Bihar, 1917–42*, Canberra: Australian National University Press, 1982; Sumit Sarkar, *'Popular' Movements and 'Middle Class' Leadership: Perspectives and Problems of a 'History from Below'*, Calcutta: K.P. Bagchi and Company, 1983. See also the evidence contained in my 'Gandhi as Mahatma', esp. pp. 53–4.

36. The phrase equating volunteer activity with 'Gandhi Mahatma's work' was actually used by a rural policeman in his testimony in the court. See evidence of Jagannath, chaukidar of Awadhpur, CCR, II, p. 362.

37. *Dada* (grandfather in Hindustani) stands for 'father' in the kinship terminology of rural east UP. The Bhojpuri exclamation, *'Ahi-ho-Dada!'* is the exact equivalent of the Hindustani, *'Bap-re-Bap!'* Both correspond to the English 'Oh my God!'

38. Naujadi offered this clarification in answer to my question. *Khariyani*, from *khalihan*, harvest floor: dues collected at the threshing floor. District Congress records mention *khaliyani* dues which were to be collected in the villages.

39. CCR, II, p. 2.

40. CCR, I, pp. 161ff; II, pp. 245, 705, 707.

41. *S.V. Chutki*, in *A New Hindustani Dictionary, with illustrations from Hindustani literature and folklore*, by S.W. Fallon, Banaras/London, 1879.

42. The full statement on chutki runs as follows:

अमीन : त ओटियर लोग का करत रहलां?

नौजादी : ओटियर! ऐसे बता देईं–ओही! चुटकिया मांगें।

अमीन : का कह कर मांगें?

नौजादी : मांगे भिखिया जैसे मांगल जा-ला–सब के जाहिल न रहे! चाहे दाल-ए-बनावे, चाहे भात बनावे, चाहे पिसान बनावे, उनके खातिर काढ़-के धारा जा।

अमीन : त काहे लोग उनकर बतिया मानत रहलां भाई?

नौजादी : बतिया ई मानत रहलां–सरकार के हुकुम दीहल रहल, सरकार के हुकुम रहल, सरकार के ओर से मांगत रहलां।

अमीन : सरकार के, कि गान्ही-बाबा के?

नौजादी : उहे! गान्ही-ए-बाबा के–त उहे दिया जाए।

अमीन : त का कह के मांगत रहलां?

नौजादी : रोज नाहिं न कहें! . . . नाहिं दुसरे तिसरे दिन चुटकी दियास रहल . . . उनके नियुति से तीन दिन रसोई बनावल जा–चाहे बढ़े चाहे घटे, उनकी चुटकी धइल रहे–त जेहिया आवें भीख मांगे, त उनके दिया जाए।

43. To quote Sita Ahir, '*Olantiyar bhik mangat rahlan. Olantiyar—koi kharcha de nahin—din-bhar ghoomen, aur khae-khatir mange—khaeke*'. The chaukidar of Bishembharpur named Buddhu and Iddan as volunteers in the Court. He '. . . found out [that] they were volunteers when Budhu *went hither and thither asking for chutki*'. Emphasis added. CCR, II, p. 423.

44. Cf. 'According to the stated rule, they must not approach a house to beg until the regular meal time is passed; what remains over is the portion of the mendicant.' Article on 'Asceticism (Hindu)', by A.S. Gedden, in J. Hastings (ed.), *Encyclopedia of Religion and Ethics*, New York: Scribner, 1910, II, p. 92.

45. Gen. [Admn.] Dept. Resolution of NWP Govt., dt. 29 August 1893, para 3(a), xvi–37/1898–1900, Commissioner's Records, Gorakhpur.

46. *Swadesh*, 10 April 1921.

47. 'Notice by Raghupati Sahai', *Swadesh*, 1 May 1921, p. 8.

48. Exhs. 114, 121, CCR; Trials of Volunteers in Padrauna tahsil, 1922, Defence of India Rules Bastas, GRR.

49. Chutki, a pinch, had become *muthia*, fistful. See 'Budget 1921–22 of the District Congress Committee, Part B', Exh. 82, CCR.

50. CCR, II, p. 593.

51. See for instance the Report on Non-cooperation in Hata Tahsil, *Swadesh*, 16 October 1921, p. 11.

52. Account of Income, dt. 4 May 1921, Budget 1921–22 of the District Congress Committee, Gorakhpur, Exh. 81, CCR.

53. See Exh. 82, CCR.

54. Testimony of Shikari, CCR, II, p. 2.

55. Judgment, Sessions Judge, p. 18.

56. There was the further problem of the distribution of this collection between the Tilak Fund and the Khilafat Fund. A meeting of the Gorakhpur Committee had agreed in early January to divide the muthia collection in a 'fixed proportion'. In some other UP districts, the ratio was 25 per cent for the Khilafat collection with 75 per cent reserved for the Tilak Fund. See evidence of Maulvi Subhanullah and Hakeem Arif, CCR, II, pp. 562, 687; Jawaharlal Nehru to Sec. AICC, 19 October 1921.

57. On public levy, see Ranajit Guha, *Elementary Aspects*: 113–15.

58. Testimony of Shikari, CCR, II, p. 8, also pp. 125, 514, 515.

59. '*Dholak baja rahe the aur jhande uthae hue the*': Evidence of Sarju Kahar, *Tajwiz Awwal*, p. 358, CCR.

60. *Sattu*, or *satua*, flour of parched barley and gram, is a common *kaccha* food in eastern UP and Bihar. Sattu is mixed with water and kneaded into a dough and garnished with chillies and onions. A few pounds of sattu is enough for a peasant to subsist on for a couple of days.

61. *S.V. Bhandara*, in Fallon, *New Hindustani Dictionary*.

62. The 'luckless peasant' in Ram Kumar Upadhyay Vaid's lament goes hungry because of all manner of imposts, including chutki demanded by babas:

हाकिम इनसे पोत मांगे, मेम्बर इनसे वोट मांगे
बाबा दुआरे मांगे दाल-ओ-पिसान हो!
देवता कराही मांगे, लकड़ी सिपाही मांगे
गंगा के तीर मांगे, पण्डा इनसे दान हो!
गुरू बाबा पूजा मांगे, लाला इनसे भूसा मांगे
माता-भवानी मांगे, चुरकी-ओ कान हो!
खसी-भेड़ा दुर्गा मांगे, गाजी मियाँ मुर्गा मांगे।

—राम कुमार उपाध्याय, 'वैध', *वैध की लचारी* (जौनपुर, 1942)

63. Gandhi regarded alms-seeking as a part of 'the beggar problem', a 'social nuisance', especially in the cities. In August 1921 he wrote strongly against the 'hundreds and thousands of people [who] do not work and live on alms, thereby putting their ochre robes to shame . . . . Today we simply have no work of a kind which we could offer to a beggar'. The answer lay with the handloom and the spinning wheel. With village industry revived, 'only Brahmins and fakirs who disseminated knowledge among the people will

continue to live on alms . . . . Rogues will no longer be able to roam around in the garb of sadhus and beg for alms'. In his speech in January 1925, however, Gandhi employed the metaphor of alms and begging to help enlist volunteers at the Petlad Cultivators' Conference in Gujarat. The sources for the above quotations are, *CWMG*, lxxii, pp. 136–7; xxii, p. 471; xxv, p. 599.

64. That *markin*, the mill cloth, was primarily white is attested by Sita Ahir's remark, '*markin jyada chale; rangin kam chale*'. See also Appx. B: 'On Cloth and the Clothes of the Natives of Eastern United Provinces' by Ram Gharib Chaube, in William Crooke, *A Glossary of North Indian Peasant Life*, ed. Shahid Amin, Delhi: Oxford University Press, 1989, para 726.

65. Evidence of Abdul Karim, CCR, I, p. 109. Emphasis added.

66. Montgomery Martin (ed)., *The History, Antiquities, Topography and Statistics of Eastern India*, II, London: W.H. Allen and Company, 1838: 267–8. *Kusum*, or safflower, in fact, formed the basis of as many as nineteen different colours, ranging from saffron-yellow, orange to green, light blue, dark blue, and even black. In the preparation of most of the darker colours it was used in conjunction with indigo. The riddle '*Bap rahal pete, put gel bariyat*': While the father, i.e., the seed, was still in the womb (i.e., pod), the son (safflower dye) went to a wedding party, indicates 'the comprehensive range of colours embraced by safflower'. Marriages, of course, were the occasion for a riot of colour. See George A. Grierson, *Bihar Peasant Life*, Calcutta: Bengal Secretariat Press, 1885, para. 1043.

67. CCR, II, pp. 38, 39, 49, 76, 115, 460. The organic dyes used in Gorakhpur to colour the white *nangilat* (long cloth) *dhotis* were: *kusum* (safflower), *haldi* (turmeric), the bark of the *tun* tree (*Cedrela toona*), and the flowers of *tesu* and *harsingar* (*Nyctanthes arbortristis*). Turmeric, an essential condiment, was used by those too poor to afford the fees of a professional dyer. Written communication, Habib Ahmad, Gorakhpur. See also 'List of Trees and Shrubs in the Gorakhpur Forest Division', *Working Plan for the Forests of the Gorakhpur Division*, by R.G. Marriott, Allahabad: Government Press, 1915, Appx. iv.

68. 'The pathetic anxiety of all volunteer bodies to model themselves on the pattern of the military and police uniforms . . .', as noticed by the Intelligence Bureau in 1939, belonged to a latter period. In August 1940, with the war in full swing, 'the wearing of unofficial uniforms bearing a colourful resemblance to military or official uniforms' was prohibited in India. See, Note on Volunteer Movement in India, Pt. III by IB, June 1939, and copy of despatch by Reuters, Simla, 5 August 1940, in L/PJ/8/678, IOL.

69. Note, dated 27 May 1922, by UP CID on Volunteer Movement, GAD File 658/1920, UPSA, Lucknow; Rahul Sankrityayan, *Meri Jeevan Yatra*: 355, 358–9.

70. Bihar & Orissa Secret Abstracts, 17 February 1921, para 2071, cited in Police Abstracts of Intelligence, UP, 7 January 1922, p. 41.

71. Instructions issued after the 3 December 1921 meeting of the (UP) *Prantiya Swayam Sevak Dal*, Exh. 118, CCR.

72. *CWMG*, xxii, p. 152.

73. Ibid., xxii, p. 273.

74. Ibid., xxii, p. 152.

75. Ibid., xxii, p. 323.

76. Ibid., xx, p. 451. The source of Gandhi's quotation was Mr Pickthall, editor of *The Bombay Chronicle*.

77. Cf. Hakeem Arif, 'founder' of Dumri mandal: 'I wear khaddar still as I did before. My upper garment is not khaddar, nor are my trousers'. Evidence dated, 12 September 1922, CCR, II, p. 685.

78. *CWMG*, xxii, pp. 463–4.

79. When the Pandit of Malaon stated that he 'remember[ed] the condition that *garha* was not to be worn and *khaddar* was', he was implying that the rough handloom cloth (garha) of the locality was fabricated from mill-made yarn. CCR, II, p. 269.

80. *The Pioneer*, 9 February 1922, cited in Sir C. Sankaran Nair, *Gandhi and Anarchy*, Madras, 1922, Appx, xii: Gorakhpur Tragedy, p. 164.

81. Report by H.N. Kunzru, Maulvi Subhanullah, and C.K. Malaviya, *Leader*, 23 February 1922.

82. See CCR, I, pp. 49, 76, 115, 161; II, 38, 49, 76, 115, 245, 705, 707.

83. CCR, I, p. 267. Emphasis added.

84. CCR, I, p. 145. Emphasis added.

85. Evidence of Pandit Mahesh Bal Dixit, Dy. Magistrate, CCR, II, p. 807. See also, 'Instructions re: Identification of undertrial prisoners in jails', UP Police A Progs., September 1910, no. 4(a).

86. Interview with Dwarka Pandey, cited in Ram Murat Upadhyay, 'Gorkahpur Janpad Mein Swatantrata Sangharsh, 1857–1947', Gorakhpur University, Ph.D. thesis, 1975: 152–3.

87. Evidence of Thag Chamar, chaukidar, Gaunar, CCR, I, p. 303.

88. Evidence of Mahatam Sukul, CCR, I, p. 287. Emphasis added.

89. CCR, I. pp. 273–4.

90. On Bhagwan Ahir's uniform, see testimonies of Bhagwan Ahir, Harcharan Singh, the Pandit of Malaon and Constable Jai Ram, CCR, I, pp. 82, 264ff, 366, 491; II, p. 473.

91. Testimony of Shikari, Chauri Chaura Trials, II, 38–9.

92. Testimony of Thakur Ahir, CCR, II, p. 49.

93. The quotations are taken from the judgment of Sessions Judge H.E. Holmes, pp. 234–5. Emphasis added.

94. CCR, I, pp. 338, 422.

95. There seems to have been general agreement about this in Dumri. 'I understand what volunteers are,' stated Subhag of Chotki Dumri in court. 'Shikari, Nazar Ali, Nageshar and Awadhi Pasi. These 4 are volunteers,' he told the Sessions Judge. 'I considered them to be volunteers because they *wore ochre-coloured clothes and demanded chutki.*' CCR, II, p. 481. Emphasis added.

96. 'Gerua' from the Sanskrit 'gairika', i.e., the colour of 'giri' or hills, is used by many Hindu sects as a prescriptive colour for garments worn by those of their members who have renounced the world. As such, it came to symbolize the spirit of world-renunciation in Hindu religious thought and practice. Adopted by Hindu nationalist discourse of both literary and political genres since the middle of the last century, 'gerua' has been operating in north Indian culture as an index of Hindu-nationalist sentiment with various idealist connotations, such as religiosity, patriotism, and self-sacrifice. A well-known Bengali (Hindu) patriotic play, based on a fictionalized version of Shivaji's conflict with the Mughals, was called *Gairik Pataka* (The Saffron Flag). As with so many other things, Bankimchandra Chattopadhyay's writings did much to promote the Hindu-nationalist symbolism of this particular colour. The armed band of sanyasis whose exploits are celebrated in his novel, *Anandmath*, were all clad in saffron robes. They called themselves *santans*, i.e., children of The Mother (=Motherland), and stepped out of fiction into real life during the Swadeshi movement when many of its nationalist volunteers adopted the appellation and the dress. The arrival of such a band at the house of the liberal-landlord hero of Tagore's novel *Ghare Baire* acts as a cue in the development of its plot. Written communication from Ranajit Guha.

97. The phrase is Ranajit Guha's. See his 'Chandra's Death', in Ranajit Guha (ed.), *Subaltern Studies V: Writings on South Asian History and Society*, Delhi: Oxford University Press, 1987: 135–65.

98. See Natalie Zemon Davis, *Fiction in the Archives: Pardon Tales and their Tellers in Sixteenth-century France*, Stanford: Stanford University Press, 1987, esp. p. 4, from where the bulk of the questions and quotation in this paragraph have been taken. My argument is in partial response to Professor Davis' comments on an earlier draft of this manuscript.

99. The official directory of accredited nationalists published by the Information Department of the UP Government in 1972 not only gives pride of place to the twenty 'martyrs' hanged for their part in the 'Chauri Chaura *kand*', it also affords an honourable mention to the five undertrials who expired (*divangat*) in jail. See *Swatantrata Sangram ke Sainik (Sankshipt Parichay)*, vol. 35, Gorakhpur, Lucknow: Suchna Vibhag, 1972: 1–2.

100. Amodnath Tripathi, 'Poorvi Uttar-Pradesh ke Jan-jeevan mein Baba Raghav Das ka Yogdan', Ph. D thesis, Allahabad University, 1981: 135; interview with Raghvendra Sharma 'Vaid', Mundera bazaar, 22 February 1989.

EIGHT

Disciplining Difference

Gyanendra Pandey

A nation is constructed not only as a bureaucratic, state-oriented community, but also as a moral one. That is what gives nationalisms their greater or lesser appeal and staying power. What constitutes this moral community? What gives us the right to call ourselves 'Indians'? 'Are we entitled to claim the status of true citizens, who have sacrificed family, caste, community and religion in the name of the nation?' as one newspaper asked in September 1947.[1]

The point I want to begin with here is the simple one of the unrealizable quality of the nationalist search for clarity and 'purity' in the midst of the blurring, mixing, and uncertainty that is the actually existing condition of all nations and nationalisms. Nations everywhere have claimed to be defined by well-marked cultural–political boundaries. Yet, such boundaries are never easily drawn. Nationalist thought, therefore, commonly proceeds to carve out a core or 'mainstream'—the unhyphenated national, the real, obvious, 'natural' citizen (Indian, Nigerian, Australian, American, British, whatever). Alongside this core, there emerge notions of the hyphenated 'national' (Indian Muslims, Indian Christians, Indian Jews, or African-Americans, Mexican Americans and Indigenous Americans): minorities and marginal groups that might be part of the nation, but 'never quite'.[2]

How do nationalists set out to cleanse the sacred space of the nation—of Pakistan (the 'Pure Land') or 'Mother India'? How are 'impure' elements to be dealt with? How do we contain, or discipline, difference? The question was posed sharply in the case of the Muslim 'minority' in India, as well as in that of 'abducted persons', at the time of Partition.[3]

THE SEARCH FOR A ONE-NATION NATION

August 1947 was the date of establishment of two new nation-states, India and Pakistan. But it was also, as we have seen (and here the date is distinctly less clear-cut), the moment of the congealing of new identities, relations, and histories, or of their being thrown into question once again. What made Partition and Independence particularly bitter was that neither of the two new states turned out to be what its proponents had hoped for. Pakistan has perhaps had the more anguished history in this respect. It had been proposed as a Muslim homeland, the country of the Muslim nation of the subcontinent. There was always going to be some doubt about the ethnic and even territorial basis of this religiously defined nation. For there was never any suggestion that the ninety million Muslims of undivided India—spread out all over that territory, with Muslim-majority regions existing in north-western and north-eastern India and in pockets (towns and sub-districts) elsewhere—could all be accommodated, or would even wish to migrate, to the areas that became Pakistan.

When Mohammad Ali Jinnah articulated his conception of a secular, multireligious Pakistan in his famous speech at the inaugural session of the Constituent Assembly of Pakistan, on 11 August 1947, the proposition produced bewilderment among many of his followers. 'How could Muslims cease to be Muslims and Hindus cease to be Hindus in the political sense when the religions . . . were, in Jinnah's passionately held belief, so utterly different from one another? Was Jinnah giving up the two-nation theory . . .?' one Pakistani commentator was to ask later.[4] On 21 October 1947, in a letter to the *Civil and Military Gazette*, Muhammad Sa'adat Ali of Lahore protested against a minister's statement that Pakistan was 'a secular, democratic and not a theocratic state'. Such a statement 'has absolutely no support of the Muslims', he wrote.

Ever since Mr Jinnah undertook to fight our case, he has on occasions without number, proclaimed emphatically that Muslims were determined to set up a state organised and run in accordance with the irresistible dictates of the Islamic *Shariat* . . . . If secularisation were our sole aim, India need not have been partitioned. . . . We raised this storm for partition because we wanted to live as free Muslims and organise a state on Islamic principles... .[5]

On the Indian side, too, Partition and Independence gave rise to an intense debate about what the character of the new nation-state should be: secular (which was to say multicommunity, with equal rights for all)? socialist? Hindu? Pakistan emerged, after the long-drawn-out moment of Partition, with its communal holocaust and forced migrations, as an overwhelmingly Muslim country, especially in its western half. As they saw this happening, sections of the Hindu nationalist press in India observed that Pakistan was on its way to establishing an '*ekjatiya rashtra*' (literally, a 'one-nation nation', or a homogenous, one-people nation), and lamented that India might never be able to achieve the same kind of unity (or homogeneity). Substantial sections of the north Indian population—especially Hindu and Sikh refugees from West Pakistan and those most directly affected by their influx—and sections of the political leadership, especially the Hindu right wing and leaders of the Sikh community, also demanded that India (or at least some parts of it, like East Punjab, Delhi, and the neighbouring districts of western Uttar Pradesh where Hindu and Sikh refugees had flooded in the weeks before and after 15 August 1947 should be cleared of Muslims; the latter should be sent to Pakistan, and the territory handed over to the Sikhs and Hindus.

Nationalism necessarily raises the question of who belongs and by what criterion. In India, in 1947, this took the peculiar form of the 'Muslim question': can a Muslim be an Indian?

THE NATURAL NATION

The figure of the 'nationalist Muslim' will serve as a useful starting point for our discussion of this question. The first point to be made is that there is no equivalent category for Hindus or, for that matter, any of the other religious groupings in India. Interestingly, in speaking of the politics of Hindus, the term is frequently reversed to read 'Hindu nationalists'. The reversal is of course not coincidental. What does the term 'Hindu nationalists' signify? It does not refer simply to nationalists who happen to be Hindus. It is, rather, an indication of their brand of nationalism, a brand in which the 'Hindu' moment has considerable weight. It is a nationalism in which Hindu culture, Hindu traditions, and the Hindu community are given pride of place.

Alongside the rise of this Hindu nationalism, and much more emphatically in the course of time, another more inclusive kind of nationalism had developed, which emphasized the composite character of Indian society and refused to give the same sort of primacy to the Hindu element in India's history and self-consciousness. This is what would later come to be termed 'secular' nationalism, 'real' or 'Indian' nationalism as Jawaharlal Nehru called it, 'something quite apart from . . . [the] religious and communal varieties of nationalism and strictly speaking . . . the only form which can be called nationalism in the modern sense of the word'.[6] This was the 'nationalism' of the Indian Constitution—nationalism, pure and simple, in Nehru's phrase. Given the existence of both these brands of nationalism from the late nineteenth century onwards, and so evidently in the 1940s and again in the 1980s and 1990s, politically conscious Hindus have readily been divided into 'Hindu nationalists' and 'secular (or Indian) nationalists.'

There were of course signs of a growing Muslim nationalism over the same period. Like Hindu nationalism, this Muslim variant developed side by side with the broader 'Indian' nationalist movement, in which large numbers of Muslims were also involved (including leading figures like Badruddin Tyabji and Maulana Mohamed Ali; Mohammad Ali Jinnah and Fazl-ul-Haq; Mukhtar Ahmad Ansari, Abul Kalam Azad, Zakir Husain, and Sheikh Abdullah). However, politically active Muslims were not divided into 'Muslim nationalists' and secular nationalists. They were divided instead into 'nationalist Muslims' and 'Muslims' —and here the proposition extended of course to more than just those who were politically involved.

The Hindus—or the majority of politically conscious Hindus, for there were in this view many who formed part of a large inert mass, and at least a few who were loyalists—were, in other words, nationalists first and foremost. Whether they were Hindu nationalists or secular nationalists was a subsidiary question. All Muslims were, however, Muslims. And the matter of political inactivity or inertia made little difference in this instance. Some Muslims were advocates of 'Indian' nationalism, and hence 'nationalist Muslims'. The remainder of that community, however—in town and country, north and south, handloom workshop or sugarcane field, modest hut or railway quarters—were not likely to be supporters of Indian nationalism, on account of their being Muslim. The peculiar history of Hindu–Muslim political differences from the later nineteenth century onwards, and British efforts to keep the Muslims on their side against the rising tide of what they saw as *babu*, Hindu nationalism, had contributed to the development of this view. But the years immediately preceding Partition and Independence, Partition itself, and the very fact of agitation for separate Muslim rights, clearly had more than a little to do with its wide acceptance as an axiomatic truth.

An editorial published in the Kanpur Hindi daily, *Vartman*, in October 1947, provides a very good illustration of 'majoritarian' nationalist thinking on this issue.[7] 'Whose country is this?' the editors ask in their opening line, and answer: 'All those who can call India their native land (*swadesh*) in the real sense of the term, this country is theirs.' They then proceed to spell out how the Buddhists and Jains, Sikhs, Christians, Anglo-Indians, and Parsis all belong in India, because they think of it as their native land. Persecuted in early times, some Hindus became Buddhists and Jains. 'However, they did not change their nationality [*sic*]. They did not leave the country. They did not start calling themselves Chinese or Japanese.' Similarly, a Sikh *panth* (community or tradition) arose. 'This Sikh community also recognizes India as their *janmabhumi* [land of their birth] and therefore their country.'

The analysis so far is simple. The Buddhists (even though they have practically disappeared from the land of the Buddha), Jains, and Sikhs treated India as the land of their birth because this is where they and their religious traditions were born. They are, in that sense, 'original', 'natural' Indians. The argument shifts in the case of the other small religious (and racial) groupings—the Christians, Anglo-Indians, and Parsis. Many of the lowest castes and classes had embraced Christianity in recent times, the editorial noted, to escape the worst oppressions of untouchability, as much as anything else. 'Yet they did not forget that they could never go and settle in Europe; [they knew that] India would always be their country.'

The Anglo-Indians had, on the other hand, remained ambivalent for some time. They were, after all, Eurasian, both English and Indian by blood, and many of them had sought to migrate (as they would continue to do during the 1950s and to some extent later). But there were two points that went in their favour, as *Vartman* saw it. First, their numbers were never very great. Second, the departing British had left them to fend for themselves: '. . . they came to their senses as soon as the British left' and recognized India as their native land.

These propositions are both patronizing and contradictory. Indian Christians could not dream of settling in Europe. The Anglo-Indians did dream of it, but were left high and dry by the departing colonial rulers. In any case, the two communities were numerically small and quite widely dispersed. They had no other country to go to and they constituted no threat to the nation or its culture. India could therefore be treated as their native land.

The logic is different in the case of the Parsis. They came to the country from Iran, but as refugees fleeing to save their lives, not as aggressors or missionaries. Nor did they give up their religion, culture, or 'language' on settling here. 'Nevertheless, many of them have contributed to the economic, intellectual, social and political development of India like true citizens.' This is a line of reasoning with which we are not unfamiliar. Wealthy Japanese business people and Arab sheikhs are welcome in England, the United States, and Australia because they contribute to the 'economic' and 'intellectual' development of these areas: not so Bradford Muslims or Sikhs of Southall, Mexican casual labourers or Vietnamese boat-people. That was what went in favour of the Parsis in India: they were a small, almost a microscopic, minority and because of the fairly privileged economic and social position they enjoyed in places like Bombay, many of them had—'like true citizens', as it was said—contributed to the economic, intellectual, social, and political development of India.

The situation of the Muslims of India was another matter altogether. Over the centuries, the immigration of small groups of Muslims had been supplemented by conversion to Islam on a fairly large scale, so that there were now ninety million Muslims in the subcontinent, 25 per cent of the total population of undivided India. The majority of these Muslims had come from the depressed classes of the Hindu population, the paper acknowledged; they had become Muslims to escape from the extreme sanctions and disabilities of the caste system. However, resisting the oppressiveness of the Hindu caste system was one thing and shedding one's 'national' culture, religion, language, and dress another.

Flesh and blood of the Hindus though they were, these Hindavi Muslims came to think of themselves as belonging to the Arab and Mughal communities [or nations, since the term *jati* can refer to either] . . . . Rulers like Aurangzeb, and later on the British, never tired of preaching that they [the Muslims] have been the governors of this country, and that their direct links are with Arabia, Persia, and Turkey. Their language, appearance, religion, and practices are all different from those of the Hindus.

The *Vartman* editorial refers to the tyranny and destructiveness of the Muslim invaders. It adds that the local converts had been no less fanatical, attacking Hindu temples, images, and religious processions, and making a point of sacrificing cows at the Baqr Id precisely because the cow was sacred to the Hindus. But these sweeping generalizations are by way of a rhetorical flourish—well-known propositions that serve only to underline the basic argument that the Muslims of India are (or may be suspected of being) alien, because 'when they changed their religion, they also dreamt up schemes of changing their country'. 'They did not think of the [other] people living in India as their own. They thought of the local language [as if there were only one!] as foreign. They cut themselves off from Indian civilization and culture. . . .'

In the course of the anticolonial struggle, the argument goes on, when people of every other community joined in a common fight for freedom, the Muslims stood in the way. They made separatist demands, played into the hands of the British and were rewarded, finally, with the prize of Pakistan—from where Hindus were now being driven out. Many Indian Muslims had earlier tried to migrate to Persia, Arabia, Mesopotamia, and Turkey, only to return disappointed. Today, 'if there was place in Pakistan, if there were agricultural lands, jobs, and if they had their way, [these Muslims] would undoubtedly go and settle there'. On other occasions, the editors of *Vartman* had declared that Pakistan was like Mecca, like paradise even, for every Indian Muslim, and Jinnah was like their Prophet.

Now, on 12 October 1947, the editorial continued, large numbers of Muslims had already gone to settle in Pakistan, and many more were waiting to go. As for the rest, who had decided to stay back, did they show signs of willingness to live in peace with the other communities of India—'Sikh, Jain, Buddhists, Christians, Parsis and Anglo-Indians'? 'These machine-guns, mortars, rifles, pistols, bombs, dynamite, swords, spears and daggers, that are being discovered daily [in Muslim houses and localities], are all these being collected for the defence of India?' There was simply not enough place for all of these Muslims in Pakistan, and the fact that many stayed on in India was no reason to think of them automatically as Indian.

It would be a waste of time to point out all the errors of fact and the blatant half-truths that pepper *Vartman*'s analysis of the Muslim condition.[8] There is one feature of the statement, however, that requires specific noting. At some stage in this articulation of the conditions of citizenship, an argument about culture gives way almost imperceptibly to an argument about politics—or, more precisely, about political power. The Anglo-Indians, unable to attain the numerical strength of the Muslims, never constituted a threat. The Parsis remained different in religion, culture, and language too, according to the paper, but they had contributed significantly to our political, economic, intellectual, and social development. The Muslims had, on the other hand, put forward their own, separatist demands and had stood in the way of the united struggle against the British. They had not accepted our conception of India: they were therefore not Indians.

There is another important aspect of this articulation. It is noteworthy that in the entire analysis, Hindus appear only a couple of times, in passing, as the people from whom the Muslims sought to differentiate themselves. An editorial that elaborates the character and place of the different religious communities of India in answer to the question, 'Whose country is this?', does not even feel the need to mention the Hindu community as a separate constituent of the nation. For the Hindus are not a constituent. They *are* the nation, the 'we' who demand cooperation from the minorities, the 'us' that the Muslims have to learn to live with.

There was a touching moment in the Constituent Assembly debates on the question of minority rights when Frank Anthony, the leader of the assembly's Anglo-Indians, referred to a comment sometimes made to him that, if he was as strongly committed to India as he claimed to be, he should drop the prefix 'Anglo' from the name of his community. Anthony's response was that, 'good or bad', 'rightly or wrongly', the word 'Anglo-Indian' 'connotes to me many things which I hold dear'. He went further, however: 'I will drop it readily, as soon as you drop your label . . . . The day you drop the label of "Hindu", the day you forget that you are a Hindu, that day—no, two days before that—I will drop by deed poll, by beat of drum if necessary, the prefix Anglo . . . .' That day, he added, 'will be welcome first and foremost to the minorities of India'.[9]

The Anglo-Indian leader's argument was logical, but misplaced. It would have appeared meaningless to many Hindus, who did not have to use the designation 'Hindu' in any case. At Partition and for a long time afterwards, they were the silent majority. They did not need to advertise the fact that they were Hindus; for some time after the assassination of Gandhi by a Hindu extremist, it was even a little difficult for the more militant among them to do so. Inasmuch as they were Hindu, they were automatically Indian. It was enough in this age of high nationalism to claim the latter designation. The question of what it meant to be a Hindu, what advantages such a classification brought to the lower castes and classes, and whether the Hindus as a whole were disprivileged, was not to be taken up in a sustained way until the 1980s or 1990s.[10]

To have given greater political visibility to the category of 'Hindu' at the moment of nationalist triumph in the 1940s would have meant running the risk of differentiating and problematizing it, and of having to recognize that history and culture and naturalness are not uncontested. To present an argument about *belonging* as a political argument would be to concede that the nation was a *political* project, first and foremost, and to acknowledge its historicity. The progress of the nation could not mean exactly the same thing to all parts of that imagined community. To acknowledge this, however, would be to foreground the question of political power and to what end that power should be used—which in turn would defeat the nationalist claim that the nation was a natural moral community.

THE NEEDS OF A MODERN STATE

For all that, even 'natural' nations must have their own states, and the needs of modern statehood must not be compromised. In this respect, too, the non-natural citizen could be a problem. The disciplining of difference was a necessity.

Everywhere, we would argue, the nation/people has historically come into being through struggles to define and advance a national interest. Everywhere, however, there is a simultaneous—and it seems almost necessary—desire to present the nation as given, an already formed totality, even a spirit or essence. Everywhere, moreover, once the nation comes to have a state of its own or (in nationalist parlance) to be realized in the nation-state, this essence, this totality, comes to be concretized in the state and its territory. The national interest comes to be equated with the integrity of the state and its boundaries; and the preservation of the latter comes to be proclaimed the primary concern of the nation.

The governance of the modern state is rooted in knowledge practices that enable the state to produce new technologies of order through technologies of objectification—statistics, budgetary models, a strong army—that embody certain rationalities and produce ever-expanding horizons for regulation.[11] These techniques of government provide vital inputs to the political imagination of 'nationalist' parties and pressure groups. 'Non-violence is of no use under the present circumstances in India', Major-General K.M. Cariappa, deputy chief of the Indian army staff, declared in October 1947; only a strong army could make India 'one of the greatest nations in the world'.[12] Durga Das, a young correspondent of the pro-Congress *Hindustan Times*, went further, demanding the building of a strong state (through the liquidation of 'enemy pockets') and a strong army on the Nazi model.[13] Nathuram Godse, Gandhi's assassin, put it no less plainly in explaining his opposition to Gandhi: India needed to become a modern nation, 'practical, able to retaliate, and . . . powerful with the armed forces'.[14] For this purpose Gandhian notions of non-violence and turning the other cheek were simply of no use.

It was in the midst of this growing statist militancy that Sampurnanand, then education minister in the Congress government of UP, wrote of the needs of the new India, two weeks before official Partition and Independence. If, 'God forbid', there was ever a war between India and Pakistan, 'our worries will be greatly increased, for it is not impossible that the sympathies of our Muslim population will veer towards Pakistan'.[15] The fear expressed here grew in strength in the weeks and months that followed, as Partition worked itself out and large numbers of Indian Muslims were pushed into a corner. Indeed the political history of India for some time afterwards, and some might say until today, has in no small part been the history of a struggle to control this fear.

In the later months of 1947, a wide range of India's nationalist leaders began to focus on the issues that Sampurnanand had raised—war, and loyalty in war. The renowned socialist leader, Dr Ram Manohar Lohia, speaking at a public meeting in Delhi on 11 October 1947, urged the people to 'rally round the Nehru Government and make it strong enough to take, when necessary, effective measures against the Pakistan Government'. This was an appeal to all communal forces, Hindu, Muslim, and Sikh, and to those who harboured doubts about the government's declared secular platform. But three days earlier, at another rally in Delhi, Lohia pointedly asked India's Muslims to 'surrender arms and . . . be loyal citizens of India, ready to fight, if need be, against Pakistan or any other country'.[16]

At the same time, Govind Ballabh Pant, Congress chief minister of UP—accomplished parliamentarian, able administrator, and a man of large, secular, human sympathies—was driving home the same point in Allahabad. Indian Muslims should 'realize clearly' what loyalty to the nation would mean if Pakistan invaded India, he declared. 'Every Muslim in India would be required to shed his blood fighting the Pakistani hordes [sic], and each one should search his heart now, and decide whether he should migrate to Pakistan or not.'[17]

Muslim leaders who stayed on in India were under some pressure to express themselves in the same kinds of terms. The Raja of Mahmudabad, secretary of the All-India Muslim League and Jinnah's right-hand man for much of the decade before 1947, provides a striking illustration. As with so many other Muslim League leaders of UP and Bihar, Mahmudabad had never contemplated leaving his native land. Broken by the experience that Partition turned out to be, he resigned from the Muslim League in September 1947. The party had committed hara-kiri, he said. To keep it alive in India now was a cruel joke. Most of its leaders—Mahmudabad actually said 'all'—had run away from India, leaving the Indian Muslims to their fate. These opportunists should now be clear in their minds that they would never be able to mislead the Muslim masses again. 'All Indian Muslims would go to war for India, even if they had to go to war against Pakistan.'[18] Taking a similar tack, M.A. Salam, a member of the Madras Legislative Assembly and the All-India Muslim League Council, declared that his community of Andhra Muslims was loyal to the Indian Union and 'shall defend it against anybody to the last drop of their blood'.[19] That last contention had become a password to citizenship, as it were: it is a password that has been demanded of Muslims in India, in one form or another, ever since.

Partition produced a plethora of statements on the question of what would constitute an adequate proof of loyalty on the part of Indian Muslims. Many called for the disbanding of the Muslim League and the giving up of any demand that smacked even remotely of separatism—such as appeals for separate electorates or an assured quota of legislative seats for Muslims. As Vallabhbhai Patel, the deputy prime minister of India and acclaimed 'strong man' of the Congress party, put it in the Constituent Assembly debate on 'minority rights', these were the measures that had resulted in 'the separation of the country': 'Those who want that kind of thing have a place in Pakistan, not here (applause) . . . we are laying the foundations of One Nation, and those who choose to divide again [sic] and sow the seeds of disruption will have no place, no quarter here . . . (hear, hear).'[20]

Others declared that Muslims alone could stop the killings in Punjab and neighbouring states. All those who had any links with the Muslim League should urge 'their Pakistani brethren' to put an end to the violence. Leaguers must make an unqualified denunciation of the two-nation theory and campaign actively for reunification. Muslims generally must step forward to help Hindu and Sikh refugees, and thereby demonstrate their patriotism. They should report fellow Muslims who collected arms or otherwise created trouble. They should be prepared to go to West Punjab and 'take up the cudgels against their Pakistani brothers for their misdeeds'.[21] Indian Muslims would of course have to be prepared to lay down their lives for the country, as already noted, but even before war broke out, they could prove their loyalty by taking up arms against 'their Pakistani brothers'!

Two comments made during the debate on minority rights in the Constituent Assembly sum up the position of the Indian Muslims in the aftermath of Partition. One came from

Mahavir Tyagi, a prominent Congress man of western UP, when the debate was being wound up on 26 May 1949:

The Muslims already know that they will not be returned [in elections to the various legislatures] for some time to come, so long as they do not rehabilitate themselves among the masses and assure the rest of the people that they are one with them. They have been separate in every matter for a long time past and in a day you can't switch over from Communalism to Nationalism.[22]

The other was a blunt statement from Vallabhbhai Patel to the Muslims, made in the course of the speech quoted earlier: '*You* must change your attitude, adapt yourself to the changed conditions . . . don't pretend to say "Oh, our affection is great for you". We have seen your affection . . . . Let us forget the affection. Let us face the realities. Ask yourself whether you really want to stand here and cooperate with *us* or you want to play disruptive tactics . . . .'[23]

Here, Hindu nationalism and secular nationalism come to be imbricated in the discourse of the new 'India'. From the late nineteenth century on, the politics of the middle-class Hindu had written the Indian people into existence by developing the modern discourse of 'the people'—imagined, on the one hand, as an ignorant, uneducated mass to be dignified through nationalism, and on the other as a 'people/nation', embodying an authentic cultural spirit. This 'people' was an empty signifier, to be filled in by political contingency. From the Hindu nationalist perspective, the violence of Partition could be seen as a kind of patriotic baptism. From the secular nationalist perspective too, it necessitated cooperation with 'us', and with 'our' cultural/political project.

THE RETURN OF THE NATIVE

Like the land and the trees, rivers, and mountains, the Hindus were the natural core—the 'us' of the Indian nation. In July 1947, Patel had written to an anxious Hindu correspondent from West Punjab that while the matter of citizenship was at that moment under the consideration of the Indian Constituent Assembly, 'whatever the definition may be, you can rest assured that the Hindus and Sikhs of Pakistan cannot be considered as aliens in India [sic]'.[24] In other words, the Hindu and Sikh communities were *natural* citizens of India, wherever they might live and whatever the constitutional definitions of citizenship might turn out to be in the two new nation-states.

If Hindus and Sikhs were 'naturally' ours, and Muslims 'naturally' theirs, as in the circumstances of Partition they were commonly declared to be, the hostile conditions of the time also raised the demand that these natural possessions be restored to their natural homes. The poignant history of abducted women caught on the wrong side of the new international border illustrates some of the tragic consequences of this curious collapsing of religious community into natural nation.

Elsewhere I have drawn attention to what amounted to an open declaration of war on the men, women, and children of the 'enemy' community. This was signalled very clearly indeed in a letter from the 'front', written by a non-commissioned officer in the erstwhile Punjab regiment of the British Indian army, two weeks after the official Partition of India. The letter reports his platoon's 'destruction' of Hindus and Sikhs in the villages of the Gurdaspur region:

Whosoever from the Hindus and Sikhs came in front of us, were killed. Not only that, we got them to come out of their houses and ruthlessly killed them and disgraced their womenfolk. Many women agreed to come with us and wished us to take them, but we were out for revenge . . . . This Indian government cannot last much longer. We will very soon conquer this and on the whole of India the flag of Pakistan will fly.[25]

Others were equally ready to take away the women, before or after 'disgracing' them. 'We took away the women. That was the system,' a retired captain of the Alwar army declared, in his recollections of the 'Meo-Jat war' of May to November 1947 in the region south and west of Delhi. 'Women do not have any religion after all (. . . *auraton ka to koi dharam hi nahin hota*).'[26] This is in line with the misogynist north Indian proverb, '*beeran ki kai jaat*' ('what caste [or nationality] can a woman have?')—for she 'belongs' to someone else, and therefore to *his* caste, nationality, and religion. Yet, the evidence from 1947 seems at times to suggest almost the exact opposite: not that 'women [had] no religion (or community or nation)', but that they came for a moment to stand for nothing else.

When the worst phase of that violence was over by November–December 1947, the question of the recovery of 'our' women, and the restoration of 'theirs', became an urgent one.[27] At the initiative of a number of women social workers, supported by some of India's most important political leaders, a programme for the 'recovery of abducted persons' was drawn up towards the end of 1947. This was to remain in operation, in one form or another, until the middle of the 1950s. Represented as nothing but the possessions of their men, their communities, and their nations, however, many of the women and children who were the victims identified by this programme became mere pawns in the crossfire of nationalist demands that came to mark it.

Gandhi pronounced it to be the foremost responsibility of the two governments, of India and Pakistan, to bring these abducted women back to their native lands. So important was the question for him that he called for intervention at the highest levels, in terms of govern-ment-to-government action—a significant departure from his normal advocacy of minimal government, self-help, and people's initiative. 'Yes, a team of women workers could be sent to East Punjab and another team to West Punjab,' he now declared, 'but I do not think that would be effective . . . . This is a task for the Governments to tackle . . . . There is only one way of saving these women and that is that the Governments should even now wake up to their responsibility, *give this task the first priority and all their time* and accomplish it *even at the cost of their lives*.'[28] Moreover, he felt that the women concerned had no real hope of considered judgement or choice in this matter. 'It is said that the [Sikh and Hindu] women concerned do not now want to return,' he said in one of his prayer meetings, '*but still they have to be brought back* . . . . I do not admit that they are not willing to return. Similar is the case of Muslim women in India.'[29]

Others put the case for restoration—and, indeed, 'reparations'—much more sharply. 'You will remember, Sir,' declared a member of the Constituent Assembly of India, debating the question of recovery of abducted persons in December 1949,

how when one [Mrs] Ellis was kidnapped by some Pathans the whole of Britain shook with anger and indignation and until she was returned Englishmen did not come to their senses. And we all know our own history, of what happened in the time of Shri Ram when Sita was abducted. Here, where thousands of girls are concerned, we cannot forget this. We can forget all the properties, we can forget every other thing, but this cannot be forgotten.

And another, in the course of the same debate: 'You are not prepared to go to war over this matter. I do not know why. If you are prepared to do so for a few inches of land in Kashmir, why not over the honour of our women?'[30]

Within months of official Partition and Independence, even Prime Minister Nehru had come to be caught up in this rhetoric to some extent. 'Please remember,' he said in a speech inaugurating the 'rehabilitation of women and children week' in January 1948, 'we may gradually forget any other hardship which we have undergone but this matter concerning our women will not be forgotten, either by our country or the world, and the longer it continues, the deeper will be our sense of shame. It will sow seeds for future bitterness and wars . . . .'[31]

That considerable force was used in the recovery programme is now well documented. It is implicit in the 'Abducted Persons (Recovery and Restoration) Act' which replaced an existing ordinance of the Government of India in December 1949: if any police officer of the rank of assistant sub-inspector or higher, or any other police official authorized by the provincial government, had 'reason to believe that an abducted person resides or is found in any place, he may . . . without warrant, enter and search the place and take into custody any person found therein who, in his opinion, is an abducted person . . .'.[32] One officer recalled that 'the operation was a raid in every sense of the word—we did many irregular things, like dipping a police officer under water and keeping him there till he told us where the women were . . . sometimes I would slap the women and tell them that I would shoot them if they didn't inform us. . .'.[33]

It is scarcely surprising that 'mistakes' occurred in the process. 'Hindu women are sometimes arrested [sic] and taken to the camp for Muslim recovered women', a leading woman social worker observed. Sardarni Santokh Singh, the Delhi Provincial Organizer of these 'recovery' operations noted that six such cases of 'wrongful arrest' had taken place within a two-month period in the Delhi region alone. Premvati Thapar and other workers also reported several examples of such mistakes.[34] If a woman was young, and pregnant, or nursing an infant, and at the same time afraid, while living in a Hindu or Sikh area, she was (in this view) likely to be a 'Muslim'. By that 'fact' alone, she could be taken for a 'Pakistani', an abducted person from Pakistan—and the logic of the new nationalism demanded her immediate 'repatriation'.

As it happened, many abducted women were hesitant about returning to their original families and countries—for fear of ostracism, because they felt they had been 'soiled'; because they could not bear the thought of being uprooted yet again and exposed (possibly) to new levels of poverty and uncertainty; or simply because they were grateful to their new husbands and families for having rescued them from (further?) assault and afforded them some protection. The governments of the two dominions decided, however, that in such cases 'they should be forcibly evacuated'.[35]

Modern technologies of government were very much in evidence, and the gathering of statistics was a central part of the exercise. One widely quoted estimate of the total number of abducted persons detained in 'foreign' territory was 50,000 Muslim women and children in India and 33,000 Hindu and Sikh women in Pakistan, although some social workers felt that the actual numbers were far greater. Of this number 12,552 women and children were said to have been 'recovered' from India, and 6272 from Pakistan, by December 1949. By 1955, the figures had increased to 20,728 and 9032 respectively.[36]

As several writers on the subject have noted, this disparity in the numbers of abducted persons recovered on the two sides produced new recriminations. Rameshwari Nehru wrote of the growing resentment and expressions of dissatisfaction in Delhi at the fact that, between November 1948 and June 1949, the number of abducted women recovered in India was four times that in Pakistan.[37] Pakistan, the 'abductor nation', had not kept its part of the bargain, it was said. There was, therefore, no reason why India should not keep recovered Muslim women as hostages at least for some time.[38] The abducted women themselves were in an unenviable position—not free to stay if the nation wanted them to go, nor free to go if it wished them to stay.

THE ILLUSION OF CHOICE

All nations, all nationalisms and nationalist discourses, are made in exceptional (that is to say, particular, if not unique) historical circumstances. It was in the particular context of 1947—building on more than a century of colonial governance premised on the division between Hindus and Muslims, and on an extended (and oft-retold) history of Muslim adventurers raiding the land, settling and setting up towns and kingdoms in which the question of religious and ethnic identities allegedly became the central determinants of privilege—that the 'we' of Indian nationalism came to be elaborated and the Muslims came to be marked out as a suspect minority.

It was whiteness that came to be constructed as the core of American, or Australian, nation-hood, and Englishness that became the core of the British nation, in spite of the substantial presence of the Scots and the Welsh and the Irish—though, in all of these cases, the demographic and political changes brought by a more recent history of substantial coloured immigration (at times actively encouraged for purposes of production, at other times severely discouraged) have pushed the 'mainstream' into other channels or, at least, different debates. In other circumstances—such as those of the subcontinent, where diverse regions and groups have fought to retain a greater degree of autonomy and political power—national cores have crystallized very differently. Indeed, even within a given set of historical circumstances, there remains the distinct possibility of national identities, boundaries, and mainstreams coming together in various ways. Surely the India of 1947 provides striking testimony to this.

The process of Partition had claimed large numbers of lives and destroyed the peace and well-being of innumerable individuals and families, even before official Partition and Independence occurred. Within weeks, it would destroy many more, and uproot practically a whole countryside in Punjab and neighbouring areas, as people fled in both directions in search of minimal safety and security. In Bengal, the movement of minorities did not assume quite the same proportions as in the north-west. The migrations were far from being insubstantial but they occurred on a smaller scale than in Punjab, and were more spread out in time, coming in waves that were observable in East Bengal in 1948, the 1950s, and even later. For all that, the minorities lived in fear all over the partitioned subcontinent in 1947–8. There was simply too much evidence of families and fortunes destroyed on account of nothing but their religious affiliation; and far too many reports and rumours of rape, abduction, and forced religious conversion—from near and far.

Towards the end of September 1947, the prime minister of India remarked that, Hindus or Muslims, only those men and women were welcome to live in the country who considered it their own nation, gave it their undivided loyalty, and refused to look to any outside agency for help. Removed from the confusion, suspicions, and violence of the time, this was an unexceptionable statement. But as the Calcutta daily, *The Statesman*, commented editorially on 5 October, how were the Muslims of India to prove their loyalty when the very act of fleeing in fear from their homes was interpreted as a sign of disloyalty and extraterritorial attachment?

Everywhere, refugees struggled to find new homes and means of survival, and in places where they had some breathing space, the minorities made desperate attempts to articulate a new sense of belonging. I have referred to leaders of the erstwhile Muslim League who called upon Indian Muslims to be prepared to shed every last drop of their blood for the Indian motherland. Consider the parallel response of the Anglo-Indian Association of Hazaribagh in Bihar on the attainment of Indian (and Pakistani) independence: 'In this new India . . ., the role of the Anglo-Indian Community in the land of their birth will be to join in co-operating with all her other children towards India attaining true and lasting greatness.' The resolution went on to say that 'an Anglo-Indian father in West Bengal with a son employed in East Bengal cannot treat one another as aliens, and the community *naturally desires a reunited India*'. At the same time the Hazaribagh Anglo-Indians noted, however, that the Congress 'has not been ungenerous and the Muslim League has shown a realistic appreciation of our position, and the Anglo-Indians hope that by loyal, ungrudging service in whatever part of the Sub-continent they happen to be, they will vindicate the *national and non-partisan* character of the Anglo-Indian community'.[39]

Or consider the course followed by Lala Murlidhar Shad, owner of Lyallpur Cotton Mills, 'the only cloth mill in Western Pakistan' as the *Pakistan Times* reported, who returned to Pakistan from Delhi as late as June 1949, 'to stay here permanently'. He was 'proud to be a Pakistani', the mill owner declared in an interview to the press; 'that is why he had brought his family back to the land of his birth'.[40]

The choices were no easier for Muslims living in India than they were for Murlidhar Shad. The consequences of Partition were hard even for the most privileged among them. In October 1947, Choudhry Khaliquzzaman—high-profile leader of the Muslim League in the Indian Constituent Assembly, long-time ally of Nehru and other Congress leaders in UP, and, subsequently, a vocal champion of the rights of India's Muslims—unexpectedly and abruptly migrated to Pakistan, leaving a bewildered Muslim League party behind. No one knew quite why he had suddenly made this decision, and his own explanations—that he wanted to make way for younger blood, that he could not reconcile himself to learning Hindi which had been made the official language of UP, and (in his autobiography, ten years later) that he felt someone who had Jinnah's continued confidence should replace him and serve as the leader of the Indian Muslims—did not set the controversy at rest.

Somewhat later, in 1949, Z.H. Lari, the deputy leader of the Muslim League in the UP legislature, also left for Pakistan, although he had by then spoken out strongly against the two-nation theory, separate electorates, reservations, and the accompanying baggage. It was, as many who lived through those times recall, primarily a question of where one could live in relative mental, and physical, peace.

Ustad Bade Ghulam Ali Khan, the doyen of the Patiala *gharana* (school) of Hindustani music, moved to Pakistan, where he lived in relative obscurity for some time, before returning to India—and to a successful revitalization of his musical career—many years before his death. Josh Malihabadi, the great Urdu poet from Malihabad, near Lucknow, who had declared along with a host of other progressive writers that 'we cannot partition Urdu',[41] went and came and went again several times over, unhappy in that he had no nation, no home now, and probably unclear to the end whether Urdu had been partitioned and what its fate would be in the two countries.

The fact is that the choice between India and Pakistan was a practically impossible one for Muslims living in what were called the 'Muslim-minority provinces' of British India, especially in the immediate aftermath of Partition and Independence. The individuals mentioned in the preceding paragraphs were part of an elite, and possessed the resources as well as the bureaucratic and political contacts that enabled them to move to and fro, at least for a time. There were innumerable others who did not have the luxury of such trial periods—or the chance of an appeal to Jawaharlal Nehru—yet who moved one way and then the other in search of security and peace.

The divisions at the borders were already being replicated at the level of localities. In November 1947, it was reported that nearly 5000 Muslim railwaymen who had earlier opted for service in Pakistan, had now 'set the authorities a serious problem' by withdrawing their preference for Pakistan and refusing to leave India. They were, of course, by this change of heart, laying themselves open to the charge of being Pakistani agents engaged in a conspiracy, although their motives were almost certainly more mundane, the result of news of trouble on that side of the border too and of the fact that working in Pakistan would create its own set of problems. However, even their co-workers in UP were not inclined to be so generous in their response to their change. Hindu railwaymen in Lucknow threatened to go on strike if the 'Pakistan personnel' were allowed to stay, and the railway authorities insisted that those who had opted for service in Pakistan must now go.[42]

A letter from one such railway worker, and the Indian government's response to it, provides another illustration of the hopelessness of many choices. The letter was written in September 1947 by Safdar Ali Khan, 'Guard, Moradabad', to the Secretary, 'Partition Department', Government of India. Headed 'Permission to revise my decision "to serve in India" ', it said:

I had submitted my final choice to serve in Pakistan . . . . The persuasions of my fellow-workers and friends favoured [forced?] me to come to this decision at which I am rubbing my hands now [sic].

. . . . My old mother is lying very seriously ill and she is not in a mood to allow me to go to Pakistan as she has no hope to survive her illness.

. . . . I have blundered in favour of Pakistan. Really speaking, as I have stated above, the decision was not my own but . . . made under compulsion. I am an Indian first and an Indian last. I want to live in India and die in India . . . .

Hence I humbly request your honoour to permit me to revise my decision and allow me to serve in India.[43]

Maulana Abul Kalam Azad, the education minister of India, forwarded this letter to the home minister, Vallabhbhai Patel, who responded briefly: 'The Partition Council decision has been that once a final choice is made it should be adhered to. I [can] see no prospect, therefore, of the gentleman, whose application you have sent me, being allowed to change his option now.'[44]

There is a bureaucratic imperative at work here. Two new state administrations are being set up, rules have to be made and followed. But there is a moral imperative as well. People simply have to decide where they stand and who they are, once and for all. This was a demand that was made insistently of *one* part of the new India's inhabitants, as the preceding pages should have shown. The modern state insists on a separation between the public and the private. Yet Partition produced a situation in which one part of the private (the 'Hindu' in India, and the 'Muslim' in Pakistan) articulated itself as the public, while denying that possibility to the 'other'. There were perhaps two voices of nationalism that could be heard in the above exchange between Patel and Azad; but it was the second that won out, as it has so often done in our times, asserting certainty even in the midst of the wholly uncertain.

The same clarity of choice was demanded of abducted, then recovered women, as we have observed. Evidence of the reluctance of many women to return to what others saw as their 'natural' homes was brought up by concerned social workers at a number of conferences in India during the later stages of the recovery programme. Following from this, it was agreed 'as a compromise', to quote Rameshwari Nehru, that 'such unwilling women should be sent to Pakistan in the first instance for one month only. At the end of this period, they should be given the option of returning to India'. This incredible solution speaks of how a whole section of the population, now classified as victims, had become unconsulted objects in an unthinking game of boundary marking. It is no surprise to find that, in Nehru's words again, 'as far as I know, no woman has come back'.[45]

At another stage, an order was issued whereby children born in circumstances of 'abduction' would have to be left behind in the countries where they were born. Once again, the protests of several women workers led to further consideration of the question. Out of this came the desperate resolution that Muslim women being repatriated from India to Pakistan, who insisted on keeping their children, would be allowed to take the children with them to the transit camp in Jalandhar where, after fifteen days, they would decide whether they wanted to keep them or not.[46] This was surely little better than the solution of sending 'unwilling women' to Pakistan for a month only 'in the first instance'.

By 1949, there was a good deal of opposition to the 'abducted women's recovery programme'. Anees Qidwai recalls people asking:

Why are these girls being tortured in this way? . . . What is the advantage of uprooting them once again? If making them homeless again is not idiocy, what is it? To take a woman who has become a respected housewife and mother in her [new] home, and force her to return to her old home and [or] her parents, is not charity but a crime. Forget this business: those [women] who are left in Hindustan and those left in Pakistan are happy where they are . . . .

Rameshwari Nehru was overcome by some of the same misgivings. Viewed from the human angle, she wrote:

I am convinced that we have not achieved our purpose, and that it is inadvisable to continue the work of recovery any longer. Two years have elapsed since the original crimes were committed, and though there may still be a considerable number of unrecovered women, to remove them at this stage from the homes, in which they have settled, would result in untold misery and suffering.[47]

The question of restoring abducted women to their respective nations, which admitted of no easy solution in any case, also generated new kinds of self-censorship and fear. Individuals who had almost gone berserk in the first phase of the violence and migrations, searching high and low for the sisters, daughters, and wives they had lost, making anxious enquiries of friends and acquaintances from their original homes, combing refugee camps and hospitals, railway stations and bazaars, sometimes preferred to withdraw and draw a blind over the subject once the recovery of abducted persons became a public issue and a matter for settlement between two governments. Thus the government of East Punjab was unable to publicize a list of abducted persons that had been compiled under its orders because a number of ministers' families were named in it. As the compiler of a two-volume *List of Non-Muslim Abducted Women and Children*, put it, 'The publication of this volume was not undertaken earlier out of deference to the feelings of the victims and their relations'.[48] When the list was published, it was in a small number of copies, for limited administrative circulation.

Where family members were abducted or otherwise taken away, and where this threatened to become public knowledge, a common response was to refuse to acknowledge the fact. The honour of the local community, household, father, husband, necessitated such suppression. At the same time, while the raped and abducted women might not be recognized by many relatives and families, the 'nation' demanded that all 'our' women must be returned—'at any cost', as Gandhi had it. On both sides of the border, the abducted women—'recovered' or not—have lived on as shadows from 1947 until today. Some have survived as quiet housewives and mothers in new lives, in which the 'past' has simply had to be buried;[49] others in so-called women's 'homes'—charities funded by the state and certain private organizations, with strict disciplinary regimes and minimal resources. Family, community, and nation take their toll in different ways.

NOTES

1. *Vartman*, 14 September 1947, editorial. (I am grateful to Saumya Gupta for giving me access to her photocopies of the files of this newspaper.)
2. Brackette F. Williams makes the point as follows in her discussion of ethnicity in the context of territorial and cultural nationalism. Like tribe, race, or barbarian, she notes, the label ethnicity identifies those who are at the borders of empire of nation. 'Within putatively homogenous nation-states, this border is an ideologically produced boundary between "mainstream" and peripheral categorical units of this kind of "imagined" social order'; Williams, 'A Class Act: Anthropology and Race to Nation across Ethnic Terrain', *Annual Review of Anthropology*, 18 , 1989: pp. 401–44.
3. For a discussion of the terms 'majority' and 'minority', especially in their Indian usage, see my 'Can a Muslim be an Indian?', *Comparative Studies in Society and History*, 41, 4 1999: pp. 608–29.
4. Shavid Javed Burki, *Pakistan: A Nation in the Making*, Boulder: Westview Press, 1986: p. 42; cf. Stanley Wolpert, *Jinnah of Pakistan*, New York: Oxford University Press, 1984: 339–40. To confuse matters even further, Jinnah's speech referred to a 'nation of 400 million souls', implying that all of British India's 400 million people belonged to one nation, among whom the question had been one of the appropriate distribution of power. See A.G. Noorani, 'The Cabinet Mission and its Aftermath', in C.H. Phillips and Mary Doreen Wainwright (eds), *The Partition of India: Policies and Perspectives, 1935–1947*, London: Allen and Unwin, 1970: p. 105.
5. *Civil and Military Gazette*, 21 October 1947.
6. J. Nehru, *Glimpses of World History*, vol. II, 2nd edn, Bombay: Asia Publishing House, 1961: pp. 1129–30.
7. *Vartman*, 12 October 1947.
8. In connection with the proposition that the 'language, appearance, religion and practices' of the Muslims were 'all different' from those of the Hindus, I might note only that all the Indian Muslims I know or have

heard of speak the Bengali, Gujarati, Marathi, Malayalam, Punjabi, Hindi, Urdu (or to break the vernaculars down further, the Awadhi, Bhojpuri, Magahi) of their regions. I should add that Urdu— designated the language of the Indian Muslims, which is also my language and the language of very large numbers of Hindus and Sikhs of my parents' and grandparents' generation—whatever else it might be, is not a foreign language, but distinctively Indian (or, now, subcontinental). And just as Indian intellectuals claim, with considerable justification, that English too is now one of the languages of India, one would also have to assert that Islam is now (and has long been) one of the religions of India.

9. *Constituent Assembly Debates, Official Report*, vol. VIII, 16 May to 16 June 1949: p. 271.

10. Ambedkar and other Dalit leaders had of course already initiated a significant debate about the relevance of the category 'Hindu' for their followers; and similar questions had been raised in connection with the *adivasis* (literally 'original inhabitants', used for various tribal peasant groups in India) in the work of anthropologists like G.S. Ghurye and Verrier Elwin.

11. For a fuller discussion of this point, see my *The Construction of Communalism in Colonial North India*, Delhi: Oxford University Press, 1990: ch. 3 and *passim*.

12. *The Statesman*, 29 October 1947.

13. *The Hindustan Times*, 28 September 1947, cited in *People's Age*, 12 October 1947.

14. Cited in Ashish Nandy, *At the Edge of Psychology: Essays in Politics and Culture*, Delhi: Oxford University Press, 1980: p. 91.

15. *Vartman*, 20 July 1947.

16. *The Statesman*, 9 and 12 October 1947. At the end of September, at a public meeting of prominent citizens addressed by Gandhi, one person declared that 'the citizens of Delhi [*sic*] were ready to live in peace with the Muslims provided they were loyal to the Union and surrendered all arms and ammunition which they possessed without a license', ibid., 2 October 1947.

17. Ibid.; see *Aj*, 22 September 1947, for a report of another, very similar speech by Pant.

18. *Aj*, 7 October 1947.

19. *Pakistan Times*, 8 October 1947.

20. *Constituent Assembly Debates*, vol. VIII, 16 May to 16 June 1949: 271.

21. See the comments of the UP Congress leaders, A.P. Jain and Charan Singh, as reported in *Aj*, 26 September and *Pakistan Times*, 11 October 1947, respectively; also other reports in *Aj*, 7 October, and *Vartman*, 27 September 1947.

22. *Constituent Assembly Debates*, vol VIII: 346.

23. *Ibid.*: 271 (emphasis added).

24. Letter to Parmanand Trehan, 16 July 1947, in Durga Das (ed.), *Sardar Patel's Correspondence, 1945–50*, vol. V, Ahmedabad: Navjivan Publishing House, 1973: 289.

25. (IOR) R/3/1/173, translation of intercepted letter from Fateh Khan, Jamadar to 'brother Malik Sher Mohd Khanji', 31 August 1947.

26. Shail Mayaram, *Resisting Regimes: Myth, Memory and the Shaping of a Muslim Identity*, Delhi: Oxford University Press, 1995: 191.

27. What follows is a summary of important research findings that have been published over the last few years, supplemented by my own archival and other research.

28. *CWMG*, vol. XC: 194 (emphasis added).

29. *Ibid.*: 193 (emphasis added).

30. *Constituent Assembly of India (Legislative) Debates, Official Reports*, vol. VI, no. 14, 15 December 1949: 642 (speech by Pandit Thakurdas Bhargava); and vol. VII, no. 1, 19 December 1949: 799 (speech by Sardar Bhopindar Singh Man). Extracts from these speeches are also quoted in Veena Das, *Critical Events: An Anthropological Perspective on Contemporary India*, Delhi: Oxford University Press, 1995: p. 70 and Ritu Menon and Kamla Bhasin, *Borders and Boundaries: Women in India's Partition*, New Delhi: Kali for Women, 1998: p. 111.

31. *Selected Works of Jawaharlal Nehru*, 2nd series, vol. V, Delhi: Jawaharlal Nehru Memorial Fund, 1987: p. 116.

32. For the text of the Abducted Persons (Recovery and Restoration) Act of 1949, see Menon and Bhasin, *Borders and Boundaries*, appendix 1: 261–3.

33. Quoted in ibid.: 117–18. Another commentator noted that 'the opinion of the Assistant Sub-Inspector [of police] determines the fate of the lad[ies]', see speech by Thakurdas Bhargava in *Constituent Assembly (Legislative) Debates*, vol. VII, no. 1: 800, 802.

34. Rameshwari Nehru Papers, 'Reports', no. 1, 'Memorandum on the Recovery of Women: Review of the Position since October 1948', by Rameshwari Nehru, 20 June 1949. See also *Constituent Assembly (Legislative) Debates*, vol. VII, no. 1: 800.

35. And again, at a later meeting, that abducted persons were to be recovered 'without any concession', Anees Qidwai, *Azadi ke Chaon Mein*, trans. Nor Nabi Abbasi, New Delhi: National Book Trust, 1990: p. 314; Urvashi Butalia, *The Other Side of Silence: Voices from the Partition of India*, New Delhi: Viking Penguin, 1998: p. 120. See also the debate on the taking away of the women's right to habeas corpus, *Constituent Assembly (Legislative) Debates*, vol. VII, no. 1: pp. 799–802.

36. Menon and Bhasin, *Borders and Boundaries*: pp. 70, 99.

37. Rameshwari Nehru Papers, 'Reports', no. 1, 'Memorandum' of 20 June 1949. Not only was there a demand for the recovery of an equal number of women on both sides, it was also necessary, as Veena Das notes, that women in their reproductive years especially be brought back; for 'this interest in women was not premised upon their definition as citizens, but as sexual and reproductive beings', *Critical Events*: 68–9 and *passim*; also *Constituent Assembly (Legislative) Debates*, vol. VII, no. 1: 796, 803. On the question of national honour, see also Butalia, *Other Side of Silence*, chs 5 and 6; and Menon and Bhasin, *Borders and Boundaries*: 110–13 and *passim*.

38. Menon and Bhasin, *Borders and Boundaries*: 113–14, see also pp. 76, 78.

39. AICC papers, File G4/1947, F.M. Holland, honorary secretary, Hazaribagh Anglo-Indian Association, to 'Secretary, Congress High Command, Delhi', 21 August 1947, forwarding a copy of the association's resolution (emphasis added).

40. *Pakistan Times*, 14 June 1949.

41. *People's Age*, 7 September 1947.

42. *The Statesman*, 23 November 1947. Cf. AICC papers, File G-18, KW I (Pt. I)/1947–48, complaint by Harikrishna Dua, 'Refugee', against Muslim postal employees who had changed their 'option' from Pakistan to India, and had been allowed to stay on, as he alleged, 'owing to [Rafi Ahmad] Kidwaiji's favour'. Note also the report in *The Statesman*, 15 October 1947, that 'By an interesting unanimity of purpose, backed, no doubt, by a firm administration of law and order, [the Muslims of UP who, it notes, form the largest concentration of Muslims outside the "Pakistan areas"] have been determined hitherto to stay put'.

43. Durga Das, *Patel's Correspondence*, vol. IV: p. 421.

44. Ibid.: 422.

45. Rameshwari Nehru Papers, 'Reports', no. 1, 'Memorandum' of 20 June 1949.

46. See Menon and Bhasin, *Borders and Boundaries*: 84, 101; and Svati Joshi, 'Torn up by the Roots' (A review and commentary on Kamlabehn Patel's *Mool Sota Ukhadela*, Bombay and Ahmedabad, 1985), *Manushi*, 48: 16, 1988.

47. Qidwai, *Azadi*: p. 313; Rameshwari Nehru Papers, 'Reports', no. 1, 'Memorandum' of 20 June 1949.

48. *List of Non-Muslim Abducted Women and Children, Part I and Part II* (1414 pages; copy in Haryana Secretariat Library, Chandigarh), 'Preface', p. i. The document gave the total number of Hindus and Sikhs abducted as 21,809 (p. ii of 'Preface', dated 24 May 1954, by A.J. Fletcher, commissioner, Ambala and Jullunder divisions and 'high-powered officer for recovery of abducted women and children, India').

49. Consider the example of Lajwanti in Rajinder Singh Bedi's eponymous story: 'Sunder Lal stopped her saying, "Let's just forget the past." . . .And Lajwanti couldn't get it all out. It remained buried inside her. She withdrew into herself and stared at her body for the longest time, a body which, after the partition of the country, was no longer hers, but that of a goddess.' Rajinder Singh Bedi, 'Lajwanti', tr. from the Urdu by Muhammad Umar Memon, in Memon (ed.), *An Epic Unwritten*, New Delhi: Penguin Books, 1998: p. 28.

NINE

Belonging

Ritu Menon and Kamla Bhasin

༚༚✦༚༚

Two nations were born on 14 and 15 August 1947, and it was thought that the issue of who belonged where had finally, though bloodily, been laid to rest. Fifty years later there are still 1100 'displaced persons' in what are called 'permanent liability homes' in India. Refugees from Bihar and Bangladesh are to be found not only in Sind and West Bengal but in Haryana and Madhya Pradesh as well. A steady stream of migration from East Pakistan continued right up to 1958, and again in 1964 after trouble in Kashmir led to riots in Dhaka and Khulna, and later in 1971, following the war of liberation for Bangladesh. A third new nation was born.

New nations, it seems, create their own refugees, or so it has been in the subcontinent. 'For the last 50 years I have travelled from one place to another,' says Ghafoor, a Bihari in Karachi, 'from Bihar to Madras to Calcutta, then to Dhaka and now Karachi. I have been travelling all my life and at 75 I am still not settled.'[1] In 1947 and again in 1971 there were those who gained a nation and those who lost a country—and, as one woman said to us, there were those who became 'permanent refugees'. For the vast majority, 'country' was something they had always thought of as the place where they were born and where they would like to die. Now, suddenly, their place of birth was horribly at odds with their nationality, had nothing to do with it, in fact. And the place now called their country, they felt little attachment to. Quite unexpectedly, and certainly unwillingly, they were violently uprooted and relocated in places and among communities they could not identify with, people they thought of as strangers. Own country? 'Now there is no country,' said Somavanti to us, 'this is not ours, that is no more ours.'

Partition made for a realignment of borders and of national and community identities, but not necessarily of loyalties. Thousands who opted for Pakistan returned a little later, an equal number, here and there, forsook allegiance to their families and never left at all. Some were unaware of Pakistan as a separate country till some years after its creation, even though they themselves had migrated to it. And any number failed to quite absorb the fact that there were borders now that could not be crossed. 'My real home?', said one woman to us in Delhi, 'the one at Sutar Mandi, Phullan Wali Gali, Lahore.' Large numbers of people chose fidelity to place rather than to religious community: they converted and remained where they were. The choice may have been expedient or not—and, indeed, often there was little choice in the matter; what it suggests is that 'country' is an elusive entity. Each time we asked the women we were speaking to whether they would die for their country, we got an eliptical response. Even Taran, who said quite clearly, 'We must fight back, we must oppose with violence if necessary', believed firmly that if women were to write history, 'men would realize how important it is to be peaceful'.

The three stories that follow all deal with how these women came to terms (or not, as the case may be) with their relocation or dislocation—for, as we realized, there can be dislocation without one's ever having been displaced. Whether the choice to go or stay was voluntary, they all speak about how they relearnt their roles in a 'new' country. Kamila,* a Hindu, chose to rejoin her husband, a Muslim, and live in Pakistan as a convert; and the three Lucknow sisters† stayed back with their parents after all other members of their extended—and very political—family had left for Karachi. When, years later as adults, they had to choose, they opted for Lucknow. Taran lived through 1947 and, as a Sikh, through the 1984 anti-Sikh riots in Kanpur. In 1947 she had no choice, in 1984, she said, she realized she had 'no country'.

Kamila: 'No Going Back'

.... On 14 August Pakistan was duly declared an independent country, and the next day British rule in India formally came to an end. India was at last free from the stranglehold of a foreign yoke after a long, long struggle. It was an occasion for great joy, but it was being spoilt by widespread reports of looting and carnage from both parts of the subcontinent. Nevertheless, frantic preparations went on in New Delhi, the capital of India, to make 15 August—India's day of independence—an outstandingly festive occasion. No police was to be posted anywhere near the site of celebrations where an impressive rostrum was set up. Cars were parked for miles around the site, from where we had to walk to our seats.

There on the rostrum stood a beaming Jawaharlal Nehru, the hero of the independence movement, now the new prime minister of the country, nodding and waving. Sitting around him were Sardar Patel and the other members of the Indian Congress hierarchy. There also sat Lord Mountbatten with his consort, the famous Lady Edwina. Everyone was smiling and seemed at ease. Speeches boomed on loudspeakers, while the audience laughed and clapped and laughed till all track of time seemed to be lost in the ensuing light-hearted banter and general friendliness. Suddenly a great cloud seemed to descend on me, till I was clutching my heart. Wildly I looked around, desperately trying to locate myself amongst all these carefree faces, and froze. Where in god's name was I? I shook myself with an effort and stood up in a panic. I felt my sister's hand pull me to her lovingly till I was drawn to her lap with my head hidden in her neck. Horses seemed to be racing inside me, thumping against my chest

---

* Not her real name.
† Names withheld at their request.

relentlessly. Somebody had forsaken someone, somewhere. Who, how, and why? Politicians seemed to have all the answers. Had I any? Was I an Indian, or had I creased to be one by marrying a Muslim who had always lived in an area now acceded to Pakistan?

. . . . I was in India when Pakistan was made, and I had a small child, he was three months old . . . so everyone was telling me, Hindus are being murdered there, this and that, don't go back, we've got good jobs for you here . . . in the PIB, in AIR,* don't go . . . your husband had no business opting for Pakistan when you're here . . . he had left me in Delhi and returned to Lahore to attend a family wedding and there they asked him, do you want to opt for India or Pakistan, and he took Pakistan. Without consulting me. There was no way he could have consulted me—the telephone lines were jammed and the operators would start expostulating —they'd say, 'Jawaharlal Nehru, murdabad!' from there and the ones here would reply, 'Jinnah, murdabad!' They'd be fighting among themselves and we'd be left saying, 'Hello? Hello?' We just couldn't talk. We booked so many urgent calls, but nothing. So we couldn't consult each other. He thought, well, she's married to me so she should come here, his whole family was there . . . . Now I had many friends who thought differently; I could understand that he hadn't been able to consult me, but still . . . I was slightly resentful. I thought, why wasn't I asked? Maybe I don't want to live in Pakistan, I want to be where my people are . . . he's secure, he has his people there, but I don't. Everyone said to me, all your links are in India except your child who is only three months old. You don't have to go back. Wait, he may come here, if he doesn't, doesn't matter.

So I was getting all this advice and then my father caught hold of me and said, 'Look, you are so confused now but when you got married I said to you, you haven't had to make any sacrifices yet, they'll come when you start living according to the choice you've made, the life you've chosen. Now the time has come for that sacrifice and you're backing out because it doesn't suit you. What option did your husband have, after all? If he had opted for India, what job security would he have had as a Muslim? Maybe he will, maybe he won't. But now that you've chosen him, you'll have to face it. You've got to keep your vows.'

I saw the truth of this. Then, I didn't know how to get back to Lahore. There was such heavy booking on trains and planes, and my husband kept sending me messages through Hindus who were coming from Lahore, asking me to return, to come home. I was in such conflict. I wanted to go, and yet not to go. Then, you'll be astonished, there were 14,000 people waiting to get on to flights to Pakistan, Muslims who were leaving India, and yet I got a booking, my father managed to get me on somehow, he was so insistent that I go back to my husband. He came with me to the airport. There—you won't believe me—many Sikhs who knew us removed their turbans and placed them at my feet, saying don't go, they are killing all the Hindus there . . . . These were people my father knew, they made me swear I wouldn't go. . . at the airport. Are you mad, they said, that you're going . . . . Now I hadn't really thought of it like that, that I was a Hindu or a Sikh, I just thought, I am a wife returning to her husband. . .

. . . . So I came to Pakistan. By then it was clear that there would be no going back, there had been so much genocide, there was no way it could be different. What had happened, had happened. Now, when I reached the Lahore airport there was a Hindu boy who'd studied with me in M.A., the police had got hold of him . . . . I don't know what he had done but he came

* Press Information Bureau and All India Radio.

and said, I want to talk to her for a minute. They were confused . . . they didn't know who I was, a Hindu or a Muslim, all they knew was that I had come from Delhi to live in Pakistan, that was good enough for them. So they allowed him to talk to me. He came up and pressed some five hundred rupee notes in my hand, 'You take them, if I ever come to Pakistan I'll take them from you, otherwise you keep them. I'd rather you have them than the police'. I didn't even remember him properly, what happened to him, I have no means of knowing . . . .

Then there was the pilot of a Pakistani plane who came up to me, he was a friend of my husband's although I had never met him. And he said, he'd sent me to receive you. I didn't believe him. I said, how could he know I'm coming today, I didn't tell him. He said, no, he knows, he's taken the day off, but there is no way you can get out of here because there is a police cordon. But I am on duty, so you get into my car and I'll take you. So there I was with this howling kid, minus a Muslim ayah who had stayed in India because she had married a Hindu cook! She said, I'm not going back . . . . He put me in his car and dropped me at the gate of our house in Model Town, this was my *jeth*'s house, he was Chief Engineer, North-Western Railways. He dropped me about a hundred yards from the house and I had to carry this suitcase and my child . . . so I left the suitcase on the road and walked the hundred yards to my brother-in-law's bungalow. There my sister-in-law ran out, saying, 'She's come, she's come!' They were overjoyed. My sister-in-law told me, 'Your husband is in your father's house waiting for you, he's taken some servants and he's waiting.' I said, 'I can't believe this, this is nonsense, he's waiting for me . . . . How does he know I am coming?' She said, 'I don't know, he's taken leave, taken my *mali* gardener and gone there.' Now that *mali* was six-foot-five, tall and strapping, and my husband had handed him a staff to protect me with.

Between my brother-in-law's house and my father's house was a garden. That's all the distance there was. My husband had already started walking towards his brother's house to collect me, and we went home. The very next day in the house next to ours, two Hindus were murdered and then, every day, an army major would visit our house saying, 'You hand over your wife to us . . . .' Yes, he would come in his jeep and demand that I be handed over to the Pakistan army so that they could finish me off. My husband never told me this, he would just walk up and down with this major outside the house saying, why don't you kill me instead of my wife? By god, every day this happened.

One day, my chachaji—he was still in Lahore in Model Town, this must have been in early September—he came to see us, very worried. Really worried. He said, give me some water, the police are after me. They had forced him out of his house at gunpoint saying, get out and take everything with you. Well, we gave him full protection, kept him in the *barsati* upstairs. If we gave him water to drink he would put it down and look abstractedly at us . . . he was absolutely broken. Somehow, with great difficulty, we managed to get him out of Pakistan but he told me later that every few miles they would stop, point a gun at him and say, 'Should we kill you? Leave you? Kill you?' They went on like this all the way . . . when he reached Amritsar, he was a wreck.

Meanwhile, my life was still in danger. That major kept coming for many days, I would see them through the window . . . . I don't know how to dealt with this problem. Now my husband had many relatives there who were well placed. Frankly, I don't know how it was sorted out, he never told me and I never asked.

I started to work in the Walton refugee camp. There I discovered all the missing quilts and blankets from our house and many other articles, like suitcases, which the Bhavra thieves must have spared. A few days later, Allah Jawai, who was the local *maalish-wali* [masseuse] appeared at our door and offered her services. She told me she had a message for me. This is what she told me. 'The Bhavras say we are sorry we had to rob you. As far as your Hindu property is concerned, we have vowed to leave you not a scrap. But your life we will protect with our own, have no doubt about that. It is not only because you have chosen to live here with us in Pakistan, but because you are the daughter of a father who saved many of our lives. Our loyalty is at your command.'

My God! What a country, what a people. My own now.

. . . . I didn't know then how they would react to our marriage, after Partition. I mean, one has seen great loves dwindle into enmities in no time—so I wasn't sure. It had been such a catastrophic change . . . .

But you see this is a great thing about Muslims, once they accept you, they take you to their hearts. Nobody resented me, treated me differently . . . my brother-in-law opened his house to us, we stayed with him, we left my father's house. The family accepted me, never ostracized me, but then one day, my mother-in-law said, 'Why don't you have a nikaah anyway.' Now in a nikaah you have to say, 'La Ilahi, Il Lillilah . . .', and so on, so I said to my husband, she's worried that she won't be able to marry off your sisters so I'm thinking, let's have a nikaah. We had had a civil marriage earlier—and, you know, in those days, you had to renounce your religion and for that, I had to say I'm not a Hindu, he had to say I'm not a Muslim. But now he said, no, you don't have to go through a nikaah, not for my sake. Please don't. But I said, I've decided, I've made up my mind, I'll do the nikaah . . . .

But then one day, in a fit of anger, I tore up the nikaahnama and my husband said, actually if you and I live together without a formal marriage it'll be much better! There'll be much less confusion. That is why he said he had torn our civil marriage certificate too! After his death I found the certificate—he had not torn it. But we never were meant to part so we never bothered. For me nikaah was just symbolic. In any case, I'm such a bad Hindu . . . . I remember I quoted Galsworthy's 'White Monkey' to him. An Englishman was surrounded by all these Muslims who said unless you say, 'La Ilah . . .' we'll murder you. So he said, if it matters so much to you I'll say it, because it matters nothing to me . . . .

So, it meant nothing to me but I thought it might be important for my children. I don't know. I wanted to belong, I shouldn't keep myself divided, half here, half there, I should be fully on one side . . . you know, this is a Hindu concept also, become one with where you are . . . . I can't say his family were orthodox but, you know, there was this social pressure . . . . I did it because I thought this will smoothen my path, I've to spend my lifetime here, why not belong to them. Once I'd made my decision I never regretted it, didn't think twice about it.

I did not feel my identity would have to change because my husband never pushed anything on me. People say Muslim society is very intolerant but I think in certain ways it is more tolerant than Hindus. Those Sanatani Hindus who are orthodox, who have so many restrictions, are terrible to live with. Arya Samajis who were converting Muslims called this ceremony, *shuddhi* [purification]. Now, *shuddhi* is a terrible word because it implies they were *napaak, ashuddh*, and they became *paak* through conversion. These were unbearable words and acts for most Muslims. I myself found them unbearable. It is because of this attitude that Pakistan was created. You treat them like *achut* (untouchable). Friends are visiting you at home and people are saying, keep their plates separate. Is this the way to treat people? Is this human? I couldn't tolerate this. Luckily my own family never did this, but if they had I would not have liked it one bit. There were many more factors which played a role, but Hindu orthodoxy *ne maar daala* (killed us). It has made a division even inside India.

I swear to you that at an individual level I did not feel any deprivation. I have said what I wanted to say, I have done what I wanted to do. In the family they just said she has different views . . . . But the cultural deprivation was something else. Things were not accessible to me, dance, music . . . all the singers had left, the only ones who remained to sing were the prostitutes and their singing was so vulgar. I had brought my sitar, my tanpura, but my husband said you'd better hide them, people will say I've married a courtesan. Very reluctantly I put them away. I was so fond of music but I was aware of the distinctions that were being made . . . . Suddenly, Muslims thought of singing as a bad thing . . . . Lifestyles also changed, but not so much because our families were of the same social and professional standing and there had been so much interaction before Partition. But I was a student of literature, wrote poetry, these things I felt much more. But, you know, those days if I said I want to go to India to see some dance, I went. Sometimes I think I had the best of both worlds.

. . . . There is resentment among Hindus and Muslims because of Partition, loss of property, and so on, otherwise where is the resentment? When Hindus and Muslims meet each other abroad, in England or America, they instantly become the best of friends, even today. It is the politicians who are responsible for the divisions, for the hatred.

The British only took advantage of these inherent divisions, they harped on these. There must have been reasons also for Jinnah's feelings going sour. It could, of course, have been his ego, his desire to become a big leader, I don't know. Jinnah was no great Muslim, he married a Parsi woman.

. . . . Even now many Indians have not accepted Pakistan. There is a friend of mine in India whom I have been inviting to visit Pakistan but she says she will visit Pakistan only when the two countries have become one, which of course means never. This is the meanest kind of possessiveness. We have to move on, we can't go back to the past.

You see, with Partition everybody lost. Pakistan lost in many ways, their faith was shaken in a way. They were a big minority, an important part of the cultural life of India. But because Pakistan was created as a Muslim country, religious fanaticism was bound to take place. They started saying, don't sing, don't dance. Those Muslims who uprooted themselves physically from U.P. and places, had to uproot themselves culturally as well. It was more difficult for them, I think. I still had my roots in India.

But it can never go back to what it was. It can never be the same again.

THE LUCKNOW SISTERS: 'INSECURE, YES. UNSETTLED, NO'

After Partition we felt an aloneness—some obstruction somewhere, in our work, lives, and there was difficulty. Our father was left here alone. Earlier all the brothers would look after the mango orchards, we had an income from there . . . then we didn't feel it so much. But after Partition when there was no work, no jobs, then we felt it.

Earlier, more people from here would go to visit Pakistan, one-way traffic, but now people come and go from both sides. The ones who come from there, they are surprised to see that we worship so freely here, observe our religious duties, can say the azaan loudly. Nobody minds.

Our Hindu neighbour, she always says when she hears the azaan in the morning, then she wakes up. So many people say how much they like the sound of voices in prayer from the masjid. . . . .

If Maulana Azad's plan had been accepted by the Cabinet Mission, the trauma of Partition could have been avoided . . . all the bloodshed and destruction . . . from Hyderabad to Punjab, the whole country was engulfed. We were fortunate in Lucknow because nothing happened here, people were extremely cultured. Hindus had economic power, nothing happened. Relations between Hindus and Muslims here were so good. Oh, don't ask . . . from the time of Wajid Ali Shah the relations were very close. Our grandfather's mazhar is here, he was a favourite of Akbar's—he gave him Lucknow and the neighbouring areas as an award. Since then the friendships have been strong . . . .

Women were all kept indoors, in parda, whether Hindu or Muslim, it was the same. The men had the same bad habits, good habits, whether they were the Rai Sahib or Khan Bahadur. Same love of good things . . . . This was a society where the bonds were so strong, feelings ran so deep, outsiders can never be a part of it.

. . . . Our uncle (Khaliquzzuman) left in 1947. It was winter, we were sitting outside when the trucks came. He came to say goodbye to Mian Jaan. We knew they were going—they didn't discuss anything with us, they might have talked to our father. A chartered plane was going to take them all and Apa would also have gone—she was older, fourteen, our parents wanted her to go because it was not safe, Ammi cried and cried—but there were too few seats. There was a cross on our house, too. Yes, we were afraid, our family was political, our Chacha was in the League. Nothing much happened but we were afraid, there was danger. Lakhs of Muslims went from Lucknow. . . .

Even if we had been able to go we would never had adjusted there. We were so attached to our parents and Abba Jaan absolutely refused to go. Ammi, too. It's very difficult to leave one's place—my uncles and others just left in the commotion, almost without thinking what are we doing . . . . He was wealthy, Chacha, he thought there was danger . . . .

Our home was a centre for the freedom struggle in the 1930s. All the big leaders came to our Chacha's house—Nehru, Patel, Sarojini Naidu, they used to come and stay during the British raj, no one else would have taken such a risk. But slowly, they began to drift apart and Chacha left to join the Muslim League. And there he became a senior officer—he must have weighed everything before deciding . . . . Our Phupa also left. Jinnah told him he had to go, there were very few people of his calibre in Pakistan. He was made the first advocate general, he felt he was required there. Our father could not have gone, he had very young children, he was 57–58, he was an artist, a zamindar. . . . And he had a strong conviction, he did not want to leave even though his family was leaving. chacha tried his best to take him, he called him many times afterwards, but our father did not once say he wanted to go. He would pace up and down, go out, come in, go out, come in. But he didn't hesitate, even for a minute. The *sukoon* (peace of mind) you get in your own place . . . . Our Dadi and one Chachi were all that was left . . . . It took Abba Jaan so long to recover from it. He didn't speak for such a long time. He never spoke about it. He went once to Pakistan, in 1952–3, his uncle had passed away and he stayed for three months. But he never wanted to live there—everything was all right, there were no problems, but return he had to. All his relatives were there but to move at his age— it wasn't possible.

He was silent for so many months. He used to go to a bookshop in Aminabad and sit there for hours, reading, reciting Hindi dohas. People loved to listen to him, dohas and Urdu poetry and stories . . . . But he was very disturbed.

We went, too, we thought we might stay back, our two brothers were there, they were working, had good jobs . . . here there was no question of their getting any work. We went to settle them into their home, we rented a place in Karachi—but we couldn't adjust. *Dil nahin laga* (our hearts were not in it), otherwise maybe we would have stayed on. We didn't like people's attitude, it was showy, loud. We couldn't understand them—they had money, everything, but they seemed rootless. *Pair nahin tike* (we could not stay). We couldn't live away from Lucknow.

If Muslims had not gone to Pakistan they would have done the sensible thing. But all the top families left—if they hadn't they would not have got as much as they did in Pakistan. They could never even have imagined such property here. So many unemployed young men have gone from here—they didn't want to go but what chances did they have here? Now they go to the Middle East. For twenty years after Partition they kept going but they never settled down. One woman was told that now pigs roam the streets of Lucknow—she said, please give my love to those pigs!

We never wanted to go because this is our country. Our roots are here. We were homesick in Pakistan. People say Muslims belong in Pakistan but this is the greatest insult, a terrible accusation. What have we to do with Pakistan? It's like any other neighbouring country but that we should be loyal to it, that is unthinkable. We belong here, this is our nationality. To suspect us, to doubt us is a grave offence. When there are riots and the government does nothing then we do feel desperate, but that passes in a little while, it's over. And people have learnt to live with riots. Those who went away have never felt settled. This didn't happen to us, we have never had the feeling of being unsettled. Insecure, yes, unsettled, no. We're in our own place. When there's danger, we may feel insecure, but we're in our own home. Still, Partition cast a shroud of silence on our entire family. . . .Why? We're all scattered, nothing remains—no Ids, no marriages, no celebrations, no happiness.

. . . . By calling it an Islamic republic, will Pakistan become Islamic? The day Muslims become Muslim you will automatically have an Islamic republic. Just by saying so, you can't make it one. *Yeh kehte kehte, Zia Saheb chale gaye* (Zia ul Huq died trying to make this happen). And you don't need an Islamic republic to observe Shariat. Nor is India secular—read forty years of our history and you won't find secularism anywhere. Every religion should be equal but this is not the case. Sometimes it seems the government is secular, at others, not.

In our history Hindu and Muslim rulers always fought—there were Hindus in the Muslim king's army and Muslims in the Hindu raja's army. The fight was between the rulers not the people. Today everyone is fighting each other, provoking the man on the street in the name of religion. The so-called custodians of religion don't know its first tenet, they cannot even read the *qalma* but they instigate fights in its name. Hinduism in danger! Islam in danger! It's all nonsense. Hindu-Muslim unity is a very old thing—they were one in 1857, two arms of the same body. But now Muslims are told, you don't belong here, you should go to Pakistan . . . . Why Pakistan was made was because there, they thought, there will be one place where Muslims will belong, find jobs . . . . So Partition happened because of religion . . . but there were other reasons too.

. . . . When we came back from Karachi because Abba Jaan had passed away we didn't realize our Chacha had made Pakistani passports for us, he thought we would stay there. We had to get a visa to come back. Then they wouldn't give us our Indian passports again. We said, it's a mistake, we live here, we don't live in Pakistan, we're Indians. They said, no, you are Pakistanis, you have Pakistani passports, you'll have to get visas. For nineteen years we had to keep getting visas because they said you're not Indian. *Ab beta, hum na Hindustan ki taraf, na Pakistan ki—hum kehte hain, aap is garib aadmin ka masla tai karen, to hum aapko jaanen* (so, we belong neither to India nor to Pakistan. We will be reconciled only when our peculiar problem is resolved).

TARAN: 'WHERE IS MY COUNTRY?'

Of course we were all emotionally affected by Partition—one of my masis (aunts) went mad in the camp at Wah—even though we never really suffered in a terrible way, we didn't lose any of our family members, we survived on what we had. We had some money and gold that we had brought with us. We managed, but for years we felt we had come to a foreign land.

I was born in 1931 in Nankana Sahib, where my father used to teach untouchables. He had an M.Sc. and a B.T. at that time. My grandfather had instructed my father never to work for the British. We were five brothers and five sisters. I went to school at Atari and Preet Nagar. When Partition took place I had studied up to class IX and had to stop for a couple of years because of all the moving—we were in a camp for a year. I finished my matriculation later, but around this time I started writing poetry, love poetry!

. . . . We saw it all. We started packing everything in huge trunks, all our trousseaus—utensils, clothes, everything—we packed the furniture and put it aside for our return. We took along just a few clothes and beddings for a month or two, after which we thought we would be back. So what if Pakistan is made? We'll stay on, anyway.

My father was a contractor; he was in Ranchi those days (August 1947) on work. When he heard about all the violence he came to take us away, and we travelled for four days before reaching Ranchi. Two of my sisters who were in Pindi and Lyallpur were evacuated by the army later. After staying with our brother for a month we moved to a camp in Ranchi because we were assured of rations. There were more than 1000 people in this camp, from all over—Sind, Gujarat, Bahawalpur. We stayed there for a year after which we bought a house, quite a big one for Rs 5000, but for years we felt we had come to a foreign land.

In Ranchi we all fell sick. There was no wheat, all we got to eat was rice and we weren't used to it. But I was still in the pink of health and looked after everyone. And we longed to meet some Punjabis—there wasn't a single one around. But, really speaking, we didn't mind all the hardship because we felt everything would be solved with Independence. All the difficulties—no food, no medicines—were minor, we just waited for Independence for our beloved country. How many songs of liberation I used to sing! I remember once when I was a little girl we had gone to Lahore and took part in a *jalsa*, singing these songs. One of them had a line in it which said: 'Throw out the invaders, throw out the foreigners!' and the police arrested us for anti-government sentiments! We were school children! On August 14 I couldn't sleep! I just couldn't imagine what the dawn of freedom would feel like. At midnight we heard the gun salute—and for a moment I thought there was going to be trouble again. But it was the sound of celebration! Our joy was so much greater than our suffering. We were unhappy about Partition, of course, but we thought it was inevitable, unavoidable because of the attitude of Jinnah and Gandhi. Yes, even Gandhiji. If he had really been against it, it would never have taken place. The way he handled things, it led to Partition. Maybe he didn't want it but he accepted it. They used to sing songs, saying Gandhi had won freedom without blood, without swords—didn't they see how much blood was spilt? How many people died? How many women were killed, burnt alive?

In 1948 itself we realized that there was no going back to Pakistan. We lost everything we had left behind but now we were in our own country, safe and free. Of course we missed our homes, our old country—I still miss it, I still roam the streets of Punjab in my mind, I loved it—but it's like bidding farewell to your daughter when she gets married. We felt we had come home.

. . . . A woman has no religion—her only religion is womanhood. She gives birth, she is a creator, she is god, she is mother. Mothers have no religion, their religion is motherhood. It makes no difference what they are, whether they are Hindus, Sikhs, Muslims, or Christians.

We girls would often talk about death—some were afraid, others thought of it as a glorious death—dying for an end, for freedom, for our honour. For me everything was related to freedom, I was dying for freedom.

But 1984 was different—it shocked me.* We went to sleep on the night of (October) 31st, worried about what would happen the next day. We had started receiving phone calls from friends in other parts of the city informing us about arson and looting. The next morning when I looked out of the window I saw little children making off with shoes, TVs, and other small things which they had looted. I was alone at home with my (deaf and dumb) daughter. I heard that they had set fire to rickshaws owned by Sikhs behind our house, near Khalsa College. In our neighbourhood a bookshop and a scooter shop were burnt—we wondered whether they had burnt the gurudwara.

Our neighbours upstairs asked me to move in with them because I was alone. I didn't know what to take along, what I might need. I didn't know what might happen. The killings had already begun. In the end I put whatever I could into a small plastic basket—one underwear, a sanitary napkin, one shawl, a sweater for my daughter, and our toothbrushes.

The memory of 1947 came flooding back, except that I feared this might be much worse. Even our neighbours had started looting—I just couldn't believe it. Our Hindu friends kept calling and informing us of what was happening elsewhere, warning us to stay indoors. I called the police station, only to be told, 'You're still alive, aren't you? We'll come when something happens'.

In the evening I told my neighbours we couldn't just sit around waiting for someone to come and kill us, we should do something to defend ourselves. But they were scared stiff and had virtually bolted themselves into their homes. My neighbour with whom we were staying said I would get them into trouble. There was another family on the top floor of our house and I went to them saying we should do something—but they didn't want to take any action.

I suggested to the family we were with that we connect the doorbell to an electric wire which could be activated if a mob arrived. Other friends said they were arming themselves

---

* For about one week after Indira Gandhi's assassination in 1984, Sikhs in many north Indian cities were deliberately targeted for arson, looting, and killing. More than 2000 were killed in Delhi alone.

with petrol bombs. I rushed down to my flat to get as much kerosene as I could. All the while my neighbour kept telling me that I would get them into trouble. But I told her I wasn't going to die like a mouse, trapped—I would die fighting.

In 1947 I was too young to resist, to fight for my life. Our elders did the thinking for us. It's not that they gave up without a fight, they also defended themselves as well as they could. One of my relatives fought till he was completely overcome, and then killed his whole family himself. He survived then, but later went quite insane and died.

And here were all these people sitting with bowed heads and folded hands, waiting to die! That's why I was so upset. Why shouldn't we fight for our right to live? Should we crawl on bended knees, begging for mercy? I refused to do that. Then, in 1947, I might have been willing to die for freedom, but now I was fighting for my survival.

My neighbours said, 'But who will fight? Where are the men?' I said, 'I will—I'm a man.' Another young woman said, 'I am, too,' and then a third. There were three of us now—although the husbands of the other two said, 'Look, don't provoke anything, just ask for mercy.' I refused. How can you succumb to criminals? But they weren't prepared to fight.

On the evening of November 2, my son's young friend rang and said he was coming around with some colleagues from the army to take me to safety. I couldn't take my neighbours' cowardice any more—one Hindu family in the neighbourhood said they would eliminate the 'troublesome' Sikhs but spare the rest. Can you believe that some of the other Sikhs agreed to this criminal bargain? 'Why meddle in other people's affairs?' they said.

I absolutely refused to go along. I told them that if anyone touched that family I personally would throw a petrol bomb at them from my house. Then they said, if they hear you talking like this they'll kill you too. 'Go and tell them what I'm saying,' I said, 'this is how they will kill us, one by one, till none of us is left.' When my son's friend arrived with the army truck I offered to take the other families along, but they were afraid that if they left their homes the neighbours would walk in. We had heard them saying drunkenly, 'I'll take flat number 3, you go for the other one.'

I felt I had lost everything. I was afraid my husband and son were both dead. They were both going to be travelling on trains and we knew what was happening on them. My neighbours begged me not to go, you're the one who's kept us together, they said. I felt I had nothing more to live for, but still I would die fighting. I said I would stay back on one condition, and that was if we all resisted together, put up a brave fight. They agreed, and I decided not to go. I told my son's friend that I would not leave.

That night we all kept vigil, made plans for the next few days. For five days we kept watch together, but I was so disheartened by their timidity, their fear. They feared for their lives, their property. They feared 1947.

But what happened in 1984 in Kanpur was very different—it happened in our own homes, our own country. 1984 was such a big shock. It was only then that I asked, 'Is this the freedom we gave up everything for?' When the Hindu mobs shouted, 'Traitors, get out!' I asked myself, 'Traitors? Is this what I sang songs of Independence for? Was handcuffed at the age of six for? Which is our home now?' I tell you, I felt a great sense of detachment from everything. Nothing mattered any more—home, possessions, people, had no meaning. 1947 was no shock, the shock is now. They have branded us by calling us traitors. I tell you truly, now even the Indian flag does not seem to belong to me. Nothing is mine any more, not even my own home. I'm not for Khalistan—I could never live in a country where they force religion down your throat, force you to pray, to wear a particular dress, certain colours, I can't stand the music that blares out of our gurudwaras. Why should I settle for one Khalistan when the whole country is ours? We fought for freedom for India, not for Khalistan. If we wanted a separate country we would have asked for it in 1947. Khalistan has been thrust upon us. But we want an open house, a big house with the breeze blowing through, not a small hut. I want the freedom to think as I like, to go where I please, to keep long hair, live like a Sikh, carry a kirpan if I want to. But I won't be forced by anyone.

Muslims had their reasons for demanding Pakistan; they had been dominated by Sikhs and Hindus for a long time. They were the working class, we were the exploiters. Hindus and Sikhs were traders, shopkeepers . . . economic reasons were important. And they knew they could never get the better of Hindus on the bargaining table, they were just too clever. And the Sikhs were with the Hindus.

We treated them badly—practised untouchability, considered them lowly. We wouldn't eat with them—on stations there was Hindu water and Muslim water, Hindu food and Muslim food. People sold tea shouting, 'Hindu chai, Mussalmani chai!' Everything was separate. When my grandmother travelled, if a Muslim happened to touch her food she would consider it polluted. At school, if a Muslim girl worked the hand-pump Hindu girls wouldn't touch the water. This was normal. They would first clean the pump with mud (mud was cleaner than the Muslim hands!) and we used to do this to our own classmates, our friends. I never practised this, nor did my father, but he could do nothing about my Dadi. I went to Muslim homes, ate there but never told her about it. Untouchability was the main reason for Partition—the Muslims hated us for it. They were so frustrated and it was this frustration which took the form of massacres at Partition, of the ruthlessness with which they forced Hindus to eat beef... .

I want to tell you about Barkat. My brother had a friend called Barkat. He was like a brother to us, we tied rakhi on him because he had no sisters. He had recently got married and the Sikhs abducted his wife . . . . But I'll tell you about when I was about twelve and he was sixteen, seventeen. He was always at our place and he was very fond of me. We were very, very close—but we could never share the same plate with them. My Dadi just wouldn't allow it. She loved Barkat but couldn't tolerate his touching our water or food. If he used water in the bathroom and she, without knowing it, used it too, she would curse him and tell him he had polluted her, violated her religion. Barkat didn't stop coming to our house but he knew exactly what Dadi thought of him.

We are still in touch with Barkat—he lives in Lahore. Some years ago I went to Atari from Amritsar and saw my old hometown. I ran around like a child, totally uninhibited, went into our old home, saw where we had played . . . . The people who lived in that house were very friendly; I went to meet our old neighbours and they recognized me. They told me Barkat had been there just the day before—he had gone to Jalandhar to see the cricket match—and my brother went all the way to Atari to meet him. They saw each other on opposite sides of the border and shouted across, telling the army to hurry up with the formalities, 'Can't you see, my friend has come to meet me? Remove these barriers, quick, let us embrace each other.' They wept when they finally met, it was so wonderful to see. They were together for four days.

I've never been able to visit Pakistan again but my older sister visited Lahore. Because

Barkat is there, for us Pakistan is inhabited. In 1947 when my brother got married, his baraat went to Lyallpur and Barkat went along. Rioting had begun so there was curfew in the city. We had to have passes to go through and tell everyone that Barkat was Barkat Ram! He was a League member, a big supporter of Jinnah's. We knew that, of course. When he came over my father would joke, 'You'll only get a paratha if you curse Jinnah!' So he would say, 'Pakistan, murdabad! Jinnah, murdabad! Now give me my paratha!'

. . . . Those were beautiful days, and it was a beautiful relationship. Now, after Partition, after 1984, where is my country? In a way, my country is where I was born, which is Pakistan. Country is where you feel at home, where you are accepted, where you know the smell of the land, the culture, where you can breathe freely, think freely. But as a woman, if I cannot call a home my own, if my home is not mine, how can a country be mine?

BETWEEN COMMUNITY AND STATE

The question of where people 'belong' when countries are divided along religious or ethnic lines has bedevilled this century more than any other. Siege, strife, civil wars that simmer or rage for protracted periods are such a present feature in so many countries that, in some ways, they seem almost to define them. But today's wars are fought by non-combatants. In every disturbed area of the world, civilians are in conflict with each other over religion, ethnicity, resources, livelihood, life itself. Five per cent of the casualties in World War I were non-combatants; in contemporary wars, 95 per cent are. As a result there are millions of refugees, political fugitives, voluntary exiles, asylum seekers, those on the run; they are to be found mostly in the developing world, and a very large proportion of them are women and children.

The designation 'stateless' is now so commonplace that it excites little comment, even as governments grapple with another category of people called 'permanent liabilities'. The repatriated Tamils of Jaffna and the Eastern Provinces, for instance, have no place to call their own in either India or Sri Lanka; 'displaced persons' of erstwhile East Pakistan are still in a kind of limbo in India and live under the threat of being declared 'infiltrators' or 'illegal immigrants' any time. Any number of second-class citizens are to be found in every country of South Asia and, everywhere, those in a minority, whether linguistic, ethnic, or religious, are vulnerable.

Kamila's anguished cry, 'Was I an Indian or had I ceased to be one by marrying a Muslim?' finds a heartbreaking echo in the Lucknow sisters' lament—'So we belong neither to India nor to Pakistan. We will be reconciled only when our peculiar problem is resolved.' Their indeterminate status is mirrored in Taran's shocked yet poignant realization: 'Traitor?' I asked myself, 'Is this what I sang songs of Independence for? Was handcuffed at the age of six for? Which is our home now?'

All the women were acutely conscious of their place and their identity as Hindu, Muslim, or Sikh in either country, and communicated a highly developed sense of self in relation of both. Although Kamila and the Lucknow sisters seem to have reconciled their lives with their choices, their accounts nevertheless reverberate with things unsaid. Kamila, for instance, was extremely reluctant to speak about her status as a convert in a rapidly Islamizing Pakistan; she kept reiterating her good fortune in being part of a cosmopolitan family and social community, both of which allowed her to gloss over the obvious tensions in her life. Any choice entails adjustment and some compromise, she said; but of course she was perfectly aware that, in her case, her choice acquired much greater significance because of Partition. Now, she had to choose one country over another, one religion over another, even though they might mean little to her, personally. Her children all have Muslim names (and she herself changed hers) because, she said, she didn't want them to be 'confused' about who they were.

In conversation, the Lucknow sisters admitted that none of them married because all the 'suitable' candidates had migrated to Pakistan. This particular condition was consequent upon, first, their father's decision to stay back and, second, their own decision to return to India from Pakistan where things might have turned out differently. The poignancy of this was not lost on them. Nor was the fact that materially they had suffered a double loss: losing their land as a result of the abolition of zamindari and losing out by not accepting the offer of plenty in Pakistan. Accepting, instead, the insecurity of belonging neither here nor there.

Taran's predicament is the most explicitly stated of all, and the least ambiguous. Super-ficially, her situation was probably more stable than that of the others, but after 1984 she felt she could never be completely at ease again, anywhere. Her insight about her status went much beyond community and country, however—as a woman, she said, she now understood that she could not even call her home her own, so how could a country ever be hers? With blinding clarity she realized that she had no part to play in determining either.

Hindu, Muslim, Sikh; India, Pakistan, Khalistan, Bangladesh—redrawn borders, new found countries, and old communities forming and reforming each other through bitter contest. The play of identity politics in South Asia has become so volatile over the last few decades (almost since Independence, in fact) that it begs the question: is there a stable national or regional identity in the subcontinent today? The definition of nationality has seen so many changes during this period that it defies any 'lowest common denominator' basis.[2] In the post-Independence period, for example, India and Pakistan both proclaimed secular national identities, even though the national movement itself was made up of two competing 'nationalisms', which eventually made for the division of India. Twenty-five years later a nationalism born of linguistic difference resulted in an earlier religion-based nationalism being replaced by a linguistic one: Bangladesh came into being. Since then, we have seen many nascent regional identities challenging the notion of a homogenous national identity as Sind, Baluchistan, and the North West Frontier Province in Pakistan, and Punjab, Assam, and Kashmir in India have come to the fore. In Sri Lanka, a Sinhala nationalism has resulted in a ten-year civil war and a demand for a separate Tamil eelam (state), and a syndicated Hinduism in India is threatening to 're-unite' the country around 'culture' and 'civilization'. Meanwhile, both the Pakistani and Bangladeshi states have moved towards consolidating their Islamic character, Pakistan now as a highly militarized Islamic state, Bangladesh as an Islamic republic. The identity of the nation-state itself is thus continually redefined.

How and when women enter this redefinition is, of course, a question of religious, ethnic or linguistic affiliation but, as we have seen, it is also contingent on their status within religious and ethnic communities and their relationship with national processes. 'Belonging' for women is also—and uniquely—linked to sexuality, honour, chastity; family, community, and country must agree on both their acceptability and legitimacy, and on their membership within the fold.[3]

The question, do women have a country? is often followed by—are they full-fledged citizens of their countries? Recent feminist research[4] has demonstrated how 'citizen' and 'state subject' are gendered categories, by examining how men and women are treated unequally by most states—but especially postcolonial states—despite constitutional guarantees of equality.[5] 'The integration of women into modern "nationhood",' says Deniz Kandiyoti, 'epitomised by citizenship in a sovereign nation-state somehow follows a different trajectory from that of men.'[6] The sources of this difference, she continues, are various and may have to do with the representation of nation-as-woman or nation-as-mother (Bharat Mata, for example) to be protected by her male citizens; they may have to do with the separation of the public-civil sphere (usually male) from the private-conjugal one (usually female); or with women as symbols of community/male honour and upholders of 'cultural values'; and most crucially, with their role as biological reproducers of religious and ethnic groups. Nira Yuval-Davis and Floya Anthias identify three other ways in which women's relationship to state and ethnicity can be seen as different from men's: as reproducers of the boundaries of ethnic or national groups; as participating in the ideological reproduction of the community; and as signifiers of ethnic or national difference. They point out that while feminist literature on reproduction has dealt extensively with biological reproduction and the reproduction of labour, it has 'generally failed to consider the reproduction of national, ethnic and racial categories'.[7]

State policies with regard to population, for instance, are a clear example of its active intervention in the reproduction of race or community. Yuval-Davis and Anthias demonstrate how fears of a 'demographic holocaust' have influenced population policies in Israel, through extending maternal and child benefits to those Jewish women who bear more children. Similarly, the Malaysian government offers attractive incentives to Muslim women graduates, urging them to play their part in maintaining ethnic superiority in multiracial Malaysia.[8] Periodic calls to women to produce more sons as warriors and defenders of the nation also form part of this scenario. Our discussion on the recovery of Hindu and Muslim women, post-Partition, and the role of the Indian state in both reinforcing ethnic difference and reaffirming the necessity of regulating women's sexuality in the interests of national honour, underlined the significance of women as reproducers of ethnic and national boundaries. It also indicated how the state participates in maintaining patriarchal control in the private and conjugal domain, and demonstrated how its anxiety regarding sexual trespass mirrors that of the male brotherhood, whether familial or communitarian. Thus is Anderson's 'deep comradeship of men' reaffirmed, and patriarchal privilege reinforced.

The intense preoccupation of the Indian state with women's appropriate sexual conduct finds legal articulation in the form of personal laws—Hindu, Muslim, Sikh, Christian, Parsi—which govern marriage, divorce, inheritance, and custody and guardianship of children and adoption.[9] The simultaneous and parallel operation of civil, criminal, and religious laws is in a paradoxical relationship to the secular nationalism of the Indian state, and it brings us back to the question of women's equality, as citizens, before the laws of a secular country. Legal intimation of how women's individual rights as citizens can be abrogated *in the interests of national honour*, was found in the Abducted Persons (Recovery and Restoration) Act of 1949. The passing of the Bill without modification, despite legislators' reservations, proves that such an interest takes precedence over the fundamental rights of (female) citizens. (The suspension of the civil and democratic rights of citizens in the interests of national *security* is a familiar case, but here the issue is different.) Thirty-seven years later, in 1986, the Indian state once again acted to demonstrate how women's rights could be suspended *in the interests of the community* when it enacted the Muslim Women's (Protection of Rights in Divorce) Bill. This Act specifically excluded Muslim women from the purview of Section 125 of the Criminal Procedure Code, a provision that enables a person to claim maintenance on grounds of indigence.[10] The law is secular and available to all citizens of India regardless of caste, creed, sex, or race. Orthodox sections of the Muslim community claimed immunity from the law in question, saying it violated the Shariat, or Muslim Personal Law, under which a divorced Muslim man has no obligation to provide for his ex-wife. Pressure from this section, as well as a fair amount of political calculation, resulted in the enactment of the Muslim Women's Bill, and the right of Muslim women to social and economic security was thus subordinated to the community's right to freedom of religious practice. Two constitutional guarantees—the equality of all citizens and the freedom to practise and propagate one's religion—were in contest, and the latter prevailed.

Women, then, simultaneously but oppositionally, belong to community and country: to the former as far as the regulation of the personal domain is concerned; to the latter in all other civil and criminal matters. The state's willingness to 'enter' the private domain in order to demonstrate its sensitivity to the question of community identity and rights is in direct contrast to its reluctance to 'interfere' with the same domain by legislating in favour of women's equality within it. It does not require much analysis to see that, in effect, both responses are the same. So, all attempts by the women's and democratic rights' movements to gain gender justice in personal matters from a secular state have come to nought.[11] Stiff opposition from religious conservatives in all communities, as well as vociferous campaigning for a uniform civil code by extremist right-wing Hindu political parties have ensured that women's status as citizens in India's secular national polity is fundamentally unequal. As Kandiyoti puts it:

> The regulation of gender is central to the articulation of cultural identity and difference. The identification of women as privileged bearers of identity and boundary markers of their communities has had a deleterious effect on their emergence as full-fledged citizens. . . evidenced by the fact that women's hard-won civil rights become the most immediate casualty of the break-down of secular projects.[12]

The rise of religious or cultural nationalism in all the countries of South Asia is cause for concern, in general, but especially for women because of its tendency to impose an idealized notion of womanhood on them. Such ideals are usually derived from an uncorrupted, mythical past or from religious prescriptions, and almost always circumscribe women's rights and mobility. When the question of ethnic or communal identity comes to the fore, women are often the first to be targeted; the regulation of their sexuality is critical to establishing difference and claiming distinction. Then the question of where women belong, of whether they emerge as full-fledged citizens or remain 'wards of their immediate communities'[13] is contingent upon how the politics of identity are played out, and how their resolution takes place between community and state.

The preceding discussions and life stories are an attempt at a gendered reading of Partition through the experiences of women. In their recall, the predominant memory is of confusion, of the severing of roots as they were forced to reckon with the twin aspect of freedom—the bewildering loss of place and property, of settled community, of a network of more or less stable relationships, and of a coherent identity. Overriding all these was a violence that was horrifying in its intensity, one which knew no boundaries; for many women it was not only miscreants, outsiders, or marauding mobs they needed to fear—husbands, fathers, brothers, and even sons could turn killers. That terrible stunning violence and the silencing pall that descended like a shroud over it have always just hovered at the edges of history; breaking the silence has exposed not only the cracks in family mythologies about honour and sacrifice but the implicit consensus that prevails around permissible violence against women during periods of highly charged communal conflict.

Family, community, and state emerge as the three mediating and interlocking forces determining women's individual and collective destinies; and religious identity and sexuality as determining factors in their realization of citizenship and experience of secularism. Partition caused such a major upheaval that it disrupted all normal relationships on a huge scale and placed women in a relationship with the state that was as definitive as that with family and community, and as patriarchal. It once again recast them as keepers of national honour and markers of boundaries—between communities, and between communities and countries. The dispute over abducted women, and who their rightful claimants were, so compromised their status as to deny them every fundamental right as adult citizens. Each of their multiple identities—as women, as wives and mothers, as members of families and communities, and as citizens—was set up against the other, making any honourable resolution of their predicament impossible. Only an arbitrary and basically communalized response won the day; this, in turn, made for women's quite different experience of citizenship, for their identity was defined primarily as that of members of religious communities, rather than as subjects of a secular state.

Yet significantly, and linked to survival, the fact of Partition also paved the way for women's abrupt entry into the economic life of the country—as social workers, wage earners, breadwinners, farmers, teachers, professionals, or students of one sort or another—in numbers that may otherwise have been spread over many years. The uncertainty of their circumstances and the break-up of the extended family pushed women and girls into the workplace and educational establishments, thus expanding their social space even as dislocation often entailed a drastically shrunk, or even completely alien, physical space. Such social mobility would no doubt have come sooner or later; Partition hastened the process. The incidence of mass widowhood, moreover, compelled the state to step in as social rehabilitator with far-reaching consequences, both, for the women and for the process of social reconstruction itself.

Neither India nor Pakistan has escaped the aftermath of Partition; their separate yet linked histories have played out the consequences of communal politics in full ingloriousness. The years 1947, 1964, 1967, 1971, 1984, 1992 are milestones not just for one country or two, but for the entire subcontinent. In between, and continuously, are the protracted battles fought over identity, national as well as sub-national. Those values and principles we took for granted in the first flush of freedom—democracy, social justice, secularism, pluralism—are besieged, bruised, and battered. Ambiguity and equivocation mark the discourse of the state on these issues in India; strident obscurantism and belligerence in Pakistan.

In either case, the predictable outcome for women is resurgent patriarchy. The endeavour has to be not for less 'secularism' or the retreat of the state, but for a proactive secularism and a genuinely neutral state apparatus. A return to self-regulating communities has very regressive consequences for women; the importance of having the choice to exit the community cannot be over-emphasized, nor can the desirability of equality as citizens of a secular state be seriously challenged. The alternative, as demonstrated most violently and soberingly by Partition, is the eternal subordination of all other identities—gender, class, caste, region—to an exclusive and confining religious or ethnic community.

NOTES

1. Azhar Abbas, 'The Twice Displaced', *Outlook*, special issue on Partition, May 28, 1997.
2. Amrita Chhachhi, 'Identity Politics', in Kamla Bhasin, Nighat Said Khan, and Ritu Menon (eds), *Against All Odds: Essays on Women, Religion & Development from India and Pakistan*, Delhi: Kali for Women, 1994: 2. See also Nighat Said Khan, Rubina Saigol, and Afiya S. Zia, 'Introduction', in Khan et al. (eds), · *Locating the Self: Perspectives on Women and Multiple Identities*, Lahore: ASR Publications, 1994: 5, 7; and Nighat Said Khan, 'Reflections on the Question of Islam and Modernity', in Khan et al. (eds), *Locating the Self*: 77–95.

    Feminist activists and academics have written extensively on the issue of the state, cultural identity, and gender in South Asia, and the last twenty years have seen widespread mobilization by the women's movements in all the countries of the region against religious fundamentalism and cultural chauvinism. It is not possible here to summarize the many debates and positions on the issue except to say that, generally speaking, their critiques have been sharp, and their analyses of the intersection of nationalism and gender, insightful. For a further elaboration of all the above, see also Kumari Jayawardena and Malathi de Alwis (eds), *Embodied Violence: Communalising Women's Sexuality in South Asia*, Delhi: Kali for Women, 1996; Zoya Hasan (ed.), *Forging Identities: Gender, Communities and the State in India*, Delhi: Kali for Women, 1994; Tanika Sarkar and Urvashi Butalia (eds), *Women and the Hindu Right: A Collection of Essays*, Delhi: Kali for Women, 1995; and Deniz Kandiyoti (ed.), *Women, Islam and the State*, Philadelphia: Temple University Press, 1991.
3. Recent writing and analysis by Indian feminists on the issue of the dalit (low caste) woman's unequal relationship to caste-community and citizenship has introduced the critical dimension of caste into the discussion in important ways. In our view, their experience of inequality, as dalits and as women, underlines (rather than undermines) the case for gender-just secular laws. See V. Geetha and T.V. Jayanthi, 'Women, Hindutva and the Politics of Caste in Tamil Nadu', in Sarkar and Butalia (eds), *Women and the Hindu Right*: 245–69; Anveshi, 'Is Gender Justice only a Legal Issue? Political Stakes in UCC Debate', *Economic and Political Weekly*, March 8, 1997; and V. Geetha, 'Periyar, Women and an Ethic of Citizenship', unpublished paper, n.d.
4. See especially, Nira Yuval-Davis and Floya Anthias (eds), *Woman–Nation–State*, London: Macmillan, 1989; Marilyn Lake, 'Personality, Individuality, Nationality: Feminist Conceptions of Citizenship 1902–40', *Australian Feminist Studies [AFS]* 19 (Autumn) 1994: 25–38; Marie Leech, 'Women, the State and Citizenship: Are Women in the Building or in a Separate Annex?', *AFS* 19: 79–91; Deniz Kandiyoti, 'Identity and Its Discontents: Women and the Nation', *Millennium*, 20, 3: pp. 429–43; Rian Voet, 'Women as Citizens: A Feminist Debate', *AFS* 19: 61–77.
5. Yuval-Davis and Anthias, 'Introduction' in *Woman–Nation–State*: 6.
6. Deniz Kandivoti, 'Identity and Its Discontents': 429.
7. Yuval-Davis and Anthias, 'Introduction': 7.
8. Chee Heng Leng, 'Babies to Order: Recent Population Policies in Malaysia', in Bina Agarwal (ed.), *Structures of Patriarchy: State, Community and Household in Modernising Asia*, Delhi: Kali for Women, 1988; Deborah Gaitskell and Elaine Unterhalter, 'Mothers of the Nation: A Comparative Analysis of Nation, Race and Motherhood in Afrikaner Nationalism and the African National Congress', in Yuval-Davis and Anthias (eds), *Woman–Nation–State*: 58–76.
9. The Pakistani state's preoccupation with it led to the promulgation of the Hudood and Zina Ordinances in 1979, the most dramatic examples of state intervention in the personal domain in the subcontinent. For discussions on women/gender and Islamization, generally, and the Shariat, in particular, see Shahla Zia, 'Women, Islamisation and Justice', and Fauzia Gardezi, 'Islam, Feminism and the Women's Movement in

Pakistan', in Bhasin, Khan, and Menon (eds), *Against All Odds*: 51–58; 70–81. Also, Hina Jilani, 'Law as an Instrument of Social Control', in Khan et al. (eds), *Locating the Self*: 96–107.

10. The Bill was enacted after the Supreme Court of India upheld a high court judgement that awarded Shah Bano, a poor, 68-year-old Muslim woman who had been divorced by her husband, maintenance of Rs 500 a month. Her husband appealed the judgement on the grounds that it violated Muslim Personal Law, by which he and his ex-wife were governed. The case became a cause celébre in many ways and was taken up by the Muslim clergy and religious fundamentalists under the rallying cry of 'Islam in danger'. The then Congress-I government knuckled under and passed the Bill in 1986.

11. There is a vast body of writing available on this subject and the debate has once more come to the fore with the Bharatiya Janta Party pressurizing the United Front government at the centre to fulfil the promise of the Constitution by enacting a uniform civil code. Women's organizations and political parties have participated in the debate and presented their views, which are by no means unanimous. For a fuller discussion see, among others, Anveshi, 'Is Gender Justice only a Legal Issue? Political Stakes in UCC Debate'; Kumkum Sangari, 'Politics of Diversity: Religions, Communities and Multiple Patriarchies', *Economics and Political Weekly* 23 December and 30 December, 1995; Working Group on Women's Rights, 'Reversing the Option: Civil Codes and Personal Laws', *Economic and Political Weekly* 18 May, 1996; Draft Resolution of the All India Democratic Women's Association, 'Equal Rights, Equal Laws', Delhi, December 1995; 'Visions of Gender Justice', report of the Women's Groups Meeting, Mumbai, December 1995.

12. Deniz Kandiyoti, 'Identity and Its Discontents': 443.

13. Ibid.

TEN

Entangled Endeavours

Saurabh Dube

❧

Do writings on the subaltern serve to inherently define self-contained ethical projects? Do accounts of subordinate peoples intrinsically designate self-realizing political knowledge? Or, are studies of subaltern subjects marked by innate limits for wider analytical inquiry? Posing these questions in a stark manner opens my writing to the charge of being trite and simplistic, in fact, of setting up straw figures. Yet the queries have immediacy. Actually, we do not have to look very far to see that these questions reflect acute representations of implicit understandings that enjoy wide presence in scholarly spaces.

Casting aside academic correctness, two examples come to mind. On the one hand, in the discipline of history in metropolitan arenas, consider the invocations today of race-class-gender as the magic mantra for a relevant historiography. (Never mind that such claims can also continue to project the West as the *habitus* of history, both consciously and inadvertently.) On the other hand, in the field of South Asian anthropology, think of the current disdain for ethnographic inquiries into caste practices, village communities, or popular religion on account of their complicities with orientalist visions. (Forget the fact that newer objects of research do not intrinsically lead to novel scholarship, and perish the thought that the charge of orientalism can also be a pigeon-holing device.) It is not only that there are several ways of 'doing' race-class-gender, even as a critical and novel scholarship on caste initiatives and popular religion is a live possibility. It is also that at stake here are overwrought orientations designating meaningful arenas of academic endeavour on the basis of *a priori* assumptions. Despite their differences, the contending questions I raised above are bound to each other through a shared logic that governs their contrasting claims. The claims are linked through their mutual presupposition regarding the object(s) of knowledge as already locked in place; and the questions are connected through their common oversight of the conceptual conventions that shape the subject(s) of analysis.

Against the grain of such orientations, this chapter underscores a mutual logic shaping the construction of ethnographic histories and the representation of untouchable pasts as entangled endeavours.[1] This shared logic is premised upon modes of reading and forms of writing in which categories of analysis and objects of understanding are not artificially separated the one from the other, particularly by stressing the latter over the former. Rather, concept and object are rendered as mutually constitutive elements, in this case within the fashioning of historical narratives. On the one hand, through this wider interplay, it is the questions asked and the categories chosen that shape the objects of inquiry, also configuring the matrices of relationships within which they are embedded. On the other hand, once there is a clear acknowledgement of the aggrandizing artifice of a meaning-legislative reason, the concepts elaborated and the narratives fashioned can also lead the objects of a singular consciousness being rendered as subjects with a different consciousness. Within the interstices of these movements, the entangled endeavours of ethnographic histories and untouchable pasts work to elaborate central analytical questions and key theoretical issues, featuring reasons of myth and rituals of history, colonial modernities and postcolonial traditions, contestations of authority and containments of power, and meanings of subalterns and margins of Hinduism. But before I turn to these themes that run as connected strands through this chapter, a brief introduction to the protagonists of this story is in order.

BRIEF BEGINNINGS

Satnampanth was initiated in the early nineteenth century by Ghasidas, a farm servant, primarily among the Chamars (etymologically, leather workers) of Chhattisgarh, a large cultural region bound through linguistic ties in the south-eastern Central Provinces, and now a separate state of the Indian Union. This group formed a little less than one-fifth of the total population of Chhattisgarh.[2] Most of its members either owned land or were sharecroppers and farm servants. Yet the ritual association of the Chamars with hides and carrion meant that the group and its members, collectively and personally, embodied the stigma of the death pollution of the sacred cow, locating the caste on the margins of the Hindu order. The Chamars—and a few hundred members of other castes—who joined Satnampanth now became Satnamis, offering a challenge to the intermeshed schemes of divine, ritual, and social hierarchies in Chhattisgarh. The Satnamis had to abstain from meat, liquor, tobacco, and certain vegetables and pulses. They were prohibited the use of cows, as opposed to bullocks, in any of their agricultural operations. There was a rejection of Hindu deities, idols, and temples within Satnampanth. The members were asked to believe only in a formless god, *satnam* (true name). There were to be no distinctions of caste within Satnampanth. With Ghasidas began a guru *parampara* (tradition) which was hereditary, and there developed in Satnampanth a stock of myths and rituals that were associated with the gurus. The subaltern religious formation combined in itself the features of a caste and the principles of a sect. These various moves in their special singularity and distinctive detail contested the tenor of ritual power and colonial authority in Chhattisgarh, but they also reproduced forms of inequality among the group. Indeed, these simultaneous processes were part of a wider logic. Over the nineteenth and twentieth centuries, the Satnamis coped with shifts in the agrarian economy and changes in the relationships of power, negotiated various efforts to regulate the community, and drew upon symbols of power to question and challenge their subordination. At the same time, across this period, the Satnamis—who continue to be an important presence in Chhattisgarh

—also elaborated schemes of meaning and power imbued with ambiguity, reworking patterns of domination within the community.

The Satnamis have formed an internally differentiated community. The articulations of property, office, and gender have shaped patterns of authority among the group. After the establishment of new proprietary rights under the *malguzari* (village proprietor) settlement, introduced by British administration in the 1860s, the Satnamis—along with the Chamars—constituted a little over one-fourth of the total tenant population of the districts of Bilaspur, Raipur, and Durg. The other members of the Satnami population stood on opposite ends in the agrarian hierarchy: a relatively small number of agricultural labourers and farm servants, and very few *malguzars*. The power of property was closely linked with the privileges of office. Important Satnami *malguzars* were not only tied to the family of the guru through bonds of kinship, but they also occupied important positions within the organizational hierarchy of Satnampanth. The members of the guru family and the organizational hierarchy of Satnam-panth, closely involved in questioning the subordination of Satnamis by dominant castes, also disciplined and regulated the community. These forms of power were compounded by critical differentials of gender within Satnamapanth. The embedding of specific practices of Satnami kinship in a wider system governed by patrilineal and patrivirilocal principles alongside a contradictory ordering of female sexuality within the group's myths and rituals had very particular consequences. On the one hand, Satnami women earned a measure of autonomy and forms of flexibility to negotiate marriages and men in everyday arenas. On the other hand, there was a double-edged construction of the agency of Satnami women, marking them with distinctly marginal attributes that spoke of an aggressive sexuality and a deviant femininity, and providing a means for their sexual exploitation by upper caste men and members of the organizational hierarchy of Satnampanth.[3] With this grim reminder of the need to guard against romanticizations of communities, I bring my introductory sketch of the Satnamis to its timely end.

HISTORICAL MARGINS

The introduction to this volume has noted that margins do not merely refer to dispossessed peoples and subaltern groups, but also to social knowledge and historical endeavour that have been subordinated by the social sciences and normalized by the humanities. In other words, margins are fluid terrain that have come to be rendered as bounded arenas, but they are also porous borders that question the dominant claims of knowledge and power.[4] In these over-lapping but diverse senses, the untouchable pasts of the Satnamis and an ethnographic history of the community fit the bill of margins as an analytical perspective.

The past few years have witnessed a vigorous debate around the question of the colonial origins of the categories of Hindu and Hinduism. While one set of scholars has seized upon etymological and philological issues to suggest that these categories are creations of colonial imaginings, the products of the nineteenth century, other historians and anthropologists have emphasized the precolonial basis of religious (and caste) categories which provided a means for colonial representations. Both sides have tended to privilege questions of the origins or foundations of these categories, and defined the meanings of Hindu and Hinduism rather exclusively in relation to other religions, mainly Islam.[5] A history of the Satnamis constructed in an ethnographic grain serves to recast the debate around this question in terms of perspectives drawn from the pasts of a group who stood on the margins of these categories—categories that were elaborated within wider cultural processes defined by power. Here a focus on the multiple negotiations and interrogations, reworkings and challenges that went into the production of different meanings of Hinduism—I speak not merely of the word, but equally of the social relationships made up of domination, subordination, and resistance that it describes—at once shows the limitations of a primary concern with the origins of the categories of Hindu and Hinduism and the dangers of reifying them as static entities.[6]

Through the filters of untouchable pasts, the categories of Hindu and Hinduism emerge as descriptive and analytical forms of shorthand that make possible an understanding of the constantly changing patterns and fluid lived arrangements of religious meanings and ritual practices, which have variously elaborated and contested the mutually intermeshed divine, ritual, and social hierarchies of Hinduism under precolonial regimes, colonial rule, and independent states in South Asia (and beyond). From the perspectives of analytical margins, these categories are equally revealed as critical resources that were worked upon in selective and contending ways by various castes and communities in their articulations of religious and political identities, particularly in the nineteenth and twentieth centuries.

On the one hand, the growing rigidities of hierarchies of caste—particularly, the norms of purity and pollution—that worked against the Chamars in the late eighteenth and early nineteenth centuries were not fabricated by the colonial regime. Rather these developments had their beginnings in precolonial Chhattisgarh ruled by the Marathas, only to be intensified further under colonial rule. These historical processes came to underlie the formation and elaboration of Satnampanth, a subaltern religious endeavour that fashioned its distinct identity by questioning the ritual power embedded within caste and by constructing (hierarchies) of otherness—and not merely the Other—within the Hindu social order in the nineteenth century. On the other hand, from the 1920s, as we shall see, the Satnamis went on to variously negotiate different constructions of the Hindu order under the regime of caste associations, within the wider context of culturally and politically constituted understandings of Hinduism by nationalists and social reformers. These dominant understandings of Hinduism were elaborated alongside measures constructed by the colonial government in relation to religious communities, and their negotiation by the Satnamis involved fashionings of novel identities, which had contradictory and unintended consequences for the group's articulations of community and nation. Indeed, such critical implications of the meanings gleaned from margins also extend to other central questions in the history and ethnography of South Asia.

It is often the case that studies of religion and ritual in South Asia tend to underplay considerations of political economy and concerns of state formation.[7] At the same time, analyses that seek to redress this imbalance often privilege the determinations and transformations of economic structures and political processes, and render religion as epiphenomenal (or at any rate derivative upon the brute realities and underlying dynamics of political economy). The difficulties with both these procedures should be evident. The first veers toward bracketing religion from wider historical processes, implicitly casting it as a static repository of timeless traditions. The second tends toward reifying the abstract workings of subterranean structures, virtually exorcizing the mediation and influence of religious meanings and historical practices upon processes of the past and the present.

I have no ready solution to an enduring problem of social theory. Instead of a singular answer, what is offered here are working suggestions. If we dispense with overriding teleological schemes and overarching theoretical models, the linkages between the analytical arenas of political economy and religious formations do not appear as predetermined verities, but rather as complex connections and conjunctural relationships whose protean forms and emergent patterns need to be unravelled and specified in particular contexts and determinate domains. If we further acknowledge the enormous extent to which the archival record for South Asia in the eighteenth and nineteenth centuries was shaped by the preoccupation of the colonial state and indigenous regimes with the extraction of revenue and the mainte-nance of law and order, it becomes clear that the difficulties of tracing the interconnections between (heuristic fields of) political economy and (analytical configurations of) religion are further compounded by the idiosyncrasies and perversities of the archive, particularly regarding quotidian subaltern endeavours and untouchable religious initiatives. Once more, the perspectives drawn from untouchable pasts suggest other possibilities—at once theoretical in scope but modest in scale, astutely analytical in their efforts but acutely aware of their limits—of attending to changes and continuities in the domain of political economy while elaborating the fluid, constant interplay between cultural schemes, social relationships, religious meanings, and ritual power. Now such modes of analysis run through my wider renderings of the pasts of the Satnamis over the last two hundred years, quite as they inform my other projects of research and writing. A single example should suffice here.

The formation of Satnampanth was informed by the wider context of Maratha rule (1742–1854) in Chhattisgarh, located within the broader processes of state formation and revenue practices in the region. We know that during the past few years imaginative historical accounts of economic and social institutions and processes in Maratha polities have revised our understanding of the eighteenth and early nineteenth centuries in India. The crude caricature of Maratha rule as a predatory empire of the saddle has been replaced by a nuanced picture which shows significant continuities between the Mughals and the Marathas, an expansion in agricultural production in Maratha territories, and a complex and sophisticated system of revenue collection in the shaping of Maratha administration.[8] Chhattisgarh as a frontier province within the Maratha dominions shared features of this wider picture, but the region also had its own peculiarities.

The administrative measures of British superintendents who governed Chhattisgarh between 1818 and 1830 compounded these complexities. Satnampanth was a response to cultural and economic processes that had a contradictory dimension for the Chamars in the region. These processes allowed members of the group to establish their own villages and thereby to negotiate and partly escape the authority of upper-caste officials. But they also led to an increasing subordination and further marginalization of other Chamars in villages dominated by higher castes in the face of a growing rigidity of the norms of purity and pollution in the late eighteenth and early nineteenth centuries. As I have shown elsewhere, the formation of Satnampanth occurred within the interstices of two simultaneous move-ments: the processes of continuity and change at the frontier of Maratha polity and the Company's dominions; and the centrality of conflict and innovation in the arena of popular religious practices.[9] Indeed, it is the processes within political economy and the elaborations of state formation—both centering upon revenue practices—in Chhattisgarh that provide meaning to the symbolic construction of a subordinate religious initiative, which carved for itself a distinct religious identity in relation to the ritual power of the social and divine hierarchies within the caste order in the region.

We have noted that Satnampanth has combined the features of a caste and a sect. The subaltern religious formation thus confounds the logical schemes of historians and anthropologists who generally conceive of caste and sect as binary categories, even as they include the possibility that sects 'degenerate' into castes. This influential understanding is a legacy of Louis Dumont's dominant model, which is based upon a Brahman householder's construction of renunciation and asceticism.[10] The work of Richard Burgahart, Peter Van der Veer, and David Lorenzen has shown that this model tends to ignore the perspectives of the ascetic and the non-twice-born caste. It overlooks thereby the permeable boundaries of the householder and the renouncer, and the interpenetration in practice of principles of caste and sect.[11] Such intertwining of the principles of these simultaneously distinct but overlapping categories has been evident in Satnampanth. I will elaborate these issues soon, but two points are pertinent here. It is not only that Satnampanth is a sectarian formation governed by an unalloyed logic of reconstituting the untouchable status of its members. It is also that the founder of this subaltern religious endeavour, Ghasidas, remained an ascetic householder guru; and from the time of his son, Balakdas, the guru as the head of the organizational hierarchy and the formal owner-proprietor of the village of Bhandar simultaneously embodied the truth of *satnam* and the symbolically constituted attributes of royalty of the raja and the dominant caste.

Yet a wider cultural acceptance of such redrawn ritual boundaries is not merely rare but often quite impossible, particularly when the protagonists are overwhelmingly lower-caste men and women. It is a truism that the Satnamis functioned within the schemes of power of the caste order in Chhattisgarh. We know now that Louis Dumont's vastly influential statement of the nature of caste society in South Asia encompasses power within the ritual hierarchy of purity and pollution and renders it epiphenomenal.[12] More recent studies by Nicholas Dirks, Gloria Raheja, and Declan Quigley have opened up possibilities for discussions of the interplay between caste structure and ritual dominance: but they have all tended to locate power, virtually exclusively, in constructs of kingship and the dominant caste constituted by cultural, ideological, and ritual attributes.[13] Here the very marginal status of the Satnamis—their lowly position in the ritual hierarchy of purity and pollution, and their exclusion from the web of relationships defined by service castes—suggests a rather different understanding of the nature of power in the caste order. An ethnographic history that draws upon Satnami myths and practices and the group's oral accounts about the late colonial period reveals that the ritual hierarchy of purity and pollution and the ritual centrality of kingship and dominant caste(s) were both symbolic schemes that elaborated modes of domination and power. These intertwined hegemonic axes worked together to secure the subordination of the Satnamis and other lower-caste groups in Chhattisgarh, and—lest we forget—elsewhere in South Asia too. The perspectives of untouchable pasts also clarify that these symbolic schemes were further entangled with the signs and metaphors of colonial power. Indeed, the colonial presence in Chhattisgarh after the nineteenth century compounded the forms of ritual dominance in the caste order: the symbols and practices of colonial governance were reworked in quotidian arenas; the upper-caste *malguzar* came to be widely fashioned as the raja of the village; and there were novel articulations of ritual power in the elaborations of caste in village life. Clearly, there was much in the local configurations of dominance that was weighted against the Satnamis.[14]

The Satnamis negotiated and resisted these relations of power in diverse ways. The creation of Satnampanth initiated the challenge to ritual power within caste society in Chhattisgarh. The subaltern religious endeavour at once drew upon popular traditions and the ritual hierarchy of purity and pollution, rejected the divine and social hierarchies that centred on the Hindu pantheon, and repositioned the signs in a new matrix to question the ascribed ritual status of Chamars as lowly untouchables. At the same time, in the new sect, the rejection of distinctions of caste among its predominantly Chamar constituency and a few hundred Teli and Rawat members was accompanied by prohibitions that governed transactions with other castes, reproducing the significance of meanings and patterns of power embedded with the ritual schemes of the caste order. From the 1850s the formalization and elaboration of the organizational hierarchy of Satnampanth—presided over by the guru who combined the twin, inextricably bound characteristics of the raja and the embodiment of the truth of *satnam*—constituted an alternative to the formidable network of relationships of village proprietors and dominant landholding groups with service castes: but this organizational structure also worked together with other institutions of the Satnamis (particularly *ramat*, the tour of the guru) to provide the gurus with means of control over the community. In the latter part of the nineteenth century, the Satnamis responded to their expropriation and exploitation under the new system of proprietary rights and *malguzari* settlement—established by the colonial regime in the 1860s—by deserting villages, continuing with the practice of *lakhabata* (the periodic redistribution of land) in Satnami villages, and revealing their solidarity in challenges to upper-caste *malguzars* over high rents and loss of land in the 1890s.

The enduring contestations of power by the Satnamis continued to be rooted in familiar arenas. The Satnami structure of beliefs, modes of worship, and social organization allowed the group to negotiate and resist the principles of ritual subordination and forms of discrimination that pervaded everyday life. Here the repertoire of myths of the Satnamis powerfully elaborated the group's imaginings of its heroic histories and current predicaments. For the purposes of the present discussion, these myths, a part of the community's ongoing oral traditions, ordered the past of Satnampanth. The Satnami gurus underwent trials, overcame obstacles, and displaced figures of authority to define the boundary and orchestrate the symbolic construction of Satnampanth. The myths of community interrogated the intermeshed principles of the ritual hierarchy of purity and pollution, the ritually and culturally constituted centrality of kingship and landholding dominant castes, and the modes of power derived from colonial administration in the region.[15] Finally, in the midst of efforts, often initiated by upper-caste benefactors, to recast the identity of the Satnamis along the lines of recently constructed authoritative blueprints of Hinduism in the 1920s and 1930s, the group fashioned distinctive uses for the key emphases of the Hinduism(s) on offer, and its reworkings of Hindu identities were accompanied by a challenge to the upper castes. Yet, these moves were predicated on the fact that the very making and elaboration of Satnampanth had carried forward the meanings embedded within the hierarchies and centres of ritual power in the caste order. Indeed, if the pasts of the Satnami reveal varieties of resistance, particularly in their refigurings of ritual forms and the fashionings of mythic meanings, it is also true that Satnami contestations, often conducted in a religious idiom, engaged with as well as subverted but were equally contained and enabled by the hegemonic processes of caste and colonial power in Chhattisgarh. Against the lingering seductions of contemporary fables that feature relentless reifications of agency and increasing inflations of power, let me illustrate the key themes that I have discussed by turning to a tiny part of the wider body of the untouchable pasts and ethnographic histories at stake here.

Engaging Stories

Around 1850, after the death of Ghasidas, the *guru gaddi* (seat of guru) of Satnampanth came into the hands of Balakdas, the founder's second son.[16] Balakdas institutionalized the practices, defined the organizational hierarchy, and elaborated the regulations of Satnampanth. The first seat of the gurus was established in Bhandar. Ghasidas lived in the village during the last years of his life and cured and healed the bodies of Satnamis with *amrit* (ambrosia), water in which he had dipped his toe or thumb. Thus, Balakdas inherited a very considerable legacy of ritual power: the absence of idols of gods and goddesses in Satnampanth meant that the guru, the only anthropomorphic icon, had become the living symbol of worship and belief for the Satnamis. Here the *darshan* (vision) of the guru carried the substance of his authority and constituted a distinct mode of worship, and *amrit* purified and regenerated the bodies of Satnamis, continuously integrating them into Satnampanth. Balakdas also built upon this legacy. He institutionalized the practice of *guru puja* (worship of the guru) on the sacred dates of the Satnami ritual calendar—Dashehra, Bhad Aathon, and Maghi Puno—that attracted ever large numbers of Satnamis to Bhandar. Moreover, the tightening of the rules of consanguinity and commensality in Satnampanth under Balakdas further swelled the numbers of Satnamis who thronged to Bhandar, as pure pilgrims were joined by those of their impure brethren who had transgressed the norms of the caste-sect and now wished to re-enter it by means of the guru. Finally, after the initiation of settlement operations and the grant of proprietary rights in the 1860s, the guru became the owner-proprietor of Bhandar, which added further prestige to this pre-eminent site of Satnami pilgrimage. Through the many vicissitudes of quarrels within the guru family, the division of the *gaddi*, and the acquisition of other villages by members of Ghasidas's patrilineage, Bhandar remained the effective locus of ritual power of the Satnami guru.

The story repeated itself with the institution of *ramat* (tour of the guru), which was the other means for the Satnamis of getting a *darshan* of the guru and obtaining *amrit*. In the true stories of the Satnamis, embodied in their myths and narrated in the course of conversations and discussions during my fieldwork, *ramat* was begun by Ghasidas but the practice was put on a sound organizational basis by Balakdas. Indeed, under Balakdas, the practice of *ramat*—which involved the gurus' travels every year to different villages so that the Satnamis gained their *darshan*, while the gurus in turn settled matters involving the violation and transgression of norm of Satnampanth—was turned into an institutionalized work of considerable finesse, even a spectacle. Balakdas outraged the feelings of the Thakurs of Chhattisgarh, who fashioned themselves as a warrior caste, by going on tour riding an elephant and wearing the sacred thread. We know that in the hierarchies of the caste order, the use of elephants as modes of transport has been reserved for dominant castes, and the wearing of the sacred thread is a mark of twice-born castes. Balakdas's appropriations here expropriated dominant groups of symbols that defined their authority through marks of exclusion and distinction, and also staged the spectacular in *ramat*, which stood fully institutionalized in the later decades of the second half of the nineteenth century.

Actually, the major fortunes made by the gurus from the offerings of Satnamis in Bhandar and during *ramat*, combined with the acquisition of the proprietary rights of Bhandar and other villages, meant that regal attributes came to be attached to the Satnami guru. The guru was both on a par with, and shared aspects of, a *raja admi* (kingly person). The presence of a large house in Bhandar, the use of elephants, camels, and horses as modes of transport, and the keeping of armed retainers formed a part of this picture. Indeed, if Ghasidas was a guru in the manner of a miraculous ascetic householder, Balakdas was much more a figure in the mould of a conqueror who invested the seat of the Satnami guru with attributes of royalty for his successors to refine and elaborate. A photograph from the late nineteenth century shows a Satnami guru with his retinue and underscores the twin aspects of the guru's authority: the provider of *amrit* and a raja-like figure with his retinue of advisors, bodyguards, soldiers, and a peon.

The structure of the guru's authority was further secured through the organizational hierarchy of Satnampanth. The foundations of this organizational structure lay in Ghasidas's appointment of *bhandaris* in villages. Balakdas went on to considerably develop and formalize the structure which was later refined by his successors. The organizational hierarchy of Satnampanth extended from the gurus at the top, moving on to *mahants*, then to *diwans*, and finally down to *bhandaris* and *sathidars* in villages and to the bodyguards and peons in the guru's entourage. The *mahant* represented the guru in a group of villages; the *diwan* was an advisor to the guru; the *sathidar* fetched Satnamis on ritual occasions and helped the *bhandari* within the village. By the late nineteenth century, Satnampanth had a firmly entrenched organizational hierarchy, which served as an alternate ritual and symbolic power centre to dominant groups and their network of relationships with service castes.

This organizational network contributed to Satnampanth combining the features of a caste and a sect. In brief, the guru regulated the prohibitions on food and controlled matters of marriage to maintain the boundedness of the Satnamis. In both these arenas, the rules of Satnampanth were tightened under Balakdas. A Satnami who broke the prohibitions and rules of commensality and consanguinity had to drink the guru's amrit, make an offering of a coconut and money to him, and feed the other Satnamis within the village. The guru's control was exercised through *mahants* and *diwans*, *bhandaris* and *sathidars*. The Satnamis were simultaneously the incorporated members of a caste and the initiated followers of a sect. Among them, concerns of *jati* (caste) and *panth* (sect) were fused together to be closely regulated by the guru.

By the middle of the nineteenth century specific symbolic markers defined the boundary of Satnampanth, and Balakdas added to this process of symbolic construction. The guru distributed the *janeu* (sacred thread), a sign of the twice-born within the caste hierarchy, among the Satnamis. The appropriation of the sacred thread, which was worn by a male Satnami after he came of age and started following the rules of Satnampanth, challenged the upper-caste monopoly over a sign of ritual purity which was constitutive of their domination. Moreover, there is a further twist to this tale. Satnamis argue that the combination of *janeu* and *kanthi*—string with wooden beads that was appropriated by Ghasidas from Kabirpanth and was worn by members of Satnampanth after their rite of initiation—distinguished them from

Kabirpanthis and Vaishnavas (who wore the *kanthi*) and from Brahmans and other upper castes (who wore the *janeu*). Finally, in the second half of the nineteenth century the Satnamis elaborated another marker in the form of *jait khambh* (victory pillar), a high pole with a small white triangular flag on top. The *jait khambh* in each village reminded the Satnamis of their boundedness as a group. A symbol of the guru, the piece of white cloth was changed on the occasions of *guru puja*. The markers within Satnampanth underscored the centrality of the guru who was the representative of *satnam*.

This past is played out in ever interesting ways in the oral mythic tradition of the Satnamis. In the period unto the 1850s, Satnampanth was still marked by considerable fluidity, which is indexed by Satnami myths about Ghasidas that bear upon the making of Satnampanth. Here, if Ghasidas initiated Satnampanth on the command of Satnampurush, the embodiment of *satnam*, the guru also questioned and offered a challenge to Satnampurush. Indeed, Satnami myths, in tune with a specific logic of oral traditions, simultaneously distinguished between the figures of Ghasidas and Satnampurush but also conflated the identities of these divine beings through a metaphoric juxtaposition of their mythic attributes and ritual power. At the same time, Ghasidas's encounters with the other major figures who populated the cosmic and social order were marked by a greater degree of caution. What was of essence here was a displacement of these figures, not by eclipsing them, but rather by demarcating their separate spheres of authority to constitute the emergent boundaries of Satnampanth. Thus, in his encounters with the Gond king of Sonakhan and *angrez raja* (English king) of Raipur, even as Ghasidas demonstrated his superior just and moral authority, he also humbly acceded to the unjust demands of these regal figures. Similarly, this demarcation of separate and complementary spheres of authority was also evident in Ghasidas's encounter with Danteshwari Devi, the goddess to whom human sacrifices were made in the chiefdom of Bastar, only now it was worked out through a play upon configurations of affinal kinship in the cosmic order.

These primary pasts that cautiously displaced mythic figures in the making of Satnampanth were to be replaced by rather more heroic histories as the sect acquired a firmer organizational and institutional basis in the second half of the nineteenth century. In the myths of the community, the sway of Satnampanth and the solidarity of the Satnamis are represented through Balakdas's rounds of *ramat*, which are rendered as successful conquests, triumphs over rival figures of authority. The forms of the guru's power are clear. Balakdas's spectacular entourage consisted, on the one hand, of two mythic gladiators, who wielded swords and guns with equal ease, accompanied by four thousand other warriors, and, on the other hand, of a thousand *sants* (holy men) of Satnampanth. The guru himself rode on a decorated elephant, carrying a spear, a gun, and a sword: but Balakdas also wore the sacred thread across his chest, and a holy ash mark on his forehead. During his travels, cast in the myths as akin to the *daura* (official tours) of kings and colonial administrators, Balakdas left the imprint of his authority upon the rajas of feudatory states and the heads of rival ascetic orders, particularly the Bairagis and the Kabirpanthis. Indeed, the ritual and moral power wielded by Balakdas, a law unto himself, also articulated an alternative legality. The sacral authority of the Satnami guru was just and true, but it was embedded within the interiority of faith. The colonial government was unjust and untrue (and corrupt and ignorant), but its orders had to be obeyed. In the myths of Satnampanth, the early caution of Ghasidas in demarcating the boundaries of the sect was replaced by Balakdas's more direct measures to vanquish rival figures of authority. Balakdas's courage and recklessness bore the hallmark of a conqueror, bequeathing much to posterity. And so it was that in the repertoire of Satnami myths, even as narratives of heroic history came to be replaced by more fragmentary tales—of quarrels within the guru family, the division of the *guru gaddi*, and the increasing importance of women in the affairs of the guru family—the later gurus continued to retain their regal attributes.[17] The major changes lay ahead, linked to the work of the newer forms of politics in the twentieth century.

CONTENDING MODERNITIES

Binary categories do not merely come in pairs. They also imply other homologous oppositions. The overarching opposition of tradition and modernity is often accompanied and animated —at the very least implicitly—by equally grand divisions between myth and history, ritual and reason, and magic and the modern. These binary schemes are actually rooted in reified representations of a singular modernity. They lie at the heart of the various traditions of social theory and political thought in Western and non-Western arenas. Elsewhere, I have questioned the persuasive power of such overriding oppositions in different institutional contexts, diverse intellectual domains.[18] My purpose here is merely to point out that totalizing renderings of a singular modernity, by both its proponents and its critics, tend to remain trapped in self-representations of the idea of the modern. Understood as transformative processes featuring capital and consumption, industry and empire, nations and colonies, citizens and subjects, public spheres and private spaces, normalizing states and secular societies, and circumscribed religion(s) and disenchanted knowledge(s), the period since the seventeenth century has seen many modernities. These plural modernities have been deeply contradictory, decisively chequered, and densely ideological. They give the lie to the self-image of modernity—now understood as an ideological construct—as a self-realizing project of progress, a self-evident embodiment of development, and a self-contained incarnation of history.

Of course, the image lives. Indeed, fabricating its reflection in the immaculate mirror of a reified West, this self-image elides the dark side of the looking glass of the Enlightenment, endorses the white mythologies of post-Enlightenment representations, and ignores its own creations of the likeness of a singular tradition, the essential other of the modern. The past and the present of the non-West, indeed of all that is not quite the authentic West—the enduring Third World and the erstwhile Second World, but equally an earlier Portugal and an anterior Spain—are cast as irremediably narrow illustrative material, the dark curiosities of a durable otherness or the modular forms of a universal history, which exemplify as exceptions and rules the *ur* passage from tradition to modernity.

The binarism of social thought extends beyond the dichotomies of the traditional and the modern.[19] It is not surprising, therefore, that all too often historical accounts, basing themselves upon classical social and political theory, set up an overarching opposition between state and community. What is missed out here are the many different ways in which the symbols and metaphors of the state and governance are drawn upon and imbricate themselves in the construction of communities, including communitarian fashionings of order and identities, legalities and pathologies. Rather than merely stressing the singular and the exceptional in untouchable pasts, it seems to me that a recognition of this interplay and interpenetration between symbols of state and forms of communities is critical for bids that seek to think through the aggrandizing analytics of overriding oppositions, posing as universal reason. And so, as this chapter draws to a close, I briefly turn to the fabrications of a colonial modernity and the makings of postcolonial traditions, involving a critical interface between state and community, in central India in the twentieth century.

We know of the vigorous politics of caste associations and movements that emerged in late-nineteenth-century India. The Satnamis were late entrants to this elaborate negotiation of colonial political forms and Indian structures of authority. It was, in fact, illiteracy among the group that created the cultural and discursive space for mediations of reform and change by those empowered by writing. These moves in turn found a niche in the structures of authority within Satnampanth. Thus, in the early 1920s a few influential Satnami *mahants*, who were also village proprietors, got together with Sunderlal Sharma, a local Brahman nationalist deeply influenced by the activities of the Arya Samaj, and G.A. Gavai, a leader of the Depressed Classes Association in the Central Provinces, to set up the Satnami Mahasabha. Soon the Mahasabha found a formidable ally in Baba Ramchandra, former leader of the Awadh Kisan Sabha move-ment in the United Provinces countryside, and also enlisted the support of Agamdas, a guru of Satnampanth. The aim of this organization was to 'reform' the Satnamis and to participate in the organizational and constitutional politics within the region and in the Central Provinces. The activities of the Satnami Mahasbha led to the community's participation in the elaboration of a contradictory and chequered colonial modernity.

The initiatives of the Satnami Mahasabha, shaped by the interventions of powerful figures who stood outside the community, led to the reworking of Satnampanth in significant ways. First, under the auspices of the Mahasabha, the 'traditional' symbols of Satnampanth were deployed to discredit and marginalize a section of the Satnami leadership that challenged the authority of the organization, and there were efforts to connect the *janeu*, *kanthi*, and *jait khambh* with the veneration of cows and a redefined and refurbished Hindu identity for the Satnamis. Second, in the period between 1926 and 1930, under the leadership of Baba Ramchandra, the Satnami Mahasabha drew upon the signs and resources of the language of law and order of colonial administration and the schemes of Brahmanical authority such as the *Manusmriti*, and situated them next to the symbols and figures of authority within Satnampanth to fashion a new legality, the true *kanun* (law) of Guru Ghasidas. Third, the casting of the activities of the Mahasabha in an idiom of law and command led to a restructuring of the organizational hierarchy of Satnampanth and a tightening of the institutional forms of the Satnami panchayat, bids to secure effective modes of intervention within the community. Here colonial administrative categories provided a blueprint for an enlargement of the earlier organizational structure with the introduction of new gradations in the ranks of *mahants*, where the *rajmahants* (a position created for the leaders of the Mahasabha) were followed by *jila* (district), *tahsil*, and *sarkil* (circle) *mahants* in a descending scale of jurisdiction, status, and power. The corollary to this was a more rationalized economy of power that replaced the somewhat fluid arrangements of the past in measures to choose the Satnami *pancha*s at the level of the village, and in the constitution of the *athgawana* (committee of eight villages) which was a firm institutional form to settle matters that could not be settled by a Satnami panchayat within a village. Finally, the orientations of the members of the community were shaped within the crucible of these wider interventionist measures. They came to recognize the centrality of the newer idioms of legality, authority, and governance within the community as the altered organizational structure of Satnampanth was established by the middle of the 1930s, and the reworked categories of colonial law and administrative organization became enduring features of the efforts of the Mahasabha leaders to discipline and control the group. But once the authority of these leaders waned, the newer idioms and categories were deployed to construct other notions of order, legality, and deviance within the community. The Satnami response to Hindu impositions and strains in the activities of the Mahasabha took the form of their situating a rehearsal of some of the key texts of Hinduism—for example, the *Gita* and the *Ramacharitmanas*—alongside the *katha*s (stories) of the gurus in some of the group's modes of worship. They also embarked on a spate of temple building activity, which was defined by the group's distinct ritual emphases and meant, for instance, that no idols of Hindu gods and goddesses were installed in these structures. These measures—two examples from a larger picture—simultaneously underscored the solidarity of the Satnamis and established the group's claims of superiority over upper-caste Hindus.[20]

Such wide-ranging interplay between meaning and power among the Satnamis has continued into recent times. Some years ago, the internal conflicts between rival politicians and power brokers in the Congress (I) party led Arjun Singh, a seasoned political leader from Madhya Pradesh, to sponsor a government initiative to celebrate Guru Ghasidas as a messiah of the poor and the downtrodden. This was part of a bid to counter the influence of politicians from Chhattisgarh in the party and the province, and to use the Scheduled Castes, particularly the Satnamis, as a political constituency. Guru Ghasidas was accorded the dignity of history when 18 December 1757 was declared as his date of birth to locate him in written and fixed, linear, and chronological time. The naming of a university in the town of Bilaspur after the guru was a recognition of Ghasidas's immense knowledge and wisdom. But arguably the most major initiative here was the support extended by the state to a *mela* (fair) held at the village of Girod, the birthplace of Ghasidas, which has served to turn a small affair featuring a few hundred Satnamis into a mammoth event involving tens of thousands of members of the community.

These state initiatives have led to unintended consequences for social organization among the Satnamis. The members of the community have found their own uses for the government sponsorship of Ghasidas. The written form and the printed word, marks of authority in 'local' cultures still defined by attributes of orality, have been pressed into the service of the worship of the founding guru. Today, the recitation and rehearsal of these newly fashioned texts—part of a collective telling and listening to songs and stories within idioms of popular religious discourse—is increasingly situated alongside modern modes of orality, technically sophisticated aural and visual messages, to constitute novel forms and attributes of Ghasidas. Indeed, the guru has been accorded a novel centrality in the belief structures of the Satnamis. Even as fresh legends accrue around the figure of Ghasidas, the myths about the later gurus, particularly Balakdas, are slowly being erased from a once widely known picture to become more esoteric forms of knowledge. All this underlies novel processes of the constitution of truths and the fashioning of traditions among the community. Thus, recent years have witnessed an ever widening spread of the performance of the Satnami ritual of *chauka*: on the one hand, the ritual has been steadily invested with ever newer meanings as it has undergone innovations, modifications, and transformations at the hands of Satnami specialists of the sacred; and, on the other hand, its novel forms are elaborated as essential parts of a timeless tradition of the community. Similarly, there are fresh fabrications of communitarian forms of worship, an eclectic and redefined ordering of time that simultaneously draws upon Satnami myths and ritual calendar and on official histories and Hindu almanacs, and increasing investments in creative cultural imaginings of the meanings of the fair at Girod alongside other initiatives, variously shored up by the state, all of which refigure the senses of the self and solidarity of the community. In the midst of dominant interventions, the Satnamis continue to construct new meanings of the group's pasts, boundaries, and identities.

CONCLUSION

In bringing together untouchable pasts and ethnographic histories as entangled endeavours, my work draws upon and develops but also extends and exceeds several important studies of untouchables and untouchability. Most anthropological writings on the dynamics of untouchable groups are primarily based upon fieldwork, severally rooted in the ethnographic present. These studies have variously elaborated questions of changing customs and 'sub-cultural' personhoods and issues of ideological innovation and religious resistance among *dalit* communities.[21] Marked by rather different points of entry, a great deal of historical work on untouchable and non-Brahman castes has discussed the caste movements launched by these groups, focusing on the organization and leadership of such initiatives, which in turn have left behind different bodies of written sources. These writings have revealed that untouchable and lower-caste endeavours played out the tensions and rivalries within caste society, where religion provided the means of negotiating an oppressive social order, and the forging of new caste ideologies involved a complex dialogue with the symbols and identities within popular traditions and local cultures.[22]

My work on untouchable pasts has taken up the salient emphases of this anthropological and historical scholarship on caste conflict and religious innovation, historical changes and ritual transformations in lower-caste arenas: but it has equally brought together varieties of both written sources and oral testimonies to discuss these issues over a much longer time period, also casting them in a dialogue with other critical questions. Indeed, distinct readings of archival and non-official sources in an ethnographic mode, the conduct of fieldwork in an engagement with the historical imagination, and considerations of wider theoretical issues in anthropology and history are inextricably bound to each other in this project, which addresses key analytical relationships between sect and caste, myth and history, religion and power, gender and order, community and hegemony, and resistance and domination over the last two hundred years, from the late eighteenth to the late twentieth centuries. Here the entangled endeavours of ethnographic histories and untouchable pasts unravel processes involving myths and the making of modernities, orality and the construction of histories, and writing and the fashioning of traditions to interrogate the place and persistence of binary categories—of modernity and tradition, state and community, rationality and ritual, and reason and emotion—within influential strands of social and political theory. Once more, these entangled endeavours question renderings of power as a totalized terrain, while avoiding seductions of staging the subaltern as an antidote to the terms of power.

Notes

1. The larger project is embodied in Saurabh Dube, *Untouchable Pasts: Religion, Identity, and Power among a Central Indian Community, 1780–1950*, Albany, NY: State University of New York Press, 1998. It is also contained in different papers, cited at appropriate moments in this chapter.

2. Firm estimates of population in the region are available only from the 1860s. In 1866 the Chamars (and Satnamis) made for 362,032 of a total population of 2,103,165 of Chhattisgarh. *Report of the Ethnological Committee, 1866–7*, Nagpur: Central Provinces Government Press, 1867.

3. These conceptual themes are spelled out in dialogue with evidence in Dube, *Untouchable Pasts*.

4. See also the related discussion in the section on Contending Modernities below.

5. Both sets of positions in this debate have been ably surveyed in a recent article by David Lorenzen. However, Lorenzen does not break with the earlier preoccupation with the origins of categories, and once more defines Hinduism in opposition to Islam. David Lorenzen, 'Who invented Hinduism?', *Comparative Studies in Society and History*, 41, 1999, 630–59.

6. A deeper and wider elaboration of these issues of the margins and meanings of Hinduism is contained in Dube, *Untouchable Pasts*.

7. It seems to me that the problem here is not one of an oversight on the part of a few studies of religion and ritual in South Asia. It has deeper methodological roots that go back to approaches in the history of religions that implicitly seek to explicate a universal grammar of religions, adducing parallels and similarities among rituals and ideologies, beliefs and practices to the neglect of processes of symbolic construction within wider relationships of power, and to the tendency in earlier ethnography of treating caste as primarily a matter of the endless play of the ritual hierarchy of purity and pollution, an ideology divorced from power. Individual works are too numerous to mention here, but for a 'classic' that has exercised enormous influence upon the study of religion in South Asia through its demarcations of the separate domains of *dharma* (ideology) and *artha* (economic and political power) in the Hindu caste order, see Louis Dumont, *Homo Hierarchicus: The Caste System and its Implications*, London: Weidenfeld and Nicholson, 1970.

8. See particularly, Andre Wink, *Land and Sovereignty in India: Agrarian Society and Politics under the Eighteenth Century Maratha Svarajya*, Cambridge: Cambridge University Press, 1986; Stewart Gordon, 'The Slow Conquest', *Modern Asian Studies*, 11, 1977, 1–40; and Christopher Bayly, *Indian Society and the Making of the British Empire*, Cambridge: Cambridge University Press, 1988.

9. Dube, *Untouchable Pasts*.

10. Louis Dumont, 'World Renunciation in Indian Religions', in Dumont, *Religion/Politics and History in India: Collected Papers in Indian Sociology*, Paris and The Hague: Mouton, 1970, 33–60.

11. Richard Burghart, 'Renunciation in the Religious Traditions of South Asia', *Man* (n.s.), 18, 1983, 635–53; Peter Van der Veer, *Gods on Earth: The Management of Religious Experience in a North Indian Pilgrimage Centre*, Delhi: Oxford University Press, 1988; and David Lorenzen, 'Traditions of Non-caste Hinduism: The Kabirpanth', *Contributions to Indian Sociology* (n.s.), 21, 1987, 263–83.

12. Dumont, *Homo Hierarchicus*.

13. Two clarifications are pertinent here. First, by making a case for certain shared orientations in the work of Dirks, Raheja, and Quigley I am not denying that there are also important differences in their emphases. Second, my critical comments should not be allowed to obscure what I have learnt from these writings in my wider body of analyses. Nicholas Dirks, *The Hollow Crown: Ethnohistory of an Indian Kingdom*, Cambridge: Cambridge University Press, 1987; Gloria Raheja, *The Poison in the Gift: Ritual, Prestation, and Dominant Caste in a North Indian Village*, Chicago: University of Chicago Press, 1988; Declan Quigley, *The Interpretation of Caste*, Oxford: Clarendon Press, 1993.

14. These themes of sects and asceticism and caste and power are discussed in much greater detail in Dube, *Untouchable Pasts*, but see also the section on Engaging Stories below.

15. See Saurabh Dube, 'Myths, Symbols and Community: Satnampanth of Chhattisgarh', in Partha Chatterjee and Gyan Pandey (eds), *Subaltern Studies VII: Writings on South Asian History and Society*, Delhi: Oxford University Press, 1992, 121–56.

16. This section takes up issues elaborated in greater detail—and somewhat differently—in Saurabh Dube, 'Rite Place, Rite Time: On the Organization of the Sacred in Colonial Central India', *Calcutta Historical Review*, 17, 1995, 19–37; and Dube, *Untouchable Pasts*.

17. On Satnami myths, see Dube, 'Myths, Symbols and Community' and *Untouchable Pasts*.

18. Dube, *Untouchable Pasts*.

19. For distinct, recent questionings of the logic of binarism, see, for example, Homi Bhabha, *The Location of Culture*, London and New York: Routledge, 1994; and Michael Herzfeld, *Cultural Intimacy: Social Poetics in the Nation-State*, London and New York: Routledge, 1997, particularly pp. 165–73.

20. These processes are elaborated in Saurabh Dube, 'Idioms of Authority and Engendered Agendas: The Satnami Mahasabha, Chhattisgarh, 1925–1950', *The Indian Economic and Social History Review*, 30, 1993, 383–411.

21. For example, James M. Freeman, *Untouchable: An Indian Life History*, Stanford: Stanford University Press, 1979; R.S. Khare, *The Untouchable as Himself: Ideology, Identity and Pragmatism among the Lucknow Chamars*, Cambridge: Cambridge University Press, 1984; Lynn Vincentnathan, 'Untouchable Concepts of Person and Society', *Contributions to Indian Sociology* (n.s.), 27, 1993, 53–82; Bernard Cohn, *An Anthropologist among the Historians and Other Essays*, Delhi: Oxford University Press, 1987: 255–83; and Owen M. Lynch, *The Politics of Untouchability*, New York: Columbia University Press, 1969. More recent studies include, Gnana Prakasam, *Social Separatism: Scheduled Castes and the Caste System*, Jaipur: Rawat Publications, 1998; Robert Deliège, *The World of the 'Untouchables': Paraiyars of Tamil Nadu*, Delhi: Oxford University Press, 1997; Viramma, Josiane Racine, and Jean-Luc Racine, *Viramma: Life of an Untouchable*, tr. Will Hobson, London: Verso, 1997; Siddharth Dube, *In the Land of Poverty: Memoirs of an Indian Family, 1947–97*, London: Zed Press, 1998; and Oliver Mendelsohn and Marika Vicziany, *The Untouchables: Subordination, Poverty, and the State in Modern India*, Cambridge: Cambridge University Press, 1998.

22. Rosalind O'Hanlon, *Caste Conflict and Ideology: Mahatma Jotirao Phule and Low-Caste Protest in Nineteenth Century Maharashtra*, Cambridge: Cambridge University Press, 1985; Mark Juergensmeyer, *Religion as Social Vision: The Movement against Untouchability in Twentieth-Century Punjab*, Berkeley and Los Angeles: University of California Press, 1982; Gail Omvedt, *Cultural Revolt in a Colonial Society: The Non-Brahman Movement in Western India: 1873 to 1930*, Bombay: Scientific Socialist Education Trust, 1976; Eugene Irschick, *Politics and Social Conflict in South India: The Non-Brahman Movement and Tamil Separatism 1916–1929*, Berkeley and Los Angeles, 1969; Eleanor Zelliot, 'Learning the Use of Political Means: The Mahars of Maharashtra', in Rajni Kothari (ed.), *Caste in Indian Politics*, New Delhi: Orient Longman, 1970, 29–69; and Lawrence A. Babb, 'The Satnamis—Political Involvement of a Religious Movement', in Michael J. Mahar (ed.), *The Untouchables in Contemporary India*, Tuscon: University of Arizona Press, 1972, 143–51. For a significant, recent study, see Vijay Prashad, *Untouchable Freedom: A Social History of a Dalit Community*, New Delhi: Oxford University Press, 2000.

ELEVEN

Reproducing Inequality: Spirit Cults and Labour Relations in Colonial Eastern India

Gyan Prakash

❦

Understanding how unequal relations are reproduced over time is as significant as comprehending inequality itself. For unequal relations exist only in human practices that reproduce them. More than a play on words, the coupling of production with reproduction in recent anthropological studies highlights processes that provide the basis for production.[1] The necessity of reconstructing practices that reproduce social relations is perhaps nowhere more neglected than in the study of South Asian history. When it comes to explaining how unequal relations between social groups were maintained, the caste system is the perennial favourite. This is particularly so where relations between landlords and landless labourers are concerned. Thus, even Jan Breman's sophisticated and rich study of dependent labourers in south Gujarat points to the *jajmani* system, the institutional form of caste relations in the agrarian context, as the basis for relations between labourers and landlords in the past.[2] While his study illuminates how bonded labour relations can be understood in the light of the *jajmani* model, it fails to explain how these relations were reproduced. Are we to assume that the transactional norms of the caste system, once in place, simply drove labourers and landlords into actions that reproduced bondage?

Implicit in the *jajmani* view of labour relations, as also in explanations that point to 'loans' advanced to labourers by landlords[3] and invoke the supply and demand theory to account for bondage,[4] is what Pierre Bourdieu calls a 'rule oriented' notion of practice.[5] That is, these three views of labour bondage assume that human practice merely executes rules and follows maps drawn by the logic of the *jajmani* system, 'debt' transaction, or the supply and demand of labour, respectively. Once practice is subordinated to the brute dominance of rules and schemes, how bonded labour relations were reproduced becomes a moot question. And so does history, because historical activities of landlords and labourers, their strategies and actions at different times, appear as mere executions of some grand design.

Focusing on relations between *kamias* (bonded labour) and *maliks* (landlords) in south Bihar, I argue in this essay that the reproduction of bondage was rooted in practice. Kamia and malik practices owed the conditions of their existence to the social structure, and they therefore articulated notions of hierarchy and bondage, in dealing with everyday life. But the logic of practices was not governed and driven by the logic of the caste ideology. Rather, the caste hierarchy and labour bondage were reproduced through practices aimed at achieving practical ends even as seemingly far removed from labour relations as the propitiation of spirits. In this essay, I reconstruct spirit cult practices in south Bihar during the late nineteenth and early twentieth centuries to show how they reproduced unequal relations between kamias and maliks, and articulated notions of hierarchy and bondage.[6] I argue that, since the social structure was composed of unequal groups whose interests were not identical, spirit cults contained ceaseless struggles between kamias and maliks over practical aims of the ritual practices. Thus, the reproduction of power went hand in hand with the struggle between kamias and maliks. In demonstrating how kamias and maliks struggled in reproducing inequality, I will examine ritual practices that constituted the spirit world, represented the caste hierarchy, and created and used *malik devatas*, that is, ghosts purchased by maliks from the southern jungles.

KAMIAS AND MALIKS IN SOUTH BIHAR

When the Turks, and following them, the Mughals, established their rule in north India, they recognized the superior rights of the local clan chiefs and incorporated them as a subordinate ruling class.[7] Owing to their superior position, these men, called maliks in south Bihar, held lands revenue-free or at preferential rates and collected a variety of payments from the peasantry in their domains.[8] Befitting their lordly position at the local level, the maliks claimed high ritual status and employed low castes to work their lands. Called kamias, these labourers in Gaya district were mainly of the Bhuinya caste.[9] Inhabiting the southern part of south Bihar, Bhuinyas were subordinated as low-caste kamias and employed in developing irrigated paddy agriculture when Hindu and Muslim clan chiefs immigrated into the region and established themselves as local lords after the thirteenth century.[10] Regional lords, drawn often from the maliks' ranks, arose and established their sway over maliks, revenue-free grants were given to religious men in their domains, but the maliks' position as local magnates remained intact well into the eighteenth century.[11]

British conquest in the mid-eighteenth century, the introduction of the Permanent Settlement making zamindars landowners and responsible for the payment of land revenue, economic changes associated with the late nineteenth century—increasing penetration of land and agricultural production by the market—transformed the terms of the maliks' domination at the local level.[12] Rather than force and social hierarchy, the maliks' position came to depend upon land control backed by legal titles and secured by the ability to turn the growing market relations to their benefit. As opportunities for land control through ownership and superior tenures opened up, different groups strove to convert premodern claims on produce and revenue into secure claims over landed property. Thus, the Hindu monastery of

Bodh Gaya secured and even extended its land control through legal tenures in the eighteenth and the nineteenth centuries.[13]

Important as it was, the maliks' control over land was not the only basis for the reproduction of their power over kamias. A kamia was not just a labourer but a Bhuinya with a past and a future, with ancestors and descendants, a living person who defined himself in relation to the dead. Nor was a malik just a landholder, but a person with a caste status, who also had to define himself in relation to his ancestors. Thus, the spirit world was a field with highly charged meanings, a field that could not escape from the representations of the maliks' power and the kamias' subordination.

THE SPIRIT WORLD

Written sources provide very little information on the practical contexts in which the spirit world was constituted. Particular circumstances and strategies that went into inhabiting the spirit world with different spirits and ghosts have been lost in the timeless discourses of colonial officials on the 'rude mind' of natives.[14] While particular circumstances and aims are lost to us, colonial descriptions of the spirit world, when combined with oral data, yield a general sense of the practical strategies that lay behind its construction.

In writing about spirit cults and worship among the people of Gaya district, L.S.S. O'Malley recorded in 1906 that spirits were classed as *dak-bhut*.[15] Ancestors, *daks*, and *bhuts* were distinct but interconnected elements in the larger spirit world. What was common to all three was that they were different forms of *preta*, or spirit of the dead. When a person died, his *preta*, or soul, survived and continued to make claims on the living.[16] Death was culturally denied by positing that physical death freed the soul from its bodily form. Thus, spirits were not separated from the living; both were distinct but related parts of an organic universe marked by the cycle of death and regeneration.

Spirit cult practices secured the endless passages and transactions between contrary categories within this world. Little mounds of clay called *pindas* were installed in a section of the house called *sira-ghar*, to represent the dead in their new form of life. Offerings were made to these ancestors in annual and life-cycle rituals. All castes had these *sira-ghars*, *pindas*, and ancestor cults. The offerings and libations were made to ancestors not only out of respect for their claims on the living, but also because of the power ascribed to spirits in general.[17] Shorn of their bodily form, the dead in their new life could see and predict things that the living could not, and could therefore prevent misfortune from occurring. This power was different in quality from the power of legendary ancestors, and different in degree from that of *bhuts* and *daks*.

Legendary apical ancestors, such as Ban Singh among the Bhogta caste[18] and Tulsibir among the Bhuinyas, were also expected to ward off misfortune and aid their caste members. But this power of legendary ancestors stemmed from the heroic character of their lives and not from their status as spirits. Whereas the power of all non-apical ancestors arose from their status as spirits (with the ability to cause both harm and good), legendary ancestors were never classed in the category of spirits and were generally regarded as benign.[19]

Like ancestors, ghosts were also forms of spirit. But their power was much greater and they were therefore more feared. Classed generally as *dak* and *bhut*, ghosts were spirits of those who had died unnaturally. Within this group there were a large number of powerful spirits.[20] There was the particularly powerful and feared *churail* or *kichin*, the spirit of a woman who had died in childbirth. There were *baghauts*, spirits of those killed by tigers in the west of the district; *barunis* and *langhandaks*, which were spirits of those who had died accidentally outside their own villages, who hovered in undefined lands and jungles between villages and at crossroads.[21]

The different forms that spirits assumed depended upon how ritual practices ordered deaths. From this arose the varying amount of power they had over the living and, therefore, the extent of harm or benefit they could cause. Those who were powerful, such as the ones described by O'Malley as 'evil', were more feared than the weaker ancestral spirits, propitiated to give succour to members of the caste.

Even ancestors could become *bhuts* and *daks*, usually those who in their lives had been *gunis*, or exorcists. Since they dealt with spirits in their lives and had control over some *daks* and *bhuts*, they became powerful ghosts after their deaths. In Sheorajpur village, for instance, Ramjani Bhuinya was a *guni* who communicated with spirits and was believed to have control over several *daks*. After his death, he became Ramjani Dak and was installed by his descendants as their *malik devata*, that is, the most prominent ancestral ghost who protected them within the house.[22] Significantly, legendary ancestors never became ghosts. For instance, Dharha, the legendary ancestor of the Dhangar caste did not become a *bhut* even though he died an unnatural death.[23] Clearly, spirits, insofar as they mediated life, the living, and the dead, were believed to have different powers from that of heroic legendary ancestors. As spirits, ancestors possessed the power to affect the lives of their descendants. If, in their lives, these ancestors, like Ramjani Bhuinya, bridged contrary categories, partook the power of the living and the dead, their *preta* became all the more powerful: they became *daks* and *bhuts*.

Ghosts came into being by the disruption of harmony in relations between contrary categories in the organic universe. The power hierarchy in the spirit world was based on the confusion of cultural categories and social roles that different spirits represented. The least powerful were spirits of those ancestors who had died natural deaths.[24] These were cases of what are called 'good deaths'.[25] Natural deaths enabled the living to define death as a controlled event leading to regeneration of life in a different form, that is, as *preta*, a regeneration that was socially constructed. In upper-caste Hindu mortuary rites, the new life was created by cremation. In the case of the Bhuinyas, it was the burial of the remains after cremation which regenerated the dead. 'When my father was buried and returned to where he came from, his *preta* resumed a new life,' explained a Bhuinya.[26] Both were cases of successful reciprocity between nature and culture. The organic unity of the socially constructed universe was maintained in 'good deaths'.

Because good deaths enabled ordered regeneration into a new life, and represented harmony in the organic universe, the spirits of these ancestors were not very powerful. When slighted, they could cause harm. But in general, their ordered cultural incorporation into cyclical death and regeneration made them less of a threat. Untimely deaths, on the other hand, were uncontrolled events. They represented disharmony in the reciprocal exchange between contrary forms of the world. These were 'bad deaths' and their power was enormous and unpredictable. O'Malley noted that the most feared ghost in Gaya district was Raghuni Dak.[27] This ghost arose when a Babhan landlord, suspecting his kamia of illicit relations with his daughter, killed them both and then committed suicide. Raghuni Dak represented the three spirits jointly. Born out of the suspected crossing of caste boundaries in real life, and representing a union of contrary categories in the spirit world, Raghuni Dak was particularly feared.

The ordering of deaths as 'good' or 'bad' highlights the role of practice in constituting the spirit world. In attributing varying degrees of power to spirits, people did not simply execute some pre-existing rules. Defining deaths had practical aims: the dead had to be reintegrated into the organic universe. Furthermore, spirit cult practices were also cognitive processes; people created notions of 'good' and 'bad' deaths, attributed a great deal of power to some spirits and not to others, and, while conceding that they existed as spirits, made their legendary ancestors wholly benign.

SPIRITS AND CASTE HIERARCHY

Upper-caste Hindus as well as low-caste Bhuinyas propitiated ancestral spirits. Ghosts and witches affected all of them. But the ordering of castes and the tensions inherent in the separation and interaction between castes were both presented and represented by spirit cults. Ritual practices associated with spirit cults not only bore the imprint of caste hierarchy but also became instruments for articulating and securing social hierarchy. By subordinating spirit cults—a field inhabited by the Bhuinya ritual specialists and wandering ghosts of low castes—to Hindu beliefs, and by bending ritual practices to conform to the social order, Hindu landlords reproduced caste hierarchy.

The upper castes subordinated spirit cult practices to the larger Hindu tradition. They were also afflicted by spirits, but their ancestral spirits occupied the world created by the Hindu cosmology. This is evident in the rites of ancestor propitiation for which Hindu pilgrims came to Gaya from all over India, and do so even today. Like Hindus from elsewhere, upper-caste men in Gaya also participated in this annual ritual.[28] Offerings, or *pindas*, were made to ancestral spirits in the Vishnupad temple at Gaya, at the Phalgu river, and at the Pretsila hill. Vishnupad is a sacred Vaishnavite temple where pilgrims as well as local upper-caste Hindus went to seek Lord Vishnu's blessing in rescuing their ancestors' souls. The Phalgu represented Vishnu and was believed to be the place where Sita (the wife of Rama in the epic *Ramayana*) offered *pinda* to Rama's father, Dasaratha. At Pretsila hill, Yama, the lord of hell, was propitiated to protect ancestral spirits.[29]

Linked to the larger Hindu world with its rich cosmology, upper-caste Hindus were able to extricate their ancestral spirits from the world of lower-caste *bhuts* and *daks*. The danger of a Bhuinya sorcerer communicating with and controlling an upper-caste ancestral ghost was removed. Furthermore, as Hindus saw the universe animated by the presence of different manifestations of God, ghosts who existed out of this universe belonged to untamed nature. Original inhabitants, such as the Bhuinyas in Gaya and tribal groups in Chotanagpur, were regarded as appropriate persons for communicating with such spirits.[30] Thus the ghost world was both separated from and subordinated to upper-caste Hindu ideology.

Although upper-caste Hindus were able to bring their ancestral spirits under the protection of Hindu gods, they could not do away with tensions in their interpersonal lives and in their relations with other castes. Ghosts and witches still provided a system of meaning to deal with contradictions in social life. When a misfortune occurred, they also consulted the *ojha* or *guni* to discover its cause.

And so when a little more than sixty years ago, a Kayasth landholder of a village near Bodh Gaya found his cattle dying suddenly, he consulted an *ojha*.[31] The exorcist disclosed that a ghost called Jaibir Dak from a nearby village was responsible for the deaths. It so happened, as the Kayasth was reported to have admitted, that he had kept a cow that had wandered into his yard along with his own cattle when they returned from the nearby village where they had been taken to graze by his kamia. The exorcist said that Jaibir Dak demanded a pig as an offering. But being an upper-caste Hindu, the Kayasth landholder would not agree to offering a pig in sacrifice. Nor would he place within his courtyard a ghost who demanded pigs. Fortunately, the *ojha* found that the ghost agreed to accept the offering of a kid. Jaibir Dak also accepted the Kayasth's backyard as its abode.

The Kayasth's propitiation of a ghost, which was obviously of a low caste since it demanded a pig in sacrifice, meant that at the very least caste boundaries were crossed. It is interesting that although the upper castes had taken care to extricate their ancestral spirits from the world of lower-caste ghosts, they ended up propitiating lower-caste ghosts. In one case, the upper castes invoked the Hindu world, in the other, they became concerned with the low-caste spirit symbols. How do we explain this?

Bourdieu has argued that one has to 'acknowledge that practice has a logic which is not that of logic, if one is to avoid asking of it more logic than it can give, thereby condemning oneself to either wring incoherences out of it or thrust upon it a forced coherence'.[32] If we view ritual practices as dynamic events where the selection of symbols and the choice of emphasis in meaning attached to them are generated by the situation, then the cultural inconsistency appears as the function of practice. If practices are not just executions of grand cultural plans, if they are discontinuous events oriented towards practical functions, then the culture they articulate will be variegated. While the cultural notions articulated by the two events were different, the practices in themselves were coherent, that is, they both employed principles and symbols appropriate to the situation. In one case, upper castes invoked Hindu symbols to reproduce the social order represented by the cycle of death and regeneration. In the other case, a Kayasth propitiated a low-caste ghost in order to remove the misfortune threatening his situation.

Because ritual practices are dynamic events, they do not simply reflect but actively construct cultural notions and social relations. So, while in social life the danger involved in the interdependence of separate castes resulted in ritual pollution requiring Hindu rites of purification, in the spirit world this caused spirit affliction requiring propitiation of the ghost. But the danger to the social hierarchy caused by the affliction from, and propitiation of, a low-caste ghost was removed by making the ghost subordinate to upper-caste Hindu notions, by making it accept a young goat instead of a pig, the backyard instead of the courtyard.

The articulation of the caste hierarchy was not the major purpose of the ritual practice; the practical aim was to restore harmony in the Kayasth landlord's world. But in doing so, ritual practices also expressed and reconstituted the social order. It was the same with the annual agricultural rite with which the cultivating season commenced. The annual *asarhi puja* was the most complex and elaborate ritual embodying the reconstruction of the social hierarchy. Beginning in the middle of June, after the monsoon had broken, it involved the entire village in a series of connected rituals:[33]

After the first rains, when the ground had become wet and swollen, the malik consulted the Brahman, giving him the names of his kamias. The Brahman then selected Shukar Bhuinya whose *rashi* [astrological sign] was favorable to do *harmantar* [plough worship]. He was fed and treated well the night before the *puja* [worship]. Next morning, he was taken to the malik's field. He ploughed one *katha* [little less than 1/20 of an acre] and sowed one corner of the field called the *bhandar kona* [storage corner] with seeds left from the previous harvest. This done, the malik chose a particular Tuesday for *asarhi puja*. All kamias were summoned to the *kachahari*, and told of the date, and were given some money and grain to perform the *puja*. First, the *manjhi* propitiated the *malik devata*. Then he and all other *gunis* went all around the village, inviting all *daks* and *bhuts* to the *puja*. In the Bhuinya quarters where all the ghosts gathered, the *gunis* began to communicate with each spirit one by one. To the beat of the Chamar's drum, the *bhagat* [shaman] danced and all ancestral spirits came to him and told everyone present what they wanted for propitiation. Then the whole procession of the Bhuinyas along with the Chamar beating the drum and the *manjhi* and *bhagats* leading the way went all around the village boundary expelling stranger *daks* who lurked around waiting to enter the village and cause commotion. Then they went to each house, beginning with the malik's. Each household offered a pinchful of rice or some money to the *daks* which was placed in a woven sieve. Then the procession gathered at the Tulsibir *sthan* [Tulsibir's shrine]. The *daks* were offered whatever they had demanded. Then with the Bhuinya men singing songs about Tulsibir whose presence was announced by the *bhagat*, a pig was sacrificed. Following this, the Hindu village goddess Bhagwati was given a young goat.

This annual rite was an integral part of the agricultural operation. Without it the crop was in jeopardy. Because the crop represented the regeneration of seeds from the previous season, death and regeneration in agriculture paralleled the cyclical process of life and death among human beings. Social life in general required the proper transition between different stages, and agricultural activity was no exception. But this transition was a potentially dangerous process.

Rains brought the wet and the dry together, the swollen ground representing fecundity. Insofar as ploughing was an act which intervened in the passage between fecundity and birth, it was a potentially sacrilegious act. It was precisely the sort of transitional stage when spirits struck. Ghosts hovered outside the village boundaries waiting to attack. *Daks* and *bhuts* thrived on this and therefore they had to be propitiated. Ritual practice intervened in the critical phase of transition between death and regeneration. To ensure a smooth transition, spirits and ancestors of low-caste Bhuinyas were brought together with ritual specialists and beliefs of upper-caste landlords in ways which reconstructed the social hierarchy of caste.

The distribution of tasks in ritual practice reproduced social relations. The paddy field chosen for ensuring proper transition from death to life in agriculture was that of the malik. But the person selected to perform the potentially dangerous act of ploughing and then impregnating the soil with the remains of the dead was a low-caste Bhuinya. The malik's field served as a symbol for the entire community. But the kamia shouldered the burden of dealing with the union of contraries. It was he who dealt with the swollen ground, tamed nature in its fecund and untamed stage, and brought death (seeds from the previous season) to life. The burden of communicating with *daks* and *bhuts* was borne by the low-caste *manjhi*, *guni*, and *bhagat*. The Bhuinya population not only provided ritual specialists for the occasion, they collectively also became central figures in the whole drama. It was in their section of the village that the ritual specialists performed. They formed the procession that went around the village. The malik distanced himself from those stages of rites when ritual specialists consorted with ghosts. By appearing only at the beginning and end of rites, by providing resources for the performance of rites, by acting as the patron of the *asarhi puja*, he asserted his social dominance.

Just as distribution of tasks in rituals reconstructed social inequality, so also cultural beliefs articulated by them represented unequal relations. Only low-caste ghosts threatened when the passage from death to life was enacted. Upper-caste ancestral spirits were removed from the field of dangerous powers which thrived on the ambivalence caused by rites of passage in agriculture. Therefore, only low-caste ghosts were invoked by shamans. These ghosts were not expressedly defined as low-caste spirits but since upper-caste spirits were separated from the rest of the ghost world, the Bhuinya ritual specialists dealt only with low-caste spirits. During the concluding part of the ritual where the malik was present as the patron, even Tulsibir, the Bhuinya apical ancestor, was invoked in assisting the rite of passage. Unlike other ghosts, however, the shaman did not negotiate with Tulsibir about what sacrifice he wanted. A pig was offered, recognizing his role as a benign ancestor.

The village goddess, Bhagwati, was treated differently. The Bhuinya ritual specialist gave way to a Brahman. As a goddess revered by the upper castes, her blessings were sought only when the lesser spirits had been appeased. She could not be inserted in the middle because that would have meant that even after appeasing a goddess associated with the upper castes, lesser spirits had to be propitiated. The sacrifice of a young goat for her therefore had to be the final act. Social hierarchy was thus inscribed in the temporal order of ritual tasks.

If spirit cult practices reconstructed the social dominance of the upper castes, it is also true that the low castes were conceded a position denied to them in other spheres of social life by the ideology of caste. No doubt, low-caste ghosts were subordinated to upper-caste cultural beliefs, placed lower than the upper-caste goddess Bhagwati, forced to accept a young goat instead of a pig, the backyard instead of courtyard, and that upper-caste spirits were separated from the potentially malevolent world of ghosts. But we should also note that this went hand in hand with the fact that the upper castes also found it necessary to appease low-caste ghosts, that they had to concede the power these ghosts had over their lives, and that they had to respect the powers that the Bhuinya ritual specialists possessed. Thus the Bhuinyas enjoyed a cultural autonomy within the overarching hegemony of the upper castes. The interdependence in social relations, obscured and denied by the ideology of caste hierarchy in other contexts, was played out in spirit cult practices. In this sense, ritual practices associated with spirits did not simply reflect the social hierarchy but represented it in forms not possible in other contexts.

GHOSTS, KAMIAS, AND MALIKS

Caste was one dimension of social relations represented in spirit cult practices. Another was the relation between kamias and maliks. The two dimensions were linked because the malik was both an upper-caste person and landlord. Spirit cults therefore represented both caste hierarchy and the unequal relations between maliks and kamias. The above section has already dealt with the caste dimension. In this section, I will examine ritual practices which represented kamia–malik relations.

As I have mentioned, there was a category of ghosts in Gaya district known as *malik devatas*, which were spirits purchased by maliks to protect their property.[34] Although O'Malley did not mention that ghosts were bought by maliks, he noted that the purchase of ghosts was widely practised to protect the village fields and crops.[35] The following account of a *malik devata* that I collected describes the process of the purchase of ghosts.[36]

During the time of Hem Narayan Gir [the chief monk or mahant of the Bodh Gaya monastery from 1867 to 1892], the *gosain* of Sheorajpur *kachahari* [the religious disciple of the Mahant who managed the math's property at Sheorajpur], went with Pancham Bhuinya, the *manjhi* of the village, to Tambe, a village to the south of Palamau in an area called Kothikunda, to buy a ghost. The people who sold ghosts there were Korba and Korain, and Turi and Turain [Korba and Turi men and women]. These people told Pancham Bhuinya that Bhainsasur and Kol Baba were best capable of protecting the Mahant's property. The *gunis* of Tambe placed a four-directional lamp on a sieve which was placed at the *pinda* of the two ghosts. Then a handful of rice was put in the sieve. The *gunis* were given some money and then Pancham Bhuinya and the *gosain* headed back. The sieve followed them back to the village. Once it reached the village, the sieve circled the village boundary and then descended on a tree. Pancham Bhuinya stayed awake the whole night looking for the light from the four-directional lamp. But once he spotted it on top of a tree, the sieve and the lamp vanished. *Pindas* were set up for Bhainsasur and Kol Baba at the place where the lamp had been spotted. The whole village was informed that *malik devatas* had arrived.

The above account is remarkably similar to the description O'Malley gave about the purchase of ghosts.[37] So it is very likely that he was also referring to *malik devatas*, even though he did not note that the purchase of ghosts occurred under the malik's direction. According to him, the ghost kept watch over the village fields.[38] Another report from a district official in 1852 also echoed the existence of this belief. He said of the Rajwars (a low-caste group residing in the hilly and forested Nawada region of Gaya district): '. . . . like all simple and uneducated people they are very superstitious and the fear they have of incurring the displeasure of their Deities (even to stealing Grain from the field) is so great that this alone is a great check to the commission of such crime amongst them.'[39] Since kamias did not own fields, and as peasant castes did not purchase ghosts or act on behalf of the village as a whole, it appears that the ghosts that, according to the report, discouraged Rajwars from stealing grain from the field were *malik devatas*.

Malik devatas were particularly powerful ghosts. They were always bought from the south, from the forested region close to or in Chotanagpur. The four-directional lamp that represented ghosts can be interpreted as a symbol of their origin in the wild. But most *malik devatas* had names connected to original settlers of southern Gaya and the Chotanagpur region. Kol Baba, Bhainsasur, and Bhuini Rani were the most common names that figured in the list of *malik devatas* of the past. Kol was the generic term used for all non-Hindu tribes, Bhainsasur was derived from Asur, a tribe regarded as the earliest settlers of Chotanagpur, and Bhuini Rani was associated with the Bhuinyas. In other words, *malik devatas* were ghosts who were believed to have tamed nature. Since the region to the south of Gaya was thickly forested and inhabited by non-Hindu tribes, ghosts who represented appropriation of nature to culture were believed to reside in such tracts. Other powerful ghosts, who were not connected to original settlers but figured in the repertory of *malik devatas*, were also bought from the south.

The southern tract was where the appropriation of nature to culture was regarded as problematic. Therefore, ghosts from there were most powerful. They were in the best position to effect a smooth exchange between nature and culture. They were propitiated annually during the *asarhi puja* by the *manjhi* with money given by the malik. In some places, expenses for propitiation were met by lands set aside for this purpose by landlords.[40] It was believed that without propitiation at crucial times of the agricultural cycle, wild animals would destroy the crop.[41]

Ghosts bought from the south were closest to nature. The reciprocal exchange with ghosts stood for relations of mutuality between nature and culture. By purchasing such ghosts and securing their assistance in agricultural rites, landlords gained control over transactions between the social and spiritual worlds. Although upper-caste landlords possessed a rich cosmology within which death and regeneration were accomplished by mortuary and ancestor propitiation rites, they still found it necessary to propitiate ghosts purchased from the south. Why? Once the ability to communicate with ghosts was conceded to Bhuinyas, the power that ritual specialization gave them had to be countered. Even if they were subordinated to Hindu beliefs in ritual practices, ghosts still represented power. Their propitiation could not be left completely to the lower caste. The power of ghosts was thus harnessed to the landlord's cause. The guardian of nature became the castellan of land and landlords because, while ghosts were custodians of nature, lands were held by landlords. Ghosts became *malik devatas*.

Controlling ghosts meant that the landlords could appropriate the power that ghosts exercised over nature, over transactions between nature and culture, over exchanges between the living and the dead. If through calculated acts of generosity, maliks could represent themselves as munificent providers, the purchase of ghosts enabled them to represent themselves as the bedrock of an orderly universe.

The transformation of a ghost into a *malik devata* through its purchase by the landlord meant that the ghost's function was not merely to mediate reciprocal exchange between nature and culture. The ghost was identified with the malik's interests, with unequal appropriation of nature as landed property. So, while in ritual practices associated with the agricultural cycle, the ghost mediated the transaction between the dead and the living, between nature and culture, as a guardian of the malik's property it also kept watch over his field and crop. It punished theft from the malik's field and crop.[42] But this was not all, as the following account of theft and punishment illustrates:[43]

There was a Bhuinya whose daughter was married to a man from Sakhwara. One day she fell ill. She could not even see properly: she mistook her father-in-law for her husband, and her husband for her father-in-law. When the *ojha* was called, he disclosed that Kol Baba, the *malik devata* from her parental home, was the cause of her sickness. On being asked to remember anything she had done to offend Kol Baba, she revealed that while taking out rice from the clay pot to cook food in her parent's home, she had found some coins which she kept and brought over to her husband's village. The woman's father-in-law had to propitiate Kol Baba in order to cure her of spirit affliction.

The revelation that the Bhuinya woman had kept quiet about the money she had found in the earthen pot came only after the *ojha* had diagnosed that Kol Baba afflicted her. But the implication of the connection made between her actions and spirit affliction was that the *malik devata* could be offended even when the theft was from a kamia's house. Relations between kamias and maliks were emphasized over all other ties. Furthermore, the event articulated a belief that was absent in other contexts. It treated the kamia's belongings as if they were part of the malik's property so that the spirit offended by theft in the Bhuinya's house was the *malik devata*. The belief was an extravagant representation of the malik's power: ritual practices did more than reflect social relations.

In spite of its association with the landlord, the *malik devata* was not identical with his person. This meant that the ghost symbol was flexible. It could be used to express the resentment that kamias felt towards landlords but could not state openly. For example, Bithal Bhuinya's move from Kharhari to Bakraur, sometime before 1914–15 because of a misfortune in his family, coincided with problems he was having with the landlord.[44] One of Bithal's two sons had died when a well he was digging for the landlord suddenly collapsed and fell on him; the *malik devata* had set a *dayan* on him. It was at this time that the landlord had taken away the land he had given Bithal Bhuinya. But the reason Bithal gave for leaving Kharhari for Bakraur was not that he had lost his land but that the ghost had turned malevolent against his family.[45]

A breakdown in reciprocal relations with the landlord was paralleled by disharmony in relations of mutuality with nature. A sudden death was just as disturbing as the loss of land. But one did not cause the other. Bithal Bhuinya did not attribute the landlord's action to the *malik devata* nor did he hold the landlord responsible for the death of his son. The two events were analogically rather than causally related. The record of Bhuinya spirit cult practices expresses the belief that nature, person, and social life exist as an organic unity. Agricultural rites, ancestral cults, death, birth, and social intercourse are analogical discourses between man and nature in which symbols become animated with meanings appropriate to the situation.

The choice of spirit affliction as the likely cause of death expressed the belief that there was disharmony in relations between different elements constituting the organic world. The diagnosis of affliction was an enquiry into the state of the social disorder, and spirit healing was the treatment of social disharmony. The exorcist looked for representation of this disorder in social life. That the death occurred while Bithal's son was digging a well for the landlord was presumably the 'factual' basis for holding the *malik devata*, rather than any other ghost, responsible for the misfortune. But involved here was an active choice of meaning. By evoking the symbol of the *malik devata* in interpreting the fact of his son's untimely death, Bithal animated the event with meanings pertinent to kamia–malik relations. Because the landlord was not identical with the ghost, he was not accountable for the death. But since the *malik devata* represented unequal social relations, the complicity of the malik in the death was not too distant. It was this ambivalent and multivocal quality of the *malik devata* which made it a powerful symbol. It allowed transmutation of tensions in kamia–malik relations into dissonance in transactions between man and nature.

Spirit cult practices allowed a fantastic representation of the malik's power over his labourers. In *malik devatas*, the power of the malik to cause harm became greatly exaggerated. The following account of affliction by a *malik devata* further reinforces this point:[46]

In Silaunja, the malik had purchased Banaut and Banautin from the south. They killed my grandfather's brother, his four sons, and his grandsons. The problem was that since the malik trusted my grandfather's brother completely, he regularly pilfered the landlord's crop at nights and became somewhat prosperous. So he and his family became victims of Banaut and Banautin.

When anyone was caught stealing from the landlord's field or his threshing yard, he was severely beaten and punished by the malik's employee.[47] But those who got away undetected had to contend with the *malik devata*. Unlike punishment by landlords, the wrath of enormously powerful *malik devatas* could bring untimely death. Disorderly and unpredictable death, however, threatened the cyclical reproduction of death and regeneration. But so did theft. Since nature, in the form of paddy fields, bore the imprint of unequal social relations, a violation of the transactional norms in the social sphere also disrupted the natural order of things. *Malik devata*s struck with terrible fury to ensure the reproduction of this order. Their power paralleled that of the landlord. But the two were not identical: in *malik devata*s, the power of landlords was reconstructed in menacing terms.

Sometimes, to pre-empt spirit affliction, kamias propitiated *malik devata*s before going to the landlord's field to steal grain. But prior propitiation meant that it was no longer theft in the eyes of ghosts: it was a gift. It may be argued that the ghost's generosity simply reflected the benefaction that the landlord showed at certain times of the year. But while the generosity of the landlord was founded on the collective apprehension of unequal reciprocity as liberality, the gift from the *malik devata* was activated by disengaging the ghost from its relation with the malik. Whereas in one case, benefaction was based on social relations, in the other, social relations were denied. Prior propitiation of the ghost established reciprocal exchange between kamias and nature unencumbered by property.

Theft was a socially illicit mode of redistributing resources. In the absence of legitimate methods, kamias resorted to stealing. But in doing so they sometimes took care to represent it as a licit act, as a gift. This was not, however, always the case. According to one account, it appears that prior propitiation was regarded successful only when the relations between the *malik devata* and the landlord were tenuous:[48]

Sodhar Manjhi told me that his grandfather, Pancham Bhuinya, used to say that kamias propitiated *malik devata* when it was angry with the landlord. Then someone could even steal the grain from the field and he would go undetected and unpunished.

Ghosts were by nature fickle. So, as the above account suggests, kamias looked for signs which expressed the ghosts' temporary alienation from landlords. At such times, they were more likely to take risks and steal grain, hoping that the ghost would not punish them. The proof that the *malik devata* was temporarily disenchanted with the landlord, and that the ghost had rewarded its propitiation by kamias, came in the results of successful theft: if kamias got away without any harm, it proved that the ghost was alienated from the landlord. But there were also times when ghosts were strongly identified with landlords. At such times, ghosts represented the power of their landlords in fantastic forms; then ghosts were potentially malevolent, capable of causing much harm.

When a Bhuinya woman gave birth in her husband's village, the *malik devata* from her natal village announced its arrival by causing sickness in the family.[49] Since the woman had grown up on grain that belonged to the landlord, the *malik devata* claimed to have a role in the birth of her child. For that, it demanded propitiation.[50] It was appeased with suitable offerings and installed in the house as *chalani devata* (literally, a travelling ghost). It did not displace the local *malik devata*, but, disengaged from its pivotal role in assisting agricultural operations in its new abode, it became unquestionably malevolent; sorcerers used it to cause misfortune.[51] As *chalani devata*, the ghost's identification with the landlord was complete, and now that it was outside the village where it had been a *malik devata*, kamias defined it as a malevolent ghost. In doing so, kamias put the maliks' power in an unfavourable light. But insofar as kamias refrained from attributing complete malevolence to *malik devatas*, they accepted the overall hegemony of maliks.

In those situations where the *malik devata*'s ties with the landlord were most prominent, the ghost was evil. When distribution of resources was involved, the ghost identified strongly with the malik. It guarded his property and represented his power as all-encompassing. It stressed kamia–malik relations over all other ties. But in the sphere of production, its role was different. It intervened, along with other ghosts, to facilitate agricultural production. In agrarian rites, the ghost's ties were stretched to include the entire community. While the social distribution and temporal succession of ritual tasks in *asarhi puja* inscribed the practice with unequal social relations, all ghosts, including the *malik devata*, intervened for the community as a whole. At these times, the *malik devata*'s connection with the landlord served to represent his power in benign terms, and the ghost did not bear a malevolent character. It was precisely because of its ambivalence that the *malik devata* was effective as a symbol of the landlord's authority.

Although neither oral nor written records exist about the practice of ghost purchase in the precolonial period, there is no reason to deny the possibility of its existence in those times. However, one feature in the practice of buying ghosts was particular to the colonial period. This was related to the reconstitution of rural power on the basis of land control in the colonial period. Unlike precolonial Bihar, when maliks exercised direct control over people, the power of landlords in the colonial period was based directly on the amount of land they controlled through various tenurial rights. Appropriation of ghosts as *malik devatas* at a time when social relations were being reconstituted through appropriation of land lent a new dimension to the dialectic between spirit cult practices and kamia–malik relations.

CONCLUSION

Like Tio, the devil worshipped by the miners in Bolivia,[52] the *malik devata* represented subordination of the Bhuinyas by landlords. But whereas Tio expressed the alienation of miners from capitalist production, as Michael Taussig so eloquently argues, the *malik devata* of colonial Gaya echoed the power of landlords over kamias, based on land control. It is tempting to conclude that *malik devatas* simply reflected unequal relations between landlords and kamias. But this would be contrary to the logic of ritual practice. Following Bourdieu, I have argued that rituals were not mere executions of pre-existing rules. In fact, ritual practices were dynamic events in which social relations were actively reconstructed. Through propitiation of ancestors and spirits, people sought to deal with 'good' and 'bad' deaths. In doing so, they made spirit cults an arena for the reproduction of social order. Upper-caste ritual practices separated their ancestral spirits from lower-caste ghosts, but, when practical life required, they also propitiated low-caste spirits and conceded ritual specialization and cultural autonomy to the Bhuinyas. The cultural notions expressed through these may appear contradictory as long as we seek their logic outside practice. But seen from the point of view of aims, these seemingly contradictory practices were coherent: both restored harmony in relations between the living and the dead. The purchase of powerful ghosts, too, was connected to the practical task of assisting the regeneration of the dead, to give life to seeds from the previous harvest. But in this process, the social power of landlords was also reproduced. Just as some practices reproduced the caste hierarchy, the purchase, installation, and use of *malik devatas* reproduced the dominance of maliks. Kamia practices responded by attributing malevolence to the ghost in situations where it was closely identified with the landlord. It was through articulation of such contrary beliefs and strategies that spirit cult practices reproduced kamia–malik relations.

NOTES

This essay draws heavily from my unpublished dissertation entitled 'Production and the Reproduction of Bondage: Kamias and Maliks in South Bihar, c. 1300 to 1930s.' University of Pennsylvania, 1984. The research was carried out in 1981–2 and was supported by grants from the American Institute of Indian Studies and the Social Science Research Council and the American Council of Learned Societies.

1. Claude Meillasoux, in particular, has stressed the pivotal role of reproduction in production. See his 'From Reproduction to Production,' *Economy and Society*, 1, 1, 1972. Jack Goody's *Production and Reproduction: A Comparative Study of the Domestic Domain*, Cambridge: Cambridge University Press, 1976, draws correlations between the organization of domestic units and mode of agriculture without drawing the tight relationship that Meillasoux develops between the social reproduction of the production unit and the production organization. While these anthropologists tend to deal with those strategies of reproduction that relate to kin relations, this essay is concerned with the reproduction of relations between classes.

2. Jan Breman, *Patronage and Exploitation: Emerging Agrarian Relations in South Gujarat*, Berkeley and Los Angeles: University of California Press, 1974.

3. Scholars have too easily accepted the legal fiction that attributed long-term bondage of labourers to loans that they had received from the landholders. For a critique of this view and an alternative interpretation, see Gyan Prakash, 'Production and the Reproduction of Bondage': 243–62.

4. For a sophisticated comparative treatment of bondage from a supply and demand standpoint, see H.J. Niboer, *Slavery as an Industrial System*, 2nd edn, The Hague: M. Nijhoff, 1910.

5. Pierre Bourdieu, *Outline of a Theory of Practice*, Cambridge: Cambridge University Press, 1977: 22–30.

6. The oral and written data used in this essay refer to the period roughly between the 1850s and the 1930s. In addition to using references in the oral data itself, I used the vivid memories the people in the region had of the revenue settlement operations in 1914–15 and the earthquake in 1934 to date the occurrences referred to by informants in their testimonies.

7. For a recent discussion on this point, see Irfan Habib, 'Agrarian Economy', in Tapan Raychaudhuri and Irfan Habib (eds), *The Cambridge Economic History of India*, I, Cambridge: Cambridge University Press, 1982: 57.

8. Bihar State Archives (BSA), Patna Commissioner's Records; vol. 21 (1839) letter from the Officiating Superintendent of Khas Mahals, dated 10 January 1839, to the Officiating Commissioner of Revenue, Patna Division. Also see, Francis Buchanan, *An Account of the Districts of Bihar and Patna in 1811–12*, II, Patna: Bihar and Orissa Research Society, 1936: 564.

9. This conclusion is drawn from the oral history fieldwork that I conducted in 1981–2, and from the summary information on the caste composition of most though not all the villages in Gaya district contained in 'Village Notes', Gaya Collectorate Record Room (GCRR), compiled during the revenue settlement operations in 1911–18.

10. For a discussion of oral and written evidence on this point, see Prakash, 'Production and the Reproduction of Bondage', chs II and III.

11. Ibid.: 145–51.

12. This is developed in *ibid.*, ch. IV.

13. For Bodh Gaya monastery's expanding land control through legal titles, see Government of Bengal, *A Brief History of Bodh Gaya Math, District Gaya*, compiled by Rai Ram Anugrah Narayan Singh Bahadur under the orders of G.A. Grierson, Calcutta: Bengal Secretariat Press, 1893: 16–18.

14. L.S.S. O'Malley, *Bengal District Gazetteers: Gaya*, Calcutta: Bengal Secretariat Press, 1906: 74 (GDG).

15. GDG : 77. The term *bhut* means ghost, and *dak* stands for sorcerer. But the two terms are used by people as a pair in referring to spirits. When *dak* is used separately, it almost always refers to the spirit of a dead sorcerer.

16. This belief is to be found in the following statement made by Karu Manjhi, who, as a young boy, moved from his parental village Kajri to his wife's home in Sheorajpur sometime before 1914–15. 'My father died a long time ago (sometime before 1934). He died in Kajri. Since I had come to Sheorajpur, I made a *pinda* [shrine] for him here. Although his *kriya-karma* [mortuary rite] was done in Kajri and his body merged with the soil there, his *preta* would have wandered around in Kajri causing problems if I had not made a *pinda* for him.' (Karu Manjhi's oral account, Sheorajpur, 6 February 1982.)

17. Referring to the earthquake, Karu Manjhi remembered asking his father's *preta* to protect him. 'He could do so because he was a *preta*. He could see everything that we could not. He warned me once that the *dayan* [witch] would cause my roof to fall if I did not propitiate the *daks*. I did so and nothing happened.' (Karu Manjhi's oral testimony, Sheorajpur, 6 February 1982.) Interestingly, in proverbs dealing with agriculture, foresight was attributed to *dak* and *dakin* (a female ghost). This is evident in aphorisms noted by George Grierson in the late nineteenth century. 'If Aradra [the lunar asterism corresponding with the end of June and the beginning of July] does not rain at the commencement, and Hathiya [the lunar asterism corresponding with the first fortnight of October] at its end, saith Dak, hear, O Bhillari, the cultivator is crushed.' See George Grierson's *Bihar Peasant Life*, Calcutta: Bengal Secretariat Press, 1885; rpt Delhi, 1975: 276. Another similar proverb recorded by Grierson was the following. ' "When the clouds fly like the wings of the partridge, and when a widow smiles," saith Dak, "hear, O Dakini, the one is going to rain and the other to marry"' (ibid.: 280). Attribution of foreknowledge to ghosts accords well with the belief that spirits could see things that the living could not.

18. GDG : 78.

19. I did not come across any account of spirit affliction by heroic ancestors such as Tulsibir or any of the other birs.

20. See GDG : 77. In general, I found that the names of such spirits mostly ended with *dak or dano*. Although the meaning of these suffixes in their apparently Sanskrit roots is demon, spirits by these names were not regarded as evil at all times. In describing these spirits, the informants frequently used the term *balwan* (powerful) and *khatarnak* (dangerous). The attribution of potentially beneficial prescience to ghosts in proverbs dealing with agriculture (see note 5) suggests that *daks* were not thought of as evil at all times.

21. Karu Manjhi's oral account, Sheorajpur, 6 February 1982.

22. Karu Manjhi's oral account, Sheorajpur, 6 February 1982. Ramjani, according to my informants, died soon after the revenue survey and settlement operations and before the earthquake in 1934, making the between period 1914 (when survey operations in the village occurred) and 1934 the time when he became a spirit. Although called *malik devata*, Ramjani Dak was different from ghosts in the landlords' service who were also known by the name *malik devata*. The ancestral *malik devatas* were simply powerful ancestral ghosts but their writ did not run beyond the house.

23. GDG : 78.

24. Most accounts of spirit affliction concerned ghosts rather than ancestors who had died natural deaths. In speaking of cases of spirit affliction by powerful spirits, informants mentioned *daks* and *dano* rather than ancestral spirits. The few cases of harm caused by ancestors that I came across involved insufficient propitiation of ancestors. For instance, Keso Bhuinya's father was once afflicted by his ancestors when he slighted them with insufficient offering. Keso concluded this account by remarking that ancestors were 'quiet spirits. They sit and watch over you, they protect you'. Keso Bhuinya's oral testimony, Bakraur, 12 February 1982.

25. Maurice Bloch and Jonathan Parry, 'Introduction', in *Death and Regeneration of Life*, Cambridge: Cambridge University Press, 1982: 15.

26. Keso Bhuinya's oral testimony, Bakraur, 12 February 1982. No doubt this reflects the present belief. But there is no reason to think that it was any different in the past. In fact, Keso Bhuinya said that his father told him the same thing when his grandfather died.

27. GDG : 77
28. Oral testimony of Chandra Shekhar Lall, Bakraur, 4 September 1982.
29. Much of the above is based on O'Malley's description. See GDG: 62–72, *passim*.
30. Throughout southern Gaya, the Bhuinyas were regarded as ritual specialists in spirit cults. S.C. Roy reported in 1932 that throughout Chotanagpur the descendants of the earliest settlers acted invariably as ritual specialists in spirit worship. See his 'Report of Anthropological Work in 1930–31: Chotanagpur, the Chutias and the Bhuiyas', *Journal of Bihar and Orissa Research Society*, 18, 1932: 51–78.
31. What follows is based on the oral testimony of Karu Manjhi, Sheorajpur, 6 February 1982.
32. Bourdieu, *Outline*: 109.
33. Oral testimony of Panchu Bhuinya, Sheorajpur, 3 September 1982.
34. Memories of these ghosts and of incidents associated with them were widespread in Gaya. But these were different from *malik devatas* which reigned within the house.
35. GDG : 76.
36. Oral testimony of Karu Manjhi, Sheorajpur, 16 February 1982.
37. 'A peculiar feature of the power of *ojhas* over *bhuts* is found in the actual purchase and sale of them, which is said to be practised by some low castes in the jungle-covered tracts to the south of the district. The *bhut*, when under proper control, is a valuable possession and becomes a marketable commodity. When the sale has been arranged, the *ojha* hands over a corked bamboo cylinder which is supposed to contain the *bhut*: this is then taken to the place usually under a tree, at which it is intended that the *bhut* should in future reside.' GDG: 76.
38. Ibid.
39. BSA; Gaya Collectorate Records, vol. 4a (issue side), letter from the Deputy Magistrate of Nawada, dated 10 May 1852.
40. GCRR; 'Village Notes', Barachatti thana no. 266, village Charaili.
41. Ibid.
42. GDG : 76.
43. Karu Manjhi's oral testimony, Sheorajpur, 16 February 1982. According to Karu Manjhi, he learnt of this incident from Sodhar Bhuinya, who, in turn, had been told about it by his grandfather, Pancham Bhuinya during whose life it had apparently happened. As Karu was a small boy at the time of the survey operations in 1914–15, and since, according to him, Sodhar Bhuinya was older than he (he was already working in agriculture as a kamia when Karu was a young boy), the date of this incident which occurred during Pancham Bhuinya's life can be placed well into the nineteenth century.
44. Keso Bhuinya's oral testimony, Bakraur, 13 February 1982. Since Bithal Bhuinya died before Pyare Lall, whose death, according to his family records, occurred in 1926, this incident can be placed in the early part of the twentieth century.
45. This is what Keso was told by his grandfather.
46. Oral testimony of Bangali Manjhi, Bakraur, 16 February 1982. According to him, this happened after the survey operations in 1914–15, but I was unable to determine a more precise date.
47. Karu Manjhi's oral testimony, Sheorajpur, 3 March 1982.
48. Ibid.
49. Deoki Bhuinya's oral testimony, Bakraur, 16 March 1982.
50. This was the explanation given by the informants. The arrival of the *malik devata* was of course known only if some misfortune occurred. Otherwise, presumably the ghost was not known to have travelled to the woman's married home. This practice raises an interesting speculation. Does this indicate that maliks exercised a tight control over the kamias' progeny in the past, that by virtue of their authority and power even over villages and lands that they did not hold directly, they controlled the marriage circles of their kamias? Control over males through a variety of transactions and domination over the progeny of women through the tight control of marriage and through ghosts would have given them a mastery over reproduction and production. Once, however, the malik's power became defined strictly by land control, as

it did in the colonial period, such a strategy of domination over the progeny of women who lived on lands not held by him directly could not work.

51. Memories of incidents of setting spirits upon one's enemies were many. One that I recorded concerned a peasant, Prasad Mahto, setting Bhainsasur (who had come to Bakraur as a *chalani devata*) on his own brother-in-law because he had taken a corn cob from Prasad Mahto's field without his permission. Soon afterwards, the brother-in-law died. (Bangali Manjhi's oral testimony, Bakraur, 16 February 1982.)

52. See Michael T. Taussig's *The Devil and Commodity Fetishism in South America*, Chapel Hill: University of North Carolina Press, 1980, pt III.

TWELVE

Minority Histories, Subaltern Pasts

Dipesh Chakrabarty

ecent struggles and debates around the rather tentative concept of multiculturalism in
Western democracies have often fuelled discussions of minority histories. As the
writing of history has increasingly become entangled with the 'politics and production
of identity' after the Second World War, the question has arisen in all democracies of whether
to include in the history of the nation histories of previously excluded groups. In the 1960s,
this list usually contained names of subaltern social groups and classes, such as, former slaves,
working classes, convicts, and women. This mode of writing history came to be known in the
1970s as history from below. Under pressure from growing demands for democratizing further
the discipline of history, this list was expanded in the 1970s and 1980s to include the so-
called ethnic groups, indigenous peoples, children and the old, and gays, lesbians, and other
minorities. The expression 'minority histories' has come to refer to all those pasts on whose
behalf democratically minded historians have fought the exclusions and omissions of
mainstream narratives of the nation. Official or officially blessed accounts of the nation's past
have been challenged in many countries by the champions of minority histories. Postmodern
critiques of 'grand narratives' have been used to question single narratives of the nation.
Minority histories, one may say, in part express the struggle for inclusion and representation
that are characteristic of liberal and representative democracies.

Minority histories as such do not have to raise any fundamental questions about the
discipline of history. Practising academic historians are often more concerned with the
distinction between good and bad histories than with the question of who might own a
particular piece of the past. Bad histories, it is assumed sometimes, give rise to bad politics. As
Eric Hobsbawm says in a recent article, 'bad history is not harmless history. It is dangerous'.[1]
'Good histories', on the other hand, are supposed to enrich the subject matter of history and
make it more representative of society as a whole. Begun in an oppositional mode, minority
histories can indeed end up as additional instances of good history. The transformation of
once-oppositional, minority histories into good histories illustrates how the mechanism of
incorporation works in the discipline of history.

MINORITY HISTORIES: ASSIMILATION AND RESISTANCE

The process through which texts acquire canonical status in the academic discipline of history in Anglo-American universities is different from the corresponding process in literature/English departments. History is a subject primarily concerned with the crafting of narratives. Any account of the past can be absorbed into, and thus made to enrich, the mainstream of historical discourse so long two questions are answered in the affirmative: Can the story be told/crafted? And does it allow for a rationally defensible point of view or position from which to tell the story? The first question, that of crafting a story, has enriched the discipline for a long time by challenging historians to be imaginative and creative both in their research and narrative strategies. How do you write the histories of suppressed groups? How do you construct a narrative of a group or class that has not left its own sources? Questions of this kind often stimulate innovation in historians' practices. The point that the authorial position should be rationally defensible is also of critical importance. The author's position may reflect an ideology, a moral choice, or a political philosophy, but the choices are not unlimited. A madman's narrative is not history. Nor can a preference that is arbitrary or just personal—based on sheer taste, say—give us rationally defensible principles for narration (at best the narrative will count as fiction and not history). The investment in a certain kind of rationality and in a particular understanding of the 'real' means that history's—the discipline's—exclusions are ultimately epistemological.

Consider for a moment the results of incorporating into the discourse of history the pasts of major groups such as the working classes and women. History has not been the same since Thompson and Hobsbawm took up their pens to make the working classes look like major actors in society. Feminist interventions of the last two decades have also had an unquestionable impact on contemporary historical imagination. Does the incorporation of these radical moves into the mainstream of the discipline change the nature of historical discourse? Of course it does. But the answer to the question, did such incorporation call the discipline into any kind of crisis? is more complicated. In mastering the problems of telling the stories of groups hitherto overlooked—particularly under circumstances in which the usual archives do not exist—the discipline of history renews and maintains itself. This inclusion appeals to the sense of democracy that impels the discipline ever outward from its core.

The point that historical narratives require a certain minimum investment in rationality has recently been made in the book *Telling the Truth about History*.[2] The question of the relationship between postmodernism, minority histories, and postwar democracies is at the heart of this book authored jointly by three leading feminist historians of the United States. To the extent that the authors see in postmodernism the possibility of multiple narratives and multiple ways of crafting these narratives, they welcome its influence. However, the book registers a strong degree of discomfiture when the authors encounter arguments that in effect use the idea of multiplicity of narratives to question any idea of truth or facts. If minority histories go to the extent of questioning the very idea of fact or evidence, then, the authors ask, how would one find ways of adjudicating between competing claims in public life? Would not the absence of a certain minimum agreement about what constitutes fact and evidence seriously fragment the body politic in the United States of America, and would not that in turn impair the capacity of the nation to function as a whole? Hence the authors recommend a pragmatic idea of 'workable truths', which would be based on a shared, rational under-standing of historical facts and evidence. For a nation to function effectively even while eschewing any claims to a superior, overarching grand narrative, these truths must be maintained in order for institutions and groups to be able to adjudicate between conflicting stories and interpretations.

Historians, regardless of their ideological moorings, display a remarkable consensus when it comes to defending history's methodological ties to a certain understanding of rationality. Georg Iggers's recent textbook on twentieth-century historiography emphasizes this connection between facticity and rationality in determining what may or may not constitute historical evidence: 'Peter Novick has in my opinion rightly maintained that objectivity is unattainable in history; the historian can hope for nothing more than plausibility. But plausibility obviously rests not on the arbitrary invention of an historical account but involves *rational* strategies of determining what in fact is plausible.'[3] Hobsbawm echoes sentiments not dissimilar to those expressed by others in the profession: 'The fashion for what (at least in Anglo-Saxon academic discourse) is known by the vague term "postmodernism" has fortunately not gained as much ground among historians as among literary and cultural theorists and social anthropologists, even in the USA. . . . [I]t [postmodernism] throws doubt on the distinction between fact and fiction, objective reality and conceptual discourse. It is profoundly relativist.'[4]

What these historians oppose in postmodernism is the latter's failure, at least in their eyes, to meet the condition of rationality for incorporating narratives into the discipline of history. *Telling the Truth about History* thus demonstrates the continuing relevance of the two conditions that sustain history's connection to public life: democracy requires hitherto neglected groups to tell their histories, and these different histories come together in accepting shared rational and evidentiary rules. Successfully incorporated minority histories may then be likened to yesterday's revolutionaries who become today's gentlemen. Their success helps routinize innovation.

From Minority Histories to Subaltern Pasts

But this is not the only fate possible. The debate about minority histories allows for alternative understandings of the expression minority itself. Minority and majority are, as we know, not natural entities; they are constructions. The popular meanings of the words 'majority' and 'minority' are statistical. But the semantic fields of the words contain another idea: of being a 'minor' or a 'major' figure in a given context. For example, the Europeans, numerically speaking, are a minority in the total pool of humanity today and have been so for a long while, yet their colonialism in the nineteenth century was based on certain ideas about major and minor. For example, they often assumed that their histories contained the majority instances of norms that every other human society should aspire to; compared to them, others were still the minors for whom they, the 'adults' of the world, had to take charge, and so on. So numerical advantage by itself is no guarantor of a major/majority status. Sometimes, you can be a larger group than the dominant one, but your history would still qualify as minor/minority history.

The problem of minority histories thus leads us to the question of what may be called the minority of some particular pasts. Some constructions and experiences of the past stay minor in the sense that their very incorporation into historical narratives converts them into pasts 'of lesser importance' vis-à-vis dominant understandings of what constitutes fact (and evidence and hence wis-à-wis the underlying principle of rationality) in the practices of professional history. Such minor pasts are those experiences of the past that always have to be assigned to an 'inferior' or 'marginal' position as they are translated into the academic historian's language. These are pasts that are treated, to use an expression of Kant's, as instances of human 'immaturity', pasts that do not prepare us for either democracy or citizenly practices because they are not based on the deployment of reason in public life.[5]

My use of the word 'minor' then does not quite reproduce the nuances of the way the word has been used in literary theory following Deleuze and Guattari's interpretation of Kafka, but there is some similarity between the two uses. Just as the minor in literature implies 'a critique of narratives of identity' and refuses 'to represent the attainment of autonomous subjectivity that is the ultimate aim of the major narrative', the minor in my use similarly functions to cast doubt on the major.[6] For me, it describes relationships to the past that the 'rationality' of the historian's methods necessarily makes minor or inferior, as something 'nonrational' in the course of, and as a result of, its own operation. And yet these relations return, I argue, as an implicit element of the conditions that make it possible for us to historicize. To anticipate my conclusion, I will try to show how the capacity (of the modern person) to historicize actually depends on his or her ability to participate in nonmodern relationships to the past that are made subordinate in the moment of historicization. History writing assumes plural ways of being in the world.

Let me call these subordinated relations to the past 'subaltern' pasts. They are marginalized not because of any conscious intentions but because they represent moments or points at which the archive that the historian mines develops a degree of intractability with respect to the aims of professional history. In other words, these are pasts that resist historicization, just as there may be moments in ethnographic research that resist the doing of ethnography.[7] Subaltern pasts, in my sense of the term, do not belong exclusively to socially subordinate or subaltern groups, nor to minority identities alone. Elite and dominant groups can also have subaltern pasts to the extent that they participate in life-worlds subordinated by the major narratives of the dominant institutions. I illustrate my proposition with a particular instance of subaltern pasts, which comes from an essay by the founder of the Subaltern Studies group, Ranajit Guha. Since Guha and the group have been my teachers in many ways, I offer my remarks not in a hostile spirit of criticism but in a spirit of self-examination, for my aim is to understand what historicizing the past does and does not do. With that caveat, let me proceed.

SUBALTERN PASTS: AN EXAMPLE

As is well known, an explicit aim of Subaltern Studies was to write the subaltern classes into the history of nationalism and the nation, and to combat all elitist biases in the writing of history. To make the subalterns the sovereign subject of history, to listen to their voices, to take their experiences and thought (and not just their material circumstances) seriously—these were goals we had deliberately and publicly set ourselves. These original intellectual ambitions and the desire to enact them were political in that they were connected to modern understandings of democratic public life. They did not necessarily come from the lives of the subaltern classes themselves, though one of our objectives, as in the British tradition of history from below, was to ground the struggle for democracy in India in the facts of subaltern history. Looking back, however, I see the problem of subaltern pasts dogging the enterprise of Subaltern Studies from the very outset. Indeed, it is arguable that what differentiates the Subaltern Studies project from the older tradition of history from below is the self-critical awareness of this problem in the writings of the historians associated with this group.

Ranajit Guha's celebrated and brilliant essay, 'The Prose of Counter-Insurgency', was published in an early volume of *Subaltern Studies* and is now justly considered a classic of the genre. A certain paradox that results precisely from the historian's attempt to bring the histories of the subaltern classes into the mainstream of the discourse of history, it seems to me, haunts the exercise Guha undertakes in this essay. A principal aim of Guha's essay was to use the 1855 rebellion of the Santals to demonstrate a cardinal principle of subaltern history: making the insurgent's consciousness the mainstay of a narrative about rebellion. (The Santals were a tribal group in Bengal and Bihar who rebelled against both the British and nonlocal Indians in 1855.) Guha put it in words that capture the spirit of early Subaltern Studies: 'Yet this consciousness [the consciousness of the rebellious peasant] seems to have received little notice in the literature on the subject. Historiography has been content to deal with the peasant rebel merely as an empirical person or a member of a class, but not as an entity whose will and reason constituted the praxis called rebellion. . . . [I]nsurgency is regarded as *external* to the peasant's consciousness and Cause is made to stand in as a phantom surrogate for Reason, the logic of that consciousness.'[8]

The critical phrase here is 'the logic of that consciousness', which marks the analytical distance Guha, the historian, has to take from the object of his research, which is this consciousness itself. For in pursuing the history of the Santal rebellion of 1855, Guha unsurprisingly came across a phenomenon common in the lives of the peasants: the agency of supernatural beings. Santal leaders explained the rebellion in supernatural terms, as an act carried out at the behest of the Santal god, Thakur. Guha draws our attention to the evidence and underscores how important this understanding was to the rebels themselves. The leaders of the rebellion, Sidhu and Kanu, said that Thakur had assured them that British bullets would not harm the devotee-rebels. Guha takes care to avoid any instrumental or elitist reading of these statements. He writes: 'These were not public pronouncements meant to impress their followers. . . . [T]hese were words of captives facing execution. Addressed to hostile interrogators in military encampments they could have little use as propaganda. Uttered by men of a tribe which, according to all accounts had not yet learnt to lie, these represented the truth and nothing but the truth for their speakers.'[9]

A tension inherent in the project of Subaltern Studies becomes perceptible here in Guha's analysis. His phrase 'logic of consciousness' or his idea of a truth that was only 'truth for their speakers' are all acts of assuming a critical distance from that which he is trying to understand. Taken literally, the rebel peasants' statement shows the subaltern himself as refusing agency or subjecthood. 'I rebelled,' he says, 'because Thakur made an appearance and told me to rebel.' In their own words, as reported by the colonial scribe: 'Kanoo and Sedoo Manjee are not fighting. The Thacoor himself will fight.' In his own telling, then, the subaltern is not necessarily the subject of his or her history, but in the history of Subaltern Studies or in any democratically minded history, he or she is. What does it mean, then, when we both take the subaltern's views seriously—the subaltern ascribes the agency for their rebellion to some god—and want to confer on the subaltern agency or subjecthood in their own history, a status the subaltern's statement denies?

Guha's strategy for negotiating this dilemma unfolds in the following manner. His first move, against practices common in secular or Marxist historiography, is to resist analyses that see religion simply as a displaced manifestation of human relationships that are in themselves secular and worldly (class, power, economy, and so on). Guha was conscious that his was not a simple exercise in demystification:

Religiosity was, by all accounts, central to the *hool* (rebellion). The notion of power which inspired it . . . [was] explicitly religious in character. It was not that power was a content wrapped up in a form external to it called religion. . . . Hence the attribution of the rising to a divine command rather than to any particular grievance; the enactment of rituals both before (e.g. propitiatory ceremonies to ward off the apocalypse of the Primeval Serpents...) and during the uprising (worshipping the goddess Durga, bathing in the Ganges, etc.); the generation and circulation of myth is its characteristic vehicle—rumour.[10]

But in spite of Guha's desire to listen to the rebel voice seriously, his analysis cannot offer the Thakur the same place of agency in the story of the rebellion that the Santals' statements had given him. A narrative strategy that is rationally defensible in the modern understanding of what constitutes public life—and the historians speak in the public sphere—cannot be based on a relationship that allows the divine or the supernatural a direct hand in the affairs of the world. The Santal leaders' own understanding of the rebellion does not directly serve the historical cause of democracy or citizenship or socialism. It needs to be reinterpreted. Historians will grant the supernatural a place in somebody's belief system or ritual practices, but to ascribe to it any real agency in historical events will go against the rules of evidence that gives historical discourse procedures for settling disputes about the past.

The Protestant theologian-hermeneutist Rudolf Bultmann has written illuminatingly on this problem. 'The historical method,' says Bultmann, 'includes the presupposition that history is a unity in the sense of a closed continuum of effects in which individual events are connected by the succession of cause and effect.' By this, Bultmann does not reduce the historical sciences to a mechanical understanding of the world. He qualifies his statement by adding:

This does not mean that the process of history is determined by the causal law and that there are no free decisions of men whose actions determine the course of historical happenings. But even a free decision does not happen without a cause, without a motive; and the task of the historian is to come to know the motives of actions. All decisions and all deeds have their causes and consequences; and the historical method presupposes that it is possible in principle to exhibit these and their connection and thus to understand the whole historical process as a closed unity.

Here Bultmann draws a conclusion that allows us to see the gap that must separate the set of explanatory principles that the historian employs to explain the Santal rebellion from the set that the Santals themselves might use (even after assuming some principles might be shared between them). I find Bultmann's conclusion entirely relevant to our discussion of subaltern pasts:

This closedness [the presupposed, 'closed unity' of the historical process] means that the continuum of historical happenings cannot be rent by the interference of supernatural, transcendent powers and that therefore there is no 'miracle' in this sense of the word. Such a miracle would be an event whose cause did not lie within history. While, for example, the Old Testament narrative speaks of an interference by God in history, historical science cannot demonstrate such an act of God, but merely perceives that there are those who believe in it. To be sure, as historical science, it may not assert that such a faith is an illusion and that God has not acted in history. But it itself as science cannot perceive such an act and reckon on the basis of it; it can only leave every man free to determine whether he wants to see an act of God in a historical event that it itself understands in terms of that event's immanent historical causes.[11]

Fundamentally, then, the Santal's statement that God was the main instigator of the rebellion has to be anthropologized (that is, converted into somebody's belief or made into an object of anthropological analysis) before it finds a place in the historian's narrative. Guha's position with respect to the Santal's own understanding of the event becomes a combination of the anthropologist's politeness—'I respect your beliefs but they are not mine'—and a Marxist (or modern) tendency to see 'religion' in modern public life as a form of alienated or displaced consciousness. '[I]n sum,' he writes, 'it is not possible to speak of insurgency in this case except as a religious consciousness,' and yet hastens to add: 'except that is, as a massive, demonstration of self-estrangement (to borrow Marx's term for the very essence of religiosity) which made the rebel look upon their project as predicated on a will other than their own.'[12]

Here is a case of what I have called subaltern pasts, pasts that cannot ever enter academic history as belonging to the historian's own position. These days one can devise strategies of multivocal histories in which we hear subaltern voices more clearly than we did in the early phase of Subaltern Studies. One may even refrain from assimilating these different voices to any one voice and deliberately leave loose ends in one's narrative (as does Shahid Amin in his *Events, Memory, Metaphor*).[13] But the point is that the historian, as historian and unlike the Santal, cannot invoke the supernatural in explaining/describing an event.

THE POLITICS OF SUBALTERN PASTS

The act of championing minority histories has resulted in discoveries of subaltern pasts, constructions of historicity that help us see the limits to modes of viewing enshrined in the practices of the discipline of history. Why? Because the discipline of history—as has been argued by many (from Greg Dening to David Cohen in recent times)—is only one among ways of remembering the past.[14] In Guha's essay, the resistance that the 'historical evidence' offers to the historian's reading of the past—a Santal god, Thakur, stands between the democratic-Marxist historian and the Santals in the matter of deciding who is the subject of history—produces minor or subaltern pasts in the very process of weaving modern historical narratives. Subaltern pasts are like stubborn knots that stand out and break up the otherwise evenly woven surface of the fabric. When we do minority histories within the democratic project of including all groups and peoples within mainstream history, we both hear and anthropologize the Santal at the same time. We cannot write history from within what we regard as their beliefs. We thus produce 'good', not subversive, histories, which conform to the protocols of the discipline.

An appreciation of this problem has led to a series of attempts to craft histories differently, to allow for a certain measure of equality between historians' histories and other constructions of the past. Some scholars now *perform* the limits of history in various ways: by fictionalizing the past, experimenting to see how films and history might intersect in the new discipline of cultural studies, studying memory rather than just history, playing around with forms of writing, and other similar means.[15] The kind of disciplinary consensus around the historian's methods that was once—say, in the 1960s—represented (in Anglo-American universities at least) by 'theory' or 'methods' courses that routinely dished out Collingwood or Carr or Bloch as staple for historians has now begun to be questioned, at least by those involved in writing histories of marginalized groups of non-Western peoples. This does not necessarily mean methodological anarchy (though some feel insecure enough to fear this), or that Collingwood, et al. have become irrelevant, but it does mean that E.H. Carr's question. 'What is History?' needs to be asked again for our own times. The pressure of pluralism inherent in the languages and moves of minority histories has resulted in methodological and epistemological questioning of what the very business of writing history is all about.

Only the future will tell how these questions will resolve themselves, but one thing is clear: the question of including minorities in the history of the nation has turned out to be a much more complex problem than a simple operation of applying some already settled methods to a new set of archives and adding the results to the existing collective wisdom of historiography. The additive, 'building-block' approach to knowledge has broken down. What has become an open question is: Are there experiences of the past that cannot be captured by the methods of the discipline, or which at least show the limits of the discipline? Fears that such questioning will lead to an outbreak of irrationalism, that some kind of postmodern madness will spread through Historyland, seem extreme, for the discipline is still securely tied to the positivist impulses of modern bureaucracies, the judiciary, and to the instruments of governmentality. Hobsbawm, for instance, provides some unwitting evidence of history's close ties to law and other instruments of government. He writes: 'The procedures of the law court, which insist on the supremacy of evidence as much as historical researchers, and often in much the same manner, demonstrate that difference between historical fact and falsehood is not ideological. . . . When an innocent person is tried for murder, and wishes to prove his or [her] innocence, what is required is the techniques not of the "postmodern" theorist, but of the old-fashioned historian.'[16] This is why Hobsbawm would argue that minority histories must also conform to the protocols of 'good history', for history speaks to forms of representative democracy and social justice that liberalism or Marxism—in their significantly different ways—have already made familiar.

But minority histories can do more than that. The task of producing minority histories has, under the pressure precisely of a deepening demand for democracy, become a double task. I may put it thus: 'good' minority history is about expanding the scope of social justice and representative democracy, but the talk about the 'limits of history', on the other hand, is about struggling, or even groping, for nonstatist forms of democracy that we cannot, not yet, either understand or envisage completely. This is so because in the mode of being attentive to the minority of subaltern pasts, we stay with heterogeneities without seeking to reduce them to any overarching principle that speaks for an already given whole. There is no third voice that can assimilate the two different voices of Guha and the Santal leader; we have to stay with both, and with the gap between them that signals an irreducible plurality in our own experiences of historicity.

PASTS DEAD AND ALIVE

Let me explore a bit more the question of heterogeneity as I see it. We can—and we do usually in writing history—treat the Santal of the nineteenth century to doses of historicism and anthropology. We can, in other words, treat him as a signifier of other times and societies. This gesture maintains a subject-object relationship between the historians and the evidence. In this gesture, the past remains genuinely dead; the historian brings it 'alive' by telling the story.[17] But the Santal with his statement 'I did as my god told me to do' also faces us as a way of being in this world, and we could ask ourselves: Is that way of being a possibility for our own lives and for what we define as our present? Does the Santal help us to understand a principle by which we also live in certain instances? This question does not historicize or anthropologize the Santal, for the illustrative power of the Santal as an example of a present possibility does not depend on his otherness. Here the Santal stands as our contemporary, and the subject-object relationship that normally defines the historian's relationship to his or her archives is dissolved in this gesture. This gesture is akin to the one Kierkegaard developed in critiquing explanations that looked on the Biblical story of Abraham's sacrifice of his son Isaac either as deserving a historical or psychological explanation or as a metaphor or allegory, but never as a possibility for life open today to one who had faith. '[W]hy bother to remember a past,' asked Kierkegaard, 'that cannot be made into a present?'[18]

To stay with the heterogeneity of the moment when the historian meets with the peasant is, then, to stay with the difference between these two gestures. One is that of historicizing the Santal in the interest of a history of social justice and democracy; and the other, that of refusing to historicize and of seeing the Santal as a figure illuminating a life possibility for the present. Taken together, the two gestures put us in touch with the plural ways of being that make up our own present. The archives thus help bring to view the disjointed nature of any particular 'now' one may inhabit; that is the function of subaltern pasts.

A plurality of one's own being is a basic assumption in any hermeneutic of understanding that which seems different. Wilhelm von Humboldt put the point well in his 1821 address, 'On the Task of the Historian', delivered to the Berlin Academy of Sciences: 'Where two beings are separated by a total gap, no bridge of understanding extends from one to the other; in order to understand one another, they must have in another sense, already understood each other.'[19] We are not the same as the nineteenth-century Santal, and that Santal is not completely understood in the few statements quoted here. Empirical and historical Santals would also have had other relationships to modernity and capitalism that I have not considered. One could easily assume that Santals today would be very different from what they were in the nineteenth century, that they would inhabit a very different set of social circumstances. They might even produce professional historians; no one would deny these historical changes. But the nineteenth-century Santal—and indeed, if my argument is right, humans from any other period and region—are always in some sense our contemporaries: that would have to be the condition under which we can even begin to treat them as intelligible to us. Thus the writing of history must implicitly assume a plurality of times existing together, a disjuncture of the present with itself. Making visible this disjuncture is what subaltern pasts allow us to do.

An argument such as this is actually at the heart of modern historiography. One could argue, for instance, that the writing of medieval history for Europe depends on this assumed contemporaneity of the medieval, or what is the same thing, the noncontemporaneity of the present with itself. The medieval in Europe is often strongly associated with the supernatural and the magical. But what makes the historicizing of it possible is the fact that its basic characteristics are not completely foreign to us as moderns (which is not to deny the historical changes that separate the two). Historians of medieval Europe do not always consciously or explicitly make this point, but it is not difficult to see this operating as an assumption in their method. In the writings of Aron Gurevich, for example, the modern makes its pact with the medieval through the use of anthropology—that is, in the use of contemporary anthropological evidence from outside of Europe to make sense of the past of Europe. The strict temporal separation of the medieval from the modern is here belied by global contemporaneity. Peter Burke comments on this intellectual traffic between medieval Europe and contemporary anthropological evidence in introducing Gurevich's work. Gurevich, writes Burke, 'could already have been described in the 1960s as a historical anthropologist, and he did indeed draw inspiration from anthropology, most obviously from the economic anthropology of Bronislaw Malinowski and Marcel Mauss, who had begun his famous essay on the gift with a quotation from a medieval Scandinavian poem, the *Edda*'.[20]

Similar double moves—both of historicizing the medieval and of seeing it as contemporary with the present—can be seen at work in the following lines from Jacques Le Goff. Le Goff is seeking to explain here an aspect of European medieval sensibility: 'People today, even those who consult seers and fortune-tellers, call spirits to floating tables, or participate in black masses, recognize a frontier between the visible and the invisible, the natural and the supernatural. This was not true of medieval man. Not only was the visible for him merely the trace of the invisible; the supernatural overflowed into daily life at every turn.'[21] This is a complex passage. On the surface, it is about what separates the medieval from the modern. Yet this difference is what makes the medieval an ever-present possibility that haunts the practices of the modern—if only we, the moderns, could forget the 'frontier' between the visible and the invisible in Le Goff's description, we would be on the other side of that frontier. The people who consult seers today are modern in spite of themselves, for they engage in 'medieval' practices but are not able to overcome the habits of the modern. Yet the opening expression 'even today' contains a reference to the sense of surprise one feels at their anachronism, as if the very existence of these practices today opens up a hiatus in the continuity of the present by inserting into it something that is medieval-like and yet not quite so. Le Goff rescues the present by saying that even in the practice of these people, something irreducibly modern lingers—their distinction between the visible and the invisible. But it lingers only as a border, as something that defines the difference between the medieval and the modern. And since difference is always the name of a relationship, for it separates just as much as it connects (as, indeed, does a border), one could argue that alongside the present or the modern the medieval must linger as well, if only as that which exists as the limit or the border to the practices and discourses that define the modern.

Subaltern pasts are signposts of this border. With them we reach the limits of the discourse of history. The reason for this, as I have said, is that subaltern pasts do not give the historian any principle of narration that can be rationally defended in modern public life. Going a step further, one can see that this requirement for a rational principle, in turn, marks the deep connections that exist between modern constructions of public life and projects of social justice. It is not surprising that the Marxist scholar Fredric Jameson should begin his book *The Political Unconscious* with the injunction: 'Always historicize!' Jameson describes 'this slogan' as 'the one absolute and we may even say "transhistorical" imperative of all dialectical thought'.[22] If my point is right, then historicizing is not the problematic part of the injunction, the troubling term is 'always'. For the assumption of a continuous, homogeneous, infinitely stretched out time that makes possible the imagination of an always is put to question by subaltern pasts that makes the present, as Derrida says, 'out of joint'.[23]

ON TIME-KNOTS AND THE WRITING OF HISTORY

One historicizes only insofar as one belongs to a mode of being in the world that is aligned with the principle of 'disenchantment of the universe', which underlies knowledge in the social sciences (and I distinguish knowledge from practice).[24] But 'disenchantment' is not the only principle by which we world the earth. The supernatural can inhabit the world in these other modes of worlding, and not always as a problem or result of conscious belief or ideas. The point is made in an anecdote about the poet W. B. Yeats, whose interest in fairies and other nonhuman beings of Irish folk tales is well known. I tell the story as it has been told to me by my friend David Lloyd:

One day, in the period of his extensive researches on Irish folklore in rural Connemara, William Butler Yeats discovered a treasure. The treasure was a certain Mrs. Connolly who had the most magnificent repertoire of fairy stories that W.B. had ever come across. He sat with her in her little cottage from morning to dusk, listening and recording her stories, her proverbs and her lore. As twilight drew on, he had to leave and he stood up, still dazed by all that he had heard. Mrs. Connolly stood at the door as he left, and just as he reached the gate he turned back to her and said quietly, 'One more question Mrs. Connolly, if I may. Do you believe in the fairies?' Mrs. Connolly threw her head back and laughed. 'Oh, not at all Mr. Yeats, not at all.' W.B. paused, turned away and slouched off down the lane. Then he heard Mrs. Connolly's voice coming after him down the lane: 'But they're there, Mr. Yeats, they're there.'[25]

As old Mrs Connolly knew, and as we social scientists often forget, gods and spirits are not dependent on human beliefs for their own existence; what brings them to presence are our practices.[26] They are parts of the different ways of being through which we make the present manifold; it is precisely the disjunctures in the present that allow us to be with them. These other ways of being are not without questions of power or justice, but these questions are raised—to the extent that modern public institutions allow them space, for they do cut across one another—on terms other than those of the political-modern.

However—and I want to conclude by pointing this out—the relation between what I have called subaltern pasts and the practice of historicizing is not one of mutual exclusion. It is because we already have experience of that which makes the present noncontemporaneous with itself that we can actually historicize. Thus what allows historians to historicize the medieval or the ancient is the very fact these worlds are never completely lost. We inhabit their fragments even when we classify ourselves as modern and secular. It is because we live in time-knots that we can undertake the exercise of straightening out, as it were, some part of the knot (which is how we might think of chronology).[27]

Time, as the expression goes in my language, situates us within the structure of a *granthi*; hence the Bengali word *shomoy-granthi*, *shomoy* meaning 'time' and *granthi* referring to joints of various kinds, from the complex formation of knuckles on our fingers to the joints on a bamboo stick. That is why one may have two relationships with the Santal. First, we can situate ourselves as a modern subject for whom the Santal's life-world is an object of historical study and explanation. But we can also look on the Santal as someone illuminating possibilities for our own life-worlds. If my argument is right, then the second relationship is prior to the first one. It is what makes the first relationship possible.

Subaltern pasts thus act as a supplement to the historian's pasts. They are supplementary in a Derridean sense—they enable history, the discipline, to be what it is and yet at the same time help to show what its limits are. In calling attention to the limits of historicizing, they help us distance ourselves from the imperious instincts of the discipline—the idea that *everything* can be historicized or that one should *always* historicize. Subaltern pasts return us to a sense of the limited good that modern historical consciousness is. Gadamer once put the point well in the course of discussing Heidegger's philosophy. He said: 'The experience of history, which we ourselves have, is . . . covered only to a small degree by that which we would name *historical consciousness*.'[28] Subaltern pasts remind us that a relation of contemporaneity between the nonmodern and the modern, a shared and constant now, which expresses itself on the historical plane but the character of which is ontological, is what allows historical time to unfold. This ontological 'now' precedes the historical gap that the historian's methods both assume and posit between the 'there-and-then' and the 'here-and-now'. Thus what underlies our capacity to historicize is our capacity not to. What gives us a point of entry into the times of gods and spirits—times that are seemingly very different from the empty, secular, and homogeneous time of history—is that they are never completely alien; we inhabit them to begin with.

The historian's hermeneutic, as Humboldt suggested in 1821, proceeds from an unstated and assumed premise of identification that is later disavowed in the subject-object relationship. What I have called subaltern pasts may be thought of as intimations we receive—while engaged in the specific activity of historicizing—of a shared, unhistoricizable, and ontological now. This now is, I have tried to suggest, what fundamentally rends the seriality of historical time and makes any particular moment of the historical present out of joint with itself.

NOTES

1. Eric Hobsbawm, 'Identity History Is Not Enough', in *On History*, London: Weidenfeld and Nicholson, 1997: 277. Hobsbawm unfortunately overlooks the point that modern European imperialism in India and elsewhere used 'good history' to justify the subjugation of peoples who, according to European thinkers, had 'myths' but no sense of history.
2. Joyce Appleby, Lynn Hunt, and Margaret Jacob, *Telling the Truth about History*, New York: W.W. Norton, 1994.
3. Cf. Georg G. Iggers, *Historiography in the Twentieth Century: From Scientific Objectivity to the Postmodern Challenge*, Hanover, N.H., and London: Wesleyan University Press, 1997: 145 (emphasis added).

4. Hobsbawm, 'Identity History': 271.

5. Immanuel Kant, 'An Answer to the Question: What Is Enlightenment?' (1784), in *Perpetual Peace and Other Essays*, tr. Ted Humphrey, Indianapolis: Hackett, 1983: 41–8.

6. See David Lloyd, *Nationalism and Minor Literature: James Clarence Mangan and the Emergence of Irish Cultural Nationalism*, Berkeley and Los Angeles: University of California Press, 1987: 19–20. Also Gilles Deleuze and Felix Guattari, *Kafka: Toward a Minor Literature*, tr. Dana Polan, Minneapolis: University of Minnesota Press, 1986, chapter 3.

7. See also Gyan Prakash, 'Subaltern Studies as Postcolonial Criticism', *American Historical Review* 99 (5) December 1994: 1475–91.

8. Ranajit Guha, 'The Prose of Counter-Insurgency', in Ranajit Guha and Gayatri Chakravorty Spivak (eds), *Selected Subaltern Studies*, New York: Oxford University Press, 1988: 46–7.

9. Ibid.: 80.

10. Ibid.: 78.

11. Rudolf Bultmann, 'Is Exegesis without Presuppositions Possible?', in Kurt Mueller-Vollmer (ed.), *The Hermeneutics Reader: Texts of the German Tradition from the Enlightenment to the Present*, New York: Continuum, 1985: 244.

12. Guha and Spivak, *Selected Subaltern Studies*: 78.

13. Shahid Amin, *Event, Memory, Metaphor*, Berkeley and Los Angeles: University of California Press, 1995.

14. Greg Dening, 'A Poetic for Histories', in *Performances*, Melbourne: Melbourne University Press, 1996: 35–63; David Cohen, *The Combing of History*, Chicago: University of Chicago Press, 1994; Ashis Nandy, 'History's Forgotten Doubles', *History and Theory* 34 (1995): 44–66; Klaus Neumann, *Not the Way It Really Was: Constructing Tolai Past*, Honolulu: University of Hawaii Press, 1992; Chris Healy, *From the Ruins of Colonialism: History as Social Memory*, Melbourne: Cambridge University Press, 1997; Stephen Muecke, 'The Sacred in History', *Humanities Research* 1 (1999): 27–37; Ann Curthoys and John Docker, 'Time, Eternity, Truth, and Death: History as Allegory', *Humanities Research* 1 (1999): 5–26.

15. The question of alternative pasts is highlighted in the following recent works in Indian history: Amin, *Event, Memory, Metaphor*; Ajay Skaria, *Hybrid Histories: Forests, Frontiers, and Wildness in Western India*, Delhi: Oxford University Press, 1999; and Saurabh Dube, *Untouchable Pasts: Religion, Identity, and Power among a Central Indian Community, 1780–1950*, Albany: State University of New York Press, 1998, chapters 5, 7, 8.

16. Hobsbawm, 'Identity History': 272.

17. See Ashis Nandy, 'From Outside the Imperium', in *Traditions, Tyranny and Utopia: Essays in the Politics of Awareness*, Delhi: Oxford University Press, 1987: 147–8; and my discussion in 'The Modern Indian Intellectual and the Problem of the Past: An Engagement with the Thoughts of Ashis Nandy', *Emergences* 7/8 (1995–96), special issue on Nandy, guest edited by Vinay Lal: 168–77.

18. Soren Kierkegaard, *Fear and Trembling: Dialectical Lyric by Johannes de Silentio*, tr. Alastair Hannay, Harmondsworth: Penguin, 1985: 60.

19. Wilhelm von Humboldt, 'On the Task of the Historian', in Mueller-Vollmer (ed.), *The Hermeneutics Reader*: 112.

20. Peter Burke, 'Editorial Preface' to Aron Gurevich, *Medieval Popular Culture: Problems of Belief and Perception*, tr. Janos M. Back and Paul A. Hollingsworth, Cambridge: Cambridge University Press, 1990: vii.

21. Jacques Le Goff (ed.), *The Medieval World*, tr. Lydia G. Cochrane, London: Collins and Brown, 1990: 28–9.

22. 'Preface' to Fredric Jameson, *The Political Unconscious: Narrative as a Socially Symbolic Act*, Ithaca: Cornell University Press, 1981: 9.

23. See Jacques Derrida, *Specters of Marx: The State of the Debt, the Work of Mourning, and the New International*, tr. Peggy Kamuf, New York and London: Routledge, 1994.

24. In using the idea of 'disenchantment' I do not deny what has been said about the 'magic' of commodities or about the magical aspects of modernity itself. That the so-called moderns can be nonmodern as well is, of course, what I myself am arguing. For a critical discussion of 'disenchantment', see Jacques Rancière, 'The

Archeomodern Turn', in Michael P. Steinberg (ed.), *Walter Benjamin and the Demands of History*, Ithaca: Cornell University Press, 1996: 24–40.

25. Personal communication from David Lloyd.

26. Robin Horton's illuminating studies of 'African thought' define 'religion' on the basis of this very European, perhaps Protestant, category, 'belief'. Robin Horton, *Patterns of Thought in Africa and the West*, Cambridge: Cambridge University Press, 1995.

27. Ranajit Guha reminded me of the Bengali word *shomoy-granthi,* literally, 'time-knot'.

28. Hans-Georg Gadamer, 'Kant and the Hermeneutical Turn', in *Heidegger's Ways,* tr. John W. Stanley, New York: State University of New York Press, 1994: 58 (emphasis in original).

THIRTEEN

Blood

Urvashi Butalia

It was around 10 o'clock on a warm summer night in 1987 that I found myself standing in the veranda of a rather decrepit old house in a suburb of Lahore. A dusty bulb, hanging from a single plaited wire, cast a pale light on the cracked pistachio green walls. I was nervous, somewhat frightened, and also curious. The enormity of what I was about to do had only just begun to dawn on me. And predictably, I was tempted to turn around and run. But there was nowhere to run to. This was Lahore; it was night; women did not walk out into deserted streets—or indeed crowded ones—alone in search of non-existent transport.

So I did what I had come to do. I rang the bell. A short while later, three women came to the barred window. I asked if this was the house of the person I was in search of. Yes, they said, but he wasn't there. He was away on 'tour' and expected home later that night. This was something I had not bargained for: had he been there I had somehow foolishly imagined he would know me instantly—despite the fact that he had never seen me before, and was probably totally unaware of my existence. Vaguely I remember looking at the floor for inspiration, and noticing that engraved in it was the game of chopar that my mother had told us about—it was something, she said, that my grandfather had especially made for his wife, my grandmother. Gathering together my courage I said to the three assembled women: 'I'm looking for him because I am his niece, his sister's daughter, come from Delhi.'

Door bolts were drawn and I was invited in. The women were Rana's wife—my aunt—and her daughters, my cousins. To this day I am not sure if it was my imagination or if they were actually quite friendly. I remember being surprised because they seemed to know who I was— you must be Subhadra's daughter, they said, you look a bit like her. Look like her? But they had never even *seen* my mother. At the time, though, I was too nervous to ask. I was led into a large, luridly furnished living room: for an hour we made careful conversation and drank Coca-Cola. Then my friend Firhana came to collect me: I knew her sister, Ferida, and was staying at their house.

This could well have been the end of the story. In a sense, not finding my uncle at home was almost a relief. I went away thinking, well, this is it, I've done it. Now I can go home and forget about all of this. But that was easier said than done. History does not give you leave to forget so easily.

* * *

Crossing the border into Pakistan had been easier than I thought. Getting a visa was difficult, though, ironically, the visa office at the Pakistan High Commission ran two separate counters, one for people they called 'foreigners' and the other for Indians. At the latter crowds of people jostled and pushed, trying to get together all the necessary paperwork while outside, an old man, balding and half-bent at the waist, offered to take instant photos, using a small bucket of developer to get them ready. Once over the border, however, everything looked familiar at the airport—the same chaos, the same language, the same smells, the same clothes. What I was not prepared for, however, was the strong emotional pull that came with the crossing. I felt—there is no other word for it—a sense of having come home. And I kept asking myself why. I was born five years after Partition. What did I know of the history of pain and anguish that had dogged the lives of my parents and grandparents? Why should this place, which I had never seen before, seem more like home than Delhi, where I had lived practically all my life?

What was this strange trajectory of histories and stories that had made it seem so important for me to come here? Standing there, in the veranda of my uncle's house, I remember thinking, perhaps for the first time, that this was something unexpected. When I had begun my search, I wasn't sure what I would find. But I wasn't prepared for what I did find. This was something no history lesson had prepared me for: these people, strangers that I had met practically that instant, were treating me like family. But actually the frontier that divided us went so deep that everywhere you looked, in religion, in politics, in geography and history, it reared its ugly head and mocked these little attempts at overcoming the divide.

Ranamama, outside whose house I stood that night, is my mother's youngest brother. Like many north Indian families, ours too was divided at Partition. My mother, who was still single at the time, found herself on the Indian side of the border. Ranamama, her brother, chose to stay behind. According to my mother and her other siblings, his choice was a motivated one. He wanted access to the property my grandfather—who was no longer alive—owned. With all other family contenders out of the way, he could be sole owner of it. Because of this, and because of the near impossibility of keeping in touch after Partition, the family 'lost' contact with Ranamama. For forty years, no one communicated with him, heard from him, or saw anything of him. Until, that is, I went to see him.

* * *

Ever since I can remember we had heard stories of Partition—from my grandmother (my father's mother), who lived with us, and from my parents who had both lived through it very differently. In the way that I had vaguely registered several of these stories, I had also registered Rana's. Not only had he stayed back but worse, and I suspect this was what made him a persona non grata in our family, he had become a Muslim. My mother made two difficult and dangerous journeys, amidst the worst communal violence, to Lahore to fetch her family to

India. The first time she brought her younger brother, Billo, and a sister, Savita. The second time she went to fetch her mother and Rana, the youngest (her father had long since died). But, she said, Rana refused to come and wasn't willing to let my grandmother go either. He denied that he wanted to hold on to her for the sake of my grandfather's property, which was in her name, and promised to bring her to India soon. This never happened. Once the country was divided, it became virtually impossible for people of different communities to move freely in the 'other' country. Except for a few who were privileged and had access to people in power—a circumstance that ensured relatively smooth passage—most people were unable to go back to their homes, which had often been left behind in a hurry. There was deep suspicion on both sides, and any cross-border movement was watched and monitored by the police and intelligence. Rana and his family kept contact for some time, but found themselves constantly under surveillance, with their letters being opened and questions being asked. After a while, they simply gave up trying to communicate. And for forty years, it remained that way. Although Rana remained in my grandfather's house, no one spoke or wrote to him, no one heard from him in all these years. Sometime during this time, closer to 1947 than not, my family heard unconfirmed reports that my grandmother had died. But no one really knew. The sense of deep loss, of family, mother, home, gave way to bitterness and resentment, and finally to indifference. Perhaps it was this last that communicated itself to us when, as children, we listened to stories of Partition and the family's history.

* * *

At midnight, the phone rang in my friend Ferida's house. We were deep in conversation and gossip over cups of coffee and the salt/sweet tea the Pakistanis call kehwa. She listened somewhat distractedly to the phone for a minute—who could be calling at this time—and handed it to me, suddenly excited, saying, 'It's your uncle'. As Ferida had answered the phone, a male voice at the other end had said, apparently without preamble, 'I believe my daughter is staying with you. Please call my daughter, I would like to speak to her'.

'Beti,' he said to me as I tentatively greeted him, 'what are you doing there? This is your home. You must come home at once and you must stay here. Give me your address and I'll come and pick you up.' No preamble, no greeting, just a direct, no nonsense picking up of family ties. I was both touched and taken aback.

We talked, and argued. Finally I managed to dissuade him. It was late, he was tired. Why didn't we just meet in the morning? I'd get my friend to bring me over. 'I'll not settle for just meeting,' he told me, 'don't think you can get away from here. This is your home and this is where you must stay—with your family.'

Home? Family? I remember thinking these were strange words between two people who hardly knew each other. Ought I to go and stay with him? I was tempted, but I was also uncertain. How could I pack my bags and go off to stay with someone I didn't know, even if there was a family connection? The next morning I went, minus bags. He remarked on it instantly—where is your luggage? Later that evening he came with me to Ferida's house. I picked up my bags, and we went back together to his home.

I stayed with my uncle for a week. All the time I was aware of an underlying sense of betrayal: my mother had had no wish to re-open contact with her brother whom she suspected of being mercenary and scheming. Why else, she asked, had he stayed back, held on to the property, and to the one person to whom it belonged: my grandmother. Over the years, her bitterness and resentment had only increased. But, given my own political trajectory, this visit meant too much to me to abandon. And once I had seen my uncle, and been addressed by him as 'daughter', it became even more difficult to opt out. So I stayed, in that big, rambling haveli, and for a week we talked. It was an intense and emotionally draining week. For a long time afterwards I found it difficult to talk about that parenthetical time in my life. I remember registering various presences: my aunt, my younger and older cousins, food, sleep— all somewhat vaguely. The only recollection that remains sharp and crystal clear, is of the many conversations my uncle and I had.

Why had he not left with his brother and sisters at Partition, I asked him. 'Why *did* you stay back?' Well, Ranamama said, like a lot of other people he had never expected Partition to happen the way it had. 'Many of us thought, yes, there'll be change, but why should we have to move?' He hadn't thought political decisions could affect his life, and by the time he realized otherwise, it was too late, the point of no return had actually been reached. 'I was barely twenty. I'd had little education. What would I have done in India? I had no qualifications, no job, nothing to recommend me.' But he had family in India, surely one of them would have looked after him? 'No one really made an offer to take me on—except your mother. But she was single, and had already taken on the responsibility of two other siblings.'

And my grandmother? Why did he insist on her staying on, I asked, anxious to believe that there was a genuine, 'excusable' reason. He offered an explanation: I did not believe it. 'I was worried about your mother having to take on the burden of an old mother, just like I was worried when she offered to take me with her. So I thought, I'd do my share and look after her.'

My grandmother, Dayawanti, died in 1956. The first time anyone in our family learnt of this was when I visited Ranamama in 1987 and he told me. For years, we'd heard that she had been left behind in Pakistan, and were dimly aware that rumour put her date of death variously at 1949, 1952, 1953, sometimes earlier. But she had lived till 1956. Nine years after Partition. At the time, seven of her eight children lived across the border, in India, most of them in Delhi. Delhi is half an hour away from Lahore by air. None of them knew. Some things, I found, are difficult to forgive.

The way Ranamama described it, the choice to stay on was not really a choice at all. In fact, like many people, he thought he wasn't choosing, but was actually waiting to do so when things were decided for him. But what about the choice to convert? Was he now a believer? Had he been one then? What did religion mean to him—after all, the entire rationale for the creation of two countries out of one, was said to have been religion. And, it was widely believed—with some truth—that large numbers of people were forced to convert to the 'other' religion. But Rana?

'No one forced me to do anything. But in a sense there wasn't really a choice. The only way I could have stayed on was by converting. And so, well, I did. I married a Muslim girl, changed my religion, and took a Muslim name.'

But did he really believe? Was the change born out of conviction as much as it was of convenience? It is difficult for me to put down Mamu's response to this question truthfully. When I asked him if I could write what he had said, he said, 'Of course, write what you like. My life cannot get any worse'. But my own feeling is that he wasn't really aware of the kinds of implications this could have. So I did what I thought I had to: silenced those parts that needed to be kept silent. I make no excuses for this except that I could not bring myself to, in the name of a myth called intellectual honesty, expose or make Ranamama so vulnerable.

'One thing I'll tell you,' said Mamu in answer to my question, 'I have not slept one night in these forty years without regretting my decision. Not one night.' I was chilled to the bone. How could he say this, what did he mean, how had he lived through these forty years, indeed how would he live through the next forty, if this was what he felt? 'You see, my child,' he said, repeating something that was to become a sort of refrain in the days we spent together, 'somehow a convert is never forgiven. Your past follows you, it hounds you. For me, it's worse because I've continued to live in the same place. Even today, when I walk out to the market I often hear people whispering, "Hindu, Hindu". No, you don't know what it is like. They never forgive you for being a convert.'

I was curious about why Ranamama had never tried to come to India to seek out his family. If he felt, so profoundly, the loss of a family, why did he not, like many others, try to locate his? Admittedly, in the beginning, it was difficult for people to cross the two borders, but there were times when things had eased, if only marginally. But he had an answer to that too: 'How could I? Where would I have gone? My family, my sisters knew where I was. I had no idea where they were. And then, who in India would have trusted an ex-Hindu turned Muslim who now wanted to seek out his Hindu relatives? And this is the only home I have known.'

And yet, home for him was defined in many different ways. Ever since television made its appearance, Ranamama made sure he listened to the Indian news every day. When cricket was played between the two countries, he watched and secretly rooted for India. Often, when it was India playing another country, he sided with India. More recently, he sometimes watched Indian soaps on the small screen. And, although he had told me that his home in Lahore was the only home he had ever known, it was to India that he turned for a sense of home. There is a word in Punjabi that is enormously evocative and emotive for most Punjabis: *watan*. It's a difficult word to translate: it can mean home, country, land—all and any of them. When a Punjabi speaks of his or her watan, you know they are referring to something inexpressible, some longing for a sense of place, of belonging, of rootedness. For most Punjabis who were displaced as a result of Partition, their watan lay in the home they had left behind. For Ranamama, in a curious travesty of this, while he continued to live on in the family home in Pakistan, his watan became India, a country he had visited only briefly, once.

His children and family found this bizarre. They could not understand these secret yearnings, these things that went on inside his head. They thought the stories he told were strange, as were the people he spoke about, his family—Hindus—from across the border. The two younger girls told me once, 'Apa, you are all right, you're just like us, but we thought you know that *they* were really awful.' And who could blame them? The only Hindus they had met were a couple of distant relatives who had once managed to visit, and who had behaved as orthodox Hindus often do, practising the 'untouchability' that Hindus customarily use with Muslims. They would insist on cooking their own food, not eating anything prepared by the family, and somehow making their hosts feel 'inferior'. Bir Bahadur Singh, one of the people I interviewed later in the course of my work on Partition, told me what he thought of the way Hindus and Sikhs treated Muslims:

Such good relations we had that if there was any function that we had, then we used to call Musalmaans to our homes, they would eat in our houses, but we would not eat in theirs and this is a bad thing, which I realize now. If they would come to our houses we would have two utensils in one corner of the house, and we would tell them, pick these up and eat in them; they would then wash them and keep them aside and this was such a terrible thing. This was the reason Pakistan was created. If we went to their houses and took part in their weddings and ceremonies, they used to really respect and honour us. They would give us uncooked food, ghee, atta, dal, whatever sabzis they had, chicken and even mutton, all raw. And our dealings with them were so low that I am even ashamed to say it. A guest comes to our house and we say to him, bring those utensils and wash them, and if my mother or sister have to give him food, they will more or less throw the roti from such a distance, fearing that they may touch the dish and become polluted. . . . We don't have such low dealings with our lower castes as Hindus and Sikhs did with Musalmaans.

* * *

As the years went by, Ranamama began to live an internal life, mostly in his head, that no one quite knew about, but everyone, particularly his family, was suspicious of. His children—especially his daughters and daughters-in-law—cared for him but they all feared what went on inside his head. For all the love his daughters gave him, it seemed to me there was very little that came from his sons. Their real interest was in the property he owned. Perhaps the one person who, in some sense, understood the dilemmas in his head, was my mami, his wife. She decided quite early on, and sensibly I thought, that she would not allow her children to have the same kind of crisis of identity that Mamu had had. They were brought up as good Muslims, the girls remained in purdah, they studied at home from the mullah, they learnt to read the Koran. For the younger ones especially, who had no memory or reference of Partition, Rana with his many stories of his family, his friends, his home, remained their father, and yet a stranger. In some ways, this distanced him further from the family and served to isolate him even more. In others, in a curious kind of paradox, his patriarchal authority was undermined, making him a much more humane father than one might normally find in a middle-class Punjabi household. But for several of his family members, he was only the inconvenient owner of the property, to be despatched as soon as possible.

I could not understand how he could have lived like this: was there anyone he could have spoken to? He told me 'no'. How could he talk about what was so deep, so tortured? And to whom? There was no one, no one who could even begin to understand. Some things, he told me, are better left unsaid. But why then was he saying them to me? Who was I? One day, as we talked deep into the evening, stopping only for the odd bit of food, or a cup of tea, and he told me about his life since Partition, I began to feel a sense of weight, of oppression. 'Why,' I asked him, 'why are you talking to me like this? You don't even know me. If you'd met me in the marketplace, I would have just been another stranger. Yes, we speak the same language, we wear similar clothes, but apart from that. . . .' He looked at me for a long moment and said, 'My child, this is the first time I am speaking to my own blood.'

I was shocked. I protested. 'What about your family? They are your blood, not me.'

'No', he said, 'for them I remain a stranger. You, you understand what it is I'm talking about.

That is why you are here on this search. You know. Even if nothing else ever happens, I know that you have been sent here to lighten my load.'

And, in some ways I suppose this was true. I did understand, and I began to wonder. About how many people had been torn apart like this by this event we call Partition, by what is known as history. How many had had to live with their silences, how many had been able to talk, and why it was that we, who had studied modern Indian history in school, who knew there was something called the Partition of India that came simultaneously with Independence, had never learnt about this side of it? Why had these stories remained hidden? Was there no place for them in history?

* * *

That first time when I came back to India from Pakistan, I brought back messages and letters and gifts from the entire family to various members on this side of the border. Ranamama sent a long letter, addressed to all his sisters (his one remaining brother was dead by then). Initially, my mother found it difficult to get over her bitterness and resentment, and to face the letter I had brought. Her sisters, all five of them, who had gathered in our house, sat in a row, curious, but also somewhat resentful. Then someone picked up the letter and began reading, and soon it was being passed from hand to hand, with memories being exchanged, tears being shed and peals of laughter ringing out as stories were recounted and shared.

Tell us, they demanded, tell us what the house looks like, is the guava tree still there, what's happened to the game of chopar, who lives at the back now. . . . Hundreds of questions. I tried to answer them all—unsuccessfully. How could I tell them who was in which room or how the house had changed, when I hadn't seen the original house myself? Mamu's letter was read and reread, touched, smelt, laughed, and wept over. Suddenly my mother and my aunts had acquired a family across the border. We kept in touch after that, occasional letters did manage to arrive. I went several times and met him again. Once he wrote to my mother: 'I wish I could lock up Urvashi in a cage and keep her here.' And she told me I had made a real difference to his life. As he had, I think, to mine, for he set me on a path from which it has been difficult to withdraw.

But old resentments die hard. And there are many things that lie beneath the surface that we cannot even apprehend. Once, when I was going to visit him, my mother said to me: 'Ask him . . . ask him if he buried or cremated my mother.' I looked at her in shock. Religion has never meant much to her—she isn't an atheist but she has little patience with the trappings of religion.

'How does it matter to you?' I said to her.

'Just ask him,' she said, implacable.

I asked him.

'How could she have stayed on here and kept her original name? I had to make her a convert. She was called Ayesha Bibi,' he said, 'I buried her.'

* * *

I often wonder what kind of silent twilight world my grandmother lived in for those nine years after Partition. Did she not wonder where her children had gone? Did she think they had all abandoned her? Did she even understand what had happened? Dayawanti, the merciful one, had indeed been fortunately named. Blessed with a large family—her surviving children numbered nine, six daughters and three sons—and a husband whose medical practice was enormously successful, she had had good reason to be happy. Then, suddenly, tragedy struck and her elder son, Vikram, died in an air crash on a practice flight. As my mother tells it, Dayawanti retreated into some kind of shell from then on, although cooking and caring for the children would occasionally pull her out of this. Then, the second tragedy happened: her husband took ill and died, and Dayawanti again sought solace in an inner world. When Partition came, the chances are that Dayawanti did not know what was happening. But the journey in and out of her twilight world must have left her with long moments of what one might call 'sanity'. What must she have wondered about her family? Who could she have asked? What must she have felt about her new identity? My mother has often described her mother as a 'kattar Hindu'—not a rabid, flame-spouting type, but a strong believer who derived comfort from her daily routine of prayer and fasting. What must it have cost her to convert overnight to a different faith, a different routine? Did it, I wonder, bring on an even more intense alienation, a further recoil into herself, or did it bring on the reverse, a kind of cold, clear sanity and understanding of the lie she had to live till she died? Who was with her these nine years? Will history be answerable for Dayawanti's life and death?

* * *

Twelve million people were displaced as a result of Partition. Nearly one million died. Some 75,000 women were raped, kidnapped, abducted, forcibly impregnated by men of the 'other' religion, thousands of families were split apart, homes burnt down and destroyed, villages abandoned. Refugee camps became part of the landscape of most major cities in the north but, a half century later, there is still no memorial, no memory, no recall, except what is guarded, and now rapidly dying, in families and collective memory.

Some of the tales I heard when I began my research seemed so fantastic, they were difficult to believe. We had heard time and again that in many villages on both sides of the border hundreds of women had jumped—or had been forced to jump—into wells because they feared that they would be taken away, raped, abducted, forced to convert to the other religion. This seemed bizarre: could the pull of religion be so strong that people—more specifically women—would actually kill themselves? And then I met Bir Bahadur Singh's mother, Basant Kaur. Basant Kaur, a tall strapping woman in her mid-sixties had been present in her village, Thoa Khalsa in March 1947, when the decision was taken that women would jump into a well. She watched more than ninety women throw themselves into a well for fear of the Muslims. She too jumped in, but survived because there was not enough water in the well to drown them all. She said: 'It's like when you put rotis into a tandoor and if it is too full, the ones near the top, they don't cook, they have to be taken out. So the well filled up, and we could not drown. . . . Those who died, died, and those who were alive, they pulled out. . . .'

And Bir Bahadur Singh, her son, had watched his father kill his sister. He described the incident with pride in his voice, pride at his sister's courage and her 'martyrdom' for she could now be placed alongside other martyrs of the Sikh religion. The first time I had been alerted to family deaths, that is, men of families killing off their women and children, was when I had met an old man, Mangal Singh, in Amritsar, during the course of the film *A Division of Hearts*. Mangal Singh told me how he and his two brothers had taken the decision to kill—he used the word martyr—seventeen members of their family. 'We had to do this,' he told me, 'because otherwise they would have been converted.' Having done this 'duty' Mangal Singh crossed over into Amritsar where he began a new life. When I met him, he was the only one left of the three. He had a new family, a wife, children, grandchildren, all of whom had heard, and dismissed, his stories. Why do you want to know all this, he kept asking me, what is the use? I told him that I wanted to know how he had coped with the grief, the sense of loss, the guilt. He said: 'Hunger drives all sorrow and grief away. You understand? When you don't have anything, then what's the point of having sorrow and grief?'

* * *

Why do you want to know this? This is a question I have been asked again and again—by the people I have wanted to interview or those to whom I have tried to present my work. Two or three times, having begun work on Partition, I gathered my courage and read a couple of papers at academic gatherings. I wanted to share some questions that had been bothering me: why, for example, had straight historical accounts not been able to really address this underside of the history of Partition, to gather together the experiences of people, to see what role they had played in shaping the India we know today? Was it that they knew they would have to deal with a story so riven with pain and grief, a story that was so close to many people—for in many ways, several of our families were Partition refugees—that some time had to elapse before this work actually began? I wanted to understand how to read the many stories I was now hearing: I knew, without being a historian, that I could not look at these unproblematically. Could I, for example, rely on the 'truth' of the stories I was hearing? How much could one trust memory after all these years? For many of those who chose to tell me their stories, I must have been just another listener, the experience perhaps just another telling. I knew that my being middle class, a woman, a Punjabi, perhaps half a Sikh, would have dictated the way people actually responded. What value then ought I to place on their memory, their recall? Often, what emerged from the interviews was so bitter, so full of rage, resentment, communal feeling, that it frightened me. What was I to do with such material? Was it incumbent on me, as a might-have-been historian, to try to be true to this material, or should I, as a secular Indian actually exercise some care about what I made visible and what I did not? A question that has dogged me constantly has been: is it fair to make these interviews public if they relate (as mine do) to only one side of the story? Doesn't that sort of material lend itself to misuse by one side or another? To this day, I have not solved this dilemma: I am torn between the desire to be honest and to be careful. And all the time, I was asked: why, why are you doing this? The question became important for another reason: the way borders were drawn between our two countries, it was virtually impossible for me to travel to Pakistan to do research, or even to carry out interviews. With the result that my work remained—and still does—very one-sided. I knew that this was not right. I didn't know—I still don't—what I should be doing. Ought I to have given up the work? There are no easy answers. But in the end, I decided that if this search meant so much to me, I simply had to go on with it. I could not abandon it.

* * *

For some years the border between Pakistan and India seemed to have become more permeable. As a result I was able to make several visits and cement my relationship with Ranamama. Once, when his second-youngest daughter was getting married, I took my mother and her elder sister with me to visit him. There was a great deal of excitement as we planned the visit, for it was really like a visit to the unknown. They didn't know what their brother would look like, how he would react to them, what their home would look like, what their beloved city would have to offer them. . . . At Lahore airport Mamu came to fetch his sisters. The last time my mother and aunt had seen their brother was forty-one years ago, when he had been a young twenty-year old: slim, tall, and smart. The man who met them now was in his sixties, balding, and greying. He wore an awami suit, the loose salwar and shirt made popular by Bhutto. I tried to imagine what he must have seen: two white-haired women: my aunt, in her seventies, and my mother, in her mid-sixties. The reunion was a tentative, difficult one, with everyone struggling to hold back tears. I stood aside, an outsider now. My friend, Lala, who came to the airport as well, tells me that she had never forgotten the look on their faces—she has no words to describe it. Everyone made small talk in the car until we reached home. Home—this was the house in which my mother and her brothers and sisters had grown up. They knew every stone, every nook and cranny of this place. But now, much of it was occupied by people they did not know. So they were forced to treat it politely, like any other house. My aunt was welcoming, warm, but also suspicious. What, she must have wondered, were these relatives from the other side doing here at the time of a family wedding? How she must have hoped that they would not embarrass her in front of her guests.

For the first two days Mamu and his sisters skirted each other. They talked, but polite, strained, talk. On the third day somehow the floodgates opened, and soon the three of them were locked in a room, crying, laughing, talking, remembering. Mamu took his sisters on a proper tour of the house: they were able to go back into their old rooms, to find their favourite trees, to remember their parents and other siblings. I, who was the catalyst at the airport meeting, was now redundant. Earlier, I had told them that I would stay with Lala, and that's what I had done. But not without a sense of guilt. Now, I was glad I'd done that—they can talk now, I thought, without having me around.

But what I didn't reckon on was that immediately one family bonded, the other grew more distant. For Mamu's own family, the arrival of the two sisters was, quite naturally, something to be concerned about. A girl was being married. What if the potential in-laws objected to Hindus in the family? What if the Hindus were there to reclaim their land? What if the Hindus did something to embarrass the family at the wedding? And, a further complication. My mother and my aunt are the older sisters. Custom demanded that they be given respect. This meant making space for them in the wedding rituals. Yet how could this be done? So, small silences began to build up between 'this' side of the family and 'that', and I was struck by how easy it was to recreate the borders we thought we'd just crossed.

* * *

Contact with Rana was maintained for some years. I managed, somehow, to go to Pakistan again and see him. But it wasn't easy. He began to worry he was being watched by the police, and he gradually stopped writing. For a while my mother continued to send him letters and gifts, but slowly, even that petered out. Several times, I sent him letters and messages with my friends until one brought back a message—try not to keep in touch, it makes things very difficult. This wasn't just something official, but also within the family, for his sons put pressure on him to break contact with his Indian family. And then, in any case, it became more and more difficult to travel from one country to the other.

It's been many years now since I have seen Rana. I no longer know if he is alive or dead. I *think* he is alive, I *want* him to be alive, no one has told me he isn't, so I shall have to go on believing that he is. And I keep telling myself, if something happened to him, surely someone would tell us. But I'm not even sure I believe myself when I say that. Years ago, when Mamu answered my mother's question about whether he had buried or cremated my grandmother, I asked if he would take me to her grave. I still remember standing with him by his gate in the fading light of the evening, looking out onto the road and saying to him, 'Mamu, I want to see my grandmother's grave. Please take me to see it.' It was the first time he answered me without looking at me: he scuffed the dust under his feet and said: 'No my child, not yet. I'm not ready yet.'

* * *

On the night of 14 August 1996 about a hundred Indians visited the India-Pakistan border at Wagah in the Punjab. They went there to fulfil a long-cherished objective of groups in the two countries. Indians and Pakistanis would stand, in roughly equal numbers, one each side of the border and sing songs for peace. They imagined that the border would be symbolized by a sentry post and that they would be able to see their counterparts on the other side. But they came back disappointed. The border was more complicated than they thought—there is middle ground—and also grander. The Indian side has an arch lit with neon lights and, in large letters, the inscription MERA BHARAT MAHAAN—India, my country, is Great. The Pakistan side has a similar neon-lit arch with the words PAKISTAN ZINDABAD—Long Live Pakistan. People bring picnics here and eat and drink and enjoy themselves. Every evening, a ritual takes place which repeats, lest anyone forget, the aggression the two countries practise towards each other. As the flags are lowered, border security personnel of India and Pakistan rush towards each other, thrusting their faces at each other, then turn smartly, and step away. The whole ritual is carried out with such precision that you wonder at how much they must have had to work together to establish their lines of difference. During the day as people arrive at the border, coolies dressed in different colours—blue and red to differentiate them as 'ours' and 'theirs'—meet at the twelve-inch line that forms the boundary, passing heavy bags and sacks across from one head to another; the boundary is crossed as their heads touch, while their feet stay on either side.

The suffering and grief of Partition are not memorialized at the border, nor, publicly, anywhere else in India, Pakistan, and Bangladesh. A million may have died but they have no monuments. Stories are all that people have, stories that rarely breach the frontiers of family and religious community: people talking to their own blood.

Presence of Europe: A Cyber Conversation with Dipesh Chakrabarty

Saurabh Dube

ᦞᦞᦞᧁᦞ

The work of Dipesh Chakrabarty offers critical reflections on history and modernity. Ten years ago, his important essay 'Postcoloniality and the Artifice of History' had raised, with care and imagination, key questions concerning the presence of Europe in the writing of history.[1] Implicitly construing his arguments against the backdrop of Heidegger's interrogation of the artifice of a meaning-legislating reason, in the essay Chakrabarty focused on 'history' as a discourse that is produced at the institutional site of the university, making a compelling case for the ways in which Europe remains the sovereign theoretical subject of all histories. By admitting that 'Europe' and 'India' are 'hyperreal' terms that refer to certain figures of the imagination, Chakrabarty critically pointed toward how—in the 'phenomenal world', of everyday relationships of power—Europe stands reified and celebrated as the site and scene of the birth of the modern, working as a silent referent that dominates the discourse of history. Here, Chakrabarty unravelled the consequences of the theoretical privileging of Europe as the universal centrepiece of modernity and history, so that the past and present of India or Mexico—or of Afghanistan or Namibia—come to be cast in terms of irrevocable principles of failure, lack, and absence, since they are always/already measured against the West.

Chakrabarty's recent book, Provincializing Europe (PE), further elaborates such critical considerations.[2] An interview with him appeared as the best means to highlight these arguments. The interchange took place via email in June 2001.[3] It briefly touches upon Chakrabarty's earlier concerns—as expressed, for example, in Rethinking Working Class History (RTWH)—while primarily tracking considerations that arise from PE.[4] Now, PE is a multilayered and intriguing work, defying conventional summary. Therefore, the questions in this interview take the form of clusters of queries that also attempt to outline the work's key emphases, as in dialogue with issues engaging reflection on history and theory. There has been very little editing of the questions and the answers as they were originally articulated, although I have added notes primarily as a means of clarification. As an abiding measure, the entire exchange circulates in cyber space.

Saurabh Dube: Your earlier writings on the working class in India, especially *RTWH*, approached community and tradition as defining the worker's quotidian experience of hierarchy in a society/culture where the assumptions of a hegemonic bourgeois culture did not apply. They were as much the mark of a 'limit' as they were the sign of an 'absence'. In *PE*, you do not explicitly engage either community or tradition. Nonetheless, are these categories not implicitly present in the book's arguments, intimating different horizons from your prior emphases?

Dipesh Chakrabarty: In *RTWH*, 'community' was opposed to what Marx called 'the dot-like isolation' of the modern individual/worker his theory of capital assumed. In *PE*, I see community as an always-already fragmented phenomenon. There is, in that sense, no identifiable 'Bengali community' or even a 'Bengali middle-class community' for whose history *PE* may be regarded as representative. That is what I try to say at the very beginning of the book, that it is not a history of the Bengali *bhadralok*. Instead, I use the more diffuse idea of 'life-world', assuming that life-worlds—even within the same speech-community, say—could be both diverse and overlapping. The life-world(s) that *PE* is most concerned with are those imagined and worlded within certain practices of modernity in Bengal, practices made possible primarily by seepage of literature into life (and vice versa). At the same time, I assume that actual people move in and out of several life-worlds at once: so I do not visualize reality as made up of colliding and insulated life-worlds. Alongside, the disavowal of the representative function of history releases me from the burden of having to speak for a community. Bengaliness I imagine (provisionally) as a collection of certain skills and competences that made it possible for some people in some particular moments of their lives to make a world out of this earth in very particular ways. Nobody is, ever, fully or exhaustively defined by these competences. My argument was that even from the limited perspective of the history of these forms of worlding, European categories seem indispensable but inadequate as explanatory or analytical devices.

So, yes, I move away from the idea of community. As for 'tradition', I do not deploy the idea. Some of the bodily and other orientations to the world I mention and describe in the second part of the book are indeed very old. Some are very new. Yet they are all present in the practices I document making for the hetero-temporality I try to explicate in the first part of *PE*. My position would be something like this: capitalist production may be a relatively recent phenomenon but the subject who lives with and under the sway of capital is not made solely by capital itself. The struggle to be at home by making a world out of this earth—a struggle that admits of no permanent resolution—both intersects with and diverges from the logic of capital. This is something I attempt to explicate in *PE* by talking about History 1 and History 2 in the chapter called 'The Two Histories of Capital'.

SD: The interplay between 'History 1' and 'History 2' entails particular understandings of capitalism and colonialism, modernity and the post-colony. How would you reflect on these categories—and the histories they contain—after *PE*?

DC: Well, then, what I say is that modernity and the post-colony, as categories, cannot be thought without some understanding of the logic of capital (or the universal history of capital). Conversely, we should not reduce them to simply this logic. What makes modernity and the post-colony inherently plural is that the logic of capital—its universal history that I have called History 1—cannot subsume into itself all the pasts that capital encounters as its 'antecedents' (to stay with Marx's expression). It attempts to subsume but the subsumption is never total. Both its success and failure in this respect are partial, and in this very partial nature of the success, paradoxically, lies the condition of possibility for the global regime of capital. If everything was reduced to the universal logic of capital, then what we loosely call 'capitalism' would have been very oppressive indeed. So this partial realization of 'capital' is the enabling condition for globalization—you will see that I make a distinction in *PE* between globalization and universalization of capital.

SD: A central strand running through *PE* is your emphasis upon, 'the fragmentary histories of human belonging that never constitute a one or a whole'.[5] Such pasts and experiences are signalled by the book's evocations of life-worlds and of ways of being-in-the world, its invocations of the pre-analytical or Heidegger's 'ready to hand' (as distinct from the analytical, 'present at hand'), and its articulations of the time of gods and spirits. These 'fragmentary histories' exist alongside the objectifications of analytical history and the social sciences, revealing the limits of historicizing and universalizing thought, indeed modifying and interrupting in practice the latter's totalizing thrusts. Here, I would like to follow upon these emphases, opening related terms of discussion.[6]

On the one hand, while you clarify that subaltern pasts come into being in the relationship of the historian to the archive, how are we to conceive of the time of gods and spirits—or subaltern practices—that you explore in *PE*? Do these primarily exist as the pre-analytical or the 'ready to hand' in your arguments? Yet, do not these times and practices contain both the 'ready to hand' and the 'present at hand', consisting at once of (prior) experiences of history and (distinct) modes of historical consciousness of subaltern subjects? Put differently, do the distinctions at hand come into play only when you question the artifice of modern reason and interrogate the limits of historicism? Should we not think of these distinctions as having a conjoint provenance, signifying different orders of reasoning and disjunctive modes of historical consciousness?

On the other hand, in the manner that ways of being-in-the-world are part of the human condition, it is not only stipulations of colonial history and postcolonial modernity in India that interrogate the limits of historicism and totalizing thought. As you hint more than once in *PE*, ways of being-in-the world or subaltern pasts everywhere, including Europe, perform this task. How then are we to conceive of the relationship—entailing not only conjunction and/or disjunction, but also possible conversation—between the life-worlds of, say, the English worker, the Bihari peasant, and the Bengali modern in the nineteenth century? For in the absence of (the positing of) such a relationship, would not the salience of ways of being-in-the-world inhere only in their opposition to 'universal, abstract, and European categories of capitalist/political modernity'?[7] Taken together, what implications arise from such congeries of considerations for imperatives of postcolonial thought and terms of historical difference?

DC: As I understand Heidegger's development of these categories in the 'Being and Time' phase of his life, it would be wrong to think of one as having any kind of historical or epistemological privilege over the other. In other words, you could not say that humans lived primarily in a 'ready to hand' orientation to the world before the coming of modern scientific rationality. Nor could you say that the 'ready to hand' is somehow more primordial compared to that which is 'present at hand'. Why? Because, there is always the phenomenon of what Heidegger calls the equipmentality of the world breaking down. One day you suddenly find that the hammer you habitually hit the nail with has broken head. In repairing it, you are forced to look on this particular hammer as 'the hammer'—that is, develop toward it an objectifying analytical relationship. That is how the 'present at hand' constantly comes into play—because the 'ready to hand' constantly breaks down. If, however, the 'ready to hand' is what we need in order to be at home, to practise dwelling, then Heidegger is also saying that the human can never be permanently at home in this world. Our 'worlds' continually break down calling into existence the more placeless logic of the 'present at hand'. Since, however, we cannot world our existence through the 'present at hand' (for the 'present at hand' is indifferent to place; it is simply analytic), and if to be human is to tend to dwell, then it follows that we cannot live by the 'present at hand' alone either, that the 'ready to hand' will also continually be called into being. Politically committed social science usually subordinates the 'ready to hand' to that which is analytic and assumes that the analytic holds the key to what's 'real' about the pre-analytic world. I was trying to resist that tendency of Marxist social thought and historical writing. The last chapter of *PE* gives examples of intellectuals both inhabiting and developing techniques of denying—historicism is one such technique— different ways of being in the world.

PE also makes another specific claim about historicism—that historicism is made possible by an unacknowledged relationship to that which resists historicism. This is what I discuss in the chapter on 'Minority Histories, Subaltern Pasts'. You are right: this happens globally and not just in colonial histories. In the case of the specific histories of the Indian middle classes, there is an interesting phenomenon. At least until now, we have never been very far from peasant or rural modes of orienting ourselves to the world. This is partly because of our practice of employing domestic servants who are often of peasant stock. This is a very complicated part of our collective biographies.

Someone like Ashis Nandy can speak very creatively and intelligently on these matters. I cannot. Yet, let me just say this. Most of us as children have intimate relations of proximity to members of the class we later come to see as objects of pedagogical exercise. In our childhood, however, these people are often our teachers. Through the stories they tell when looking after us, through the affections they shower on us in our childhood, they impart to us orientations of the world we often later disavow. I did not have to read the history of plague riots of 1898 to understand the opposition of subaltern classes to hospitalization or modern medicine. When we were kids, the city authorities used to send vaccinators to our homes to vaccinate against cholera, typhoid, smallpox, and other diseases. Who would hide under the bed for fear of the needle? It would be my sister and me, and our adult servant. My father would drag us out of there. While we the children got a modernizing lecture on public health and hygiene, the servant was bullied into submission. I have often wondered if Subaltern Studies did not have some roots in this aspect of the collective biography of the Indian middle classes.[8]

As to how the life-worlds of the Bihari peasant and the Bengali intellectual would come together, you will remember that I do not regard life-worlds as constituting hermetically sealed entities. Nor do I see people as being marked by their belonging to only one life-world. Life-practices for anybody are manifold and would resist being summed up into the description of one life-world. There is, for instance, an academic life-world you and I share, and that is irrespective of from where our parents came. People move in and out of life-worlds, and life-worlds, as I think of them, are permeable entities. An example of this actually occurs in the chapter in *PE* on Rabindranath Tagore, 'Nation and Imagination'. Take the case of 'darshan' as I discuss it there.[9] Tagore aestheticizes the practice while the everyday temple-goer is not required to do that. Yet a connection remains between the different locations of this world, and even in Tagore's aestheticization, the word does not lose all connection with the other location of its use.

Again, for me, *PE* was a way of saying that European social thought only gives us a limited—though critical—purchase on the life-practices through which we world the worlds (and we do not do this in one single way). Hence, the need to know European thought as giving us a particular, and not universal, genealogy of thought which we translate into other genealogies. Indeed, to know it as a particular genealogy is to move away from its trans-historical pretensions.

SD: My next set of questions precisely concerns the place of universal categories in your work. *PE* emphasizes the simultaneous indispensability and inadequacy of universal categories of European thought in considerations of political modernity and social justice in India and beyond. Indeed, you return to the question several times, in different ways. Here, particularly interesting is the manner in which you set up a distinction between the necessity of the universal and the avowal of the local, only to find the one entailed in the other. For example, you argue that 'On inspection the universal turns out to be an empty place holder whose unstable outlines become barely visible only when a proxy, a particular, usurps its position in a gesture of pretension and domination'.[10] Yet, it seems to me, at several crucial junctures in the book, the universal intimates itself in the form of rather fully fabricated entities, a given corpus of categories, already in place, ever there. Rather than pointing an accusatory finger, here is what I wish to ask—Can your practice of reading difference into and against universals be at all possible without bringing into play such formations of totality, which tend to retain the prior given-ness of universal categories? Put another way, alongside difference and heterogeneity, is there perhaps a critical tension circulating through your own configurations of the universal, insinuating disjunctive registers that deflect and disrupt one another? Finally, how do you construe the constitutive contradictions and founding exclusions—looking far beyond the gap usually invoked between preaching and practice—of universal categories within your advocacy for the 'need to think in terms of totalities while at the same time unsettling totalizing thought by putting into play non-totalizing categories'?[11]

DC: The question of universals is solved for me by two observations. The first is that they are all around us in everyday life and inform much of our everyday sense of justice. Take the newspaper, for instance. Ideas of rights and representation, of equal punishment for equal crime, equal pay for equal work—these are all there around us at least as rhetoric if not as concepts. Any engagement with the political has to begin with the everyday, the common-sensical. The universals are there, I think. Secondly, we deal with institutions that, in their ideal form, see themselves as based on certain universalist ideas. Their own ideational structure requires us to engage the universals. In a footnote in *PE*, I think, I give the example of the parliament. To be a parliamentarian in India, one does not have to know, even in outlines, the global history of 'the parliament' as an institution. But imagine writing about 'the parliament' for a civics course for high-school students. Then an abstract and universal conception of the parliament will be your thought-object. My point in *PE* was that being modern did not involve us in thinking universals (though it may find us using universal-sounds words pragmatically and rhetorically). Yet thinking about political modernity is impossible to do without engaging some universals of 'European thought'. The problem with these universals is this. They, as thought-concepts, come packaged as though they have transcended the particular histories in which they were born. But being pieces of prose and language, they carry intimations of histories of belonging which are not everybody's history. When we translate them—practically, theoretically—into our languages and practice, we make them speak to other histories of belonging, and that is how difference and heterogeneity enter these words. Or, in thinking about them and self-consciously looking for places for them in life-practices we have fabricated using them, we sometimes rediscover their own plural histories in the history of European thought. I try to do this with the category 'imagination' in one of the chapters in *PE*.

So, unlike many postmodernist thinkers, I do not rail against totalizing concepts. I think they are unavoidable if one takes contemporary critiques of our lives seriously. As Indian historians, I think we have to remember the investment that Dr B.R. Ambedkar developed as a 'dalit', or Untouchable, leader in Enlightenment universals in the first half of the twentieth century. This does not stop me from critiquing these universals for the problems of thought they pose for me. Yet how could I deny their political appeal when I see someone representing some of the most oppressed sections of my society finding them inspiring and helpful. *PE* reflects this tension. It is not a simple tension between thought and practice. Thus, I am not saying that we need the universals practically but should think without them. No. I think we need to think the universals as part of immanent critique of structures of domination that predicate themselves on the same universals; but we also need to think about what problems of thought they create because of our having to make them speak to histories of life-practices from which they did not originate. I guess I try to resolve this tension by talking about different ways of being in the world. In saying this, I am not just following Heidegger. I am also drawing on my lessons of high school and undergraduate physics. Physicists deal with both the Newtonian and quantum worlds without having to claim that only one must prevail. Something similar can be said of the two tendencies of thought that I try to build on—the totalizing and the non-totalizing ones.

SD: Your essay on 'Postcoloniality and the Artifice of History' of the early 1990s had spoken of a 'politics of despair' as a critical component of the project of provincializing Europe,[12] but in *PE* you declare that such politics do not any longer drive your arguments. 'Historicism can circulate only in a mood of frustration, despair, and ressentiment', you state, questioning your own, prior propositions.[13] This is a powerful but intriguing statement. Could you say more about it? What are its implications for a radical critique and transcendence of liberalism that you propose? How might such considerations bear upon possible practices of history writing that critically (and carefully) engage with universals and that carefully (and critically) attend to histories of belonging and the 'non-integral' nature of historical time?

DC: The despair I felt then came from an exclusive dependence on the vocabulary of critique that Marxism and liberalism provide us. I accepted this vocabulary in toto. I knew, instinctively and from having unsuccessfully struggled with the problem in my labour-history book, *RTWH*, that the 'ends of human life' encoded in this vocabulary did not necessarily represent the whole—or even the best—of human experience. Yet I knew no other place where I could turn to look for critical perspectives on life-practices that I have grown up with.

In other words, I was aware of the inadequacy of European thought but also of its indispensability (for reasons explained above). Yet I did not know where to go from there, hence the despair. I thought that articulating one's sense of helplessness in the face of the assumed inevitability of what Heidegger once called 'Europeanisation of the earth' was the only political option one had. Not only was this politics motivated by ressentiment, it also failed to acknowledge the positive debt one may owe to Europe and European thought. This sense of despair lifted, however, once I paid more attention to the translationsl processes through which concepts and practices are made one's own. I saw that these processes make available to us—if we are prepared to see and listen—many other vantage points of criticism that are not necessarily indebted to European thought but that do not come in a separated package either. They come blended into our conceptual artifacts of modernity.

The chapter on widows in *PE* is a good case in point. There is no doubt that that chapter documents the emergence of a citizenly voice in social critiques of Bengali patriarchal arrangements. Yet the voice actually contains grains that have very little to do with any theory of citizenship or rights. They could be about human-god relationships and the critical perspectives they lend on the world, or about familial relationships, or about other things. In other words, being attentive to the translational processes makes us aware of horizons of human existence that speak of histories other than those encoded into European political thought.

Now it is up to us to build an archive or repository of these other horizons so that we can use them creatively to fabricate our lives as we live them. It means further that while one can acknowledge, without seeking revenge, what one owes to Europe, one can at the same time also investigate the histories that provided the grounds on which European thought was situated and translated in our pasts. At present, most of us studying modern Indian history do not do this digging. We lack the training, although that we can rectify through collective effort. At the same time, there are other histories still living among us. They remain hidden because their intimations come delivered through words and practices that we use or conduct in an everyday laziness of spirit. Yet it is also up to us to reawaken those histories, doing this for both elites and subalterns. There would be interesting overlaps as well as critical differences between the two groups. But none of this will happen if we simply allow the concept-metaphors of 'citizen' and 'rights' to obscure from view the tremendous heterogeneity they actually gather under their umbrella at the same time as we enter the historical process of making these concepts our own.

SD: These are profound challenges for the practice of history. What do you consider as the limits and the possibilities of critical histories and postcolonial perspectives today to respond to these challenges?

DC: Thank you for the generosity of spirit that inheres in all your questions. It is difficult for me to spell out all the 'challenges' that *PE* may have for the practice of writing history. A text has its own life, and not simply in terms of the diversity of reception that it may encounter. Anything in prose contains a certain degree of heterogeneity over which no author has complete sovereignty. So let me only mention some of the points that I myself was aware of as I worked on *PE*.

I think *PE* tries to hold some kind of a middle ground between taking categories of thought seriously, particularly the categories we need to think through issues of political modernity, and the tendency to reify these categories themselves into historical actors. This happens, for instance, with the category 'capital'. Obviously, I think that we need to understand the internal construction of this category—I deal, of course, only with the Marxist construction of it—in order to think about political modernity. But I do hope that I have said enough about the politics of belonging and dwelling and its intersection with the 'logic of capital' to help interrogate the plausibility of statements such as 'capital has done this or that in the world'. (Similar remarks could be made about the nation-state. There is a widespread scholarly tendency to reduce it simply to its form—as monopoly of violence, etc., which, as such, is not problematic—and then blame this formal abstraction for many instances of actual governmental violence in the world.) I also hope that *PE* has something to say about the relation between historical narratives and literary imagination. Of course, the literary imagination I have explored is that exhibited by the established writers of the Hindu-Bengali middle classes of the nineteenth and twentieth centuries. But the middle classes are not the only source of literature. This is, in a way, also a plea for histories written out of bilingual or multilingual positions. And, finally, *PE* is involved in investigating the different ways the European message about human sovereignty in organizing public life—what else is modern European political thought?—has been worked on and hybridized by a certain group of people in the world as they tried to evolve their politics of dwelling under conditions of modernization initiated by colonial rule. This hybridization, by the way, happens in all areas of the world, including Europe, for we must not equate thought-traditions with actual historical processes. I have tried to demonstrate this for a small part of the world, which I have had the privilege of knowing somewhat intimately. I simply hope that the exercise is relevant for others as well. Thank you, once again, for your own stimulating and generous reading of *PE*. I have learned from listening to you.

NOTES

1. Dipesh Chakrabarty, 'Postcoloniality and the Artifice of History: Who Speaks for "Indian" Pasts?', *Representations*, 37, Winter 1992, 1–26.
2. Dipesh Chakrabarty, *Provincializing Europe: Postcolonial Thought and Historical Difference*, Princeton: Princeton University Press, 2001.
3. The interview had its beginnings as an exchange in Saurabh Dube (ed.), *Enduring Enchantments*, a special issue of *South Atlantic Quarterly*, 101 (4), 2002, published by Duke University Press.
4. Dipesh Chakrabarty, *Rethinking Working-Class History: Bengal 1890–1940*, Princeton: Princeton University Press, 1989.
5. Chakrabarty, *Provincializing Europe*: 255.
6. The queries that follow bring into play what is widely considered as a central insight of Heiddeger, described by Paul Ricouer as Heidegger's recognition of the capacity of '*Dasein* to project its most proper possibilities inside the fundamental situation of being in the world', so that understanding itself entails 'the mode of being before defining the mode of knowing'. Here, in the understanding of history, for example, the implicit awareness of exposure to the labours of history precedes the objectifications of documentary historiography, which is to say that (what is frequently understood as) historical consciousness barely covers the experience of history. The questions that I sent to Chakrabarty clarified these premises, and his response registers this. Paul Ricouer, cited in Zygmunt Bauman, *Intimations of Postmodernity*, London: Routtedge, 1992: ix–x.
7. Chakrabarty, *Provincializing Europe*: 255.
8. As is generally known, Chakrabarty is one of the founder members of the South Asian Subaltern Studies project.

9.   Here the reference is to the activity of *darshan* (to see), connoting 'the exchange of human sight with the divine'. Chakrabarty, *Provincializing Europe*: 173.
10. Ibid.: 70.
11. Ibid.: 21–22.
12. Chakrabarty, 'Postcoloniality and the Artifice of History'.
13. Chakrabarty, *Provincializing Europe*: 248–9.

Notes on Contributors

Shahid Amin is Professor, Department of History, University of Delhi, and a founding-member of the Subaltern Studies collective. His books include *Sugarcane and Sugar in Gorakhpur* (1984), *Event, Metaphor, Memory* (1995), and several edited and co-edited works.

Kamla Bhasin worked with the Freedom from Hunger Campaign of the FAO for over twenty years, and is a well-known gender trainer. She has written extensively on participatory training, women, and sustainable development, and also composed several songs on these issues.

Urvashi Butalia co-founded Kali for Women, India's first feminist press, and has been active in the women's and civil rights movements in India. She has written *The Other Side of Silence* (1998), edited *Speaking Peace* (2002), and co-edited *Women and the Hindu Right* (1995) and other works.

Dipesh Chakrabarty is the Lawrence A. Kimpton Distinguished Service Professor at the University of Chicago where he teaches in the Departments of History and of South Asian Languages and Civilizations. A founding-member of the Subaltern Studies collective and a founding-editor of *Postcolonial Studies*, his books include *Rethinking Working-Class History* (1989), *Provincializing Europe* (2000), and *Habitations of Modernity* (2002).

Partha Chatterjee is Director, Centre for Studies in Social Sciences, Kolkata, and Visiting Professor of Anthropology at Columbia University. A founding-member of the Subaltern Studies collective, his many books include *Bengal 1920-1947* (1984), *Nationalist Thought and the Colonial World* (1986), *The Nation and its Fragments* (1993), and *A Princely Impostor?* (2002).

Bernard S. Cohn is Professor Emeritus, Department of Anthropology, University of Chicago. A founding-figure of the wider field of historical anthropology, his books include *An Anthropologist among the Historians* (1987) and *Colonialism and its Forms of Knowledge* (1996).

Nicholas B. Dirks is the Franz Boas Professor of History and Anthropology at Columbia University. He has written *The Hollow Crown* (1985) and *Castes of Mind* (2001), and edited *Colonialism and Culture* (1992) and *In Near Ruins* (1998).

Saurabh Dube is Professor of History, Center for Asian and African Studies, El Colegio de México. His books include *Untouchable Pasts* (1998), *Sujetos subalternos* (2000), *Stitches on Time* (2004), and *Genealogias del presente* (2003).

Ranajit Guha is a founding-member of the Subaltern Studies collective. He has held academic appointments at universities in Australia, England, and the U.S., and now lives in Austria. His books include *A Rule of Property for Bengal* (1963), *Elementary Aspects of Peasant Insurgency in Colonial India* (1983), *Dominance without Hegemony* (1998), *History at the Limits of World History* (2002), and several edited volumes.

Sudipta Kaviraj is Reader in Politics, School of Oriental and African Studies, University of London, and a member of the Subaltern Studies collective. He has written *The Unhappy Consciousness* (1995), edited *Politics in India* (1998), and co-edited *Dynamics of State Formation* (1997) and *Civil Society* (2001).

Ritu Menon co-founded Kali for Women, India's oldest feminist press, and is active in the women's movement across South Asia. She has written (with Kamla Bhasin) *Borders and Boundaries* (1998) and (with Zoya Hasan) *Inequality and Community Disadvantage* (forthcoming). She has also co-edited several works, and is presently editing two volumes of essays from Pakistan, India, and Bangladesh on the Partition.

Gyanendra Pandey is Professor of Anthropology and History at the Johns Hopkins University, and a founding-member of Subaltern Studies. His books include *The Ascendancy of the Congress in U.P.* (1978), *The Construction of Communalism in Colonial North India* (1990), *Remembering Partition* (2001), and many edited works.

Gyan Prakash is Professor of History, Princeton University, and a member of the Subaltern Studies collective. His books include *Bonded Histories* (1990), *Another Reason* (1999), and, as editor, *After Colonialism* (1994).

Anupama Rao is Assistant Professor of History, Barnard College, Columbia University. She has edited *Caste and Gender* (2003), co-edited other works, and is currently completing a book-manuscript entitled *The Caste Question: Untouchable Struggles for Rights and Recognition*.

Index